AUTHOR'S

The Honorable Allen B. Clark

The Honorable Allen B. Clark graduated the United States Military Academy at West Point in 1963. In 1966, he volunteered for service as an Army Intelligence officer in the Republic of Vietnam, in which assignment he was involved in clandestine activities to include debriefing a defector, training anti-Communists in helicopter insertions into Cambodia, and organizing intelligence-gathering operations against enemy base camps in the tri-border area of South Vietnam.

On June 17, 1967, Allen was wounded in an enemy mortar barrage and was returned for fifteen months of hospitalization that included amputation of both legs below the knees, multiple surgeries and a fourteen-week residency in a closed psychiatric ward at Brooke Army Medical Center, for what would later be described as Post-Traumatic Stress Disorder (PTSD). For his service in Vietnam, he is a recipient of a Silver Star, America's third-highest decoration for Gallantry in Action, a Purple Heart, and the Combat Infantryman's Badge.

His political service began in 1979, when he served as a special assistant to Texas Governor Bill Clements until 1981. In 1982, he represented the Republican Party as a candidate for Texas State Treasurer. Between 1989 and 1993, he served in the President George H.W. Bush Administration as the Assistant Secretary for Veterans Liaison and Program Coordination, and Director of the National Cemetery System in the United States Department of Veterans Affairs.

He authored *Wounded Soldier, Healing Warrior*, his autobiography with a foreword by Ross Perot which was published in 2007 by Zenith Press. He also authored *Valor in Vietnam*, a collection of personal stories of the war with a foreword by Lieutenant General Dave R. Palmer, Superintendent of West Point (1986-1991). *Valor in Vietnam* was published in 2012 by Casemate Publishers of Philadelphia and Oxford. In 2014, the book was recognized by the Military Writer's Society with the Bronze Award in the History category.

For many decades, Allen has been a seasoned and frequent presenter and motivational speaker for numerous youth groups, churches, and religious organizations. Over the past several years, he has been a guest speaker at military bases for their Wounded Warrior Battalions and has mentored many young veterans of our Nation's conflicts.

In 1993, Allen was designated as the Citizen of the Year of the Military Chaplains of the United States. In 2010, he was recognized by the Chaplains Commission of the National Association of Evangelicals with their Centurion of the Year Award. In 2018, Allen became the proud recipient of the Patriot Award from the Greater Dallas Military Foundation, as well as the Sons of the Flag Legacy Award.

Visit the following sites for more information and helpful resources:

Website: www.allenbclark.com
Website: www.combatfaith.com
Blog: www.combatfaith.blogspot.com
Book site: www.woundedsoldierhealingwarrior.com
Book site: www.valorinvietnam.com
Book site: www.soldiersblood.com

SOLDIERS' BLOOD
AND BLOODIED MONEY

Wars and the Ruling Elites

ENDORSEMENTS FOR SOLDIERS' BLOOD

"Few understand the price of war better than Allen Clark. This is a man who has lived an extraordinary life in service to his country. Allen is a patriot, maintaining the highest respect for the American experiment, despite the incredible toll taken on him personally. So, when a man of his great character undertakes a project of this magnitude, representing four years of in-depth research, it is essential that we hear him out. *Soldiers' Blood and Blooded Money* deserves our attention."

- Kevin D. Freeman, CFA
Global financial analyst commissioned by the Pentagon; *New York Times* best-selling author of *Secret Weapon;* author of *Game Plan: How to Protect Yourself from the Coming Cyber Economic Attack;* www.globaleconomicwarfare.com

---

"Allen Clark has shed flesh and blood for his country in support and defense of our treasured values as he has demonstrated in this work. An astute scholar, a believer in the Gospels and an observer of latter-day history, Allen Clark has plunged into perhaps the most in-depth, incisive and revealing documentary of the year, if not the century! He has permitted the unfettered facts of our history and those of mankind to speak for themselves. Herein, he has revealed much of the real world that is often skirted or muted entirely so as not to offend sensitivities, perhaps the guilty themselves. I invite you to join me and delve into this incredibly researched and thoughtful work by this equally scholarly author."

- Major General Chris Adams (USAF-Ret.)
Author of *Requiem of a Spy* and *Notable Encounters*

"I have known Allen Clark for some time. He is a writer, soldier, businessman and Christian who talks the talk and walks the walk.

In his newest book, he stands up extra tall and speaks truth to power as he peels away the layers of political chicanery and greed that corrupted our generation of warriors.

We went to war for the noblest of reasons, perhaps too naive, but we answered our Nation's call not realizing that we were being used as pawns for profit. As Allen says, our leaders saw money and position, we saw blood and death and returned unknowingly carrying the cancerous ghosts of war.

In his book, he and former Master Sergeant Johnson dig into those dark corners that denied the survivors' suffering and that of their families, for as they point out, the casualties of war are not just the soldier, but the families and generations yet to come. The double dealings of so many of our institutions failed us and instead became corrupt themselves. Clark uses the term "plutocracy" in his introduction as being abhorrent to a republic as it threatens our democracy.

Our faith has been deeply challenged, and as former President Jimmy Carter decries in his newest book, Clark and Johnson open doors and bring light into the dark corners of the corrupt power that deepens and spreads the casualties of war."

- J.L. "Bud" Alley
Silver Star and Purple Heart recipient; author of The Ghosts of the Green Grass; Battle survivor, Ia Drang Valley, Vietnam, 1965

"Allen Clark, as a West Point graduate, was 'shot full of the glory-gun' during his four years as a cadet. He heard the stirring speech of General Douglas MacArthur's farewell to the Corps of Cadets. The hallowed words of Duty, Honor, Country were emphasized as the guiding principles for Allen's future service to his country.

With that motivation, Allen has painstakingly researched the reasoning behind wars in which the youth of countries sacrificed life and limb, mind and bodies, to protect and defend their countries. His conclusions will surprise some. Yet, those conclusions have been made after a careful investigation into the countries' leaders' motivations before, during, and after these conflicts."

- Michael J. Vopatek
Combat veteran, Vietnam War; graduate of the United States Military Academy (USMA), 1963

"Allen Clark's latest book is an invaluable accurate account that ranks as a most worthy scholarly work on the subject of wars and their hidden and real causes by a man of outstanding credentials, impeccable integrity, and unsurpassed qualifications. This meticulously documented comprehensive book is a treasure for anyone wishing to learn about the history of warfare and its casualties."

- Amil Imani
Author and National Security Expert

"Having known Allen Clark for several years, I've had the privilege and pleasure of long and detailed conversations with him on a variety of topics. Our discussions have ranged from America's current military conflicts, to our historical wars, to the state of law enforcement and border security in our nation, and perhaps most importantly, to the impact of Christian values, morals and faith on our personal and professional lives. As such, I can state without reservation that Allen's book is an incredible MUST READ!

Allen Clark is a true American hero, a proven combat warrior that sacrificed his body and some of his soul for the nation that he holds so very dear. Allen's research, his documentation and his conclusions are above reproach and offer an insightful and enlightening education into the true nature of American wars, their origins and the impact that they have had on our country and on us all. Allen Clark sets the bar high and lifts us all by his example, his perspective and his incredible faith in God, Country and the True Patriots of America."

- Kenneth W. Cates

Special Agent in Charge (Ret.), Department of Homeland Security/U.S. Immigration and Customs Enforcement (ICE), North TX and Oklahoma; former U.S. Army Military Intelligence Specialist (E-4), 1972-73; former Special Agent, Bureau of ATF, U.S. Customs Service and U.S. ICE, 1976-2006; Senior Law Enforcement Advisor/Operator, U.S. Army's Asymmetric Warfare Group (AWG), Special Advisory Group (SAG), Iraq and Afghanistan, 2007-2012; Senior Law Enforcement Advisor, A-4/Commanders Advisory and Assistance Team (CAAT), International Security Assistance Force (ISAF), Afghanistan, 2013; author of Handbook *Leaders Tactical Guide to Threat Finance*, Asymmetric Warfare Group, Center for Army Lessons Learned

---

"I am honored to endorse my friend, The Honorable Allen Clark, and his latest book, *Soldiers' Blood and Bloodied Money*. Allen Clark's military service in Vietnam, and his extended suffering through tragic permanent injuries, both changed his life and proved to be character building and faith sharpening. Allen has committed tremendous time, research and thought to more deeply exploring world and American military history, along with studying the Bible's message and meaning, with a goal toward finding the truth about the causes of war. His research, service, and sacrifice warrant him a place at the table of conversation among America's serious thinkers about the roots, justifications and purposes of war.

On a personal level, Allen Clark is a man of earnest Christian faith, and unquestioned integrity and sincerity. For all these reasons, this book is worthy of your consideration."

- Debbie Georgatos

Conservative Radio Show Host of "America, Can We Talk?"; author of *Ladies, Can We Talk?*

"In my teens, I once saw a sign, 'War is good business; invest your son.' Over the years, I have pondered the meaning. It took a war hero, a standard bearer of freedom, enterprise, and justice, Allen Clark, to reveal the true meaning of investing our children in endless wars. Allen's journey uniquely qualifies him to reveal the hidden things that through this enlightenment, we may have the wisdom to break the cycle of wealth by war while preserving our liberty."

- Bill Wilson
Founder and Editor of "The Daily Jot"

"In this world, we are constantly fighting battles. Whether the battles we fight are mental, physical, or spiritual, we all want to know that any amount of suffering was for the good of mankind or for the benefit of future generations. In these world-battles, we must stay vigilant to understand what is good or evil.

Allen Clark has fought these different battles all his life. With his thorough research and wisdom, his book describes the battle between truth and hypocrisy. He proves himself still a warrior fighting as a soldier of truth, with a pen, against the dangerous enemy called hypocrisy."

- Christopher Vopatek

"Excellent perspective that masterfully evaluates the balances among the Warrior Ethos, foundation of Faith, and that of the Civilian governance that summoned military action. Allen's first-hand experiences in each of those areas make him uniquely qualified to present this holistic perspective on our history. His passion incites a reader to open their minds to comprehend beyond the obvious. I'm looking forward to Allen's future works containing other valuable lessons about our Nation's history."

- Rick Makowski
USMA graduate, 1976

"Allen Clark is a combat-wounded hero whose faith, writing, ministry, and personal story inspire those of us who know him, and thousands who have taken his inspiration into their daily lives to find meaning not only in their own travails but in what God has planned for us all..."

- Roger Cirillo

OTHER BOOKS BY ALLEN B. CLARK

Wounded Soldier, Healing Warrior: A Personal Story of a Vietnam Veteran Who Lost His Legs but Found His Soul; Hardcover – March 15, 2007; Foreword by Ross Perot.

Valor in Vietnam: Chronicles of Honor, Courage and Sacrifice: 1963 – 1977; Hardcover – Aug. 7, 2012; Foreword by Lieutenant General Dave R. Palmer, Superintendent, United States Military Academy at West Point (1986-1991). (Paperback released in 2019.)

TRIBUTES TO ALLEN B. CLARK AND PREVIOUS BOOKS

"There are a host of heroes to whom this country owes a debt it can never repay. Allen Clark lost both his legs while serving his country in Vietnam. When he came home, his body was broken, but his spirit never faltered. He went back to school. He earned his masters' degree in business administration. He served his state in a high government post and is now a successful businessman. He's an inspiration to all who know him."

- President Ronald Reagan

"*Wounded Soldier, Healing Warrior* is a book needed by those in the process of physical recovery from wounds of war, accident or heritage, as well as by the families and loved ones ... The reader will come away uplifted in body, mind and spirit. Sharing in this brave warrior's experience, through his adversities, gifts, and blessings reveal the inner strength of the human spirit."

- Purple Heart Magazine

"Allen's story has the potential to touch many lives. It is a message of struggle, perseverance, courage, and hope."

- Ross Perot

"*Wounded Soldier, Healing Warrior* is an exceptional read – captivating, inspirational and educational. Allen Clark is an American patriot who has lived the West Point values of Duty, Honor, and Country every day. From experiencing the rigors of combat during the War in Vietnam to becoming Assistant Secretary of Veterans Affairs, he did not allow physical disabilities to detract from his intent to care for others and serve his nation.

Allen provides a clear message – through strong values and faith in God, we can overcome adversity and be all we want to be."

- Lieutenant General Robert F. Foley (USA-Ret.)
Medal of Honor Recipient, Vietnam; Director, Army Emergency Relief, 2005-2016; USMA graduate, 1963

"When I first met Allen Clark in the early 1970s, I knew instantly this was a young man struggling to come to terms with his experiences, to make sense of tragedy and the conflict of his country's claim on his allegiance and the consequences of his patriotism. His spirit touched me then, as this book does now. He is an unusual American, and a pilgrim whose quest the reader will find poignant and illuminating."

- Bill Moyers
Former Press Secretary to President Lyndon B. Johnson, 1965-1967

"From my own experience, I know how much determination, courage, and faith it took for Allen Clark to travel his long journey back to life. But, he has made it, and in telling his story he will help others make it, too."

- Senator Bob Dole
U.S. Senator, KS, 1969-1996

"Allen's life story reflects rich experiences from his military service, his support of our veterans and his active political involvement. He is a patriot who raised himself from a battlefield in Vietnam to dedicate his energy and passion for helping others. It is a story full of encouragement and inspiration."

- Senator Kay Bailey Hutchison
U.S. Senator, TX, 1993-2013

"*Wounded Soldier, Healing Warrior* by Allen Clark is an inspiration to all soldiers who are injured in the field, especially in the case of mortar attacks and IED bombs. I enjoyed reading how he and other wounded soldiers managed to rehabilitate themselves with the help of the military and VA hospital systems, their faith in God, and their determination not to let their injuries destroy their lives."

- Robin Moore
Author of *The Green Berets* and *The French Connection*

"Allen's story of quiet unpretentious heroism will introduce the reader to the sights and sounds and smells of an ugly part of history and the triumph of God's grace through the meanest of circumstances."

- Richard Halverson
Chaplain, The United States Senate, 1981-1995

"*Wounded Soldier, Healing Warrior* is a captivating recount of a combat veteran's encounter with the enemy both on the battlefield and in life. This honest, open and insightful account of Allen Clark's life is a story everyone can relate to with their own challenges and struggles. Allen's faith journey is inspiring, and a must read for all."

- Scott O'Grady, Former Captain USAF
Author of *The New York Times* bestseller *Return with Honor*

"I've known Allen Clark for many years! His story is a must read for all who are interested in preserving the freedom we all enjoy in our great country. You'll also discover how to find true personal freedom. Allen made that discovery one day as I was teaching the Word of God. The message of Jesus Christ changed his life. I'm honored to recommend this book!"

- Dr. Gene A. Getz
President, Center for Church Renewal; Pastor Emeritus, Fellowship Bible Church, North Dallas, Texas; author with Holmon Bible Staff of *The Life Essentials Study Bible: Biblical Principles to Live By*

"WOW!!! What a sensational story of a heroic life and service for our dear country and our dear Lord Jesus. There are few accounts today of such dramatic demonstration of the Lord's power to not only save a life but to use that life for His glory. Your book is bound to help so many who suffer from Post-Traumatic Stress Disorder, as well as those returning from war, now."

- Dr. Bobby Welch
President, Southern Baptist Convention (2004-2006); author of *You, The Warrior Leader;* former Green Beret and Vietnam Veteran awarded a Purple Heart; Pastor Emeritus, First Baptist Church, Daytona, FL

"A fascinating tale vividly told. Allen Clark's account of his two wars – one for America and one for himself – is intimately personal yet broadly applicable to the larger audience of mankind. Set against the backdrop of the Vietnam War and its aftermath, the story traces Clark's trajectory from professional soldier to shattered veteran to civic leader to active lay ministry. He recounts his stark struggles to restore himself physically and emotionally, and unblushingly describes his inner spiritual pilgrimage. Particularly pertinent reading for veterans present and future."

- Lieutenant General Dave R. Palmer (USA-Ret.)
Author of *George Washington and Benedict Arnold: A Tale of Two Patriots;* author of *The River and the Rock: The History of Fortress West Point 1775-1783;* author of *Summons of the Trumpet;* USMA graduate, 1956; former Superintendent of West Point, 1986-1991

"Two centuries ago, George Washington set forth his ideal for the perfect soldier, declaring: 'To the distinguished character of Patriot, it should be our highest glory to add the more distinguished character of Christian.' Allen Clark fulfills this standard, being both a distinguished Patriot and Christian. As a patriot, in defense of freedom in Vietnam he lost both his legs. As a Christian, his faith is the centerpiece of his life and a source of inspiration for millions of others. *Wounded Soldier, Healing Warrior* is the story of a Patriot and Christian and a must read for every American."

- David Barton

Founder and President, author of The Founders' Bible (NASB); created and delivered famous patriotic speeches and sermons called *Celebrate Liberty!*

"Allen Clark's story, *Wounded Soldier, Healing Warrior*, is one of hope, help and healing. It will move your heart and stir your soul. Don't miss his deeply personal and powerful insights into inner healing, spiritual growth and personal triumph."

- Dr. Jerry Falwell (1993-2007)

Founder and Chancellor, Liberty University, Lynchburg, VA

"'Oh, God, I'm dead!' cried Captain Allen Clark when a North Vietnamese mortar burst landed 18 inches behind his left leg, June 17, 1967. ... From the pages of this remarkable memoir ... Wars in a sense never end, for victor or vanquished either one. How enriching to learn that Vietnam, which broke so many hearts and lives, gave – and gives – a sort of victory to one of the supposedly vanquished. Few 'dead' men in our time have lived with so much vigor, so much capacity to inspire."

- Bill Murchison

Radford Distinguished Professor of Journalism, Baylor University, 2002-2007; author of *There's More to Life Than Politics* and *Reclaiming Morality in America*

"I am proud to know Allen Clark. He is one of those rare individuals who has not only faced death, but has learned from the experience as well. That is enough, but that is not all. The insights found in *Wounded Soldier, Healing Warrior* are deeply felt and eloquently expressed. They are insights which remind us that the pain that comes from loss, the joy of overcoming adversity, and the sweetness of success need not cause barriers to be erected between us and God. I am always inspired and uplifted when I hear Allen's story. It is a pleasure to recommend this book."

- Lewis R. Timberlake, CPAE (1931-2012)
Professional Speaker; co-author with Marietta Reed of *Born to Win;* author of *It's Always Too Soon to Quit*

"For the more than forty years I have known him, Allen Clark has been a man of passion, courage, integrity and faith. All four of these qualities pulse through the experiences of his life. His honesty and authenticity as he tells his story is both heartwarming and challenging. It is today commonly agreed that one of the critical elements that develops people as leaders is hardship. Allen has had his share of hardship, more than most of us face in a lifetime, and it has helped to develop him into a man of strength, honor, humility and faith. We desperately need more men like him to help guide America through the challenges of the years ahead."

- Dr. Andrew B. Seidel, Colonel (USAR-Ret.)
Former Executive Director, Center for Christian Leadership; graduate of Dallas Theological Seminary; USMA graduate, 1963; author of *Charting a Bold Course*

"The story behind Allen Clark's journey from a casualty of the Vietnam War to a champion of the faith remains in my heart and mind as one of those all-time great reads. It is truly an enthralling account of the overcoming spirit Green Berets seemed to be endowed with as they go about their task of military service, and freeing the oppressed. Today, Allen is still freeing the 'oppressed,' but in a new and exciting way. *Wounded Soldier, Healing Warrior* is not one of those books you will merely read and put on your shelf-it is one you will study time and time again for years to come."

- Chuck Dean
National Chaplain, Emeritus, 173d Airborne Brigade; author of *Nam Vet: Making Peace with Your Past*; co-author with Bridgett Cantrell of *Down Range: To Iraq and Back*

"Allen Clark's book is a powerful, moving account as he takes the reader on a most harrowing but ultimately triumphant ride. His early days of service as a dutiful West Point graduate are followed by a grievous wounding that left him without legs in a world that waits for no one. Cast into a pit of understandable depression, he refuses to quit, and his own unquenchable spirit ultimately lifts him back up and allows him to find his own triumph over tragedy. His resilience and unquenchable spirit make up a powerful model for all, especially when he turns his efforts to the selfless cause of helping others in need. Spiritually refreshing and boldly inspirational, I give this wonderful book my highest recommendation."

- Tom Carhart, Ph.D.
Author of *Lost Triumph: Lee's Real Plan at Gettysburg – and Why It Failed* and *From West Point Brothers to Battlefield Rivals*; USMA graduate, 1963

"*Wounded Soldier, Healing Warrior* is a compelling testimony of courage and redemption. Allen Clark describes in riveting detail the battle in Vietnam where he was severely wounded and with uncompromising honesty his recovery from physical disability and emotional self-doubt. Like most combat-wounded veterans, Clark's post-war journey was not easy. But the power of faith enabled his understanding that true healing comes through the inner peace that comes of understanding God's forgiveness, love and grace.

As a battle-tested veteran, I recommend Allen Clark's story as vital reading for veterans and their families of any war who have experienced the crucible of combat and the spiritual challenges of coming to terms with their experiences."

- Al Santoli
Founder and President, Asia America Initiative; author of *Everything We Had* and *To Bear Any Burdon*

"All of us encounter challenging and potentially life-changing events at some time. *Wounded Soldier, Healing Warrior* is proof that despite the cards we are dealt, each of us can persevere and overcome obstacles to lead a fulfilling, meaningful life. Allen Clark's autobiography inspires us all to see the possibilities and encourages us to make a difference."

- Roger Staubach
Heisman Trophy Winner, 1963; Pro Football Hall of Fame Quarterback; Executive Chairman, Jones Lang LaSalle; USNA graduate, 1965

SOLDIERS' BLOOD
AND BLOODIED MONEY

Wars and the Ruling Elites

by

The Honorable Allen B. Clark
Captain, U.S. Army, Retired

and

J.W. "Jess" Johnson
Former Master Sergeant, U.S. Army
Contributor

www.soldiersblood.com

SOLDIERS' BLOOD AND BLOODIED MONEY
Wars and the Ruling Elites

ISBN: 978-0-692-1198-7

Author: Allen B. Clark

Contact the author at www.soldiersblood.com or www.allenbclark.com.

DEDICATION

To our Creator, our Lord in Heaven, who sent His Son, Jesus the Christ, to die on the cross to offer for our faith the gift to live forever.

To all the laborers of the harvest, who have imparted to me their love, knowledge, understanding, and prayers throughout my life.

To my patient wife, Linda, who makes life worth living.

To all the men and women on both sides of conflicts, who have gone off to fight in wars and become casualties in body, mind, and soul, to their suffering families, and to all the innocent civilians on both sides who died or sustained wounds as "collateral damage."

TABLE OF CONTENTS

PREFACE BY AUTHOR

Allen B. Clark, Captain (USA-Ret.)

Now in the middle of my eighth decade of life, I reflect often upon how one day in my third decade of life transformed my life forever, and I have recalled it mournfully every day since. On June 17, 1967, three days before my twenty-fifth birthday, as a soldier in the Vietnam War, twenty pints of my blood were shed! As an Army captain assigned to the Fifth Special Forces in Vietnam, the clandestine mission of my unit was the collection of intelligence on our enemy, the Communist North Vietnamese regular troops, by utilizing the safe haven of Cambodia as a privileged sanctuary.

On that fateful day my Special Forces "A" camp at Dak To came under an intense mortar and rocket barrage from a Communist battalion, which had moved to fight Americans from its Cambodian sanctuary to our west. In the pursuit of my modest actions during the attack, it was seen fit by my superiors to award me a Silver Star, our Nation's third-highest decoration for "Gallantry in Action."

I wear most proudly this Silver Star and a Purple Heart medal for my wounds incurred in this attack that caused the amputation of both my legs below the knee.

[Author's note: My survival despite my horrendous wounding was due only to the medical care I received from Special Forces combat medic Jimmy Hill, also wounded in the attack. Jimmy braved the barrage to obtain plasma and morphine for me, and even despite his own shrapnel wound, treated seventy more wounded in the camp before assistance finally arrived the following day in the form of another combat medic.]

Eight years of psychotherapy and antidepressants followed. My healing process at an Army Medical Center lasted fifteen months and included twelve surgeries, more than one hundred stitches, and fourteen weeks in a closed psychiatric ward in 1968.

Despite this abrupt jolt to my life through this trauma, I went on to a rewarding and satisfying life. In my life, I've experienced America's capitalist system in the investment industry as a Chartered Financial Analyst in a large bank trust department, where I was involved with Wall Street investment firms. In the real estate industry, I brokered residential transactions. In the energy industry, I was employed by a small independent oil exploration company and served as president of three oil industry service companies in Midland, Texas. Returning to real estate, I was involved in the real property investments industry as founding president of an investment and management company in multi-family limited partnerships. Finally, I also gained experience in the mortgage lending industry.

It has been my honor as a citizen of the United States to serve my state of Texas as a senior political appointee of a Texas governor and as a political candidate for statewide elected office as well as a local county office (both contests were unsuccessful). Additionally, I served my country as a senior political appointee with a four-star general protocol rank in a presidential administration. My two presidential appointments with senatorial confirmation at the U.S. Department of Veterans Affairs led to roles as the Assistant Secretary for Veterans Liaison and Program Coordination, as well as to serving as the Director of the National Cemetery System, where I oversaw 115 national cemeteries with two million burial sites. In this capacity, I visited many of the cemeteries where our war dead were buried.

Over nine years at a big-city Veterans Affairs Department medical center, it was my great privilege to serve many soldiers, sailors, Marines, airmen and women, and veterans also of the Coast Guard, many with severe wounds incurred while serving our country in our myriad of wars. While it was difficult to understand the underlying purposes behind our wars, we rode to the sound of the guns as loyal and patriotic citizens, inspired perhaps merely by jingoism and sometimes convoluted explanations and causes, if any were defined for us at all.

My father was an Army officer, who served in the Korean War. Following in his footsteps, I, too, became an officer by graduating the United States Military Academy with a regular Army commission before my twenty-first birthday as the youngest man in my class of 504 graduates. A *New York Times* article by Scott Shane on November 27, 2016, came to my attention because it related succinctly to my service academy culture. The article profiled Steve Bannon, who was later selected by President Donald Trump as a special political counselor on his White House staff. Bannon's daughter graduated from West Point in 2010.

In the *New York Times* article, Peter Schweizer, a conservative author and president of the Government Accountability Institute, stated:[1]

> "But through his daughter's service, he saw an inequity that fueled his anger at the privileged Americans among whom he had long worked. At West Point, 'he saw a complete, utter lack of people from the upper economic levels of American society,' said Mr. Schweizer, the conservative writer. 'He thought it was appalling, especially because the elite set so many policies that sent these kids into war.'"

Bannon's sentiments were like those that had intermittently crossed my mind for decades.

Despite a "safe" opportunity for assignment to Korea in 1966 as a general's aide-de-camp, my sense of duty and allegiance to my country prompted me to volunteer for service in Vietnam. After volunteering in-country, I was assigned to the Army's Special Forces, the Green Berets, as an airborne-qualified officer without attendance at any of the specialty Fort Bragg schools.

In my post-military advanced education, I obtained an MBA at

Dallas' Southern Methodist University. Before West Point, my high school education consisted of two years in a Catholic Jesuit High School (Gonzaga in Washington, D.C.) plus one year at Phillips Exeter Academy, an elite New England preparatory school founded in 1783 in New Hampshire.

It is my purpose to recount my biography only to establish my roles as loyal soldier, experienced businessman, and dedicated public servant who feels deeply privileged to have been raised in a proud military family in this great land of the free and home of the brave. The extraordinary opportunity I received to pursue a good education laid the groundwork for me to serve my country in military service and to experience a variety of endeavors in our free market system.

Throughout the decades, I have always been an avid reader of religious, patriotic, historical, and business books. The bottom line is that I suppose many would define me as a "loyal American, evangelical Christian, populist-leaning Republican, patriotic citizen, proud veteran, typical businessman, and finally, a representative member of my country's 'establishment.'" Typically, "liberals," "anti-war activists," and "progressives" write books such as this one. Their purpose often seems to be to denunciate and tear down the America so beloved, and bled for, by me.

So, why would a seemingly pro-establishment person such as I embark upon producing a manuscript that brings forth apparent historical truths as opposed to the typical historical revisionism? These truths illustrate that we young patriots, who have gone off to fight in wars, are merely pawns in a much larger chess game of life – a game where the captains and kings and knights and bishops are the ones who often profit immeasurably in terms of financial gain or increases in power. Meanwhile, we perish or suffer immense physical and emotional wounds from which many of us never heal. One must also consider the casualties in the unassuming innocent citizen bystanders in the wars of history, or the so-called "collateral damage."

My studies have revealed the stories "behind the curtains" as to the REAL reasons men and women like me have shed our blood through the centuries, and perhaps even the millennia, so that blood money may be made by the unseen (but now revealed herein) manipulators of world events. Careful analysis indicates that the full truth has not always been documented and that authentic motivations have not always been revealed.

The following quote by Davis Aiken that appears in the foreword of a book about the Civil War makes a clear case for the title of this book:

> According to the sources used by Graham, the death of the American Republic, that shining light to oppressed humanity everywhere, was not caused by slavery. Nor was the death caused by unfair tariffs, or even by States asserting the right of secession. No, the great American experiment in constitutional government by the consent of the governed was ruined by a plot to gain control of banking and currency-the love of money, the root of all evil according to St. Paul. Blood money. (Graham: 12).

Perhaps our real reasons for some of these wars and their attendant profits are that the citizenry has not been sufficiently attuned to the important matters of state and politics and have been "low-information" voters much too often. I am no longer uninformed and remain hopeful that the readers of this book will also be enlightened by the truth.

I have adopted one comment from a *Newsweek* article dated November 14, 2005, penned by Jonathan Darman, as my "right," and almost also as my obligation, to write this manuscript: "It is the privilege of the old soldier, then, to speak realistically of war, and idealistically of peace. Another privilege: speaking for those who did not live to speak for themselves." The same article included a letter from an American Army private Paul Curtis in May of 1944 at Anzio, Italy, stating, "... peace will be settled by men who have never known combat and ... hold no dread of another war for they do not know."

I acknowledge with extraordinary gratitude the contributions of my dear Vietnam War comrade, J.W. "Jess" Johnson, who shed his blood twice in our Vietnam War. His real-world experiences and research into a variety of world arenas have proven to be invaluable in the completion of the manuscript.

The following YouTube videos reflect the suffering endured by some combatants and their families in warfare. The first video, entitled "The Band Played Waltzing Matilda," (John McDermott, composed in 1971, and later revised) is about an Australian soldier who lost both legs at the Battle of Gallipoli in 1915. [Video link: https://www.youtube.com/watch?v=VktJNNKm3B0]

The second video relates to the horrors of death in war: "For all the 'Willie McBrides' The Green Fields of France Celtic Thunder." [Video link: https://youtu.be/h6qK_PRaf_8]

These two videos will serve as a fitting and compelling contextual backdrop to reading the following histories of conflicts and casualties.

PREFACE BY CONTRIBUTOR

J.W. "Jess" Johnson, former Master Sergeant, U.S. Army

After an idyllic childhood, what I experienced in Vietnam jarred every fiber of my being, damaging both my mind and heart. Infantry combat in the jungle with its horrific experiences of landmines and memories of the wounded, blood, limbs, agony and screaming are as vivid today as if I were to have been there this morning. As a combat medic, I needed to achieve a balance in my life - mentally, physically, emotionally and spiritually.

Then in the mid-80s, I began to become aware of what went on behind the scenes in the causes of the war. I have served as a young, idealistic American patriot. What I began to discover as I matured, was that wars were for profit at the expense of uniformed military personnel. I began to study and understand the causes of my war in which so many served and sacrificed with the loss of our youth, our lives, and in some cases, our minds. I began to study what was happening up the food chain. When I was in the jungle, I could only see a few meters ahead. At night, you could not see your hand in front of your face.

There were individuals in higher places of power in my government and corporations. They sat in plush leather chairs in oak-paneled boardrooms across corporate America. The leaders of these corporations could clearly see the future for themselves. They saw the green of dollars for profit while I saw the red blood of my fellow platoon members. What I began to learn about Vietnam motivated me to study the causes, casualties, and consequences of my war and other wars.

These corporate leaders and those in the military-industrial complex made decisions that put the youth of America into situations where sometimes we could hardly breathe in the heat of combat. It was my privilege to travel all throughout Southeast Asia, Africa, Europe, Russia, Central America, and South America.

I have derived much of what I know from being "boots on the ground" in many dangerous hotspots around the world.

I agree with Allen that it is not our purpose to bash this magnificent America, our homeland, which we so proudly served as soldiers in a war zone. We desire to lend our efforts to this work of ours to enlighten our readers to what we have discovered in our research. We will relate what has gone on backstage behind the strategic curtains of history as we young patriots have played out the tactics on the battlefields.

My parents were members of the greatest generation. They experienced the Depression as well as WWII. My father lost his right leg when his Sherman tank hit a mine after they crossed into Germany. As a member of the Baby Boomers generation, everything was new. I grew up in Commack on Long Island in the '50s with three sisters and a brother. Our home looked the same as all our neighbors. Twenty schools were built in town to accommodate the thousands of new children as families moved into the area.

Our parents wanted to provide us with a life they had not had; a brand-new home, nourishing food, warm clothing, a quality education, church attendance each week as a family, and a stable home environment. This was what my father fought for and my mother longed for since both grew up as orphans. As children, we were sheltered from the ongoing events of the world. As far as I knew, my universe was Commack, New York.

Vietnam was 8,874 miles away or halfway around the world. The United States had entered a war that we did not understand. Vietnam was a very small nation of thirty million people and divided into two countries in 1954. North Vietnam was under Communist ruling and the South was supposedly free but was really run by a supposedly benevolent dictator.

On April 7, 1954, President Dwight Eisenhower described the "Domino Theory" to America, which predicts that a political event in one country could cause similar events in neighboring countries, like a row of falling dominoes. Communism, the all-pervasive socialist system centered in the Soviet Union that was originally established in 1917 through a violent revolution and maintained with much bloodshed and suffering, is probably the best example of the domino effect. We had been involved in a Cold War since after World War II but were consumed with Communism as our major enemy. At the very lowest level in the jungles of Vietnam, I was doing my small part in combatting Communism.

In 1969, my Army time began as a paratrooper and combat medic. After my initial military training, my assignment was to the 101st Airborne Division in Phu Bai, Republic of Vietnam. My platoon would walk and fight through the jungles of Vietnam on missions lasting for 45 days at a time. One morning, four men were sent out on a patrol where they were ambushed with all being severely wounded. A medevac helicopter was summoned to evacuate them to our rear area surgical hospital. That night, another nine were wounded, when one of them stepped on a landmine. My medical supplies had become depleted and helicopter evacuation support was almost impossible due to the heavy ground fire from the North Vietnamese soldiers in our area. At midnight two more soldiers suffered concussions and were evacuated to the rear hospital as was I shortly thereafter.

I had arrived in Vietnam at age 18 and departed feeling 40. Initially, I had believed my enlisting for active Army duty would help stop Communism in Vietnam. Soon I realized a much-lessened purpose which was to be there medically to save the members of my platoon. We sustained a 75% casualty rate and all we desired was to survive long enough to return to the "world" we all called home. My complete story is written in a chapter in Allen Clark's book, *Valor in Vietnam*.

My growth has been exponential from those days of my youth in the jungles of Vietnam to where I am today as a much wiser and more informed citizen of my country.

[Author's note: Johnson received two Purple Hearts for his wounds in Vietnam. He continued to serve his country as a weapons specialist in our Nation's Special Forces.]

FOREWORD

Lt. Col. Allen B. West (USA-Ret.)

Member of 112th U.S. Congress

Author of *Guardian of the Republic:*
An American Ronin's Journey to Faith, Family and Freedom

When the Honorable Allen B. Clark asked me to write the foreword to his book, *Soldiers' Blood and Bloodied Money – Wars and the Ruling Elites*, I felt completely unworthy of such a task. Mr. Clark humbly said to me that no one else is better suited to write the foreword to this literary endeavor than you. He also gave me a warning that this would be a controversial book and that I may not want to have my name in association. Nothing could be further from the truth, as this book presents a critical exegesis on a very important question, why are wars started, and who benefits from them?

If there is one thing that we must embrace, it is a simple maxim that truth should never be considered controversial. And history should never be examined from the revisionist perspective. In objective analysis and reflection, we can oft time learn incredible and valuable lessons that refine our present and shape our future.

So, why would a distinguished and accomplished man and veteran such as Allen B. Clark ask me to write a foreword to his book?

The story of my life and family's service to our Nation in times of war is the reason. My dad was a simple young man born in Ozark, Alabama, who answered the call to arms in World War II. Here was an American black man who would fight for his Nation when it was his own Nation that did not afford him all the rights and privileges it did others. It was not his personal sense of entitlement, or rights, but rather my dad realized that his Nation needed him. He realized that America was facing a determined enemy, a true evil which if triumphant, would redefine liberty and freedom for future generations. My dad knew that in Nazi Germany there was an enemy that wholeheartedly represented a belief in racial superiority. Herman West, Sr. knew that he had to step up and make a stand against this abhorrent philosophy, and he did.

My dad was not seeking to earn any great accolades. He was not a college graduate but ended up being just a simple Army Corporal in the supply branch. Dad was joining a legacy of black men who would fight for this Nation, serve, sacrifice, and commit to its principles and values, even when they did not enjoy them. It started with a freeman named Crispus Attucks, one of the first killed in what would become known as the Boston Massacre. It was followed by great freed men who first wore the uniform of the United States as Union Army Soldiers, the 54th Massachusetts Infantry Regiment, who distinguished themselves at Fort Wagner during the Civil War.

It continued with the men of the 9th and 10th Calvary Regiments who helped protect the settlers heading west and were often denied entry into the very towns they helped to protect. In World War I, it was the 369th Infantry Regiment, the famed "Hell Fighters from Harlem," who when rebuffed by General Pershing, fought with the French and earned great honors. In World War II we saw American black men who distinguished themselves, like Dorie Miller, a Navy cook, at Pearl Harbor. The 332d Fighter Group, famed "Tuskegee Airmen," the 333d Field Artillery Battalion, and the 761st Tank Battalion were all black units, consisting of men who, like my dad, answered the call to arms to defeat an ideological enemy whose belief was rooted in abject racism. Units like the Montford Point Marines and the 555th Parachute Infantry Battalion evidenced that these American warriors wanted to fight, that their purpose was clear, and that their hearts were true to a cause. The sacrifices of these men over all these years were rewarded when President Truman desegregated our armed forces by Executive Order 9981 on July 26, 1948.

The fight was hardly over for our Nation when it came to Civil Rights, but the first step had been taken. It happened because these black soldiers, sailors, Airmen, and Marines from Crispus Attucks to my dad knew why they had to fight for America, to prove their equality.

And so, we entered the Korean War to stem the tide of a new evil, communism. And then came another battle between liberty and collective subjugation, Vietnam. It was then my older brother, Herman West, Jr. answered the call to arms, volunteering, not drafted, to be a Marine Infantryman. My older Brother, Lance Corporal West, sought the discipline and honor of the United States Marine Corps and during his tour of duty was wounded during the siege of Khe Sanh. My dad had also been wounded in World War II in Italy during an artillery shelling causing him to wreck his motorcycle while running supply dispatches.

My older brother's purpose for serving was to prepare him for a law enforcement career, and he did serve in the Atlanta Police Department.

And then my time came.

It was a simple day when I was 15 years of age when my dad sat me down on the steps of 651 Kennesaw Avenue in Atlanta's historic Old Fourth Ward and gave me a purpose. My dad stated to me that there was no greater honor than to wear the uniform of the United States of America. He said that being in the military one is not judged by their skin color but rather on merit and their abilities. Corporal Herman West, Sr., a disabled veteran from World War II, challenged me to be the first commissioned officer in our family. And so it was that I began my quest as a Henry Grady High School Army JROTC cadet as a 10th grader. Seven years later, on July 31, 1982, there I stood in the Army ROTC conference room in Stokely Athletic Center at the University of Tennessee, Knoxville with Mom on one side, and Dad on the other pinning on my gold Second Lieutenant bars as a commissioned U.S. Army officer.

I had fulfilled the challenge that Dad, and Mom, had made for me. However, I did not yet know my real purpose as a young Army officer, a Soldier. That came for me in January 1985 as an officer in the 4th Battalion, 325th Airborne Battalion Combat Team (4/325th ABCT) when I went through Checkpoint Charlie transiting from West to East Berlin...from freedom to tyranny. It was then that I knew why I was a Soldier. It was then that I knew my purpose as a Soldier. It was then that I came to know why I stood upon freedom's rampart as a Guardian of the Republic. Later during combat tours in Desert Storm and Iraq, I saw the face of evil. And even after retiring, as a civilian/military adviser to the Afghanistan National Army, I knew why I was serving.

And today, the fourth generation of our family is a young Army Major, the second commissioned officer, my nephew, Major Herman Bernard West III. Bernie was there on June 6, 2002, at Ft. Hood, Texas, when I took Battalion Command with his dad, my older brother. That day after the ceremony was over, Bernie, who was a cadet at North Georgia College, confessed to me that he wanted to be an artilleryman just like his uncle, and so he is. As of the time of my writing this foreword, Major Bernard West III is on his third combat tour of duty.

Why did I tell this story of the service, sacrifice, and commitment of our family to these United States of America? Because it is a story that is repeated in many families across our great land. It is the story of soldiers willing to make the ultimate sacrifice, the last full measure of devotion, to shed their blood for our freedom.

However, the interesting aspect of warfare is that there are oft times a conflicting purpose, a competing purpose that is not so honorable, nor noble. This is the purpose of the book written by the Hon. Allen B. Clark and contributed to by former Master Sergeant J.W. "Jess" Johnson. We must learn about and understand the interests of the industrial, political, religious and ecumenical, and financial elites who sometimes benefit from the wars fought by those with true intentions. Why through history have soldiers, sailors, Airmen, and Marines...warriors, shed blood?

Could it be that they have done so for providing money, bloodied money, for those who sit far away and manipulate events to advance their dishonorable, perhaps even nefarious, purposes?

This is the real riddle of warfare, the juxtaposition between the honorable young men, and women, who leave home and hearth to do as *Washington Times* film critic and essayist Richard Grenier stated in 1993: "As George Orwell pointed out, people sleep peacefully in their beds at night only because rough men stand ready to do violence on their behalf." This belief stands in contrast to those who profit or gain higher office due to the exertions of others.

It was John Stuart Mill who said, "War is an ugly thing, but not the ugliest of things: the decayed and degraded state of moral and patriotic feeling which thinks that nothing is worth a war, is much worse. When a people are used as mere human instruments for firing cannon or thrusting bayonets, in the service and for the selfish purposes of a master, such war degrades a people. A war to protect other human beings against tyrannical injustice; a war to give victory to their own ideas of right and good, and which is their own war, carried on for an honest purpose by their free choice — is often the means of their regeneration. A man who has nothing which he is willing to fight for, nothing which he cares more about than he does about his personal safety, is a miserable creature who has no chance of being free, unless made and kept so by the exertions of better men than himself. As long as justice and injustice have not terminated their ever-renewing fight for ascendancy in the affairs of mankind, human beings must be willing, when need is, to do battle for the one against the other."

The Honorable Clark's and Master Sergeant Johnson's book is all about the quote by John Stuart Mill. The four generations in my family embodied the fight, the war, the purpose of protecting human beings against tyrannical injustice. Yet, we cannot disavow that there are those who exist in powerful positions, even elected office, who seek to use warriors as mere human instruments for their own selfish purposes. One is a worthy endeavor, and as Mr.

Mill says, the other degrades a people.

When I was a Member of the 112th U.S. Congress and sat on the largest oversight committee, the House Armed Services Committee, I was shocked at how many had never served in uniform. No, I do not believe we need a draft in America, but I do hold the belief that certain elected offices and political appointee positions should require military service. Especially if these elected officials and political appointees have anything to do with the decisions to employ and deploy young men and women into combat.

I do believe that the defense industrial complex should be providing the weapons and equipment that our military requires. They should not be in the business of making things they want to profit. The funds we appropriate to our Department of Defense must no longer be tied up in a profit-driven weapons acquisition and procurement process. I have no problem supporting the free market, but not at the expense of our troops in contact (TIC).

Soldiers' Blood and Bloodied Money – Wars and the Ruling Elites is a vital read for this generation so that we do not commit the same mistakes. We must ensure that our wars are fought for honorable purposes, because those who fight them are the most honorable this Nation can produce. Those who are willing to lay down their lives for another...and not for a selfish purpose.

INTRODUCTION

This work will be most controversial. However, as a severely disabled veteran (double-leg amputee from the Vietnam War) who reads extensively and began to learn about the behind-the-scenes causes of wars, it became my tireless quest to document what I have discovered. To put it succinctly, as a "patriot" volunteer soldier, I am appalled by what I have learned and what I narrate in the following pages. In every case, I necessarily do not make a judgment as to whether the warfare outcome was in fact merited by any criteria that had been propagated as to its origination. However, it has become imperative for me to know and impart the facts I have learned. Above all, I love my country, the United States of America, and desire that its sovereignty be preserved.

Rest assured that my work will not blame capitalism or the free-market system for the egregious examples of the seekers of money and power who have not been averse to wars occurring for their own financial gain.

The machinations of history are replete with hidden factions that actually govern the real world in lieu of "official" governing bodies, like kingdoms, dictatorships, democracies, representative republics, autocracies, and monarchies that appear to be in charge. Hidden powers even guide ideologies such as capitalism, socialism, anarchism, fascism and communism.

William Jennings Bryan, a one-time candidate for president of the United States, expressed in a speech at Madison Square Garden on August 30, 1906, words that most definitely reflect what I would define as a "populist" philosophy:

> Plutocracy is abhorrent to a republic; it is more despotic than monarchy, more heartless than aristocracy, more selfish than bureaucracy. It preys upon the nation in time of peace

and conspires against it in the hour of its calamity...The time is ripe for the overthrow of this giant wrong.

Plutocracy comes from two Greek words meaning wealth and power. A plutarchy, which is a form of oligarchy, exists when a society is controlled by a small minority of the wealthy people in a society. Wikipedia defines the concept of plutocracy as a system that "may be advocated by the wealthy classes of a society in an indirect or surreptitious fashion, though the term itself is almost always used in a pejorative sense."

The eloquent words of a fictional character in Taylor Caldwell's *Prologue to Love* add fuel to the fire that the wealthy live to propagate gain:

> Great fortunes, immense fortunes, are rarely made honestly, and certainly not very fast. It was not my intention to start a dynasty slowly and carefully. And legitimately. That would have taken too long for my purposes. Besides, what is 'legitimately'? Some of the mightiest fortunes in America, now honored and scraped to reverently, were made in a fashion similar to mine. The Delanos, for instance, made their fortune through opium, the Astors through their exploitation of the Indians and their furs, the Vanderbilts through their ruthless manipulation of railroads and the stock market. Yet who despises them? Presidents and kings are delighted to entertain them and are as delighted to be entertained in turn. One of the most tremendous fortunes in America was made by gun-running to the South during the war; another, equally tremendous, was made by black birding, the running of naked black savages from Africa to America despite intricate and punitive laws. The heirs of all these have married into some of Europe's noblest families; their children are now aristocrats. Their marriages and their deaths and their births make notable headlines in the newspapers.

Murder of the helpless, ruin of the weak, theft, exploitation and despair and death have attended the making of these fortunes for a few. Not to mention, of course, the subornation of politicians, princes, and statesmen, who profited by glancing the other way or by quietly assisting.

'Yet who cares? Who denounces?'

No one who has ever been like or is like this fictional character would ever admit it, except perhaps in a deathbed confession.

It is the shared purpose of the author and contributor of this book, both of whom have shed "soldiers' blood," to relate the true and apparent behind-the-scenes manipulations and movements propagated by "plutocrats" to serve their financial needs, economic motivations, greed, and lust for power. For these selfish purposes, we young patriots and other innocent civilians sacrifice our lives, our limbs, our blood, and sometimes our very minds and emotions to fulfill their ambitions, bank accounts, and positions of power.

Whenever one studies history, one should be mindful of what President Calvin Coolidge once said: "It is even probable that the supremacy of nations may be determined by the possession of available petroleum and its products." Many wars and machinations have truly occurred solely for the purpose of procuring and securing energy resources.

It is my purpose to explore and relate the behind-the-scenes events that have brought about so much pain, agony, and suffering for so many due to the acts of the "Captains and the Kings" of many nations to enrich themselves. As my research became deeper and deeper, my displeasure increased, and I agonized over how these cooperative business endeavors could have been accomplished, many times to the detriment of my very comrades in the profession of arms.

Charles Higham, in his *Trading with the Enemy*, answered my question and expressed the "Big Picture," when he wrote that individuals were "... introduced ... to the idea of a world community of money that would be independent of wars and empires." He went on to speak of certain high-level American businesspeople who, "... shared ... views on international financial solidarity," intent on fulfilling their own financial, economic, or spiritual purposes through cooperative efforts.

My research has been attained through extensive readings of authors in four categories: 1) authors who were published a hundred years or even longer ago; 2) authors who are not citizens of our nation, and therefore not necessarily wedded to the history we are taught in our country's textbooks; 3) authors who might be considered by some as "liberals, leftists, or even anti-war"; and 4) authors whose research quotes sources in other books, not all of which have been added to my already extensive personal library. When authors have utilized other original sources, the author of the original source will usually be footnoted in the chapter notes section. Years after wars, our referenced authors have sometimes discovered information that has been declassified or newly discovered.

It is not my intention to be seen as capable nor learned enough to produce a work that is academic in nature, nor qualified or eligible for "peer review." It will never be an example of extraordinary scholarship. That result will be left to the many learned scholars and historians in the hallowed halls of higher education. Any published work will have its critics who will question its sources and its conclusions. So be it. An author such as I must be prepared for a denunciation of some of the quoted authors, who will be criticized for their own personal prejudices or for bias in their writings. Referenced authors may be castigated for their own anti-Semitic or anti-Christian biases.

Therefore, any negativity directed toward my sources must differentiate between their perceived biases and their quoted research and facts. Apparent to readers is that older published books do not necessarily adhere to current standards of documentation of sources and footnotes. Some of these authors speculate about discussions at which they were not personally present, but the conversations are eminently expressive of what might have been related. When such situations are referenced, this book attempts to designate them as such.

Many "sacred cows" will be explored, including major money center bankers, Wall Street lawyers, City of London financiers, politicians, presidents, people of both Gentile and Jewish heritage, members of various faith walks, unscrupulous capitalists, propagandists, media moguls, and captains of industries who profit from wars. No work on topics about sources of oil, wars, and lending to governments to finance wars should leave unmentioned controversial families such as the Rothschilds of Europe, the Rockefellers, the Morgans, the Fords, and the Dulles family of the United States. Nuggets of involvement by members of the venerable New York law firm of Sullivan & Cromwell crop up throughout many periods of our history. These "usual suspects" have been written about as participants in the "conspiracy theory of history," the Illuminati, and the New World Order. It is not our purpose to suggest that all subjects in the above circles are complicit in malfeasance, misfeasance, guilt, or involvement in the various conspiracies written about so completely in depth by other writers. This book adheres to my disciplined goal of presenting the facts as learned.

Included here and in potential future writings is documentation related to the unknown or little-known history and causes of our wars through the influence of cabals and elitists. This book covers wars such as the American Revolution, our Civil War, the Spanish-American War, and episodes in Mexico and Central and South America. A potential later volume could include subjects such as the Anglo-Boer War, Russo-Japanese War, World War I, the Bolshevik Revolution, trading with Nazi Germany and Japan in the 1930s, China and Japan, WWII, the Korean War, Vietnam, the Balkans, and the recent conflicts in the Middle East. (God willing for my longevity.)

You may, in the future, be able to read my recounting of the real stories behind the assassination of Archduke Ferdinand, the sinking of the Lusitania, the leaders of the Bolshevik Revolution, the warnings of a possible attack on Pearl Harbor, and other provocations of conflicts. Most importantly, a later volume would delve even further into the never-ending quest to control energy sources so that mankind can enjoy the very definite benefits of "the good life" provided by petroleum and its products.

Why would this book be of interest to readers? It will be compelling because, for perhaps the first time in this and a potential future volume, someone will have reported upon some of the principal causes of major wars and conflicts with the attendant casualties, consequences, and the suffering of the masses and the combatants. A subtitle for this book could also well be, "All You Ever Wanted to Know about the Causes, Casualties, and Consequences of Wars, But Did Not Have Time to Learn."

This book will bring readers up to speed on many fascinating points of historical study. It is not my purpose to tear down the exceptional country that is our United States of America, which Jess Johnson and I both served as young men, nor to dissuade our citizens from fighting for legitimate causes of national security in the future. It is, however, my objective to call attention to the reasons behind our past wars that may not be well-known by our citizenry due to the questionable actions of individuals who propagated the wars for their own financial gain.

As one of my original sources taking me on this journey of discovery, author Deanna Spingola wrote:

> ... politicians choose war instead of open negotiations, but it is the youth of many nations, indoctrinated to hate the 'enemy,' who die in those wars. The U.S. government, often without public support or knowledge, has intervened in countries worldwide...During the course of those interventions, millions have perished. If people consider

their moral values, resist the propaganda and follow the proverbial money, they will discover that the same people who advocate warfare frequently profit in its aftermath.

Typically, those who initiate wars have not necessarily served in uniform themselves. This book connects the dots for wars fought by us and others to demonstrate Spingola's thesis.

This book describes individuals whose actions reflected greed, selfishness, and the pursuit of power, all of which are far from altruistic motivations. It is recognized that the underlying character and actions of many of the subjects were in many instances individual actions and expressions, divorced from some overall nefarious, organized, and concerted evil efforts.

However, others took part in the concerted effort in secular world history through the action of being participants in larger conspiracies, wittingly or unwittingly. An example taken from the Boer Wars, a plan by elitists to foster a controlled world (possibly being defined by the much-repudiated concept of "One World government") came out through a statement made in 1891 by Cecil Rhodes. Rhodes, who amassed a fortune in South African diamond and gold mines, stated, "The only feasible [way] to carry this idea out is a secret one [society] gradually absorbing the wealth of the world to be devoted to such an object."[1]

Perhaps this could be interpreted as a "smoking gun" relative to plans being laid to control world systems (see future references to the influence of Great Britain). Recorded history is replete with attempts to control and acquire power at the expense of others, especially the powerless or uninformed pawns who likely comprise 99% of the population. These pawns were moved by their "handlers" space by space until all were swept off the boards of life by the proponents of the power grabs. As a war-wounded soldier, I am especially cognizant of these movements.

Originally, my thesis and thrust of this book were only meant to encompass a secular recounting of the causes and results of wars.

Of and by itself, I expected this book to be most controversial and possibly not capable of being published by any publisher, even as a secular book. Finally, I chose not to submit myself to the agonizing timeframe of examination and editing for acquisition by a publisher.

Once I made the decision to self-publish, it was a quick realization that a rendition of the secular events of our wars really had a spiritual undergirding and foundation. Therefore, what is before you is an all-encompassing attempt to document my own journey of faith, along with a recounting of the spiritual dimensions and explanations behind all of the turmoil that so many have suffered through conflicts across the ages.

Jesus became my personal Savior in my teen years. However, it was not until my early thirties after surviving the amputations of both my legs from war wounds, a 14-week residence in a closed psychiatric ward, and several years of psychotherapy and anti-depressants that my faith had progressed to the level at which Jesus became Lord of my life. I believe that my healing from Post-Traumatic Stress Disorder only occurred due to my serious faith as a Christian, not from medication nor psychotherapy.

From that time forward, as my faith walk progressed, and I stumbled through attempting to appropriate the gifts my Lord Jesus had available for me, I began to recognize, understand and develop certain aspects of my faith that have served me in good stead. There is no formal (or informal) doctrinal or theological education in my background. My understanding of my Christian faith and its applicability in a larger worldly sense has been derived through OJT (on-the-job training).

This book expresses my hope and prayer as an American patriot that it will prove beneficial as an expression of a walk of faith to help others grow in their Christian faith. I also hope that my story serves as a helpful introduction to those not of Christian faith, as they consider how my life has been enhanced through a personal relationship with Christ and how that could also become so for them.

The lessons and history I recount offer a deep spiritual explanation of why young men such as myself have suffered so horribly in Caesar's world. It is my way of explanation as to what and who have caused the misery, sorrow, and suffering of so many for so long. It is a call to Godliness and a quest to explain the struggles on a macro (strategic) and micro (tactical) level of humanity.

The Books of Revelation, Daniel, and Ezekiel relate prophecies about the End Times. These prophecies track secular trends. One needs only to connect the dots. "The danger in the rise of authoritarian government is that Christians will be still as long as their own religious activities, evangelism, and life-styles are not disturbed." (Schaeffer: 256). My research found significant movement by acquisitive individuals in a concerted fashion to take away freedoms from all on earth, not just Christians. Our wars have their origins in the eternal struggle between good and evil, between God and Satan, who was exiled from Heaven with his own contingent of warriors to attack the saints and the lowly.

What you are about to read answers intriguing questions related to the official tales of history and also uncovers and surfaces the accurate and bigger picture of what has transpired throughout the history of our Nation and other nations. It is the ultimate "follow the trail of 'bloodied money'" tale.

Non illegitimi carborundum.

THE TRUTH SHALL MAKE YOU FREE!

SECTION I:

CONFLICTS – SECULAR AND SPIRITUAL

Chapter 1:

The Personal Appearance of Jesus
on the Stage of History

Ancient Words:

> *Holy words long preserved for our walk in this world,*
>
> *They resound with God's own heart.*
>
> *O, let the ancient words impart.*
>
> *Words of life, words of hope, give us strength, help us cope.*
>
> *In this world where'er we roam, ancient words will guide us home.*[1]

Author Gloria Copeland once wrote, "The Bible is not just a textbook, a storybook, or a history book. It's a handbook for living. It's the wisdom of Almighty God written down so that you can apply it to your everyday circumstances."

When I was younger, the "ancient words" of the Old Testament seemed to be just that – old, dried-up, dusty, and outdated. When I read, but rarely ever really studied, those old books, the stories did not seem connected and were seemingly unimportant. I wanted to concentrate on the meat of the Bible, the story of that divine being born in that manger in Bethlehem. My first actual recollection of any Bible story was the one about building one's house on a firm foundation rather than on sand. Even in my third grade Sunday school class that made sense.

Never having been trained or educated by formal Bible classes other than sermons and Sunday school classes, I never really grasped the firm foundation for my life that was represented by knowledge and understanding of the Old Testament.

With an Army officer as a father, my childhood interests naturally turned to military history and warfare. As a West Point cadet and Army officer, leadership was the name of the game. As a citizen and observer of everyday life, and particularly as a news reader, the prevalence of evil and wrongdoing was constantly evident.

[Author's note: When North Korea attacked the South on June 25, 1950, we lived in Japan and saw off the troop trains transporting the 7th Infantry Division troops from Sendai, where we lived at the time, to fight the Communists. In 1952, when I was hospitalized in Tokyo, adjacent to our ward was the head injury ward. It was most sobering at age nine to peek through the lattice barrier to view the horrendous wounds. Therefore, at an early age, I was exposed to warfare in a highly personalized fashion. My father's best friend, Bud Flook, was killed at the Chosen Reservoir in late 1950, when the Chinese "volunteers" overwhelmed our forces.]

Despite this early exposure to warfare, it took some time before I grasped the strategic and tactical aspects of the ultimate battlefield of spiritual warfare, that of good versus evil.

The Old Testament ended up being truly a rich repository of military history, lessons on leadership, and a seemingly endless cycle of wrongdoing and clashing of good and evil. Especially compelling and fascinating is the Hebrew Bible, the Torah, by Rabbi Scherman, (Ed.), et al.

Once I decided to become serious about my faith, the Old Testament was no longer "ancient," but current, alive, compelling and important for me in understanding my place in the world as a man of faith. It would be critical to grasp whether everything, especially planet earth, began only 6000 years ago. If so, what about everything I read about fossils, dinosaurs, carbon dating, and the Cro-Magnon man? What was the big picture about those Jews to whom I became exposed at age six when I heard in 1948 about that war they were fighting in their new country, Palestine? That really became confusing when my train that year passed through Texas, and the conductor yelled out, "Palestine," which is a town southeast of Dallas.

How it all tied together was a source of mystery and wonderment to me. My wife, Linda, performs dramatic presentations of women of the Bible (http://voices.name) and one of her more fascinating characters is Esther, who saved her people from annihilation by the Persians. We began to attend groups where I would follow her with the stories of the modern-day, seemingly miraculous victories of the Israeli Defense Forces. Then one day a junior high student asked her about the Persian kings in Esther's time. Deriving that answer, which was unknown to us at the time, motivated a quest to corroborate the biblical stories with a secular history of Bible times. Not too surprisingly, secular sources of history tracked the Old Testament stories, of which I had only superficial knowledge.

Books I had previously read seeped back into my consciousness about the spiritual heritage of primitive civilizations, the importance of the ups and downs of the Jewish tribes, and the clashes of good and evil amongst all those "ancient" characters of the Old Testament.

The true bottom line of all those stories and lessons before New Testament times was that our mighty God was preparing humanity on this planet, created by Him, to enter history as an actual Person to demonstrate visibly and concretely how much He loves us. God portrayed how our lives can achieve a definite degree of peace and contentment amidst lives torn asunder, not only by unwise choices, but by the continual warfare present not only from earthly enemies, as well as by soulful and spiritual enemies.

Are you ready for the ride of your life? Hold on for a very practical explanation that answers the question, "What's it all about, _____?" (Fill in your name.)

One of my goals is to awaken readers to a beginning or a renewal of their spiritual dimension and knowledge. Secondly, I hope to bring readers to the recognition and belief that Jesus the Christ was sent by God to earth so that we could have a relationship with Him, not just a religion, wherein we follow rules. Thirdly, I desire to motivate readers to want to study the Christian Bible, not only to glean the facts, but to internalize the underlying "why" of the stories, and to apply the morals of those stories to their lives in a practical way. Later chapters will relate the stories of many throughout history, who cared little about their spiritual lives.

Some readers may say there is much skepticism about the Biblical Creation story. I will not dogmatically say that I believe the Biblical Creation story, and therefore, so should you. However, it will be my goal to develop the plausibility and even the truth of the Biblical Creation story from numerous sources that have come to my attention through my years of study.

The Old Testament begins very simply, "In the beginning God created the heavens and the earth" (Genesis 1:1). Many scholars speculate as to whether the "beginning" was only 6,000 or so years ago, as dated by the genealogy down through the centuries from the first man, Adam, down to Jesus Christ, the last Adam. Significant circles of belief also profess the existence of an "old earth" prior to the so-called "seven-day creation" in our Old Testament. Carbon dating and questions about fossils, especially the dinosaurs, lend some credence to these arguments.

Evolutionists, disputing the Biblical accounts, have their theories about how humanity evolved. I believe in the simple explanation; therefore, the age of our earth is really of no importance to me. However, it remains critically important to me to believe faithfully that someone very intelligent created our good old Mother Earth.

Dr. John Coleman, a distinguished scholar, wrote a paper titled, "How the Earth Was Created." In it, he maintains, "The new science of anthropology, combined with geology, supports entirely the account of creation contained in the book of Genesis." (*Coleman Earth*: 4). The central question in the creation story is the source of matter. Some believe matter just evolved. If so, from what did it evolve? From what did the original matter emanate? For the first time in my studies, Dr. Coleman introduced to me the proposition of the miracle of the molecules.

Molecules have always remained the same and have not been changed. Molecular structures had to have been created and not to have been developed from nature nor by chance. When one studies molecules, it is not too difficult to believe that only a Creator with extraordinary intelligence could have created the building blocks of all seen and unseen. The design of the molecules and how they fit together is proof enough scientifically of their creation not by any simple natural means. (Coleman *Earth*: 13). A child experiencing a simple snowflake through a microscope sees the miracle of creation in that alone.

I am a big fan of a writer who graduated from my own prep school, The Phillips Exeter Academy, in New Hampshire. The writer is Dan Brown, author of *The Da Vinci Code* and *Angels & Demons*, both blockbuster novels and movies. Both novels are full of religious and scientific topics and subjects. I wondered where Brown stood in his own religious enlightenment. Prior to the release of his fifth novel, *The Lost Symbol*, Brown was interviewed in the September 13, 2009, edition of *Parade Magazine*. In the piece, Brown admitted that he was a religious young man, an Episcopalian. However, the Big Bang Theory caused in him a conflict regarding the seven-day creation story. However, he stated in the interview, "The more science I studied, the more I saw that physics becomes metaphysics and numbers become imaginary numbers. The farther you go into science, the mushier the ground gets. You start to say, 'Oh, there is an order and a spiritual aspect to science.'" (Parade: 4).

The NIV Archaeological Study Bible (hereinafter referred to as ASB), represents a fascinating discovery for me. This Bible, published in 2005, provides a prodigious amount of information on "Archaeological Sites, Cultural and Historical Notes: Ancient Peoples, Lands and Rulers; The Reliability of the Bible; and

Ancient Texts and Artifacts." (ASB: xiii).

Archaeological digs, discovered artifacts, and epigraphical finds in the Near East over the past hundred years or so have lent worldly credibility to the truthfulness of what we read and study in our Old Testament. The Old Testament's happenings, places, and people are real and increasingly are held up as being authentic by modern day findings. A study of the cultures, chronology, characters, and geography of ancient lands and nations provides an unequivocal decision for a belief that the Old Testament is quite simply true.

In 1727, an English clergyman, Dr. Samuel Shuckford, wrote a voluminous amount of information in a series of several volumes titled, *The Sacred and Profane History of the World Connected*. A Cambridge graduate and chaplain to King George II, he lived from 1694-1754. Dr. Shuckford compared the information written by the non-Biblical writers to that of the Bible. Through his scholarly research, it became his belief that the Bible represented an account "...of the truth and exactness of the ancient Scriptural history by showing how far the old fragments of the heathen writers agree with it." (Shuckford: v).

In an interesting finding, Dr. Shuckford uncovered that Aristotle characterized creation by claiming that, "...all things lay in one mass, for a vast space of time, but an intelligent agent came and put them in motion and so separated them from one another." (Shuckford: xxxix).

Dr. Shuckford then makes a strong, unequivocal case that the one true God either imparted to Moses through divine revelation what to write about in his account of the creation and early history of humanity, or it was revealed by God to the early humans and they passed it on down through their children. Paul writes in 2 Timothy 3:16 (NIV), "All Scripture is God-breathed...." Therefore, I believe that what God wanted us to know, He gave to certain believers to relate for posterity.

Dr. Shuckford also professed that God himself introduced humans to the practice of worshipping Him. Unfortunately, beginning early in history, people began to worship idols. Dr. Shuckford wrote, "The descendants of Abraham were true worshippers of the God of Heaven, when other nations, whose great and wise men pretended to consider and reason about the works of the creation, did in no wise rightly apprehend or acknowledge the workmaster." (Shuckford: 327). Many decided to worship the elements God created such as the stars, the sun, fire, or wind rather than the Creator.

Dr. Shuckford concluded that man, despite what had been revealed in ancient times directly by God, decided to apply their own reasoning to what constituted God's revelation of the Earth and early times. The result of this independent thought process led to many inaccuracies. (Shuckford: 330). These misunderstandings, false reasonings, and departures from the worship of the true and only God explained the eventual need of the judgment due to the evil in the world as reflected in the Great Flood. Survived only by Noah, his family and the animals, the Great Flood represents the most memorable Bible story heard by many of us in our first Sunday school classes in early childhood. However, early peoples knew of other stories in the Bible and not only about accounts of the flood.

The author of Ecclesiastes 3:11 (NIV) wrote, "He has made everything beautiful in its time. He has also set eternity in the hearts of men...."

In the book by Don Richardson, *Eternity in Their Hearts*, the author discovered that many peoples and tribes in remote areas of the world believed in an omnipotent being.

The builder of Machu Pichu in Peru, Pachacuti, the Incan Empire Ruler from 1438-1471 A.D., believed in an ancient creator and directed prayer to be addressed to this being rather than to the sun god of his culture. Unfortunately, his beliefs were only communicated to the upper classes, which, when obliterated by the Spanish Conquistadors, meant the lower classes would have to wait for the Catholic priests to introduce the God concept. (Richardson: 33-41).

In 1867, missionaries reached the Santal tribe, living north of Calcutta, India. When the gospel message began to be told, it was not a hard sell. The Santals believed in a Thakur Jiu, "Genuine God," whose story had been passed from generation to generation by mouth (confirming Dr. Shuckford's beliefs). This God created the first man and woman to the west of India. Their successors became corrupted and a flood followed (there it is in the ancient folklore of these people), destroying mankind except for a "holy pair," (possibly Mr. and Mrs. Noah?). Their descendants traveled east and were blocked by mountains, fell into spiritism and lost faith in their ancient Thakur Jiu, but the story remained in their culture. A Norwegian missionary, Lars Skrefsrud, found the message of Jesus Christ, son of Thakur Jiu, to be easily grasped and understood by the Santals. (Richardson: 41-48).

In 1948, Ethiopia's Gadeo people eagerly received missionaries and their message because they had heard of a benevolent being called Magano in their culture. (Richardson: 54).

In the early 1920s, members of the Mbaka tribe of the Central African Republic were receptive to the gospel message, because they related the story passed down from their forebears, "Koro, the Creator, sent word to our forefathers long ages ago that He has already sent His Son into the world to accomplish something wonderful for all mankind. Later, however, our forefathers turned away from the truth about Koro's son. In time they even forgot what it was that He accomplished for mankind." (Richardson: 57). Does this sound familiar? The falling away of so many after hearing the story of the one True God and His Son has repeated itself over and over. This story was heard in the wilds of Africa. The Genesis, and yes, even the salvation story, were planted in the hearts and minds of the previous generations of this culture.

In approximately the year 2600 B.C., a figure called Shang-Ti-Lord of Heaven was worshipped by only the privileged classes in China. His story was lost to the masses, who gravitated to the newer religions of Confucianism, Taoism, and Buddhism. (Richardson: 63).

In 1795, the British found the Karen tribes people in Burma. In their cultural heritage it had been reported that someday someone would bring them a "book." They sang hymns, proclaiming the eternity of a "Y'wa," obviously very close to "Yahweh," the God of Moses' time in the terminology of Judaism and Christianity. (Richardson: 73-78).

All these stories from primitive cultures add to the compelling and underlying truth of a Creator, a flood, and a Son of the Creator known for many centuries in earthly locations far from the so-called "civilized" world. In addition to its confirmation of many parallels to Old Testament stories in primitive cultures, recent archaeological discoveries in ancient cultures of Biblical times also lend extraordinary authority to the ancient Biblical texts.

Known as Mesopotamia, Sumer (Biblical Shinar), an ancient civilization situated in the southern part of modern-day Iraq, produced literature mirrored by many parallels in the Bible. (ASB: 10). Teachings from the ancient land of Sumer produced a genealogical list of kings divided into reigns before and after a flood. Just as in the Biblical genealogies from Adam to Jesus, the Sumerian kings had shorter reigns after a great flood. (ASB: 12).

One of the most compelling non-Biblical accounts with extraordinary comparability to the Genesis story relates to Noah and the flood. A Babylonian version belonged to the library of the Assyrian King Ashurbanipal. This story in the Epic of Gilgamesh tracks amazingly closely to the Biblical account of God's becoming fed up with humanity and His subsequent decision to bring the great inundation. In this epic, one of the highest-ranking gods, Enlil, also becomes upset with humanity and orders a boat to be built and a flood to follow. (ASB: 13).

The translation of the cuneiform tablets (in the Babylonian creation myth Enuma Elish) dated from 750-200 B.C. in the Babylonian Akkadian culture also describes a creation story. (ASB: 888).

Descendants of Noah in Genesis 11, Serug, Nahor, and Terah, all have towns in south central Turkey named after them in the original homeland of the Biblical stories. (ASB: 22).

In the Sumerian Eridu Genesis, which was studied from texts as early as 1600 B.C., stories were told of old cities and rulers. Similar renditions from the time spoke of humans displeasing the gods to such an extent that a flood was called down. A boat was ordered to be built and filled with pairs of animals. This story, too, tracks very comparably to the Genesis story. (ASB: 576).

Comparable Akkadian and Sumerian accounts of the flood also exist. (ASB: 13). The actual story in the Bible in Genesis (6:5-7) relates to God's extraordinary displeasure with created man. Much sin and evil precipitated a consequent extreme example of God's judgment coming down upon humanity through the flood. Many more corporate judgments of Israel would come throughout history.

Individually, we will suffer not only specific judgments, but will suffer what I believe to be a withholding of blessings when we do not obey our God and do not live righteously. Our obedience should emanate from our desire to be righteous, because it is right, not because we will be judged. This becomes our supreme challenge as humans once we believe in God and His Son.

In Genesis 6:8 (KJV), it is written, "But Noah found favor in the eyes of the Lord." This outcome exemplifies my own constant goal, to merit the favor of God. Pastor Arni Jacobson expressed it this way, "When you are living right and desire God's blessings for you to undertake a vision He gave you, God will bless you with His favor in your home, your neighborhood, your church, your work place, your life." (Jacobson: 51).

64

The Old Testament recounts many negative situations holding instructional value for our own lives. In the book of Jeremiah, the prophet Jeremiah spoke to the people of Judea circa 626-580 B.C. about their apostasy in falling away from the worship of God for the worship of idols, especially one known as "The Queen of Heaven." (ASB: 1267). Jewish women burned incense to their idols. Jeremiah called them to repentance, but they refused to turn to the only true God.

In these modern days, we, too, have many idols that we worship – our possessions, our money, our power and influence, our leisure time, our entertainment choices, and our reading selections that are not the Bible. Judgment may not be direct yet may appear in an indirect form through a withholding of God's blessings.

The people of Judea turned their backs on God, worshipping idols and refusing to change in their hearts. These individuals, thinking that God would protect them unconditionally, became complacent in their faith. Jeremiah prophesied what was required. God would not indefinitely overlook their wrongdoings and meted out justice, once his mercy had run out. He prefers that we obey Him because it is the right thing to do, not to merely obey based on the motivational factor of fear.

The Old Testament book of Isaiah outlines the prophecy of the fall of Israel because it would not repent of disobedience. (ASB: 1055). This story is an important example of God's judgment carried out by the kingdoms of Assyria and Babylonia by means of the captivities of the Hebrews. Isaiah elucidates the major criteria for the favor of God in Isaiah 66:2 (NIV) by saying, "This is the one I esteem: he who is humble and contrite in spirit and trembles at my word." This behavioral condition of our hearts is very challenging in a world built upon materialism, status, impressing others with our toys, and competitiveness. Based on this passage, we should adopt the characteristics and behavior of humility and contrition.

In my leadership education and experiences as a West Point cadet and Army officer, I learned about many of the great military leaders of all time. The Bible, a significant repository for learning significant leadership lessons, also contains great moral and ethical wisdom. No one can read Proverbs without gaining incredible insights into the practical wisdom required for success in our everyday lives. The Old Testament holds many great lessons regarding how to handle people and develop our EQ, or Emotional Quotient. Worthy of in-depth study, the Bible teaches us these lessons.

Pastor Gene Getz wrote a series on men of character, with Moses representing perhaps the most dynamic and important personage. It took a magnificent leader to accomplish what Moses accomplished. As Getz wrote, "Imagine leading a mass of people the size of a major American city into a wild and desolate desert, a wilderness where the natural resources for providing food and water were almost non-existent. How could Moses provide for two million-as well as their livestock?" (Getz *Moses*: 94). That situation presented some serious leadership challenges. Admittedly, Moses had divine help!

Joshua's leading of the Jewish people into the Promised Land presents another classic example of leadership, following in the footsteps of Moses. Given those challenges, how could Joshua possibly have succeeded? Yet somehow, he did. A very successful military leader, his principal characteristic was that of courage, both physical and moral. (Getz *Joshua*: 26). After serving under Moses for forty years, Joshua was ready to step up into a leadership role. Full of examples like these, the Old Testament embodies for all its students, scholars, and mere readers an important treasure of philosophy and lessons for life.

The Epic of Gilgamesh appears to track Ecclesiastes and the story of failure of kings during approximately the 2000 B.C. timeframe to achieve eternal life. (ASB: 1027). The epic describes an "eat, drink and be merry" philosophy due to the impending death of all. However, Ecclesiastes proposes that all of life's tribulations can be balanced with a belief and fear of God. According to Ecclesiastes 8:12 (NIV), "Although a wicked man commits a hundred crimes and still lives a long time, I know that it will go better with God-fearing men, who are reverent before God." In Ecclesiastes 8:15, one is encouraged to enjoy life in the days given by one's God.

Ecclesiastes concludes in Chapter 12 (NIV) with a piece of extraordinary counsel. Verse 1 teaches, "Remember your creator in the days of your youth, before the days of trouble come and the years approach when you will say, 'I find no pleasure in them.'"

Verses 13-14 (NIV):

> *Now all has been heard;*
> *here is the conclusion of the matter:*
> *Fear God and keep His commandments,*
> *for this is the whole duty of men.*
> *For God will bring every deed into judgment,*
> *including every hidden thing,*
> *whether it is good or evil.*

This sobering and compelling wisdom from the Old Testament embodies a rich mother lode from which all can achieve incredible guidance for life. Prophecies revealed in the pages of the Old Testament epitomize important, credible, reliable and relevant real-world outcomes across history. Bursting with amazing stories of dreams, the book of Daniel overflows with credible examples of prophecies coming true. When one studies the book of Daniel and grasps the significance of his rendition of the chronology of the empires that would follow that of the Assyrian Empire, one sees that Daniel, who had become a trusted advisor to the king after his banishment from Israel, was a true prophet. The prophetic chronology became true when the Babylonian, Persian, Greek and Roman empires did in fact transpire exactly in the order prophesied in Daniel's dream.

The Old Testament remains a true treasure trove of history, inspiration, wisdom, and prophecy. The ultimate value of the Old Testament must include that of laying the groundwork for the coming into history of God in the human form of Jesus, who walked the earth. Over 100 prophecies in the Old Testament tell the specifics of Jesus' life, ministry, and death, all of which were fulfilled in the New Testament (Pamphlet: 100 Prophecies Fulfilled by Jesus). For the more mathematically inclined amongst us, the statistical probability of all these prophecies being fulfilled as they were actually fulfilled, is truly astronomical. Interestingly, most Old Testament prophecies have been fulfilled. Most of the prophecies that have not yet been fulfilled relate to the end times as further described principally in the last book of the New Testament, Revelation.

Pastor Tony Evans describes what may be the final expression of the incomparable value of studying and grasping Old Testament teachings. He wrote, "...one thing that sets the Bible apart is its prophetic accuracy. A large portion of biblical prophecy has already been fulfilled with flawless accuracy. Events that one author wrote about were fulfilled precisely hundreds of years later." (Evans: 17).

One incredible example appears in Micah 5:2 (written o/a 750 B.C.), when it was prophesied that Jesus would be born in the obscure village of Bethlehem. The materialization of obscure predictions such as this one about the birthplace of Jesus lends tremendous credibility to the truth of the Bible.

The Old Testament indeed consists of ancient words, but these words can change both you and me. The song Ancient Words expresses it best:

> *Ancient words, ever true, changing me and changing you; we have come with open hearts, O, let the ancient words impart...Holy words long preserved for our walk in this world.*[2]

For many of us, our faith walk has become a daily sprint. The Old Testament holds much knowledge for us to help us recognize our place in history and our individual personal significance to our God, the Creator of everything in our lives.

In the beginning of Genesis 12 (KJV), God speaks of the Abrahamic Covenant in verse 3, "...and in thee shall all families of the earth be blessed." This means us. In fact, Don Richardson writes of a "4000-year connection," of all peoples together from the time of the patriarch Abraham in the Old Testament. (Richardson: 163).

A good life exists in contrast to the many lives that will be described in later chapters of those who choose to live their lives based on the pursuit of the fulfillment of power, self-aggrandizement, and satisfaction of the baser instincts of behavior. However, the ultimate expressions of human behavior, for good or for bad, devolve upon being explained in the realm of "spiritual warfare."

Seeing ourselves within this long line of humanity, and feeling blessed as members of God's family, is awesome. I have always felt a great sense of personal pride in being a member of the Long Gray Line of West Point graduates, who have served our country and the cause of freedom since 1802. Another source of pride has been receiving the Purple Heart, originally designated as a Medal of Merit by General George Washington on August 7, 1782. It is a distinct privilege to be associated with this group of our military, who have been killed or wounded in action.

However, these two Caesar's world heritages pale in comparison to the significance of my Godly heritage all the way back to Abraham. My belief system bequeaths to me participation in a lineage that will last into eternity, since I was grafted into the lineage of my Christian faith the moment when Jesus Christ became my Savior. This may also become a part of your heritage. Keep reading and learn what we have learned of God's Son, who came to earth as a human example of what a life may become.

Chapter 2:

Between Two Worlds – Spiritual Warfare

The moment that Adam and Eve succumbed to Satan's temptation to disobey God 6,000 years ago in the Garden of Eden established a battlefield on earth. The struggle between good and evil, darkness and light, has ensued in the hearts and minds of men and women since that fateful day.

<u>Battlefield Earth</u>

Satan desires complete authority over the earth and his goal is to rule and reign in the place of God. The Luke 4:5-6 (NIV) passage tells us that Satan tempted Jesus and "showed him in an instant all the kingdoms of the world" – adding the chilling phrase, "...for it was given to me."

Thankfully, Christ rejected Satan's offer and continued to His sacrifice on the cross. He leveled out the battlefield by retaking the high ground of control of Mother Earth previously controlled by Satan and his angels who had fallen to earth with him in the rebellion against God in heaven. (Rev. 12:4).

Man is continually being tested, generation after generation, to separate those, who prove worthy by faith, for admission into the eternal kingdom. Just as military soldiers are continually tested in training and combat, so, too, are we in our daily lives. If we desire success in the daily battles and struggles of life, we must be disciplined in God's ways as are the military. We are all sinners in one way or another at different times in our lives. Romans 3:23 (KJV) tells us, "For all have sinned and come short of the glory of God."

The secret of restoration is:
1. To identify our sins

2. To confess and repent of our sins
3. To turn and sin no more

With this approach, we achieve balance and peace and are restored to the state we were intended to occupy. We reclaim the ground taken from us.

Satan desires us to be dysfunctional, confused, addicted to substances or other evils, and filled with fear and anger, for then we become a part of his side of the line of battle. In 1 John 3:8-9 (NIV) it is written, "He who does what is sinful is of the devil, because the devil has been sinning from the beginning."

Demonization occurs not only due to sin, but to faulty freewill choices we make in life and to false beliefs we hold from times of trauma and injury. These injuries (physical and emotional) cause us to be taken into emotional and spiritual captivity and kept from freedom in our lives.

The goal of our own life is to be returned to the "friendly lines" where God is in charge.

This defines our enemy.

This defines the battlefield.

This is the time to get on the victorious side for God and for you.

Spiritual Warfare

It is written in Ephesians 6:12 (KJV):

> For we wrestle not against flesh and blood, but against principalities, against powers, against the rulers of the darkness of this world, against spiritual wickedness in high places.

The Christian New Testament is the fulfillment of the Old Testament. Jesus was born in Bethlehem and began a three-year ministry in what was then Palestine. He was crucified, died, and was buried, and is the only "leader" of any faith, who is still alive, because He rose from the sepulcher and returned to Heaven to exist with His and our Father. He left the third Person of the Trinity, the Holy Spirit, to indwell us and be our spiritual guide, when we call on the Holy Spirit for help.

Through conflicts in the Old Testament ranging from the Garden of Eden to other timeless stories like the fall of David to lust and murder and to the temptation of Christ in the Wilderness, we learn lessons. From the time in the Garden of Eden when the Adversary, the Devil in the form of a serpent, tempted Eve and Adam to disobey God, the Adversary has worked humanity over through his demonic spirits attacking us when "pathways" of evil exist.

Various authors I have read allude to the work of the evil spirits in the world. In 1939, secular author Yeats-Brown, prior to the overwhelmingly evil World War II, wrote:

> If you are not a Christian, it may appear fantastic to suggest that there are forces of evil in the world working against the powers of good. The Devil has become unfashionable. He has gone 'underground' like the Communists. But unless you believe in the Devil this book will provide no explanation of what is happening in the world. We shall always have to wrestle with an Adversary.

Satan incarnates sometimes in those who cannot support the burden of our civilization and would shatter it to bits, and sometimes in the body of a man of genius, to scourge the earth, and sometimes in amiable and idealistic geniuses, capturing the minds even of the Saints and others, unconscious of the parts they play. (Yeats-Brown: 20).

In the gospels of Matthew, Mark and Luke, Jesus was asked about whether the Jews should pay taxes or not. He answered in Matthew 22:21 (NIV), "Give to Caesar what is Caesar's and to God what is God's." This differentiation and definition are in their essence the major questions of our lives. No, not whether we should pay taxes or not! The question for us all is: In which world shall we truly live? Will we live enveloped, engaged, and employed only in Caesar's world, for us today, the "world's system," or will we live in God's world? We may make a living in the "world's system," but we must live, prosper spiritually and soulfully, and grow in God's world. When one applies God's world to "Caesar's" world in an integrated fashion, our daily mundane existence becomes deeply enhanced, contented, satisfied, and productive.

The description of a profound change that occurred in my life one day in a church service in the mid-1970s is best described in my autobiography, *Wounded Soldier, Healing Warrior*. The first time I really pursued an exploration of the two worlds was in Dallas' original Fellowship Bible Church, founded and pastored by Gene Getz.

One of Getz' sermons made a distinct impression on me and changed my life forever. The real war in this world, he said, "...is the war between good and evil--Satan and the Lord. They are fighting for the very hearts and souls of all people."

I could certainly relate to war. Getz' words got my attention and made me think. Here I was a dedicated citizen and sincere patriot. I loved my country—I always had. I had dedicated my life to community and civic endeavors. I had almost given my life to fight the Communists who, in my mind, represented the ultimate evil, their dedication to bring socialism by violent means and to obliterate and destroy Christianity. I had not, however, given all of myself to the ultimate Provider—God and His son, Jesus Christ.

I sat in church and listened to Getz' words while hot, burning tears formed in my eyes. One by one, the tears trickled down my cheeks as I remembered the many battles I had fought — both on and off the battlefield. They seemed small now in comparison to the battles waged every day between the forces of good and evil — battles with more lives at stake than all the wars of history put together. As I wrote in my autobiography:

> During that service I heard, believed, and reaffirmed my acceptance of John 3:16 (KJV) 'For God so loved the world that he gave his only begotten Son, that whosoever believeth in Him should not perish, but have everlasting life.' As a teenager in the 1950s, I had really believed in Jesus Christ and became a 'Born Again' Christian. However, at that time, not only had I not understood what it all meant, but I had also not surrendered my life to Christ. In 1973, at age thirty-one, it all began to come together. That evening I began my mature walk in faith. (Clark *Wounded*: 202, 203).

On that day, I entered a new world. Once each of us achieves that point in our lives (and the sooner it happens, the better), we have made a choice between the two worlds.

A very wise and dear friend of mine, Jim Ash, once sent me an "Eternity Ticket," which I printed and laminated. This is what it states:

> The Bible states, 'That if thou shalt confess with thy mouth the Lord Jesus, and shalt believe in thine heart that God hath raised Him from the dead, thou shalt be saved. For with the heart man believeth unto righteousness; and with the mouth confession is made unto salvation.' (Romans 10: 9,10 KJV).

To receive Jesus as your personal Savior, pray this prayer from your heart:

> "Dear Jesus: I believe You died for me and that You rose again on the third day. I confess to You that I am a sinner and that I need Your love and forgiveness. Come into my

life, forgive my sins and give me eternal life. I confess You now as my Lord. Thank You for saving me. Amen."

Next, confess to someone, "I am a Christian," for Jesus said, "Whosoever therefore shall confess me before men, him will I confess also before My Father which is in heaven. But whosoever shall deny me before men, him will I also deny before my Father which is in heaven." (Matthew 10: 32,33 KJV).

The writings on Jesus and the Holy Spirit by the Reverend Hugh Morgan, my personal pastor, reflect that each of us is in one of three states: 1) solidified in your belief that Jesus truly came so that you personally can have eternal life; 2) turned off to all this doctrine and theology and ready to stop and continue on your merry way of life undiminished by anything deeper than making a living, having fun, and trying to be as "happy" as possible; or 3) ready to begin a new life with Jesus at the center of your world. You are ready to move forward for Jesus to be "Lord of your life." This stage is wherein you can attain the joy of the soul and spirit, not just earthly pleasure and happiness in life.

Very seldom does anyone perform an audit of one's life. We all are aware of the audits of businesses by accountants. The assets and liabilities of an entity must be equal on the balance sheet upon completion of the audit. In real life, we tend to focus on our assets and minimize our liabilities.

Between Caesar's and God's worlds there are different attitudes and convictions of assets and liabilities in each world. In a world without God, one's assets relate to cars, homes, beauty, power, position, and the attention one receives. In a world without God, liabilities include being "too religious, a Jesus freak, one who wears religion on one's sleeve, or too goody-goody." In God's world, our assets become striving to adopt Jesus' values taught in His ministry on earth. Our liabilities become failing to appropriate in our own lives and in our decisions how Jesus taught us to address the never-ceasing challenges we face daily. Leading a life characterized by Jesus as the epicenter allows one once and for all to have the ultimate game plan and life manual to overcome one's liabilities. My research for this book has led me to discover throughout history those who have not adhered to a life that reflects love for others, justice, and a balance for good.

Those that live in God's world contrast with those who have not surrendered their soul to being led by the grace and love of Jesus, with whom we desire to have a personal relationship, not just a religion. Unfortunately, many see faith as only a "religion," allowing them to act not always in accordance with God's ways.

From now, proceeding forward, this work of mine is essentially one of a recognition that Caesar's world has prevailed at the higher secular "strategic" level. This condition is reflected in the rampant evil in the world, exemplified by individuals who have demonstrated "cupidity" in its most horrific form while pursuing the achievement of power and wealth in a nefarious fashion at the expense of many others. Unfortunately, the victims of these wicked individuals are often used as instruments for the fulfillment of their schemes, deception, and deceit.

Author Curtis Dall, President Franklin Roosevelt's son-in-law, expressed a compelling opinion of the propagation of evil in the world in his book titled *F.D.R. My Exploited Father-in-Law:*

> For centuries the Forces of Evil had combatted the Forces of Good. The Forces of Evil use carefully selected and trained persons, of all religious faiths, and also those from nonreligious groups, to carry out their objectives. These trainees and their followers are made up to include some Jews, Christians, Mohammedans, Hindus, atheists etc. (171).

Chapter 10 of Daniel describes the twenty-one days the prince of the kingdom of Persia battled Michael. A footnote to this reading of Daniel 12:21 states, "This suggests the very real possibility that Satan who is 'the prince of the power of the air' (Eph. 2:2) may well have his demons indwelling world rulers, attempting to thwart the plans of God for mankind." (Bible PSB: 915). This theory takes the concept of evil, along with its impact on individuals, far and beyond simple individual influence to that of the macro-world level.

On the "tactical" spiritual warfare level throughout recorded history, many "elitists" have never been introduced to a Godly way of life or have chosen to ignore it. Caesar's world is consumed with sin that is expressed in manifest evil in both corporate and individual lives, causing extraordinary pain, hurts, harm, distress, and death.

Very simply explained, when one commits sins and they are not confessed to God in the Name of Jesus and repented of in order to obtain absolution (which is what Jesus taught us is the way we should live), then there is that open "pathway" of evil. The Devil then has the legal authority to assign his "soldiers," his demon spirits, to enter us, take charge, and direct us to lives of impurity, emotional weakness, and failure. These spirits remain with us until removed by spiritual restoration. "Pathways" of evil are opened to our soul (our mind, emotions, and will). A lack of forgiveness to others is another avenue for the opposing forces of the Adversary to take root in us to keep us from God's good Word and to motivate us to make evil and wrong choices.

In my thesis and thrust in this work, a strategic-level struggle between God, our benevolent Creator, and the Adversary, the exiled Satan, has existed for 6,000 years of recorded history, with Satan's influence causing much avarice, greed and violence in the highly malevolent Caesar's world. Satan, thrown from Heaven with one third of the angels who now roam the earth seeking abodes within individuals who do not know God, continues to influence the world with evil today.

It is from this world that the causes of most of our wars emanate. It is in this world that widespread pain, sorrow, and suffering of the masses with all the attendant casualties reside.

The cautionary verse of 1 Peter 5:8 (KJV) states, "Be sober, be vigilant; because your adversary the devil, as a roaring lion, walketh about, seeking whom he may devour." History demonstrates the Devil's success targeting many significant individuals.

Two of my favorite authors, C.S. Lewis and Derek Prince, have both written very compellingly about spiritual warfare and lend distinct credibility to this concept.

C.S. Lewis was a professor of Medieval and Renaissance Literature at Oxford's Magdalen College and Cambridge University. He wrote thirty books in his lifetime and died in 1963. He was the author of *Mere Christianity* and a rather short work titled *The Screwtape Letters*, in which "a senior fiend advises his young apprentice in leading humanity astray." (Lewis: Back cover). On the topic of devils, Lewis wrote:

> The proper question is whether I believe in devils. I do. That is to say, I believe in angels, and I believe that some of these, by the abuse of their free will, have become enemies of God, and as a corollary, to us. These we may call devils. They do not differ in nature from good angels, but their nature is depraved. Devil is the opposite of angel only as Bad Man is the opposite of Good Man. Satan, the leader or dictator of devils, is the opposite, not of God, but of Michael. (Lewis: 6).

Lewis also expresses his informed opinion regarding "elitists":

> The greatest evil is not now done in those sordid 'dens of crime' that Dickens loved to paint. It is not done even in concentration camps and labour camps. In those we see its final result. But it is conceived and ordered (moved, seconded, carried, and minuted) in clean, carpeted, warmed, and well-lighted offices, by quiet men with white collars and cut fingernails and smooth-shaven cheeks who do not need to raise their voice. Hence, naturally enough,

my symbol for Hell is something like the bureaucracy of a police state or the offices of a thoroughly nasty business concern. (Lewis: 7, 8).

Born in 1915 in India, where his father was a British Army officer, Derek Prince wrote more than 60 books before dying in 2003. Educated at Eton and Cambridge University, he also studied at Hebrew University in Jerusalem and served in the Ambulance Corps during WWII's North Africa fighting. He became acquainted with Lewis during his oversight of a worldwide ministry. Prince wrote about the vast increase in knowledge over the two or three centuries prior to the time of his ministry, and expressed an interesting opinion about science:

> This explosion of science has not, however, solved humanity's most basic problems: injustice, cruelty, war, poverty, disease. In fact, in some ways, it has increased them. Science has provided man with weapons of mass destruction that could obliterate the entire human race and turn the whole earth into a desolate waste. Furthermore, some of these weapons are in the hands of cruel and wicked individuals who would not be deterred from using them by any means of mercy or morality. (Prince: 14).

Prince was well-aware of spiritual warfare. He maintained that we must never allow ourselves "...to forget that we are in a spiritual conflict with unseen forces of darkness who are continually watching for an opportunity to catch us unprepared." (Prince: 24). On the individual level, assaults are "tactical." On the global scale, the combination of these tactical assaults transforms into strategic spiritual warfare. We find ourselves in individual battles daily, while my writings cover the broader historical strategic wars that have brought so much death and suffering to humankind.

No less an unimpeachable and immensely credible source than Billy Graham weighed in on spiritual warfare as follows:

> Lucifer [another name for Satan], our archenemy, controls

one of the most powerful and well-oiled war machines in the universe. He controls principalities, powers, and dominions. Every nation, city, village, and individual has felt the hot breath of his evil power. He is already gathering the nations of the world for the last great battle in the war against Christ--- Armageddon. (Duck *Daniel*: 265).[1]

A hymn (Hymnal 551) written by Martin Luther in 1529 offers a very appropriate summation of this chapter:

And tho' this world with devils filled, should threaten to un-do us: We will not fear, for God hath willed His truth to triumph through us: For still our ancient foe Doth seek to work us woe: his craft and power are great, And, armed with cruel hate, on earth is not his equal. Christ Jesus, it is he; Lord Sabbaoth his name, from age to age the same, and he must win the battle.

History played out until the end is a bit like a chess game. The majority of the pieces consists of pawns, while the royalty, bishops, knights, and "elitists" snugly tucked away in their castles, scheme behind the scenes. Behind the curtain is the Devil. Those of us in the spiritual "know" are aware that the final movement is "Checkmate, Evil One." Our Lord will shut him down!

Chapter 3:

Connecting the Dots –
Conspiracies and Prophecies

[Author's note: The Biblical quotes in this chapter are from the King James Version of the Tyndale Life Application Study Bible unless otherwise noted.]

This chapter will be my most controversial one, potentially rendering me "an endangered species." Be aware that I am in no way suicidal. I drive very defensively, and prior to the writing of this book, I am not aware of any mortal enemies. I suffer from no life-threatening illnesses. Everything I quote comes from other authors, usually from their original written sources. My analysis just connects the dots.

My demise soon after this publication under any suspicious circumstances should be inferred as first-hand evidence that at least something I wrote bears merit as the truth. In this book, I will step on many toes, least of which are my own. Interest in this topic began more than forty years ago when my co-worker John Strauss and I traveled together in a carpool from far north Dallas to the then Republic National Bank downtown.

I had read *The Late Great Planet Earth* by Hal Lindsey and became intrigued by my first exposure to terms like the End Time prophecies, the Rapture, the Tribulation, the Antichrist, and the false prophet. Thankfully, one of our fellow carpoolers, Chuck Lamb, was well-versed in these topics. The topics were fascinating to me, but, alas, the carpool broke up when one member tired of hearing about all these "crazy" spiritual and religious subjects. Concurrently, my secular education on the one world government began at a bookstore in Dallas.

Francis J. Schaefer, who resided at a Swiss retreat center called L'Abri near Geneva, wrote a book in 1976 titled *How Should We Then Live*. Recently, I pulled it off my bookshelf because I recalled that I had marked several very memorable passages upon my original reading, and I have never forgotten them:

> Overwhelming pressures are being brought to bear on people who have no absolutes, but only have the impoverished values of personal peace and prosperity. The pressures are progressively preparing modern people to accept a manipulative, authoritarian government. Unhappily, many of these pressures are upon us now...History indicates that at a certain point of economic breakdown people cease being concerned with individual liberties and are ready to accept regimentation. (Schaefer: 246,247).

These thoughts tracked what I had begun to learn about a one world government, both Biblically and secularly. In his book, Schaefer quotes Harvard Professor Daniel Bell:

> Bell sees that in the final analysis the whole state----its business, its education, its government, even the daily pattern of the ordinary man's life----becomes a matter of control by the technocratic elite. They are the only ones who know how to run the complicated machinery of society and they will then, in collusion with the government elite, have all the power to manage it. (Schaefer: 225).

Schaefer continued:

> An elite will offer us arbitrary absolutes, and who will stand in its way? ... I believe the majority of the silent majority, young and old, will sustain the loss of liberties without raising their voices as long as their own life-styles are not threatened. (Schaefer: 227).

Schaefer wrote about the loss of Christian principles leading to the evolution of an elite, authoritarian state, manipulated by the use of psychological techniques as well as by the media. Remember this point when I discuss Great Britain's Tavistock Institute.

Quoting Schaefer again:

> An elite, an authoritarianism as such, will gradually force form on society so that it will not go on to chaos. And most people will accept it----from the desire for personal peace and affluence, from apathy, and for the yearning of order to assure the functioning of some political system, business, and the affairs of daily life. That is just what Rome did with Caesar Augustus... The danger in regard to the rise of authoritarian government is that Christians will be still as long as their own religious activities, evangelism, and lifestyles are not disturbed. (Schaefer: 245, 256).

Supposedly, we as Christians have real absolutes to live by and we must not remain silent. Remember in Ezekiel about the Watchman on the Wall?

> Then whosoever heareth the sound of the trumpet, and taketh not warning; if the sword come, and take him away, his blood shall be upon his own head. (33:4).

> But if the watchman see the sword come, and blow not the trumpet, and the people be not warned; if the sword come, and take any person from among them, he is taken away in his iniquity; but his blood will I require at the watchman's hand. (33:6).

Fulfillment of Old Testament Prophecies

The New Testament prophecies in Revelation relate to events that could happen in this century. Should we pay any attention to them? I maintain that, yes, we should, because examples of fulfilled prophecies are eminently evident in the Old Testament. For example, in Daniel 2:32-45, Daniel the Jew told the

Babylonian King Nebuchadnezzar not only what he had dreamed, but what the dream meant.

The dream was about his Babylonian Empire's yielding to a Medo-Persian Empire, then in turn followed by the Greek and Roman Empires. All of this appeared in symbols, but ultimately became fulfilled. The fourth one, the Roman Empire, broke up, then was intended to be renewed, then eventually resulted in ten kingdoms coming forth before "another" comes to power. This final one will be controlled by the "Antichrist." If the prophecy from the 6th century B.C. related to the major empires all came to pass, should we not likewise expect the modern-day- to-come prophecies in the books of Daniel and Revelation to be fulfilled?

Of course, the ultimate fulfillment of Old Testament prophecy became fulfilled in the 100, yes, I repeat, 100 prophecies, as early as 1200 B.C. that foretold the coming of Jesus the Christ in intimate detail. Jesus fulfilled them all! (Pamphlet: 100 Prophecies Fulfilled by Jesus). This, my friends, is the evidence. If all these came true as prophesied, would it not be prudent also to pay attention to the others in Daniel and those given to the Apostle John in 95 A.D. on the island of Patmos about what is to happen in the End Times to include the seven-year Tribulation period? The prophecy in Daniel chapter 7:23 relates to a final kingdom that will devour the whole world by trampling and crushing it. This metaphor is believed by many to be a pre-cursor for a one world government.

Revelation 13:8 states, "And all that dwell upon the earth shall worship him (the Antichrist), whose names are not written in the book of life of the Lamb slain from the foundation of the world." The fulfillment of the elevation of this ruler at the top is as the head of this "One World Government and New World Order," spoken about by the elitists of the world for decades. This new realignment always must come about with the reorganization attendant to the demise of the sovereign nation-states.

Here are some examples of elitists who have referred to these terms:

1. Henry Kissinger's book is titled *World Order*. Imagine that!

2. President George H.W. Bush, in whose administration I served

3. Strobe Talbott, Asst. Secy. of State under the Clinton administration

4. Zbigniew Brzeziński, adviser to President Jimmy Carter

5. President Bill Clinton

6. Presidential candidate Barack Obama stated on July 24, 2008, that he supported a "globalized world."

Perhaps the most telling statement regarding the "New World Order" was made by David Rockefeller in his own words in his autobiography *Memoirs*, where he is quoted as saying:

> Some even believe we [Rockefeller family] are part of a secret cabal working against the best interests of the United States, characterizing my family and me as 'internationalists' and of conspiring with others around the world to build a more integrated global political and economic structure-One World, if you will. If that's the charge, I stand guilty, and I am proud of it. (*Memoirs*: 45).

This is quite telling, lending credence from the ultimate "elitist" about the "Conspiracy Theory of History." Of course, even the most die-hard non-conspiracist will dispute that this represents anything of consequence and will proclaim that it is just another "conspiracist" calling attention to a topic best kept under wraps. Enough is enough from these nay-sayers.

People, wake up! There has always been a concerted effort to pull a curtain over all that represents the movement of the "internationalists" to control the world. It is in the interests of a supposed "secret" movement to deny it exists. Furthermore, it may be too late before it is discovered and achieves its final purpose as prophesied!

The Rockefeller Dynasty

This dynasty will be addressed more fully in the chapter on elitists, however some of the efforts of the Rockefellers touch on the conspiracies as they relate to religion.

What were the motivations of Rockefeller's son, John D., Jr.? Here are some indications of his state of mind and heart in contrast to the supposed Baptist belief of his father. "At the time of the creation of the Rockefeller Foundation, fundamentalist preachers had noted the advocacy of John D., Jr. for a 'new' and 'liberal' theology that decried sectarianism as pragmatically unsound and veered toward Marxism and 'higher criticism.'" John D., Jr. was still around at the end of WWII and gave a talk on Jan. 31, 1945, titled "The Christian Church, What of Its Future?" He suggested, "...its transformation into the 'Church of the Living God,' and eliminating or subordinating 'ordinance, ritual, creed, all non-essential.'" (Josephson *Rockefeller*: 35).

Josephson believed that this Rockefeller fostered Marxism in the churches through such agencies as the Federal Council of Churches of Christ in America, with support of the Rockefeller Foundation. I quote Josephson, "...there emerges the idea that the real intent and purpose is the destruction of religion as the modern world knows it and its replacement by ancient concepts of religion in which the 'Living God' is the ruler of the state." (Josephson *Rockefeller*: 35). Josephson questioned whether, even way back in 1952, this could have been one of the objectives of the Rockefeller Empire.

A key element in connecting the dots behind this conspiracy is to focus some attention on foundations. Josephson wrote:

> The Rockefeller Foundation together with the other foundations of import, of which it seized control, became the spearhead of a world-wide drive for totalitarianism. Its vaunted 'internationalism' implied a drive to crush competition and rival powers; world conquest by both indoctrination and force; and the ultimate welding of the world, thus conquered into a united totalitarian world, 'One World'----a Rockefeller world. (Josephson *Rockefeller*: 155).

Here it was 1952 and the term One World was already in use in describing "Rocky's World." After 1928, the Rockefeller Foundation began to sponsor, aside from medical sciences, also natural sciences, the "social sciences," and the humanities.

Later, I will return to my new favorite researcher and author on the Rockefellers, Josephson, who has much to say about the Council on Foreign Relations, which he repeatedly mentioned as the "Foreign Office" of the Rockefeller Empire.

David's other brother, Nelson, well-known to all of us above a certain age, wrote in the Future of Federalism in 1962 that "current events demand a 'new world order.'" He stated that there exists:

> ...a fever of nationalism---but the nation-state is becoming less and less competent to perform its international political tasks...These are some of the reasons pressing us to lead vigorously toward the true building of a new world order...sooner perhaps than we may realize...there will evolve the basis for a federal structure of the free world.

These people have been using these terms for decades. Where have we been?

Amazingly, the term goes back even further to 1919 when Samuel Zane Batten published for the American Baptist Publication Society something titled, "The New World Order." In it, believe it or not in a so-called "Christian" publication, he wrote, "World patriotism must be a faith. The only alternative is World Federation...with a world parliament, an international court, and an international policy force." Did not anyone construe that to be a bit of mixing of church and state? Further, he advocated, "Internationalism must first be a religion before it can be a reality and a system." Is it possible a Rockefeller entity planted this story? At any rate, the secular movement toward the fulfillment of Biblical prophecy regarding a One World Religion is not something merely cooked up.

Global Governance by the Antichrist

In Daniel 7:23-25 (PSB), Daniel puts forth the following prophecy:

> Thus he said, the fourth beast shall be the fourth kingdom upon earth, which shall be diverse from all kingdoms, and shall devour the whole earth, and shall tread it down, and break it in pieces...and another shall arise after them;...And he shall speak great words against the most High, and shall wear out the saints of the most High.

Houston Pastor Ed Young indicated a similar belief:

> There will come along an Antichrist who will at first appear to be a savior, at first will appear to be very moral and very brilliant, and in the crisis in which the world will find itself at this particular moment in history, the Antichrist will begin to dominate. And three of those ten nations will be destroyed. Then he will become supreme. (Duck *Daniel*: 200).[1]

That it has been happening, or is happening, right before us spans more and more machinations to achieve international control at the expense of national sovereignty. Let's look at some modern-day examples of how this prophecy is being fulfilled:

1. Global behavior modification, as defined by transformation of the world's economic, environmental, and social agenda

2. "Free trade agreements" such as the Trans-Pacific Partnership and the Transatlantic Trade and Investment Partnership.

3. The World Economic Forum in 2009 suggested a global TV network to help usher in "global governance."

4. President Obama and Bill Gates globalized education through Common Core.

Furthermore, suggestions are being made for cyberspace and the internet to come under "global governance," such as:

5. Advocacy is progressing for a "world currency."

6. Globalized taxation is another utopian scheme.

7. Submission to world courts for our own judicial system.

What about the prophecy of the Ten Horns? The prototype under development to lead to nine more is the European Union. Decades ago, the Club of Rome advocated ten regional governments. It is amazing how events are unfolding before us that were written millennia ago.

The prophecy of Daniel 2:41-44 speaks of the breaking up of the Roman Empire to later become reborn in an unstable manner. This fulfillment is illustrated most aptly by our multitudes of dictatorships, strict communist states, social democracies, and theocracies.

One World Religion

Revelation 13: 12-14 (PSB) prophesies of a figure coming forth as a beast known as the "false prophet," who will bring together all faiths in a one world religion:

> And he exercised all the power of the first beast before him, and caused the earth and them which dwell therein to worship the first beast, ... And he doeth great wonders, ... And deceiveth them that dwell on the earth by the means of those miracles which he had the power to do in the sight of the beast...

In his book titled *Revelation*, author Duck wrote, "The second beast, the False Prophet, will hold as much authority as the first beast, the Antichrist...but he will not use his great authority to exalt himself. He will use it to exalt the Antichrist." (195).

Is this being fulfilled? Let us look at the signals.

A now deceased author, Grant Jeffrey, whose works I studied, wrote, "Just like the growing apostasy in the Protestant denominations many of the modern Catholic leaders have rejected the fundamentals of the New Testament faith." (Duck *Revelation*: 196).[2] Constant ecumenical activities occur to set the stage for a more "tolerant and socially conscious" society. In Berlin, plans exist to build one single structure to house a church, a mosque, and a synagogue. Saves on building costs, for sure. The Parliament of the World's Religions met in Salt Lake City in 2015. Joseph Smith is probably rolling over in his grave. On January 12, 2009, Henry Kissinger said, "To bring about the New World Order, we need to have a new consciousness." He advocates this while most of us continue living obliviously in our unconsciousness.

There exists much information relative to the movement toward a One World Religion and I will leave it up to my readers to do their own research. Anything I would list could edge over into negativity toward some other faiths.

Prophecy in the end times focuses on wars and rumors of wars. I guess the signs of the times for this indicator remain obvious with our own military's high level of engagement since 9-11 against Al Qaeda, the Taliban, and the latest "bad actor," ISIS. The threat of ISIS may be leading the Middle East to become another of those ten regional blocs we have discussed, leading to a solution to the chaos and horrors of that demonic and barbaric group.

Illuminati

Who are the suspects for all this turmoil, and what do I believe to be the unstoppable stampede to the fulfillment of Biblical prophecy?

In my opinion, a most complete reference for one Adam Weishaupt, the reputed founder of the modern-day Illuminati, is Nesta H. Webster in her 1921 book titled *World Revolution or the Plot Against Civilization*. Webster provides many sources for her writings, although many are in foreign language footnotes, so I will proceed to express her research and just reference the pages of her work.

A comprehensive background history of the Illuminati must go back to 1250 when a Hungarian ex-priest named Jacobi began to fight the priests and nobles. Very soon thereafter, the Knights Templar came on the scene. It was reputed that they had two sides, one public, and one not even known to lower levels of the Knights. (Webster: 5).

Weishaupt, born on February 6, 1748, was educated by Jesuits and turned against them. He began to develop a new system for the world, the modern-day Illuminati, based on the concept that kings and nobles should be removed. He adopted the concept of Reason serving as man's motivating force, not Religion or the State. (Webster: 9). He unveiled his new organization on May 1, 1776, two months before the unveiling of the Declaration of Independence and the birth of the United States. (Webster: 10). It is fascinating to know that May 1, May Day, is celebrated in the Communist world on May 1st of each year!

Communication between members was conducted in code, and although he was opposed to Jesuitism itself, nevertheless Weishaupt's grades and ranks in the Illuminati were based on the Jesuit and the Freemason systems. (Webster: 12).

It is also important to recognize from the initiation of the Illuminati that it was based on a goal of world domination, the eventual aim of which was to remain unrevealed to the lower level initiates. (Webster: 12). The whole secret of the order was eventually to be exposed as initiates progressed, "Behold our secret...If in order to destroy all Christianity, all religion, we have pretended to have the sole true religion..." (Webster: 13). The members were expected to hide the term Illuminati. Espionage was a major tenet of the movement. Soon after its formation, there was an agreement made with one of the branches of Freemasonry to coordinate their efforts. (Webster: 18).

The initial history of the Illuminati will be left by your author in quoting what Webster quotes as their goal: "All religion," they declared, "all love of country and loyalty to sovereigns, were to be annihilated ..." (Webster: 21). She continues, "In the lodges death was declared an eternal sleep; patriotism and loyalty were called narrow-minded prejudices and incompatible with universal benevolence ..." (Webster: 22).[3] The original precepts of the Order were distributed throughout Europe by officials in Bavaria to call attention to the plans of the Illuminati and therefore to justify their banishment. The precepts were titled the Original Writings of the Order of the Illuminati. The banishment served the Illuminati's purposes because now they could claim they no longer existed. (Webster: 25).

Therefore, would it be too far-fetched to speculate that what we are witnessing today in our world could be the culmination of a steady drive of this organization to accomplish its purposes to usurp and remove Christianity and national sovereignty through secrecy, espionage, deception, and concealment?

Illuminism

Much more relevant today to the foundations of this movement toward a One World Government and One World Religion is a discussion of "Illuminism," which came to my attention in early 2015, for my own "illumination."

On December 14, 2014, a new book was published that as of October 2018 had already received an astounding 2,196 reviews on Amazon. Its title is *Illuminatiam: The First Testament of The Illuminati*, and the book was the number-one rated book in the category called Controversial Religious Knowledge in 2015, when I discovered it. The writeup on Amazon implores, "Join the millions who have discovered the light...Fear not your war-stricken, poverty-ridden planet: the age of illumination will soon begin...the Illuminati's path for humanity - our Universal Design - has spanned throughout the centuries to safeguard the human species from extinction." I guess the secret is out! There is not a need for further speculation. One can find out how to join the Illuminati at www.illuminati.am. I have not done so, because I am in God's Book of Life and do not want any confusion regarding my status.

Then there is the paperback published on Sep. 26, 2013, titled *66 Laws of the Illuminati*, which states in its marketing, "The House of the Illuminati, has broken years of silence with this publication. This should bring the world great enlightenment as its 'Laws' which they indicate are the secrets of success for anyone who embarks upon the path of light." I don't know about you, but I find these two very recent books truly sensational in their promotional verbiage, much less in their content and in the timing of their publications!

Secular Fulfillment of Prophecy

Now, it is time to direct my efforts toward discussing the secular "usual suspects" that are fulfilling the prophecies of Daniel and Revelation right in front of our blinded eyes. A discussion of these groups usually encompasses the Round Table, the Council on

Foreign Relations, the United Nations, the Bilderberg Society, and the Trilateral Commission. Wading through all these groups presents a never-ending and puzzling series of enigmas.

My bottom line is that three basic motives exist for those involved in this myriad of endeavors to move us to an inevitable one world government and religion. One group is basically oriented in a distinctly, though misguided, humanitarian motivation to bring peace to a troubled and divisive world. I define these as the sheep and the lambs. The second, with a seemingly benevolent, but decidedly avaricious motivation, is driven by economic power and financial gain. These are the wolves. I have concluded that a third group of these "Illuminists" are behind it all and using the first two groups to attain the ultimate purpose, which is to oversee a world dominated by Lucifer, God's antagonist, since the attempted coup in Heaven. These are the serpents.

My conclusion comes from a side of mine derived from assignment in the Vietnam War as a military intelligence officer assigned to Fifth Special Forces, the Green Berets. In my assignment, I served as a case officer (i.e., "handler") utilizing Cambodian and Montagnard agents to obtain intelligence from Cambodia, which was purportedly, but not really, a "neutral" country.

Order of Battle

In military terms, the Order of Battle relates to the opposing forces arrayed against each other. Regarding my personal order of battle, it is my own distinct and definitive belief that Jesus Christ came to earth to save sinners. My belief in Him allows me to know with certainty that I have a ticket to eternal life upon my demise. The strategic purpose for the Son of God's coming to earth 2000 years ago is that it signaled that God was taking back His Kingdom. The forces of Lucifer represent our enemy and believe that they will keep control and that all these efforts equal their battle plan. We may fail as God's people in some of the secular battles, but we will win in the final war. Lucifer will be checkmated after playing out this game on a large chess board.

The "Illuminists," hard-core believers in fulfilling their objectives, use the first two groups as their players on the board. I believe they have as major entities "spiritual" groups like the "New Age" movement and the "Age of Aquarius" as their cover groups, as well as the secular "usual suspects" discussed earlier. Acting as Lucifer's case officers behind the scenes, these serpent-like Illuminists directly or indirectly guide the activities of the sheep and the lambs, as well as those of the wolves.

A probable assumption is that many in the power group have become co-opted and have become true "Illuminists" themselves. Their movement has been based on a satanically-inspired heresy in building a "benevolent" peaceful kingdom on earth to shepherd the sheep and the lambs. Of course, the sheep and the lambs will be led to the slaughter by the serpents, and the wolves will prevail at the top of the pyramid. The strategic plan of my God, also prophesied, upholds that this final peaceful kingdom only occurs after two things come to fruition. First, the one world government and religion must have been established and destroyed. Second, Jesus must return a second time to establish the final one-thousand-year period of history, the Millennial Kingdom.

Building the Kingdom of God on Earth

A book titled *Building the Kingdom of God on Earth* by Dr. Martin Erdmann discusses "John Foster Dulles' participation in the ecumenical movement from 1919 to 1945." Dulles, who became our Secretary of State in 1953, was the principal force working with the Federal Council of Churches. This organization legitimately desired peace and order in the world, and the entity believed it would be possible through an international group that ended up becoming the United Nations, largely due to their influence. In my opinion, Erdmann's book serves as a tremendous resource to trace the underlying drive that culminated in the UN all the way back to the history in England of an original Oxford University group, the later Round Table, and our own Council on

Foreign Relations. The UN fulfilled John Foster Dulles' view of a new world order.

Dr. Pearse of the London School of Theology wrote the foreword for Erdmann's book, and professed that Erdmann's work tied together the internationalist use of the churches to facilitate the formation of the UN. In his foreword, he wrote:

> The ironical conclusion was that the age that was in full retreat from Christian orthodoxy and supernaturalism witnessed a paradoxical confidence that the Kingdom of God-established of course, by human management skills-was just around the corner....(Dr. Erdmann) demonstrates how key, highly placed individuals in both Britain and America attempted to harness the churches for a secular technocratic programme to build a new world order-and ultimately a world government-that would rest upon a minimalist theology of a vague Christian ethic.... As these pages show, the individuals like John Foster Dulles who come together to make 'big plans' for us lesser mortals are not dispassionately benevolent intelligences.

John Foster Dulles, through all his efforts, still took time to take care of his legal business that he pursued from 1934-1939, which included numerous business interests with the Nazis. The Nazis very shortly afterwards were killing our young men and enslaving the countries they took over. He was despicable! He and his brother Allen served as the attorneys for Shroeder/Rockefeller & Co., who conducted business with the Nazis all the way through most of the 1930s.

In my opinion, the bottom line of the formation of the UN is that after 1932, the social gospel was "propagated with renewed vigor." This culminated in the principles of the social creed designed to attain the Kingdom of God on earth rather than to reach lost souls with the Gospel of the Lord Jesus Christ.

Propaganda and "PSYOPS"

Previously, it has been written that Schaefer said people would be manipulated by the use of psychological techniques or psychological operations (i.e., PSYOPS). One of my reference books was written by Dr. John Coleman, a former British MI6 officer, who studied in the back archives of the British Museum for five years. He wrote *The Tavistock Institute of Human Relations*, and originally revealed the existence of this operation in 1969. His conclusion states that this British entity is responsible for the psychological manipulation techniques utilized for decades to effect what the establishment desired to accomplish. Major General John Rawlings Reese, one of the leaders of the Institute explained their methodology in 1954:

> Their job is to apply the advanced techniques of psychological warfare as we know them to whole population groups that will grow ever larger, so that whole populations may be more easily controlled. In a world driven completely mad, groups of Tavistock psychologists linked to each other, capable of influencing the political and governmental field must be arbiters, the power cabal. (Coleman *Tavistock*: 145).

I would say they have been doing their job exceedingly well and should get pay raises.

Control Group

Dr. Coleman wrote another book titled *The Illuminati in the U.S. 1776-2008*. He wrote about the subversion of America by a "Committee of 300," as he terms it. He gives his opinion as to why most of us lend no credence to any kind of "conspiracy." He states, "It is part of the catalog of deception being practiced upon the public by our thought-conditioners, who teach that there is no conspiracy worth mentioning. This ploy is designed to discredit the belief that there is a massive conspiracy going on against the United States in many of its institutions."

Coleman wrote extensively about the Rockefellers and pulls no punches as he elaborates on the Illuminati:

> Naturally, there is no means of proving that they work to overthrow the Christian religion, family, and the sanctity of marriage, especially as they themselves honor these codes, but documents I got sight of in the British Museum in London, make reference to these anti-Christian-anti-family goals of the Illuminists. (Coleman *Illuminati*: 60).

Coleman was on to these Illuminists a few decades before me. He maintains that part of the strategy is to overcome traditional forms of Christian worship. Per Coleman, the main target has been the Catholics, but their resistance has been so strong that they have gone after an easier target, I am sad to say, my Protestants. He maintains as a bottom line that the Illuminist master plan is to destroy Christianity worldwide, and especially America's Christian heritage. Now we know why everything including all the assaults on our cherished traditions and history have come from the Illuminists. Suspicions confirmed!

Coleman found confirmation of this Committee of 300 in a statement made by a Walter Rathenau in 1922. Now Rathenau was no ordinary peasant. He was chairman of the giant EEG Company in Berlin, a socialist, politician and financial advisor to the Rothschilds. In an article, he wrote, "Only three hundred men, each of whom knows all others, govern the fate of Europe. They select their successors from their own entourage. These men have the means in their hands of putting an end to the form of the State, which they find unreasonable." (Coleman *Committee*: 203). Apparently, some or possibly all those 300 took offense at being made public, because six months later, he was assassinated.

The Armies of The Conspiracy

On the topic of conspiracy, Dr. Erdmann wrote:

> These high-minded diplomats put their confidence in a

steady stream of internationalist propaganda. Public opinion would be persuaded to clamour for a voluntary abrogation of national sovereignty. To this end, the Institute of International Affairs was formed. It later received a royal charter and united more or less informally with the American Council on Foreign Relations...The Council on Foreign Relations attracted many influential members, among them many 'high-ranking officers of banking, manufacturing, trading, and finance companies, together with many lawyers.' In most cases these members were directly aligned with the financial network of J.P. Morgan & Co. (Erdman: 18,19).

The lawyers must be included and the bankers who love to lend money to finance wars.

James Perloff in *Shadows of Power* captured what Admiral Chester Ward, a twenty-year member of CFR, said:

Once the ruling members of the CFR have decided that the U.S. Government should adopt a particular policy, the very substantial research facilities of CFR are put to work to develop arguments, intellectual and emotional, to support the new policy, and to confound and discredit, intellectually and politically, any opposition.

The Admiral said the CFR has a goal of "submergence of U.S. sovereignty and national independence into an all-powerful one-world government." (Perloff: 9).

Emanuel Josephson, newly-established in my mind as the "hit man" for the Rockefellers (perhaps Chase Manhattan Bank turned him down for a loan along the way), said in 1952, "The top Rockefeller agency, the Communist-riddled Council on Foreign Relations, openly boasts, as stated in the chapter on that organization, in its annual reports, that it has planted innumerable agents in policy-making Federal posts, for which it trains them." (Josephson *Rockefeller*: 228). Josephson termed the positions so pervasive that the CFR could be called the invisible government of the United States. Why would he term it Communist-riddled? A classic reason is because the U.S. contingent to form the UN consisted of almost all CFR members led by an Alger Hiss, who was suspected of being a Communist.

Conclusion

In conclusion, I must make some more personal remarks. In no way do I intend to leave you with an opinion that all CFR members are involved in this documented conspiracy. The CFR, thousands in number, are delighted to have the enhancements on their resume and the networking opportunities that are benefits of being "tapped" for this auspicious organization. Are some unwitting and unknowing as to what I believe to be the immense power wielded by this group, not necessarily in the interest of the peasants, but for a goal of globalism? By all means.

Through the movement to form the UN, were there idealistically-minded individuals truly interested in world peace? Of course. Are there selfish and greedy individuals who will do anything to further their power and personal wealth? Most assuredly, and we witness more of them every day than we do of the conspirators.

Has it been Satan's goal since the Garden of Eden to kill and destroy and subvert God's plan for humanity? The answer to that is a resounding and unequivocal affirmative!

My personal belief is that there will be a pretribulation "Rapture" of the faithful Believers, who have accepted Jesus as personal Savior. They will be gathered up in an instant to Heaven, thereby absenting themselves from the traumatic events of the seven-year Tribulation period, thereby "missing" all the horror of God's judgment for the sins of the world and its inhabitants. Wolves and serpents beware!

At the end of the Tribulation period, Chapter 16 of the Book of Revelation (KJV) reads:

And I saw three unclean spirits like frogs come out of the mouth of the dragon, and out of the mouth of the beast, and out of the mouth of the false prophet. (13).

For they are the spirits of devils, working miracles, which go forth unto the kings of the earth and of the whole world, to gather them to the battle of that great day of God Almighty. (14).

And he gathered them together into a place called in the Hebrew tongue Armageddon. (16).

If some of these terms are alien to the reader, some personal research on End Times prophecy could prove to be very helpful.

According to the book of Revelation, the Battle of Armageddon will be fought in the Jezreel Valley (Esdraelon), located north of Megiddo and south of Nazareth, Jesus' home. My visit to the plain north of Megiddo confirmed a huge flat expanse of ground which could easily accommodate one huge tank battle! Author Tenney quantified the size of this space by saying, "This plain is a triangular shape and is 15 by 15 by 20 miles in size. Several passes enter into it making it easy of access and important commercially and in military operations." (Tenney: 259).

This plain near Megiddo, the oldest battlefield in the world, is quite historic. Through the millennia, much blood has been spilled on its ground. The latest battle was fought there in September of 1918, when British Lord Allenby, commanding the Egyptian Expeditionary Force against the Turkish Army of the Ottoman Empire, routed the Turks under the command of Mustapha Kemal Pasha (the future Kemal Ataturk). The Turkish Army was chased all the way to Damascus and Aleppo. (Do these sites sound familiar given the conflicts in present-day Syria?). On October 30, 1918, the British signed an armistice with the Turkish authorities. (Taylor: 139-145). And surprise, surprise, surprise:

Palestine was overrun with the U.S. Standard Oil agents

thinly disguised as Red Cross workers, a subterfuge which was particularly obnoxious to Allenby whose efforts to expose it however were not entirely successful owing to the fact that at the head of the American Red Cross was...Davidson, one of the head partners in Morgan's Bank, the Allies' principal creditor in the U.S.A. (Taylor: 150).

The footnote in my Bible for Revelation 16:16 reads:

Sinful men will unite to fight against God in a final display of rebellion. Many are already united against Christ and his people-those who stand for truth, peace, justice, and morality. Your personal battle with evil foreshadows the great battle pictured here, where God will meet evil and destroy it once and for all. Be strong and courageous as you battle against sin and evil: you are fighting on the winning side.

I prefer to be on God's side in the Order of Battle!

Do I believe there is a concerted and well-planned effort of long standing in the secular world to effect what God has in fact prophesied? If I have not yet made that case, I can do no more.

As seen in Romans 8: 18-22 (KJV):

The future glory

For I reckon that the sufferings of this present time are not worthy to be compared with the glory which shall be revealed in us.

For the earnest expectation of the creature waiteth for the manifestation of the sons of God.

For the creature was made subject to vanity, not willingly, but by reason of him who subjected the same in hope.

Because the creature itself also shall be delivered from the bondage of corruption into the glorious liberty of the children of God.

For we know that the whole creation groaneth and travaileth in pain together until now.

This is an accurate description of the New World Order taking place. But the footnote brings it all together for the Eternal World Order: "They look forward to the new heaven and new earth God has promised, and they wait for God's new order that will free the world of sin, sickness, and evil."

I will be more comfortable in God's New World Order instead of the one being planned by the forces of evil.

SECTION II:

CUPIDITY – PLAYERS AND CONSEQUENCES

Chapter 4:

Cupidity and the "Usual Suspects"

> Definition: CUPIDITY, *n.* [L. *cupiditas*, from *cupidus*, from cupio, to desire to covet.] "An eager desire to possess something; an ardent wishing or longing; inordinate or unlawful desire of wealth or power. "

Galatians 1:4 reads, "Who gave himself for our sins, that he might deliver us from this present evil world..." (*LASB KJV*: 2051). And in the footnote of Galations 1:3-5, it reads, "God's plan all along was to save us by Jesus's death. We have been delivered from the power of this evil world – a world ruled by Satan, full of cruelty, tragedy, temptation, and deception." Note that we are not taken out of this world until death and in the interim we must suffer, while the tentacles of Satan remain wrapped around some of my "usual suspects," described in the following chapters. However, we have the means to know how the world system works and has worked for centuries

The individuals and institutions cited in this chapter may be considered the "Cast of Characters" for reappearance in the succeeding chapters. They may even be considered the "Usual Suspects," as most appear again and again at some point in our stories. Quotes are representative of what some individuals, many in high-level political positions, and others, including authors, believe is indicative of conditions operative and historical in the political, financial, and economic arenas of world societies and life. An extensive use of quotes appears in the upcoming chapters, because paraphrasing renders a significant diminishment of the impact of the original writing.

My efforts toward accountability will be reflected in the truths I've discovered in exhaustive research to tell the true stories, not the revisionist ones of history, so that we may hold our elected officials and titans of business to the truths of our future conflicts that send the patriots of America into harm's way.

It will be my fate in several circles of today's society that I will face extraordinary disdain for possessing the effrontery to describe and write about many "sacred cows" of our world's demographics, many close to me personally.

As Burke maintained, "No property is secure when it becomes large enough to tempt the *cupidity* of indigent power." (*Noah Webster's 1828 Dictionary*). One of the Seven Deadly Sins is Greed, greed for power, acquisition and enslavement. The subjects in this chapter and many throughout this book commit this sin. Many make their money from the blood of our soldiers.

After writing the three preceding chapters, which focused on the spiritual and religious aspects relevant to the thesis of this work, I was prepared to go secular. But then my research led me to a 23-page pamphlet written by Vincent Cartwright Vickers, who fits into several of the categories of my "usual suspects," that will be addressed in this chapter.

The first category is as an elitist (Eton and Magdalen College, Oxford), followed by politician (deputy lieutenant of the City of London), then arms maker (Director of Vickers Limited for 22 years), and finally, banker (Governor of the Bank of England for 9 years). Startled by the revelations about international finance made by this insider, I address them in due course in this book. However, I wish now to relate some information that he addressed within what are basically his views on economics and finance in England.

Vickers, who died in 1939, two years before his son published this pamphlet, wrote:

> Is it not time to see that in the future we are no longer to be enslaved by the methods of the old order, but that we are to be equitably governed under principles which will

indeed be sacred, because they will be founded upon Christianity itself and will be Christian principles?

Furthermore, he wrote:

But, it will be asked, how can we as practical man with mundane mentalities, combine Christian principles with business abilities? ...you must be able... to play the same throughout by the Christian principle of honesty.

Expounding upon this topic, he also stated that:

Fundamental laws, originally designed for the common welfare of the individuals of a community, have been broken – community laws which were never intended to permit the individual to grow fat upon the poverty of others; nor to permit him, in pursuit of his own personal profit, to base his standard of honesty upon his own flexible conscience, consoling himself with gratitude that he is within the law. (Vickers: 4).

This "usual suspect" finally saw the light! Would that more of his fellow "usual suspects," to be mentioned in future chapters, have been of the same level of enlightenment.

Marine Major General Smedley Butler wrote an extraordinary work titled *War is a Racket* in 1935. As a bona fide war hero (two-time Medal of Honor Recipient), he qualifies himself with the wisdom of his insights, grounded in military and political experiences. Therefore, he will be quoted often in this book. He wrote of "blood money" related to the arms merchants as one of the most blatant "usual suspects."

In one of Butler's most outstanding quotes, he stated:

Don't you realize that the money you'll get for your ammunition will be covered with blood? And as time goes on this blood will be the blood of your children. Has blood money ever brought anything but misery to those who got the money? (Butler: 84).

Chapter 5:

Warfare and Casualties

No less an authority on warfare than Ernest Hemingway shared a very compelling opinion about warfare. During World War I, Hemingway served as an ambulance driver for the Red Cross. Soon after his arrival on the battlefield in Italy, he was severely wounded by an artillery shell. At the age of thirty in 1929, he published *A Farewell to Arms.* Later, he served as a correspondent in both the Spanish Civil War and World War II.

In 1948, his novel was republished, and in that edition, he wrote:

> Some people used to say, why is the man so preoccupied and obsessed with war, and now, since 1933 perhaps it is clear why a writer should be interested in the constant, bullying, murderous, slovenly crime of war. Having been to too many of them, I am sure that I am prejudiced, and I hope that I am prejudiced. But it is considered belief of the writer of this book that wars are fought by the finest people that there are...but they are made, provoked and initiated by straight economic rivalries and by swine that stand to profit from them. I believe that all the people who stand to profit by a war and who help provoke it should be shot on the first day it starts by accredited representatives of the loyal citizens of their country who will fight it.[1]

The old poet Shenstone penned:

> Let the gilded fool the toil of war pursue
> Where bleed the many to enrich the few. (Hurt: 323).

Author Walter Hurt writes very succinctly about why wars are fought:

Wars are waged for various economic reasons--- but always for economic reasons only, whatever the putative purpose; for commercial advantage when intensive competition restricts the world-market for rival powers; for territorial expansion to relieve by colonization a painfully congested population with its consequent economic evils that breed a dangerous discontent; to restrain aggressions that threaten national industrial interests; to divert the minds of the masses and restore the spirit of solidarity when economic oppression at home impels to revolt; to protect the loans of large combinations of capital and the interests of powerful investment groups; to afford greater opportunity for graft, and from many similar motives. (Hurt: 31).

As one proceeds to learn about the different conflicts described herein, one or more of the above purposes can explain the underlying rationale for the conflicts.

Major General Smedley Butler, one of my obviously favorite sources, writes:

A racket is best described, I believe, as something that is not what it seems to be to the majority of people. Only a small 'inside' group knows what is about. It is conducted for the benefit of the very few, at the expense of the very many. Out of war a few people make huge fortunes. (Butler: 11).

General Butler goes on to describe what he believes is the principal cause of wars, and as he pursues his analysis of warfare, his reasoning may be the bottom line rather than what the public is led to believe. He is most credible because, as we say in the military, "he has been there, done that."
Butler continued:

Stripped of all camouflage, competition for world trade stands out as the cause of nearly every major war in the history of the United States and the world at large. In the term 'world trade' I refer to international financial loans and credits, and the purchase of foreign bonds by investors, as well as the buying and selling of ordinary merchandise and commodities. (Butler: 182).

Another of my favorite authors is Curtis Dall. In the dedication of his very compelling book, he wrote:

Dedicated to young Americans--- may you benefit from observing how certain shadowy forces contrive to ruthlessly advance their own financial and ideological objectives at your expense. They select, then groom, and ultimately control many of our highest government officials. They plan the wars and through 'foreign policy' arrange to set the stage for incidents to initiate hostilities. They overwork the word 'peace' to mislead you and create a plausible smoke screen in order to conceal their real operations. You can recognize who 'they' are.

At the end of the following chapters, many of "they" will have been identified and described. Not all are necessarily guilty of any wrongdoing or transgression, nor do they necessarily fit the cupidity profile, however many are subjects of significant controversy and coverage in various literary works. I will address numerous categories of groups in our societies in the interest of the extraordinary parts they have played on the stages of history. These chapters individually could be books in themselves, but I will confine myself only to the highlights of their histories.

History is rampant with disarmament conferences. Butler is very forthcoming relative to his negative opinion about these so-called "disarmament" conferences. He maintains that these conferences were conducted so that the opposing sides could utilize the negotiations to better arm themselves against their opponents. Butler believes that disarmament conferences are staffed by militarists, politicians, and diplomats who really do not want to disarm as much as they really want to perpetuate their preparations for conflict. Note the 2018 situation relative to the past decades of ongoing negotiations and attempts at disarmament relative to Iran and North Korea. (Butler: 202). All to no avail.

In his fascinating pamphlet, Vincent Cartwright Vickers levels a frightening charge about the "usual suspects" in the industries of finance and banking, whom he maintains carried on their activities without what he proposed as much-needed industry changes. He wrote, "And it has therefore devolved upon the directors and managers of the money industry and of banking and finance, headed by the Bank of England with its charter, to exercise the existing monetary system even if it entails war."[2] Vickers was not some academic scholar. Rather, he was deeply involved all his life in the "money" industry. It was only near his demise that he felt he could call to question one of his own industries and its connection to wars. This late-in-life enlightenment was like that of my highly admired President Dwight D. Eisenhower, who availed himself only at the end of his term of office to reflect upon the "Military-Industrial Complex."

Casualties and Ill-Gotten Gains

Butler nailed this topic when he said:

> Out of war a few people make huge fortunes. Nations acquire additional territory (which is promptly exploited by the few for their own benefit) and the general public shoulders the bill---a bill that renders a horrible accounting of newly-placed gravestones, mangled bodies, shattered minds, broken hearts and homes, economic instability and back-breaking taxation of the many for generations and generations. (Butler: 208).

Upon his retirement, General Butler perhaps became the Nation's most vocal advocate for the veterans of World War I. He wrote an in-depth account of his thoughts on that subject:

In the government hospital at Marion, Indiana, 1,800 of these boys are in pens! Five hundred of them in a barracks with steel bars and wires all around outside the buildings and on the porches. These already have been mentally destroyed. These boys don't even look like human beings. Oh, the looks on their faces! Physically, they are in good shape; mentally, they are gone.

There are thousands and thousands of these cases, and more and more are coming in all the time. The tremendous excitement of the war, the sudden cutting off of that excitement---the young boys couldn't stand it.

That's a part of the bill. So much for the dead---they have paid their part of the war profits. So much for the mentally and physically wounded---they are paying now their share of the war profits. But the others paid, too---they paid with heartbreaks when they tore themselves away from their firesides and their families to don the uniform of Uncle Sam---on which a profit had been made. They paid another part in the training camps where they were regimented and drilled while others took their jobs and their places in the lives of their communities. They paid for it in the trenches where they shot and were shot; where they went hungry for days at a time; where they slept in the mud and in the cold and in the rain—with the moans and shrieks of the dying for a horrible lullaby. (Butler: 28).

Upon real reflection, does anyone believe the civilians in their comfortable offices and homes during wartime really care about the front-line soldiers, Marines, sailors, and Air Force personnel? One of the saddest, but truest comments I have ever heard was stated by a soldier who served two years stateside during World War II. He said, "If I'd been home as a civilian, I would have made a lot of money." My wife's father returned from World War II wartime in Europe and North Africa and was never the same again emotionally.

The Army Song, "The Army Goes Rolling Along," is a distinct part of my personal heritage. I close this chapter with a few of its words:

Valley Forge, Custer's ranks, San Juan Hill and Patton's tanks.

Men in rags, men who froze, still that Army met its foes.

Faith in God, then we're right, and we'll fight with all our might.

Our traditions will never be trampled upon.

Soldiers' Blood

Total U.S. Casualties: ~2,852,901
- 1,354,664 deaths
- 1,498,240 wounded

Total U.S. Deaths (1775-Present):[3] ~1,354,664
- 666,441 combat-related
- 673,929 by other causes

Total Missing in Action (MIA): ~40,031

Chapter 6:

Arms Merchants

<u>Introduction</u>

In their writings, Dr. Engelbrecht and Mr. Hanighen show that arms merchants are not prejudiced against any potential buyer base:

> To give arms to all men who offer an honest price for them without respect of persons or principles: to aristocrats and Republicans, to Nihilist and Czar, to Capitalist and Socialist to Protestant and Catholic, to burglar and policeman, to black man, white man and yellow man, to all sorts and conditions, all nationalities, all faiths, all follies, all causes and all crimes.--- Creed of Undershaft, the arms maker, in Shaw's '*Major Barbara*.' (Engelbrecht: 1).

> "I appreciate the fact that the manufacturers of arms and ammunition are not standing very high in the estimation of the public generally." - Samuel S. Stone, President of Colt's Patent Fire Arms Manufacturing Co. (Engelbrecht: 1).

> Dr. Engelbrecht and Mr. Hanighen...thoroughly expose all the evils of the armament industry, but they remain at all times conscious that broader forces such as patriotism, imperialism, nationalistic education, and capitalistic competition, play a larger part than the armament industry in keeping alive the war system...They expose the corruption, graft, and disloyalty of the armament makers with a thoroughness sufficient to gratify the most determined pacifist...They recognize that they are no more corrupt than, for instance, our own great investment bankers. Moreover, even though the armament makers have played a prominent role in encouraging wars,

rebellions and border raids, they never exerted so terrible an influence upon the promotion of warfare as did our American bankers between 1914 and 1917. Armament makers and bankers alike are the victims of human cupidity." (Engelbrecht Foreword by Harry Elmer Barnes: *vii, viii*).

Many retired military officers work for the arms industry. This cast of "villains" in this deadly play roam the globe!

Merchants of Death: United States

DuPont:

The original DuPont dynasty had its beginnings in France with Pierre Du Pont on June 24, 1771, becoming the father of Eleuthere Irenée (E.I.), founder of the DuPont empire. The Du Ponts entered Newport Rhode, Island on New Year's Day 1800. The family, 13-members strong, consisted of rich American immigrants who originally settled in New Jersey. Quickly, gunpowder became the family "product." (Colby: 44). With assistance from Napoleon's Foreign Minister Talleyrand by means of machinery, designs, and techniques of powder-making, E.I. Du Pont was on his way to establish in America a competition to England's lock on the gunpowder business. (Colby: 45). The industry established its headquarters in Delaware with the DuPont gunpowder mills.

By 1905, the DuPont Company had a monopoly on all powder orders for the United States military after which they imposed price-fixing. In 1907, they were charged with a violation of the Sherman Antitrust Act. (Engelbrecht: 35).

E.I. Du Pont, the founder of the DuPont Company had a son, Henry Du Pont, who graduated the United States Military Academy at West Point in 1833. He was involved in a DuPont subsidiary and reentered the Union Army in 1861 for service during the Civil War. His son, Henry Algernon Du Pont, graduated first in the class of

May 1861 at West Point and received the Medal of Honor as a Union officer at the Battle of Cedar Creek. He joined the family operation and eventually was elected to the United States Senate. Graduate records of West Point indicate no other graduates from the Du Pont family at least by the Du Pont last name since 1861. (Source: 2010 *Register of Graduates of the U.S. Military Academy, West Point, NY.*)

Bannerman & Sons of New York City:

This company came into prominence after the Civil War, when it bought massive quantities of military items at auctions. At one point they owned an island north of West Point on the Hudson River, upon which they built a veritable arsenal in a Scottish castle design. They became somewhat of a catalog supplier of discarded weaponry to multitudes of foreign buyers. *The Army and Navy Journal* of March 26, 1904, reported that the Panamanians, who revolted against Colombia, were armed with weaponry suspiciously like the weapons that been seized in the Spanish-American War by the United States. The American Secretary of War proclaimed weapons from that conflict were sold in an auction to Bannerman and the United States had no responsibility for their ultimate destination. (Engelbrecht: 61-65).

Remington Arms:

This company, formed in 1816, became a major supplier of rifles during the Mexican and Civil Wars. After the Civil War, sales were made to foreign markets such as France, Puerto Rico, Cuba, Spain, Egypt, Mexico, and Chile. (Engelbrecht: 45). The company was on the verge of a huge order in Turkey at one point, but the company halted the order when Turks demanded "royalties" (i.e., bribes). (Engelbrecht: 46). During the 1879 Russo-Turk War, Remington filled orders for both sides. Officers from both sides were civil to each other as they interacted at the factory ensuring quality control. (Engelbrecht: 47). A curious case ensued in the Franco-Prussian war. The United States government collected 37,000 Springfield breechloaders, and together with 17 million cartridges, many of which were made at the Frankford U.S. Arsenal, Remington was able to fill a French order. Accordingly, in this case the "neutral" country of the United States sold munitions to one side in the war. (Engelbrecht: 49). Repeatedly, sales by companies domiciled in "neutral" countries occurred.

The Germans were winning the war against France and the supplying by the United States to France really did not bother Germany's Bismarck. However, a German-American, Senator Carl Schurz, made a most eloquent speech that condemned his own supposedly "neutral" country for facilitating the arms sales to be used against friendly Germany. (Engelbrecht: 51).

Bethlehem Steel, Carnegie, and Midvale Steel and Ordnance:

Shortly after 1880, three companies joined together to produce armor plating for battleships. By 1894, Germany's Krupp operation produced the armor plates through a new process and the U.S. consortium purchased the rights. By 1916, Bethlehem reported in their *Mobile Artillery Material* catalog that they had obtained customers in Russia, Greece, Italy, England, France, Argentina, Chile, Cuba, and Guatemala. (Engelbrecht: 53).[1]

In September 1893, charges were brought against the Carnegie, Phipps & Company for production of defective armor plating. (Engelbrecht: 53).[2] A fine of $288,000 was assessed. No mention of the scandal was printed by the press. On December 20, 1893, Andrew Carnegie met with President Cleveland, and lo and behold, the fine was reduced to $140,484. Many naval officers and members of the investigating committee did not approve of how the president downplayed the issue Engelbrecht writes, "Others see in this incident merely another instance of profiteering on the part of the arms makers." (Engelbrecht: 55).

Merchants of Death: Great Britain

Maxim:

An American named Hiram Maxim became a British citizen, and by 1884, he had perfected a machine gun that fired 660 shots a minute. Engelbrecht described its power by saying, "As a slaughtering machine it was unspeakably effective." Soon thereafter, the British Vickers Company added this gun to its inventory. (Engelbrecht: 87). The Boers of South Africa were one of the first customer groups for the new gun. Even though Maxim (and Vickers) supposedly surmised that the gun might be used against British soldiers since a conflict was looming against the Boers, their focus on bottom-line profits became more important to these purveyors of their awesome instruments than injury to humans. Gun orders were obtained from France, Switzerland, Italy, Germany, Russia, and many other military forces. A Swiss officer witnessed the guns' spewing of death and commented, "No gun has ever been made in the world that could kill so many men and horses in so short a time." (Engelbrecht: 88-89). This was music to the ears of these merchants of death and their stockholders.

George Bernard Shaw wrote in *Major Barbara:*

> The Government of your country! I am the Government of your country, I and Lazarus. Do you suppose that you and half a dozen amateurs like you, sitting in a row in that foolish gabble shop, govern Undershaft and Lazarus? No, my friend, you will do what pays us. You will make war when it suits us and keep peace when it doesn't... When I want anything to keep my dividends up, you will discover that my want is a national need. When other people want something to keep my dividends down you, will call out the police and military. And in return he shall have the support of my newspapers, and the delight of imagining that you are a great statesman. (Dialogue by the character Undershaft, the armament maker).

Co-authors Engelbrecht and Hannigan maintain that the above passage is an exaggeration of the actual influence and power in evidence of the armament companies, especially Vickers, but that they were known to wield significant influence. In 1914, stockholders in British armaments companies included Lord Balfour; Lord Curzon; Earl Grey; Lord Kinnaird, the president of the Y.M.C.A.; Sir J.B. Lonsdale; Sir Alfred Mond; the bishops of Adelaide, Chester and Hexham; and Dean Inge, the" gloomy dean" of St. Paul's. (Engelbrecht: 149).[3] This list is obviously a "Who's Who of the British elitists" to include even Anglican bishops! Shame on ministers to own stock in the makers of arms!

Vickers:

Vickers began in the early 19th century as only a general engineering and iron works. In the 1840s, Germany's Herr Krupp visited England. Both Vickers and Krupp began by manufacturing only gun parts, then proceeded to build the entire gun. Super salesman Sir Basil Zaharoff expanded their sales territory outside of Britain. Vickers bought a shipbuilding company in Glasgow and one in Italy, and then sold to Spain, and both Russia and Japan in the Russo-Japanese War. (Engelbrecht: 109-110).

In 1901, Vickers was a part of a huge international trust of arms dealers including Krupp and Dillingen in Germany, Terni in Italy, the American Bethlehem Steel company, the French Schneider, Chatillon Steel Co., and the St. Chaumont Steel Co. – all producers of arms. The group included the Nobel Dynamite Trust. (Engelbrecht: 111).[4] Many former retired military officers became employed by the arms dealers. Naturally, they were very familiar with the procurement systems as well as with the officers still on active duty. Engelbrecht defined them as "shills." This phenomenon still exists today, of course. Vickers placed former very high-ranking British officers on their Board of Directors. (Engelbrecht: 112).

By 1911, many of the "elitists" of British society, including dukes, earls, barons, knights, members of Parliament, and on and on, *ad nauseam,* to include even bishops, served on the boards of the three major arms manufacturers. These nobles and titled class members were the largest members of these boards. (Engelbrecht: 114).[5]

One Lord Welby indignantly proclaimed, "We are in the hands of an organization of crooks. They are the politicians, generals, manufacturers of armaments and journalists. All of them are anxious for unlimited expenditures and go inventing scares to terrify the public and to terrify Ministers of the Crown." (Engelbrecht: 114,115).

Nathaniel Rothschild financed the merger of the Maxim Gun Company with the Nordenfelt Guns and Ammunition Company and became very active in the company's management. The Austrian Rothschild branch invested in the country's arms business. "If late nineteenth century imperialism had its 'military-industrial complex' the Rothschilds were undoubtedly part of it." (Ferguson: 413).

Merchants of Death: France

Schneider:

In 1833, Joseph Eugene Schneider bought the Creusot foundries, suppliers of arms since Louis XIV. Under the reign of Napoleon III, his business thrived. The Franco-Prussian war made Schneider very wealthy. In the "radical eighties," when Communists came up against his company, French troops were called out to help him overcome the union pressures. (Engelbrecht: 123). Eugene Schneider was elected to the Chamber of Deputies. He began to move into the international markets and competition with Germany's Krupp developed. When Schneider competed for Brazilian orders in 1903, the media aided Krupp. Krupp won out over Schneider in both Argentina and Chile. (Engelbrecht: 124,125).

Schneider assisted his country in its alliance with Russia and arms were sold to Russia after French bankers provided loans to Russia.

The loans took the form of bonds sold to French investors. Czarist archives in Russia indicate that in 1904 and 1905, bribes and retainers were paid to the French press to ensure that the bond sales proceeded due to significant unrest at the time in Russia. The Russians corrupted the French Havas Agency, affiliated with and the counterpart of the Associated Press of the United States. Ten thousand francs per month were placed at the disposal of this press association to doctor Russian news. (Engelbrecht: 126,127).

In Paris, the Russians utilized as their Russian Imperialist agent a man named Arthur Raffalovich, who reported his machinations and payments to French media organizations. The Banque de Paris advanced the funds to pay off the French press for favorable or incomplete news on the turmoil in Russia, which if known, would have derailed the bond offering. The payments were "bribes." (Engelbrecht: 127).

Merchants of Death: Germany

Krupp:

The Krupp Company in Germany had its beginnings in a steel works, which by 1842, produced a crucible steel cannon, originally opposed by the Prussian military generals. Then a breakthrough occurred in 1856 when the Khedive of Egypt, Said Pasha, bought Krupp's cannon. Krupp learned to influence his own country with a dual-approach of emphasizing his patriotism, but also threatening to sell to other nations. In 1863, Russia came through with cannon orders. (Engelbrecht: 70-75). Krupp's cannon design was decisive for the Prussians in 1866 against the Austrians, but the Krupp dominance was evidenced in the Franco-Prussian war when the Krupp cannons used by Germany signified a major reason for their victory. (Engelbrecht: 79). According to one account, "[Krupp's Company] agents were everywhere; taking advantage of every political friction, bribing their way, using ambassadors and diplomatic officials to secure them an open door." (Engelbrecht: 79).[6]

Krupp guns were found in practically every war. If the Turks fought the Greeks or the Serbians fought the Bulgarians, both sides used Alfred Krupp's guns. (Engelbrecht: 79).[7]

The arms merchants sometimes acquired odd bedfellows such as when China's Krupp guns were used against Germans in the Boxer Rebellion. (Engelbrecht: 80).

By 1914, the naval forces of many of the opponents all utilized Krupp's armor plate, including Great Britain, France, Italy, Japan, Germany, and the United States. When the company reorganized in 1903, Emperor William II became a major stockholder. For 10 years prior to World War I, Krupp filled all the armaments needs of Germany. (Engelbrecht: 81).

By the beginning of World War I, Krupp had helped Russia rearm. Russia had become allied with France, Germany's perpetual enemy. Krupp had expanded its influence by owning or controlling three powerful German newspapers. Through these media mouthpieces, Krupp was able to rouse patriotic German support to war scares or the arms activities of other nations. Krupp went so far as to place on their payroll even active duty officers. Krupp was a giant in the cannon business by 1912, having sold 26,000 to Germany and 27,000 to 52 foreign countries. (Engelbrecht: 82,83). Killing machines were just waiting for the young of warring nations to throw themselves into battle and shed their blood for the honor and glory of their homeland!

Merchant of Death: Basil Zaharoff (1849-1936)

"Reputedly one of the richest men in the world, he was described as a 'merchant of death' and the 'mystery man of Europe.' During World War I he was involved at the highest levels of the Allied efforts in the war!"[8]

Basil Zaharoff was the quintessential arms salesman. Of Greek nationality, he originally represented the Swedish company Nordenfeldt in the Balkans. He sold the first submarine to Greece, but worried not about patriotism to his homeland. He also sold submarines to Turkey, Greece's enemy. Again, he worried not about patriotism to his home country. His pocketbook was his guide. Zaharoff, ever the opportunist, eventually allied with Maxim and traveled the world to peddle machine guns. (Engelbrecht: 95-100).

He became a most shadowy figure enmeshed in many scandals and much intrigue. He became friends with powerful Frenchmen and Englishmen such as Lloyd George and Lord John Murray. He was a man of the world, always courting powerful figures, all the while serving as an agent for the arms merchants. His influence and wealth got him mentioned in the same conversations as Rockefeller and Morgan. He was indeed a man of consequence, with his finger in many European pies wherein he increased his wealth. His own chapter in the Engelbrecht and Hanighen book is titled "Super Salesman of Death." (Engelbrecht: 106).

Author Guiles Davenport's 1934 book offers a complete and compelling biography of Zaharoff, who was possibly the most preeminent arms merchant and salesman of all time. Zaharoff was showered with honors, such as the Knight Grand Cross of the British Empire, Knight Grand Cross of the Bath, and Recipient of the Grand Cross of the Legion of Honor of France. The massive wealth acquired in his career could never have been enough to wash away, by any number of baths, the bloodshed caused by his exploits all over the world.

In his foreword, Davenport lays out his thesis for Zaharoff's career: "Until the Zaharoffs and that gang of international bandits, who intend to profit by the world's disorder, are exorcised by a thorough thrashing, we are always in danger of assault." (Davenport: x). This book enumerates countless "bandits of warfare," but undoubtedly the one who maintained a mask of mystery so very well was this shady character, whose principal connection was to Vickers, Limited, the English munitions firm. (Davenport: 38).

The process of budgeting for the purchase of weapons was explained as "… a strange and terrible process which always leaves a few the richer and the masses poorer." As indicated earlier, Zaharoff once arranged for submarines to be acquired by both sides in the enmity between Greece and Turkey. He and others of his ilk were a part of an evil system, "… whose function has been to bring mankind to its knees by killing it off and impoverishing its human components by war." (Davenport: 85). He was undeniably the best example of fostering "war for profit." As Davenport wrote, "… his task was to sow the seed. Depression, strikes, blockade, revolution, starvation, and destruction are essential corollaries to the harvest." (Davenport: 91).

Davenport expressed amazing warfare history. In the Russo-Japanese war, Japan received financing from an American bank, Japanese weapons were acquired through Russian contacts then used against Russians, and "England sold arms to both sides without discrimination." In 1914 Bulgaria, powered by French loans, bought weapons through French company Schneider-Creusot, weapons that were later used to kill French soldiers. The lists and facts never ceased about weapons, bought from a certain country, and eventually used against the combatants of that same country. (Davenport: 99). In the Russo-Japanese War, Zaharoff sold machine guns to both sides. The bottom line for all of these machinations by the arms merchants throughout history is that their profits were only exceeded by the blood spilled on the battlefields they equipped. I trust they are agonizing throughout all eternity in the heat of Hell!

As closure on the topic of Zaharoff, I was scanning through Acorn, the British Television streaming service, in early April 2018, and a series titled *Reilly Ace of Spies* (1983) came to my attention. Basil Zaharoff has a major part in episode 1 of the one-season series about a real British spy by the name of Sidney Reilly. Zaharoff is featured as a cast character in three more episodes. Admittedly the series is fictional, but it brings to viewers a very compelling picture of Zaharoff as an extremely powerful and connected arms merchant based in England.

Merchants of Death: Sweep of Influence

Bankers:

Throughout history, arms merchants either obtain control over banks or work on the trust of bankers. For Schneider-Creusot, it was the Banque de l'Union Parissienne. For the Krupps, the Deutsch Bank. For the Americans, J.P. Morgan. Influence through a country's borrowings were utilized by the arms merchants to obtain contracts. (Engelbrecht: 145).

Press:

By the early 1930s, the arms merchants utilized the press to their great advantage. Sometimes they just bought the newspapers, but other times, they made it profitable for press executives to be on arms company payrolls or boards. DuPont controlled every daily in Delaware. The companies bought advertising for their non-weapons products to ensure the coverage needed for their nefarious schemes and plots. (Engelbrecht: 146).

Merchants of Death: The Nye Report

On February 24, 1936, the U.S. Senate published the "Report of the Special Committee on Investigation of the Munitions Industry" (Nye Report).[9] I examined the entire report and profess that it is a sad commentary on the munitions industry. More on my conclusions may be covered in possible future writings, but for the present time, it will suffice to quote directly some of the more conspicuous judgments reached.

H.C. Engelbrecht, Ph. D. and F.C. Hanighen have been amply utilized as a resource for this chapter from their *Merchants of Death* work. On the first page of their Foreword, it is written:

> ... this study reveals illuminating information with respect to the organization and sales methods of a very considerable industry. The propaganda and high-pressure salesmanship

which has characterized contemporary business find his prototype in the activities of armament manufacturers long before our generation. (Engelbrecht: *v*).

In 1936, two years after the publishing of Engelbrecht's and Hanighen's book, the Nye Report was completed. The following quotes from the Nye Report represent some of the more surprising, damaging, explosive, and significant instances of profit-seeking, law violations, bribery, and other examples of cupidity that are shameful!

> The committee finds, under the head of sales methods of the munitions companies, that almost without exception the American munitions companies investigated have at times resorted to such unusual approaches, questionable favors and commissions, and methods of 'doing the needful' as to constitute, in effect, a form of bribery of foreign governmental officials or of their close friends in order to secure business. (1).

The industry's activities concerning peace efforts are further summarized in this manner:

> ... There is no record of any munitions company aiding any proposals for limitation of armaments, but that, on the contrary, there is a record of their active opposition by some to almost all such proposals, of resentment toward them of contempt for those responsible for them and a violation of such controls whenever established, and of rich profiting whenever such proposals failed. (2).

On the effect of armaments on peace, the committee found:

> ... That some of the munitions companies have occasionally had opportunities to intensify the fears of people for their neighbors and use them to their own profit.... The very quality which in civilian life tends to lead toward progressive civilization, namely the improvements of

machinery, has been used by the munitions makers to scare nations into a continued frantic expenditure for the latest improvements and devices of warfare. The constant message of the traveling salesman of the munitions companies to the rest of the world has been that they now had available for sale something new, more dangerous and more deadly than ever before and that the potential enemy was or would be buying it.... The committee finds it to be against the peace of the world for selfishly interested organizations to be left free to go and frighten nations into military activity.... Munitions companies engaged in bribery find themselves involved in the civil and military politics of other nations, and that this is an unwarranted form of intrusion into the affairs of other nations and undesirable representation of the character and methods of the people of the United States. (3).

Military-Industrial Complex

On January 17, 1961, immediately prior to the conclusion of his public service after his two-year term as president of the United States, President Dwight Eisenhower fired a warning shot across the bow of one of America's powerful entities:

Those who expected the military leader and hero to depart with a nostalgic 'old soldier speech,' like Gen. Douglas MacArthur's, were surprised at his strong warnings about the dangers of the military-industrial complex... Though he did not say so explicitly, his standing as a military leader helped give him the credibility to stand up to the pressures of this new, powerful internet group.

Furthermore, he explained:

... we have been compelled to create a permanent armaments industry of vast proportions... This conjunction of an immense military establishment and a large arms industry is new in the American experience ... we must guard against the acquisition of unwarranted influence, whether sought or unsought, by the military-industrial complex. The potential for the disastrous rise of misplaced power exists and will persist.[10]

Conclusion

The Arms Merchants of Death have clearly profited substantially from warfare. Few of their stockholders or executives have ever touched the blood-soaked sod of the battlefields, where their weapons of mass destruction have been used to annihilate young patriots, who marched off to wars signaled by the bugles calling forth the young to ride to the sound of the guns! Elitists of all countries make their fortunes and the patriots and common folks do the dirty work!

Chapter 7:

Bankers – Morgans and Rothschilds

[Author's note: In regard especially to international banking community, in no manner do I desire to impugn nor cast aspersions on the integrity and decency of the vast majority of the banker population. The majority are of an inestimable value to the masses of humanity in providing vital services to societies in daily business operations. In fact, in one of my past lives, I worked at a bank!]

<u>Banking: Overview</u>

David Rockefeller, Sr., the Chairman and CEO of Chase Manhattan Bank from 1969 to 1990, wrote in his *Memoirs* about a secret cabal, internationalists, and a conspiracy to which he admitted his family was a part. He basically said it was his story and he was sticking to it. I believe there has been, and still exists, a "conspiracy." The world of money is the major "Usual Suspect" and international financiers have been the major players in these "games." These bankers have prospered immensely. Castles, palaces, ostentatious and luxurious mansions, enclaves in gated communities, and elegant homes pay tribute to their successes and prosperity throughout modern history.

I will take literary license to quote from the many sources I have researched to express opinions of others relative to bankers and international financiers. It would be difficult to paraphrase much of what is included across such a variety of sources.

Author Quigley names the banking giants of history: Baring, Lazard, Erlanger, Warburg, Schroeder, Seligman, the Speyers, Mirabaud, Malle, Fould, and especially Rothchild and Morgan. It is upon their stories that this chapter will focus. They were called "merchant bankers" in England, "private bankers" in France, and "investment bankers" in the United States. Quigley wrote, "…they were almost equally devoted to secrecy and the secret use of financial influence in political life." (Quigley *Tragedy*: 52).

Several well-known figures from history have this to say about bankers and financing.

Napoleon Bonaparte said this:

> When a government is dependent upon bankers for money, they and not the leaders of the government control the situation, since the hand that gives is above the hand that takes. Money has no motherland; financiers are without patriotism and without decency; their sole object is gain.[1]

Obviously, one could assume that he probably did not have many social engagements with the bankers!

Thomas Jefferson, third president of the United States who served from 1801 to 1809, and principal author of the United States Declaration of Independence in 1776, said in a letter written to John Taylor on May 28, 1816, "I sincerely believe with you, that banking establishments are more dangerous than standing armies."

John C. Calhoun, vice president of the United States from 1825 to 1832 and former U.S. Senator, said in a speech on May 27, 1836, "A power has risen up in the government greater than the people themselves, consisting of many and various powerful interests, combined in one mass, and held together by the cohesive power of the vast surplus in banks."

In 1935, Dr. R.E. Search wrote a book on finance that he began researching in 1933 at the Library of Congress. Yes, I question his name, but there have been instances in which authors have used pseudonyms, perhaps to mask their names as "whistleblowers" or for protection due to the controversial nature of their writings.

He wrote:

> ... and it was a continuous wonder to me that the rotten crookedness and corrupting of Legislators and the extending of the grasp of the 'money changers' into our financial and business system could have gone on year after year, and generation after generation getting progressively worse, with a mountain of bonded indebtedness growing higher and higher, with the chains of national mortgage debts growing closer about the life of our people year after year, and not to be stopped somewhere, some way. (Search: 109).

Another sensational opinion expressed by Dr. R.E. Search in 1935 stated:

> I had found to my own enlightenment and conviction, that the desire for money, together with the power it carries with its possession and its uses and abuses, had been at the very foundation of most of the world's greatest crimes, tragedies, and murders of many ages and nations, causing the fall of one civilization after another, right down to the present time. (Search: 7).

Deanna Spingola, a prolific author, wrote her opinion on the topic:

> The international bankers, who profit most from warfare, have controlled the entertainment and documentary media for decades. Media moguls, often in conjunction with the Pentagon, produce movies that glorify war, promote immorality, immodesty, and profanity, all in an effort to subtly shape our opinions, alter our culture and persuade us to abandon traditional Christian values. If Christians forfeit so-called small ideals, they are more likely to relinquish Christ's prohibition against warfare.[2]

My personal library contains three books by Spingola, encompassing 2,214 pages and 6,042 footnotes. Other gems by

Spingola (whose writings were one of my original motivators to begin my studies and I have also personally communicated with her):

> International bankers, without particular national loyalties or regard for those used as cannon fodder, typically fund both sides of every war and often have major investments in, or outright ownership of, ammunition production facilities. Guaranteed contracts for tons of one time use bullets and bombs are tremendously more lucrative than selling cars and washing machines to consumers.

The statement below, attributed to the matriarch of the Rothschild family, is found repeatedly in many sources including Spingola's website, however no original reference has been located:

> Gutele Schnapper Rothschild, the wife of Mayer A. Rothschild, who grew enormously wealthy by collecting usury while funding European wars, [purportedly] said, "If my sons did not want war, there would be none."

Spingola continues to express a further believable opinion:

> Given the manner in which individual governments exploit soldiers to enrich the bankers, those troops are evidently expendable. Their bloodied bodies create massive profits for the international bankers, the original advocates of globalism, acquired through warfare, usually followed by sanctions, reparations and finally obedience to an international entity. A nation uses warfare to impose its policies on another nation.

In 1918, author E.C. Knuth was released from active duty as an officer after World War I, and, "Like many servicemen, he was filled with resentment as the deluge of utterly obvious and brazen falsehoods by which participation in that war had been forced upon the American people, was exposed and became more evident day by day after the war was won." By 1946, when he wrote *The Empire of the City the Jekyll/Hyde Nature of the British Government* (Second Edition), he had done extensive research on what he termed a very powerful and well-financed secret organization. The organization to which he alludes plans and directs American foreign affairs, and for lack of a more specific identification, this suspected international secret organization is popularly referred to as the International Financiers. (Knuth: 4).

Knuth's book is a short, but information-packed book. Naturally, if there has ever been, and still exists, a behind-the-scenes efforts to control the world, when anyone such as Mr. Knuth, or an obscure disabled war veteran such as I, ever dares to write about what our research has discovered, we will be attacked as "conspiracy theorists." So be it. Just as one large Eastern publisher declined to publish Mr. Knuth, so, too, was I declined. Following in the footsteps of Mr. Knuth, I decided to self-publish my findings.

The following are some of Knuth's more controversial opinions:

> It is said that only a few dozen men in the world know the nature of money; and therefore these few men are allowed to practice the manipulation of money and of that mysterious commodity known as credit as a mystic right, despite the fact that their machinations costs recurrent giant depressions in which many of the life savings of the people are lost, and cause recurrent gigantic bloodshed in which the people must sacrifice their lives to protect the manipulators from the fury of those nations and peoples who have been their victims; and despite the fact that eminent students of high business, financial and social position, such as Vincent C Vickers and Arthur Kitson, have condemned this money system as a fraud; have condemned the men who manipulate it as super-criminals and traitors to their own lands and peoples, and have condemned the recurring economic depressions and wars as the deliberate products of the money power! (Knuth: 95,96).

He also wrote:

> The late Vincent Cartwright Vickers stated, '... financiers in reality took upon themselves, perhaps not the responsibility, but certainly the power, of controlling the markets of the world and therefore the numerous relationships between one nation or another, involving international friendships or mistrusts... Loans to foreign countries are organized and arranged by the City of London with no thought whatsoever of the Nation's welfare but solely in order to increase indebtedness, upon which the City thrives and grows rich... This national and mainly international dictatorship of money, which plays off one country after another and which, through ownership of a large portion of the Press, converts the advertisement of its own private opinion into a semblance of general public opinion, cannot for much longer be permitted to render Democratic Government a mere nickname. Today, we see through a glass darkly; for there is so much which 'it would not be in the public interest to divulge'... (Knuth: 65).

After World War I, the power of the financiers strove mightily to organize internationally. Perhaps this could be viewed as evidence that disputes the theory that there is no attempt to conspire and control the systems of humanity for total power, nor to move us to fulfillment of the End Times prophecies as outlined in the book of Revelation.

The ever-analytical author Quigley wrote after World War I:

> In addition to these pragmatic goals, the powers of financial capitalism had another far-reaching aim, nothing less than to create a world system of financial control in private hands able to dominate the political system of each country and the economy of the world as a whole. This system was to be controlled in a feudalist fashion by the central banks of the world acting in consort, by secret agreements arrived at in frequent private meetings and

conferences. The apex of the system was to be the Bank for International Settlements in Basel, Switzerland, a private bank owned and controlled by the world's central banks which were themselves private corporations. Each central bank, in the hands of men like Montagu Norman of the Bank of England, Benjamin Strong of the New York Federal Reserve Bank, Charles Rist of the Bank of France, and Hjalmar Schacht of the Reichsbank, sought to dominate its government by its ability to control Treasury loans, to manipulate foreign exchanges, to influence the level of economic activity in the country, and to influence cooperative politicians by subsequent economic rewards in the business world. (Quigley *Tragedy:* 324).

Quigley summarizes the overall effect of bankers in his 1966 writings by saying, "The history of the last century shows, as we shall see later, that the advice given to governments by bankers, like the advice they gave to industrialists, was consistently good for bankers, but was often disastrous for governments, businessmen and the people generally." (Quigley *Tragedy:* 62).

Bankers: Schiff

It is significant to point out the entry into American banking circles of several prominent men, who were immigrants from Germany. One was Jacob H. Schiff, born in Frankfurt, Germany in 1847. Naomi W. Cohen has written presumably the definitive autobiography on Schiff in *Jacob H. Schiff-A Study in American Jewish Leadership* (Brandeis Series in American Jewish History, Culture and Life. October 1, 1999). Schiff was a banker, who had experience in the House of Rothschild Frankfurt before his employment by the New York banking firm of Kuhn-Loeb and Company in 1875. He was "part of a wealthy and powerful German Jewish circle that included the Warburgs and Rothschilds."[3]

Abraham Kuhn and Solomon Loeb were two successful German merchants who made a fortune in being the supplier of Union

Army uniforms. Their profits financed a New York investment operation, which eventually became Kuhn, Loeb with close affiliation to the Rothschilds back in Frankfurt. They recruited Jacob Schiff, a supremely qualified banker with experience in Europe, to run their operation in America. (Docherty: 214).

A large part of his significance is derived from the fact that he was instrumental in financing Japan in the Russo-Japanese War, in being a principal backer of the Bolshevik Revolution, and in personally financing Communist Trotsky's trip from New York to Russia for Trotsky to influence overthrowing Russia. (Griffin: 210). In the three-way presidential election of 1912, he and Paul Warburg, another Kuhn, Loeb partner, supported Democrat Woodrow Wilson, while partner Felix Warburg supported Republican Taft. For the partners to ensure they would be able to influence the winner, Otto Kahn supported Roosevelt of the Bull Moose Party. (Griffin *Creature:* 453).

Bankers: Warburgs

The Warburgs, another prominent American banking family of German Jewish origin, are noteworthy for accomplishments in a variety of fields. Felix and Paul emigrated to the United States from Germany. Felix married Jacob Schiff's daughter, Frieda. Paul Warburg married Nina Loeb, daughter of Solomon Loeb. These marital alliances kept the families connected.

Around 1927, a son of Felix Warburg named Freddy became acquainted with Curtis Dall, the son-in-law of President Franklin D. Roosevelt, when Freddy became a Lehman firm associate on Wall Street, as was Dall, on "loan" from Kuhn, Loeb. Freddy Warburg and Curtis Dall became friends, and Freddy related a most fascinating anecdote about his uncle, Max Warburg, a senior member of the German Kaiser's Secret Service. This nephew of Max Warburg related that after the 1918 World War One Armistice, Max oversaw the movement across Germany in the first sealed train of $500,000 in gold to finance Leon Trotsky's revolution. (Dall: 29). Amazing what tidbits of information are revealed in memoirs!

Paul Warburg was a member of the six-man cabal, who met together in November 1910 at the Jekyll Island club in Georgia, the private resort of J.P. Morgan to discuss the eventual formation of the Federal Reserve Bank of the United States. Henry Davison (a Morgan partner) was also at the meeting. (Chernow: 129,130). Warburg "became the dominant and guiding mind throughout all the discussions" because he was the expert on the European model of a central bank. (Griffin *Creature*: 17). Paul had immigrated to the United States only in 1901. With Rothschild group funding he and Felix bought partnerships in Kuhn, Loeb and remained as partners in Warburg of Hamburg. (Griffin *Creature:* 18). He was one of the first members of the Federal Reserve Board and became the vice governor, from which position he resigned due to his German banking connections, when World War I began. (Griffin *Creature*: 481). He became a naturalized U.S. citizen in 1911, meaning, presumably as a "consultant" at the Jekyll Island meeting, he participated as a non-citizen.

Bankers: Morgans and Rockefellers

The Morgans and Rockefellers were the big financial moguls of the United States between 1880 to 1933. They held immense control of America's economic and financial as well as political life during this time frame. A combination of effort of these two giants was described as follows: "The influence of these business leaders was so great that the Morgan and Rockefeller groups acting together, or even Morgan acting alone, could have wrecked the economic system of the country." (Quigley *Tragedy*: 72). For almost fifty years (1880 to 1930), the power structure in the United States was a "feudal system" controlled by the Morgans and the Rockefellers. Other powers included Kuhn, Loeb and Company; Dillon, Read and Company; Brown Brothers and Harriman and others. (Quigley *Tragedy*: 530).

As mentioned, bank operations such as Barings (who financed the Louisiana Purchase) and the Rockefellers were termed "merchant banks," private partnerships, free from control by shareholders or depositors. Eventually, London banker Junius Morgan maneuvered to attain the same status. (Chernow: 250). Morgan, the founder of the Morgan dynasty, established himself as an American-bred banker in London, competing against the big boys of Europe. In 1837, his son, John Pierpoint, was born, and would later oversee the U.S. operation. Junius attained his desired and enhanced financier status in 1870, when the Prussians after their victory at Sedan and seizure of Napoleon III, were laying siege to Paris in the Franco-Prussian War. France needed funds. The Rothschilds deserted France as a hopeless cause. Barings had supported the Prussians. Junius Morgan came to France's rescue with the bond offering for France that was paid off in 1873, even though the French had lost the war to the Prussians. This financing put the Morgan operation on the international map. (Chernow: 26, 27).

The competition between Jewish and Gentile bankers on Wall Street began about 1870 with Joseph Seligman, who had German investors, and J. Pierpoint Morgan, who had access to London money. Pierpoint began to reflect his new wealth. He bought a several-hundred-acre country estate called Cragston near West Point. He was coming into prominence as the preeminent financier in America. (Chernow: 32). In early 1871, Pierpoint was approached by Tony Drexel of a Philadelphia financial powerhouse and their eventual partnership was a merger named Drexel, Morgan.

In 1873, the United States decided to refinance the remaining 300 million in debt from the Civil War. The Drexel, Morgan syndicate obtained half the refinancing in competition with a Jay Cooke syndicate teamed with two Jewish groups, the Rothschilds and Seligmans. This was a major coup for an American syndicate. (Chernow: 35, 36). The panic of 1873, which was a major disaster for railroad stocks, convinced Pierpoint to focus only on companies that were gold-plate entities.

A financial crisis for the United States government in 1895 brought further brilliance to the Morgan name, when he maneuvered a partnership with the Rothschilds to bailout the U.S. treasury. (Chernow: 76). A populist movement began equally attacking the elitist bankers, Gentile and Jewish. In 1901, Pierpoint faced an assault from a group which included Edward H. Harriman, William Rockefeller, the National City Bank and Kuhn, Loeb for control of the Nation's railroads. Harriman's banker was the German-born Jacob Schiff of Kuhn, Loeb. The Jewish firms began to be the financiers for companies considered too small by the Christian financial houses. (Chernow: 89). Schiff was able to tap French and German money. Chernow writes; "Political, ethnic, and religious differences among bankers permeated Wall Street in the early 1900s." (Chernow: 90).

The Rockefeller fortune derived from Standard Oil allowed the Rockefellers to team up with Harriman and Schiff against the Morgan group. National City Bank became the Rockefeller bank of choice. This became the forerunner of partnerships between industrial giants and banks in U.S. financial history. (Chernow: 90).

Jack Morgan, Pierpoint's son, came on the scene by 1898 in the London office of Morgan. During Jack's tenure, the British government prevailed upon the Rothschilds in London and Morgans in New York to obtain the financing of bonds to fight the Anglo-Boer war. This began the ascendancy of the Morgans over the Rothschilds as a financial powerhouse. (Chernow: 99). At this time, Pierpoint was the leader in the evolution of U.S. Steel coming into its ascendancy as an industrial power. Another cross-current internationally at this historic juncture was the move by Pierpoint to enter the shipping business through a trust combination with Albert Ballin of the Hamburg Amerika Steamship Line. Chernow describes Ballin as; "...the court Jew of his day," with Germany's Kaiser Wilhelm. Eventually the combination was consummated. (Chernow: 102).

The political power of the Morgan dynasty was evidenced in 1904 and 1924 when both candidates were in their circle of power and influence. In the 1924 election, the Democratic candidate was an attorney for J.P. Morgan and the Republican one went to school with and was picked to run by Morgan's partner, Dwight Morgan. (Quigley *Tragedy*: 74).

Many personages throughout America's history, not necessarily publicly known, but influential in corporate and government circles nonetheless as being related to the Morgans, were in fact connected. They were connected at 23 Wall Street with J.P. Morgan. These individuals included Walter Burns, Clinton Dawkins, Edward Grenville, William Straight, Thomas Lamont, Dwight Morrow, Nelson Perkins, Russell Leffingwell, Elihu Root, John W. Davis, John Foster Dulles and S. Parker Gilbert. They were all part of a presumably obscure private partnership affiliated with the Morgan dynasty, originally founded in London in 1838 as George Peabody and Company. The partnership lasted until April 24, 1959, when it merged with the Guaranty Trust Company. (Quigley: 53). Another major entity that evolved was Morgan Stanley, an investment banking firm. The London affiliate was Morgan Grenfell.

Thomas Lamont was undoubtedly one of the most influential members of this Morgan circle. He became chairman of J.P. Morgan, and also served as an advisor to Woodrow Wilson in his second administration, as well as to President Herbert Hoover. Lundberg described Lamont as someone who "...has exercised more power for 20 years in the Western Hemisphere, has put into effect more final decisions from which there has been no appeal, than any other person... a man consulted by presidents, prime ministers, governors of central banks, the directing intelligence behind the Dawes and Young plans.... diplomat, an editor, a writer, a publisher, a politician, a statesman--an international presence as well as a financier." (Lundberg: 33).

Quigley summarized the power of the bankers, as follows:

> The influence of financial capitalism and of the international bankers who created it was exercised both on business and governments, but could have done neither if it had not

been able to persuade both these to accept two 'axioms' of its own ideology. Both of these were based on the assumption that politicians were too weak and too subject to temporary popular pressures to be trusted with control of the money system; accordingly, the sanctity of all values and the soundness of money must be protected in two ways: by basing the value of money on gold and by allowing bankers to control the supply of money. To do this it was necessary to conceal, or even to mislead, both governments and people about the nature of money and its methods of operation. (Quigley *Tragedy*: 53).

The bankers have succeeded!

Bankers: Rothschilds

On October 11, 1863, a *New York Times* article originally published in the *London Globe* appeared during our Civil War. A major reorganization of the Rothschild financial dynasty had been accomplished. The Rothschild sitting over their Naples bank was dethroned and now "... there [were] to be but four kings of the House of Rothschild, with secure thrones at London, Paris, Vienna, and Frankfort."

The dynasty, founded by Mayer Anselm, a close confidant of the German Serene Elector of Hesse Cassel, celebrated its hundredth anniversary. Mayer was a very shrewd investor. The American Revolution chapter of this book talks about the German Hessian "mercenaries," hired by Great Britain to fight in America. Mayer's five sons established their financial domains in the above capitols prior to Anselm's death in 1812, changing their names to Rothschild, and so developing unarguably what became the strongest international financial powerhouse ever in history.

London's shrewd Nathan Rothschild, due to early news of Lord Wellington's victory at Waterloo in 1815, was able to make a financial killing before it became public. Insider trading, as it could most assuredly be described! The same *Times* article reported that the Naples branch manager, Charles Gustavus, imperiled his family reputation by having a generous liberal streak reflected by Charles' philanthropic donation of 10,000 ducats to the orphan asylum St. Carlo at Naples. However, he did not depart the family ranks poor and homeless. His fortune, already consisting of six million sterling, was taken with him upon his exile from the family.[4]

In the final years of the Napoleonic Wars and Napoleon's Empire, the five brothers had banded together to finance Wellington's British-led Army. Nathan Rothschild received the official government commission and the strong family ties of the brothers and their extraordinary communications network ensured the success of their financing efforts.[5]

The House of Rothschild biographers reported that the Rothschilds, due to loans to nobility all over Europe, were in the debt of many of the high and mighty. (Knuth: 70). The Rothschilds were responsible for Queen Victoria and Prince Albert being able to buy the lease on Balmoral Castle in Scotland as well as the purchase of Sandringham Palace. (Docherty: 24).[6]

Knuth wrote:

> ... One of the most effective devices employed by the House of Rothschild through the years to destroy their competitors and to discipline recalcitrant statesmen has been that of artificially creating an over-extended inflation by extended speculation, then to cash in and let others hold the bag. (Knuth: 70,71).

Knuth believes that British capital had an extraordinary influence on America's 1929 crash. He states, "The fact that the House of Rothschild made its money in the great crashes of history and the great wars of history, the very periods when others lost their money, is beyond question." (Knuth: 71). The family valued its privacy to such a degree that it frequently operated through what we would define as "cut-outs," or other businesses. (Knuth: 68).

In his 1887 book, John Reeves asserted that, in the early 1800s, "… no war could be undertaken without the assistance of the Rothschilds, since the control exercised by them in the money markets was such that they could eventually withhold or procure the requisite funds." (Reeves: 66). Reeves wrote that at one period of history the Rothschilds were the "dictators of Europe." (Reeves: 71). The purpose of the Rothschild fortune to be employed, at least during Napoleon's time, was defined as follows:

> The Rothschilds belong to no one nationality, they are cosmopolitan, and, whilst on the one hand they provided supplies for the armies of Napoleon, on the other, they raised loans for his foes, who used the funds thus obtained in defraying the cost of their campaigns against him; they belong to no party, they were ready to grow rich at the expense of friends and foe alike. (Reeves: 86).

A hallmark of their success was the apparent ability and power to be supportive of one side while encouraging the other. (Docherty: 23).

It is obvious that Reeves in his 1887 book had very little positive to write, ever, about the Rothschilds. Even though contemporary writers today find it difficult to write negatively about certain centers of power, Reeves obviously did not feel constrained in the same way. He reported their amassing of their fortunes and how their business ethics were expressed, at least in some quarters, in the following way:

> Through operations calculated to bring about a fall or a rise, as the case might be, in the prices of particular stocks, the Rothschilds went on unceasingly amassing their millions, and these operations, by the violent fluctuations they produced, formed the basis on which the fortunes of the firm were laid. In order to render these great speculative operations successful, every means at their

command was employed. Every method that could be devised was resorted to; every Stock Exchange manoeuvre and artifice called into requisition; every sort of rumour and false news promulgated; and money in large and small sums sacrificed to secure the success of their schemes. This, then, was how the earlier Rothschilds amassed their millions, which the present representative strive to keep and augment steadily and cautiously, without grasping at the handsome, old-fashioned profits of bygone days. (Reeves: 93,94).

Reeves wrote that much of the financial success of the Rothschilds (at least as portrayed in his 1887 book) was due to their extraordinary communications systems, especially during times of war and crisis in the political realm. The Rothschilds also ensured that they became connected with people in business and political circles in order to receive information in an early and timely fashion. (Reeves: 94,95).

The Rothschilds were given an immense amount of credit for their power. Reeves stated "... that his (Anselm's) sons would in after years come to exercise such an unbounded sway that the peace of nations would depend upon their nod." (Reeves: 104,105).

The power they held in the 1800s is almost unfathomable. Reeves described this Rothschild operation at one time as "...the ruling power in Europe..." (Reeves: 105). In Anselm's favor (one of the sons), he was a very religious Jew. (Reeves: 117). Nathan's son Baron Lionel became the agent for Russia for 20 years. He was instrumental in funding the debt of the United States, and also arranged the financing to purchase the Suez Canal. (Reeves: 208). Lionel was known to be a most generous philanthropist.

The following passage further illustrates the vast reach of the Rothschilds:

Throughout the nineteenth century, the Rothschild family banking, investment and commercial dealings read like a list of international coups. Entire railway networks across Europe and America were financed through Rothschild bonds; investments in ores, raw materials, gold and diamonds, rubies, the new discoveries of oil in Mexico, Burma, Baku, and Romania were financed through their banking empires, as were several important armaments firms including Maxim-Nordenfeldt and Vickers. (Docherty: 23).[7]

The view of the Rothschilds as being second-to-none in terms of financial power is described well below:

It was no exaggeration to assert that in many a land the minister of finance who could not come to an agreement with this firm might as well close the doors of his exchequer. 'There is only one power in Europe,' was a dictum well-known about the middle of the 19th century, 'and that is Rothschild; a dozen other banks are his underlings,'... (Sombart quoting from A. Weil: 99).

Beginning in 1870, England's major export was money. The international banks headquartered in London, "The City," included the Baring, Lazard, Morgan, and of course, the Rothschilds. Quigley wrote that all the way up to 1931, the Money Power under domination by the international money cartels were able to influence completely both businesses and governments. (Quigley *Tragedy:* 60). "The great investment houses made billions, their political allies and agents grew wealthy, ... The Bank of England was completely in the hands of these powerful financiers, and the relationship went unchallenged." (Docherty: 211).

America created many millionaires during the nineteenth century. The Rothschilds, very powerful representatives for Great Britain through either front companies or other controlled entities, were instrumental in financing activities in America. (Docherty: 211). The Rothschilds were always willing and able to bail out troubled financial or corporate entities, but the support came at a price. The bank or company then became just a front for Rothschild control. This included our J.P. Morgan, Barings, and armament firms. (Docherty: 213).

Published in 1988, a more current book on the Rothschilds by Derek Wilson includes research corroborating the immense financial power of the Rothschilds. Wilson writes extensively of the different Rothschild European families, much of it relating to social aspects.

It is important to note that in World War I many Rothschilds served in the British military. (This impresses me.) World War I changed and diminished the past influence of the Rothschilds. During and after World World I, members of the Rothschilds family found themselves on opposite sides during wartime. Some supported Zionism and colonization in Palestine, some suffered deaths from Nazism, and some members found refuge in new business opportunities in America. The world was changing and the former connections of influence between bankers and politicians were lessened. More competition in the financial field became prevalent.

After World War II, author Knuth in his 1946 book wrote that the recent history of the Rothschild Empire reflected that the Vienna house was closed by the Nazis and the Paris house relocated to New York in 1940. (Knuth: 69).

Carroll Quigley's epic book *Tragedy and Hope* is very complimentary towards the Rothschilds for their generosity in a variety of endeavors, and he writes that in the 1830s and 1840s they were a force for peace. (Quigley *Tragedy:* 51,52). Perhaps history's juries have yielded different verdicts at different periods of time for this family.

In conclusion, for now, about the Rothschilds, despite new competition and losses, it is quite significant that in 2018 one source reported that the combined incomes of all the Rothschilds were estimated to be between $400 billion-$2 trillion.[8] This is the miracle of compound interest from those riches amassed in the

1800s!

The website https://thesiriusreport.com/geopolitcs contains a very comprehensive timeline and history of the Rothschild dynasty in six parts. Although it is extensive and comprehensive, it is impossible for me to make an informed judgment on its accuracy and conclusions.

As I was completing my final editing, I watched two fascinating YouTube videos by a Dutchman, Ronald Bernard, who was deeply involved in the higher levels of banking and finance. His "whistleblower" revelations are worthy of consideration. His credibility is questioned in some circles, but his depth of emotion as he described some of the initiation rites of passage in his circles is unquestionably sincere.

Chapter 8:

Industrialists

Introduction

The beginning of this section relates to the period between World Wars, but is illustrative of what is actual history, rather than omitted or "glossed over" history. Rest assured that my work will not blame capitalism or the free market system for the egregious examples of the seekers of power and money, who have not been averse to wars occurring for their own financial gain.

Antony Sutton, author of *Wall Street and the Rise of Hitler*, wrote:

> In brief, American companies associated with the Morgan-Rockefeller international investment bankers---not, it should be noted, the vast bulk of independent American industrialists---were intimately related to the growth of Nazi industry... This book is not an indictment of *all* American industry and finance. It is an indictment of the 'apex'---those firms controlled through the handful of financial houses, the Federal Reserve Bank system, the Bank for International Settlements, and their continuing international cooperative arrangements and cartels, which attempt to control the course of world politics and economics. (Sutton: 31, 32).

[Author's note: Especially, it is not my desire necessarily to cast aspersions on these same corporations as they are constituted and directed today, nor on their present-day executives.]

His sources include "previously unpublished evidence, a great deal from files of the Nuremberg Military Tribunals." (Sutton *Hitler*: 13).

The bibliography of this book contains some very conspicuous, remarkable, and fascinating information about the American and international corporate landscape that are merely summarized in this chapter. The topics will be more elaborately covered in later chapters.

Industrialists

In March of 1908, Senator Robert M. La Follette, Jr. gave a speech in the Senate, claiming that no less than 100 men control the business of America. That claim received due attention, mostly negative, however his later research from the Directory of Directors established that, in actuality, only one dozen men were in the seats of power for American business due to the technique of interlocking directorships. The two real powerhouses distilled down to the Rockefeller and Morgan groups. On December 13, 1911, George M. Reynolds of Chicago's Continental and Commercial Bank confirmed La Follette's conclusion by saying, "I believe the money power now lies in the hands of a dozen men. I plead guilty to being one, in the last analysis of these men." (Knuth: 64).

Knuth wrote that as late as 1940, the business machine of Rockefeller-Morgan-Aldrich still controlled the reins of power in business and politics due to "...the manipulations in the presidential election of 1940, ...charged to Thomas W. Lamont, President of J.P. Morgan and Company, and others; which has been made the subject of a Senate investigation." (Knuth: 64).

War hero General Smedley Butler in his antiwar classic *War is a Racket* was not timid about indicating what might even be defined as the "obscene" profits of American businesses in World War I. He wrote that at the end of the war there were at least 21,000 new millionaires and billionaires. He asked the pointed questions that really tie together the thesis of this work:

> How many of these war millionaires shouldered a rifle? How many of them dug a trench? How many of them knew

what it meant to go hungry in a rat-infested dugout? How many of them spent sleepless, frightened nights, ducking shells and shrapnel and machine gun bullets? How many of them parried the bayonet thrust of an enemy? How many of them were wounded or killed in battle? (Butler: 13).

The consummate propagandist Edward Bernays could not have been prouder of the effect that propaganda had in terms of motivating our young men to leave factories, farms, and day-to-day comforts to go off to fight. As Butler put it, "...when patriotism, love of country and 'we must all put our shoulder to the wheel'" [attitudes] are evoked as propaganda, young men do not hesitate to march to the battlefields. (Butler: 19).

A remarkable example before and during World War II came to light in the following situation. On April 25, 1948, Senator Brewster, while on the floor of the Senate, said that "...the Aramco action [i.e., shipments of oil to the enemy] [are] 'an amazing picture of corporate greed when our country was in its most bitter need.'" (Higham: 90).

In addition, Senator William Langer of North Dakota said, "The men who have put over this oil deal ought to be in the penitentiary. These men, who have called upon American boys to go into foreign lands to protect their oil interests, are traitors to America. They ought to surrender their citizenship or have it taken away from them." Investigations of these scandals were blocked by three former Navy Department employees in the Justice Department. (Higham: 90). Higham discovered that International Telephone and Telegraph (ITT):

> ...supplied ingredients for the rocket bombs that fell on London, selenium cells for dry rectifiers, high frequency radio equipment, and fortification and field communication sets. Without this supply of crucial materials it would have been impossible for the German air force to kill American and British troops, for the German army to fight the Allies in Africa, Italy, France, and Germany, for England to have

been bombed, or for Allied ships to have been attacked at sea. (Higham: 99).

Patriotic Americans should all be ashamed of the facts discovered by Higham in his book, in which he wrote:

> It thus came as a severe shock to learn that several of the greatest American corporate leaders were in league with Nazi corporations before and after Pearl Harbor, including I.G. Farben, the colossal Nazi industrial trust that created Auschwitz. Those leaders interlocked through an association I have dubbed The Fraternity. Each of these business leaders was entangled with the others through interlocking directorates or financial services. All were represented internationally by the National City Bank or by the Chase National Bank and by the Nazi attorneys Gerhardt Westrick and Dr. Heinrich Albert. All had connections to the crucial Nazi economist, Emil Puhl, of Hitler's Reichsbank and the Bank for International Settlements. (Higham: *xiv*).

Shame on these people! Furthermore, Higham said, "The tycoons were linked by an ideology: the ideology of Business as Usual. Bound by identical reactionary ideas, the members sought a common future in fascist domination, regardless of which world leader might further that ambition." (Higham: *xiv*). The corporate leaders should have been tracked down after WWII just as were some Nazis after the war. Of course, they had no shame. Their stockholders and their asset balances were maintained while the true Americans served the "cause."

Author Buckminster Fuller served as the head mechanical engineer of the U.S.A. Board of Economic Warfare during World War II. He was a student of patents, and in this capacity, he listened to many international telephone conversations that had been originally received by censors. After their deciphering, he studied the strategic patents held on both sides (enemy and our big corporations). From this experience, he discovered that "...the

same money was often operative on both sides in World War II."
(Fuller: 104).

In 1953, the Arbenz government in Guatemala decided to take
possession of 178,000 acres of land owned by United Fruit
Company, for which the government offered only four dollars per
acre. An argument could be made that this was a fair price
because that was the tax assessment. Obviously, this would have
been catastrophic for the corporate giant, so the company
commissioned a report which pointed toward a Communist
conspiracy in Central America instigated by the Russians.
(McCann: 49).

Author Thomas P. McCann was in the know about United Fruit
Company as he was a senior executive who penned his company's
history in 1976. McCann's bottom line was this: "Companies like
United Fruit and ITT and Standard Oil became political
instruments and carried out political relations by other means,
usually in secret, whereby the government got what it wanted
through the use of the company and the company got what it
wanted as well." (McCann: 50).

In 2004, author John Perkins wrote and published *Confessions of
an Economic Hit Man*. He has written about the life he led, and
the nickname he gave himself, the "Economic Hit Man" (EHM). He
stated, "...telling the real-life story about his extraordinary
dealings as an EHM, has exposed the world of international
intrigue and corruption that is turning the American Republic into
a global empire despised by increasing numbers of people around
the planet." (Perkins *Confessions:* 248).

It is with great disdain that I write about much of what I've
discovered in my research for this book. But facts are facts. I'm
inclined to be positive toward corporate America for the jobs it
provides to countless employees. However, I hold in contempt any
enriching of senior officers and owners in the instances when they
succeeded by means of achieving revenues in the manner Perkins
describes. Typically, no "conservative" such as I would write this

book. Usually only a "progressive' or "liberal" would do so. All sides of the political spectrum share a desire for truth and fairness and justice. But, when young people such as I suffer as I did, it becomes a crusade to find out why we as a capitalist nation did what we did. My work hopefully sheds light upon the answers to many of these questions.

Perkins describes the methodology by which part of our global empire has been built. He witnessed and reported that he was a member of "... an elite group of men and women who utilize international financial organizations to foment conditions that made other nations subservient to the corporatocracy running our biggest corporations, our government and our banks." (Perkins *Confessions: xvii*).

The methodology to fulfill this strategy has been to provide loans to build electric generating plants, highways, ports, airports and industrial parks. The loan comes tethered to a requirement that U.S. companies must be used. (So far so good.) The problem appears down the line when the large loans must be repaid, then often they cannot be repaid. So, then we demand our "pound of flesh" to obtain influence in the country. (Perkins *Confessions: xvii*).

Admittedly, part of the strategy during the Cold War was to counter the influence of the Soviet Union amongst these countries (a valid and worthy purpose indeed.) Some of the U.S. companies involved at the time included Bechtel, Halliburton, Stone and Webster, and Brown and Root. (Perkins *Confessions:* 15). Perkins writes that our schools and press have reported all our magnificent efforts in other countries as truly compassionate and selfless. We could be described as "Guardians." However, the projects, according to Perkins, "... create large profits for the contractors, and to make a handful of wealthy and influential families in the receiving company very happy, while assuring ... the political loyalty of the governments around the world. The debt service however took away many services needed by the poor." He concluded, "The rich get richer and the poor get poorer." (Perkins *Confession:* 16). Instead of "guardians" we became "predators." What else is new? I am not so naïve as to believe that other financial power houses such as China and Russia do not also benefit in the same manner. Again, it is the "cupidity" theme being exercised by many entities.

To bring history up to date, here is what another world power is perpetrating today! Hot off the press in 2018! On page A8 of the *Wall Street Journal* on Monday, March 5, 2018, China has learned lessons from the "Masters":

> China is emerging as a massive creditor to its economic allies taking up projects to upgrade roads, harbors and airports, making it an increasingly important financial influence on the world stage. China is financing as much as $8 trillion in deals as part of its 'Belt and Road Initiative' in 68 countries winding through Asia, Africa, and Europe... 'The Chinese companies are getting blanket tax assessments,' says a Kaiser Bengali from Baluchistan, 'and instead of buying materials from here they buy in China. So the multiplier effect of development happens in China, not here.'

These countries are assuming great debts owed to China.

[Author's note: At a speech once, I had a private conversation with an officer who had been a U.S. Navy medical doctor in a certain tribal area in Afghanistan. He told me that the tribal leader had sold to a Chinese interest the underlying mineral rights of the tribal area ruled by him. Perhaps, if, and when, we finally depart from Afghanistan, having dedicated much blood, sacrifice, and money to bringing "freedom" there, the Chinese will swoop in to reap the economic benefits paid for by us. Of course, they will have different and more severe "rules of engagement" to counter any opposition by the Taliban and ISIS.]

The original world industrial behemoth that integrated up and down the line to produce a giant organization unarguably must be

John D. Rockefeller's Standard Oil described in one corner at its inception as follows: "The company operated according to the merciless methods and unbridled lust of late 19th century capitalism; yet it also opened a new era, for it developed into one of the world's first and biggest multinational corporations." (Yergin: 19).[1]

In Cleveland in 1865, John D. Rockefeller separated from his partner and he struck out on his own. One author said he was "admired by some as a genius of management and organization, [and] he also came to rank as the most hated and reviled American businessman-in part because he was so ruthless and in part because he was so successful." (Yergin: 20). Eventually, the previously mentioned Jacob Schiff was closely tied to the Rockefeller's Standard Oil. (Docherty: 215). Some readers may have already discerned a pattern of interlocking financial and business relationships becoming intertwined within a small powerful group.

Rockefeller's company headquarters and home state, Ohio, was at the top of 19th century politics. How could any other state dispute this when, within 1869-1901, it produced five of seven presidents (all Union Army veterans): William T. Sherman (Treasury Secretary), Senator Phil Sheridan, and Secretary of State John Sheridan, as well as Senator John B. Foraker, who wielded great influence in our policies toward Cuba and Puerto Rico. (Spingola *Elite Power*: 60).[2] Do you think possibly that Rockefeller's political contributions had any influence on this locus of political power?

Industrialists: Conclusions

General Smedley Butler, who has become my personal hero for reasons far and beyond his heroism on the battlefields, summarized most succinctly an excellent closure to this section on industrialists and their corporations:

> America must face the cold brutal facts. The people must eventually decide whether or if we want to sacrifice our

manhood on the fields of battle, and struggle under the load of taxation that is created by wars, merely to save the business enterprises and profits of a handful of our citizens. (Butler: 185).

A possible position to consider adopting is presented by General Butler:

Let us be the first to admit to the world that our greed for profits through world trade is an irritation to war we intend to remove. Let us resolve that henceforth the United States—as a nation—will confine the strength of its military forces strictly to protection against any invasion that threatens America—not merely to preserve the rights of the privileged few who make money in world trade—but the rights and the welfare, the happiness, and the homes of all our citizens. (Butler: 188).

Charles Higham, in his beginning pages of *Trading With the Enemy* published in 1983, summarized the purpose of his work as follows:

I have tried to write this book as dispassionately as possible, without attempting a moral commentary, and without, of course, intending implication of present corporations and their executive boards. It will be claimed that the people in this book, since they are dead, cannot answer and therefore should not be criticized. To that I would reply: Millions died in World War II. They, too, cannot answer. (Higham: *xx*).

Echoes of President Dwight D. Eisenhower in 1961

On May 19, 2019, President Donald Trump was interviewed by Steve Hilton of Fox News. As music to my military person's ears, the Commander-in-Chief of the United States declared an opinion that would be met with derision in certain circles of the American economy. He said, "We have tremendous power economically. If I

can solve things economically, that's the way I want to do it."
Shane Trejo wrote:[3]

> Trump doubled-down from there, explaining that despite
> his push for a stronger military that takes care of the
> troops, he wants to avoid any wars caused by the 'military-
> industrial complex,' that President Dwight D. Eisenhower
> once warned about before leaving office.

> 'Well, I'm the one that talks about these wars that are 19
> years and people are just there, and don't kid yourself, we
> do have a military-industrial complex. They do like war!'
> Trump exclaimed.

Shane Trejo continued his report with:

> Trump ... criticized the military-industrial complex for using
> these instances [rogue terrorists in Syria] to agitate for
> endless war.

> 'You have people here in Washington, they never want to
> leave!' Trump said in an exacerbated tone.

Originally, President Trump declared that all our troops in Syria
would return, but he acquiesced and left a few hundred there "to
get the military-industrial complex off his back." Trump added in
his interview, "... you do have a group, and they call it 'the
military-industrial complex.' They never want to leave. They
always want to fight. No, I don't want to fight."

In truth, the military-industrial complex would rather produce
swords than plowshares. Trump's war philosophy would definitely
not be music to the ears of neoconservatives!

Chapter 9:

Elitists – Rockefellers, Politicians, Lawyers, and Masons

<u>Overview</u>

> "*O cives, cives, quarenda pecunia primum est; virtus post nummos.*" Horace, Roman Poet. [Translation: "Greed and money first, and all the rest after." (Hamill: 122).]

The term "elitist/elite" was not known in 1828 because Noah Webster included no definition of the terms, but the *Oxford American Writer's Thesaurus* (2004) defined elite in this manner: "Hobnobbing with Southport's elite BEST, pick, crème de la creme, flower, non-pareil, elect; high society, jet set, beautiful people, beau monde, haut monde, glitterati, aristocracy, nobility, upper class."

The classic example of elitism is repeated and was expressed by Walter Rathenau, a German industrialist and advisor to Kaiser Wilhelm II, who stated in 1909:

> Three hundred men, who all know each other direct the economic destinies of the Continent and they look for successors among their friends and relations. This is not the place to examine the strange causes of this strange state of affairs, which throws a ray of light on the obscurity of our social future.[1]

As previously indicated, he was assassinated in 1922. Could it possibly have been because he revealed the existence of an elitist group on the Continent?

Recorded history is replete with examples of a grouping in every society from the beginning of time that considers itself above the masses either through money, royal titles, positions, power, or education. Furthermore, these groups utilize their influence to accomplish their goals and purposes to enhance the group and its "favored" members, sometimes overtly and sometimes covertly, and often at the expense of the masses of us mere mortal beings.

Perhaps we can more distinctly identify some original elitists from the Christian Bible, such as the Sadducees and Pharisees in the Hebrew society. Throughout history there have been successive waves of powerful elitists. So much compelling fodder exists on this topic that this section could easily be expanded into its own book.

Author R.E. Search wrote:

> We should not be surprised when we find that when the government of old Egypt fell, four percent of the people owned all the wealth. When the Babylonian civilization collapsed, three per cent of the people owned all the wealth. When old Persia went down to destruction, two per cent of the people owned all the wealth. When ancient Greece went down to ruin, one-half of one per cent owned all the wealth. When the Roman Empire fell by the wayside, two thousand people owned the wealth of the civilized world and then followed the Dark Ages from which they did not recover until wealth was scattered by continuous wars, a great share of it being therein destroyed. It is said at this time (1935) that less than two (2) percent of the people control ninety (90) percent of the wealth of America." (Search: 3).

In my opinion, the ultimate source for the history and modern-day definition of "elitists" is Dr. John Coleman, who is described thusly by Prof. Carlos St. John Reuterman:

> Author, constitutional scholar, economist, British Museum researcher, historian, lecturer, political scientist, Middle East specialist and radio talk show guest speaker. Dr. Coleman is a master of more than one hundred subjects.

He is not one of the rather plentiful newcomers who have lately appeared on the scene. Stationed in fourteen countries around the world and speaking five foreign languages, puts Dr. Coleman at the head of the field of all writers of conspiracy and secret society books in the United States. (Coleman *Committee:* 489).

Dr. Coleman identifies himself as a former member of Great Britain's MI6, the counterpart to the CIA of the United States, who spent five years in a research role in the back sections of the British Museum in London. Several years back, I came across in his writings (and in those of Deanna Spingola) information about oil deposits offshore in Vietnam that could have been the origination for the interest in pursuing control of Indochina. Obviously, the historic background to my Vietnam War piqued my curiosity in the causes of wars and my work on what may encompass a future volume began.

Several years back, I called and talked to Dr. Coleman. In mid-2017, I again attempted to contact him, but to no avail. Either he has died or "mysteriously disappeared." Many, even close personal friends of mine, dispute the existence of any conspiracy. It is my belief, after extensive study, that it does indeed exist, that elitists do indeed exist, and that they care not for the masses. I will stand by my belief.

At any rate, much of the depth of my understanding of the ultimate elitists relates to a wide-ranging history expressed in his most-fascinating book, *The Conspirator's Hierarchy: The Committee of 300* (4th edition) published in 2006, previously referenced in this book. This is how he describes the Committee of 300:

> For decades the British East India and Dutch East India companies amassed fortunes from their opium trade with China and now through the Committee of 300 they continue to wage phony drug wars... There is no need to use 'they' or the 'enemy' except as shorthand. We know

who they, the enemy, is. The committee of three hundred with its Eastern Liberal Establishment 'aristocracy,' its banks, insurance companies, giant corporations, foundations, communications networks, presided over by a hierarchy of conspirators—this is the enemy...

Coleman continues in his definition of the Committee of 300:

The Committee of 300 is the ultimate secret society made up of an untouchable ruling class, which includes the Queen of England, the Queen of the Netherlands, the Queen of Denmark, and the royal families of Europe. These aristocrats decided at the death of Queen Victoria, the matriarch of the Venetian Black Guelphs that, in order to gain worldwide control, it would be necessary for its aristocratic members to 'go into business' with the non-aristocratic, but extremely powerful leaders of corporate business on a global scale, and so the doors to ultimate power were opened to what the Queen of England likes to refer to as the 'commoners.' (Coleman *Committee*: 338).

An elitist royalist, King Leopold of Belgium, controlled the rubber production in the Belgian Congo. About him, it has been said, "The soldiers of King Leopold of Belgium, to satiate his greed for money to satisfy his concubines, were massacring, torturing, and mutilating the natives of the Congo who did not bring in enough rubber." One of the King's loyal soldiers was Emile Francqui, who will reenter our history in the aftermath of the Anglo-Boer War as a partner with Herbert C. Hoover (yes, the future U.S. President) in slave trading of Chinese workers. (Hamill: 156, 157).

Buckminster Fuller has also researched the power of the elites:

In 1600 Queen Elizabeth I and a few intimates founded the East India Company. Exercising her crown privileges, the queen granted the company limited liability for losses on the part of enterprise backers...Elizabeth's East India Company scheme was to have her national navy (and armies) first win mastery of the world's sea-lanes. This advantage would thereafter be exploited by her-owned enterprise...All the other world-power-stature individuals who vied for supreme mastery of the world's high seas lines of supply also operated invisibly through monarchs and nations over whom they had sufficient influence. Through such behind-the-throne influence the influenced nations' resources could be politically maneuvered into paying for the building and operation of the navies and armies that would seek to establish and protect their respective privately-owned enterprises. (Fuller: xxi).

I can but scratch the surface as to the intricate spider webs woven by these elitists throughout history back to the oligarchic families of Venice and Genoa, to the royal dynasties of Europe, to British East India Company, to the Rockefellers and Rothschilds, to the Jewish and Gentile international bankers, and to modern day titans of banking, politics and industry. These modern-day titans include such organizations and figures as Philander C. Knox, Thomas Lamont, George Mandel, J. Pierpoint Morgan, National City Bank, Jacob Schiff, J. Henry Schroeder Bank, Wall Streeters, the Warburgs, Bernard Baruch, Chase Manhattan Bank, Dillon, Read, and the Federal Reserve.

Ferdinand Lundberg died in 1995. His obituary[2] in the *New York Times* indicated he had been a former financial writer for *The New York Herald*. In 1937, he wrote *America's Sixty Families* in which:

> ...[he] proposed that a small group of wealthy families held sway over the economy and the body politic, while their financial interests controlled the press...The United States is owned and dominated today by a hierarchy of the richest families, buttressed by no more than ninety families of lesser wealth. (Lundberg: 3).

Elaborating on his research, Lundberg states:

> Every great fortune that rolled out of the nineteenth

century was rooted in fraud and the literature and documentation and proof of this broad statement is voluminous.[3] In their absorbing passion for the accumulation of wealth, says David Saville Muzzey, a cool historian, 'men were plundering the resources of the country like burglars looting a palace.'[4] Fraud and trickery were the revolutionary devices resorted to by the northern industrialists to complete the job begun by Grant's cannon and bayonets; by fraud a realm oozing riches, and far surpassing in value the Russian Empire seized by the Bolsheviks, was wrested from the American people in the years 1860 to 1900. Whereas in the Civil War it was the Southern planters who were mowed down and summarily divorced from their property, in the postwar decades it was the farmers, laborers, professionals, and small merchants who were indirectly expropriated by unscrupulous revolutionary improvisation upon the Constitutional machinery. (Lundberg: 53).

Elitists: Modern Day

My extensive research (now consisting of over two hundred books in my personal library) brought across my radar two books by John Perkins, who was described earlier as the "Economic Hit Man" (EHM). He wrote of his work to prepare inflated economic reports in foreign countries to justify the assumption of massive debts to fund extensive projects in their countries of dubious value to the "downtrodden masses." (Perkins *Confessions: ix*).

In his opinion, Perkins lends no credence to any "organized conspiracy." Perhaps his experiences lent themselves to be described as strictly expressions of raw "cupidity." He believes that the economic and financial conditions brought a system upon many foreign countries that is more damaging than a conspiracy (so extensively covered by my writings).
Perkins wrote about this system:

It [the system] is driven not by a small band of men but by

concept that it become accepted as gospel: the idea that all economic growth benefits humankind and that the greater the growth, the more widespread the benefits. This belief also has a corollary: that those people who excel at stoking the fires of economic growth should be exalted and rewarded, while those born at the fringes are available for exploitation.

He believes that, when greed is rewarded, of and by itself, greed becomes a motivator. He continues by saying that "...when we define huge sections of the population as subservient to an elite minority, we asked for trouble, and we get it." (Perkins *Confessions: xii*).

He also wrote that a "few swim in riches and the majority drown in poverty, pollution and violence." (Perkins *Confessions: xiii*). This relates to my thesis that the elitists benefit from wars and those who fight them suffer.

Perkins describes what one of his foreign contacts indicated as an anguished cry reflecting her opinion of the "haves" of the world:

> 'Stop being so greedy,' she said, 'and so selfish. Realize that there is more to the world than your big houses and fancy stores. People are starving and you worry about oil for your cars. Babies are dying of thirst and you search the fashion magazines for the latest styles. Nations like ours are drowning in poverty, but your people don't even hear our cries for help. You shut your ears to the voices of those who try to tell you these things. You label them radicals or Communists. You must open your hearts to the poor and downtrodden, instead of driving them further into poverty and servitude. There's not much time left. If you don't change, you're doomed.' (Perkins *Confessions*: 46).

As a severely wounded soldier, I ask for a deep and searching public discourse before our young patriots go off to wars. I also ask for deep searching of our hearts as to how we constantly can help the "downtrodden masses" of the world. By this, I do not advocate massive immigration into our country. Many millions of the "downtrodden" throughout the world have already come to the United States illegally or desire to come. We cannot end up being for the world what was termed after World War II and also after the Korean War, by some who witnessed our logistics backing up our troops, "the land of the big PX" (i.e., Post Exchange).

On April 4, 2016, a colossal story hit the world. It was reported that a Panamanian law firm, Mossack Fonseca, "...helped register offshore companies for Americans who are either accused or convicted by federal prosecutors of serious financial crimes, including securities fraud and running a Ponzi scheme." Apparently at least two hundred Americans were discovered to have accounts in what are described as "shell companies," established to shelter money or assets. The document leak totaling 11.5 million documents was called the "Panama Papers." Obviously, all subjects identified were not necessarily indulging in incredible criminal activity.[5] Some were 'merely" avoiding taxes.

The *New York Times* says that the Panama Papers "exposed how some of the world's most powerful people may have used offshore bank accounts and shell companies to conceal their wealth or avoid taxes." Some of those identified include prominent politicians, businesspeople and other high-profile individuals "involved in a web of suspicious financial transactions." A list of individuals mentioned include "close associates of President Vladimir V. Putin of Russia, the father of Prime Minister David Cameron of Britain and relatives of President Xi Jinping of China and members of the Chinese Communist Party Politburo Standing Committee."[6]

Do you think that perhaps elitists not only make money, but also want to hide it? 99%+ of us in the lower ranks need not be concerned about tax shelters. Many billions of people are simply satisfied with going to sleep on a full stomach and having sufficient clean water on any given day!

It can be very risky to write about controversial issues, especially if the elite are involved. Witness the car bombing death in Malta on October 15, 2017, of an investigative journalist, Daphne Caruana Galizia. Ms. Galizia reported in the "Panama Papers" on her island's links, and those of some of its people, to offshore tax havens.[7] Telling the truth about some members of the elite can be deadly! Confront an elitist at one's own risk!

Elitists: Rockefellers

To begin with the original "elitist" family of America, one must address the Rockefellers. Lundberg researched the Rockefeller-Standard Oil power base and described it covering all bases:

> The Standard Oil Company was conniving with the chieftains of both parties before 1880. John D. Rockefeller habitually contributed large funds to the Republicans in return for lucrative concessions; Colonel Oliver H. Payne, his partner, gave liberally to the Democrats, and did not hesitate to call upon them peremptorily for delivery of the political quid pro quo.[8] James A. Garfield, the successful candidate for the presidency in 1880, anxiously asked an associate 'if Mr. Rockefeller would be willing to assist.'[9] Rockefeller gave heavily for the Garfield campaign, and Mark Hanna, the statesman of Standard Oil, sent four checks for $1,000 each to the Ohio State Republican Committee.[10] It was the settled policy of the company to use its money everywhere and anywhere, in state and national councils, to produce results.[11] (Lundberg: 54).

Higham wrote the following about the Rockefellers:

> I turned to the matter of the Rockefeller-controlled Chase National Bank, which had conducted its business for the Nazi high command in Paris until the war's (WWII) end and from the Chase Bank it was a natural progression to Standard Oil of New Jersey, the chief jewel in the crown of

the Rockefeller Empire. Records of standards dealings with the Axis were contained in the Records Rooms of the Diplomatic Branch of the National Archives and were specially declassified. (Higham: *xviii*).

[Author's note: I knew personally many of our veterans of World War II, who were Prisoners of War (POW) or Wounded in Action (WIA) by the Nazis and Japanese. It incenses me to learn about corporate collusion with our enemies.]

Deanna Spingola said it simply, but eloquently, when she stated, "The ultimate price is paid by those who are squandered in battle without a moment's thought by the elite purveyors of war and bloodshed."[12]

Founder John D. Rockefeller was perceived as a most generous philanthropist, but there may have been another purpose as seen in this depiction: "The Rockefeller 'philanthropies' were conceived for the dual purpose of taking the curse off the Rockefeller name and enabling the Rockefeller-Standard Oil interests to carry on without interference from a hostile public or the government." (Josephson *Rockefeller:* 72).

Why the Rockefeller family and dynasty could be considered the "elite" of the "elite" families of America is further explained by Lundberg:

> These are only a few examples of the interlocking of the Rockefellers with families of wealth; some Rockefeller marriages to be sure have taken place outside of the pecuniary circle. The rich families with which the Rockefellers have interlocked in turn have been interlocked by marriages with other wealthy families, so that one can trace an almost unbroken line of biological relationships from the Rockefellers through one-half of the wealthiest sixty families of the nation. Mary E. Stillman, for example, became Mrs. Edward S. Harkness (Standard Oi). Anne Stillman is, as we have observed, Mrs. Henry P Davison, Jr.

The Stillmans also married into the Pratt (Standard Oil) family. (Lundberg: 11).

Enough documentation on the life of John D. Rockefeller, Sr. exists to make it easy to accept the summary by Docherty and MacGregor of this original elitist in American history. There will be discussion later in this work or a possible future volume also about the elites, Britain's Secret Elites, and Round Tables, but for now, realize that Rockefeller was one of the funders of New York's Round Table. These dual-authors do not appear to have much respect for Rockefeller, describing him as "...an unscrupulous thug, ruthless in his determination to trample opposition and throttle competition...He indulged in secret deals to undercut his competitors and expanded his control of the oil business across the entire American Continent." (Docherty: 215). This scathing commentary was pulled from the 1935 book *Years of Plunder* by Proctor W. Hansl (pp. 37-38). It deserves its own place in the text rather than being buried in an endnote. The previous depiction may describe business as usual for some, but not all, of our millionaires.

Now is the time to go behind the scenes and raise the curtain veil to reflect upon the Rockefeller family back into the 1800s and to review the major influence they had on bringing forth the one world government and one world religion. Allow me to connect some dots.

The original Rockefeller philanthropically supported educational operation was the General Education Board. Rockefeller's head man in philanthropy was Reverend Frederick T. Gates, who was recruited from the American Baptist Education Society. In 1904, Gates wrote a passage in *Occasional Paper No. 1* titled "The Country School of Tomorrow," which set the groundwork for the attitude toward us "peasants" by John D. and his "elitist" compatriots:

> In our dreams we have limitless resources and *the people yield themselves with perfect docility to our molding hands*.

The present educational conventions fade from our minds, and *unhampered by tradition, we work our own good will upon a grateful and responsive rural folk*. We shall not try to make these people or any of their children into philosophers or men of learning, or men of science. We are not to raise up from among them authors, editors, poets or men of letters. We shall not search for embryo great artists, painters, musicians. Nor will we cherish even the humbler ambition to raise up among them lawyers, doctors, preachers, politicians, statesmen, of whom we have an ample supply. The task we have set before ourselves is a very simple as well as a very beautiful one to train these people as we find them for a perfectly ideal life just where they are. So we will organize our children and teach them to do in a perfect way the things that their fathers and mothers are doing in an imperfect way, in the homes, in the shops and on the farm. (Gates: 6).

In other words, do not change their circumstances or any aspirations towards improvement, just control the masses! Frankly, I am incensed that, in America, a group of rich elitists in New York would have thought and planned one hundred years ago an endeavor akin to totalitarianism – then perhaps even dare it to be described as what could within a few years be termed "communistic?" Even back then, to have done so would not have been deemed as "politically correct." This is what they were planning to do with their millions to control the common people of our land!

In his 1952 book, Josephson really tears into John D. Rockefeller, who becomes highly vilified in funding a bewildering group of philanthropies, supposedly only to elevate his humanitarian concerns for mankind. Josephson believes that:

That purpose from the very start, was, and still is, a 'new social order,' the establishment of a dictatorship in the United States. The objective is to convert our republic into a totalitarian state, into what Hillaire Belloc has named a

'Servile State,' a state of slaves. This Rockefeller proposed to attain by propaganda, 'thought control,' bribery, corruption, and force. And it is to be ruled by him or his heirs. (Josephson *Rockefeller*: 73,74).

Never mind that the "servile rural folk" would be many of the foot soldiers of America in 1917 thrown into the gas attacks, mud, bombardments, dying, and maiming of the trenches of WWI. Obviously, both rural and city folks in warfare sometimes are overwhelmed by their war experiences. Today, it is termed Post Traumatic Stress. Throughout the history of warfare, the medical professionals have termed it differently. In the Civil War, it was termed "condition of the heart." In more recent wars, it has been called "combat fatigue" and various other terms.

The history and far-reaching influence of the Rockefeller family is most broad and deep. It would require its own volumes of books. In very short fashion, my writing is sufficient to explain the background of this "elite" American family. Please recognize that in no way would I impugn the integrity, goodwill, or philanthropic thrust of many Rockefellers, then or now. Several distinguished members of the family have attended The Phillips Exeter Academy (some even simultaneously with me when I spent my one year at the school). It is my understanding that many members of the family have been very philanthropically-oriented in various worthwhile causes.

Elitists: Politicians

My section on politicians and political activity was fine-tuned in early 2018, immediately after the revelations were reported about the intrigue, politicizing, and conspiring, that had possibly occurred at the highest levels. I am not talking about the rank-and-file of our Federal Bureau of Investigation and various intelligence agencies, organizations which had previously been left relatively untarnished.

In 2008, Deanna Spingola, wrote her opinion as it relates to the history of the world and its realm of rulers, royalty, and politicians. After three years of my own intensive study, I agree with her. Spingola's following passage explains her views on:

> ... the long-term diabolical deeds of America's ruling class. Alternative information exists despite their dedicated efforts to control information through compulsory education and the Free Press. And because history is prologue, one may acquire an accurate perception of the events and political schemes of the current power base. Yet, due to disinformation, deception and calculating rhetoric, ethical moral people frequently underestimate, justify or even dismiss this suspicious behavior of their political leaders."[13]

GK Chesterton, a British author, related his opinion about political leaders in a 1921 interview with the Cleveland Press:

> The man whom the people ought to choose to represent them are too busy to take the jobs. But the politician is waiting for it. He's the pestilence of modern times. What we should try to do is make politics as local as possible. Keep the politicians near enough to kick them. The villagers who met under the village tree could also hang the politicians to the tree. It is terrible to contemplate how few politicians are hanged.

This attitude is probably much too radical for me. In my several decades of life, I have known of and been associated with many politicians who have the people's interest in mind and cannot be bought. However, the examples of ineptitude and ability to be swayed by lobbyist contributions are rampant today and throughout history.

In the early 1500s, Machiavelli, a statesman from Florence, Italy, studied the attainment of power by the rulers. He wrote *The Prince,* which was published in 1532. He did not paint a very pretty picture of the acquisition of power:

... to obtain power it is essential to ignore the moral laws of man and of God that promises must be made only with the intention to deceive and mislead others to sacrifice their own interests, and that the most brutal atrocity must be committed as a matter of mere convenience. (Knuth: 76).

Civilization surely has advanced over these hundreds of years past the time of "brutal atrocities," unless one could, and should, define warfare and the assassinations of political adversaries as realms of brutal and atrocious behavior.

Throughout my research, I have discovered multitudes of instances wherein politicians have fulfilled the bidding of powerful interests to protect their investments, centers of power, and non-competitive arenas of endeavors.

Edward Bernays weighs in on political leadership and propaganda, subjects about which he is without peer. He wrote, "...fortunately, the sincere and gifted politician is able, by the instrument of propaganda, to mold and form the will of the people." (Bernays: 109). In 1928, he also wrote, "... Political campaigns today are all sideshows, all honors, all bombast, literature, and speeches. (Bernays: 111). In my humble opinion in 2019, not much has changed. If the main task of politicians is to win elections and to solidify their positions, money must be raised, and therefore politicians must be "slaves," especially to their major contributors.

It is naïve to believe that some elected officials will not listen to the compelling "reasoning" offered by individuals, special-interest groups, and political action committees, after they have contributed to campaign funds. Unfortunately, in my opinion, some votes and governance directions are achieved as a result of outright graft, corruption payments, and even surefire investment opportunities. Dare I declare that some politicians are compelled or even forced to vote a certain way because they have been guilty of immoral or unethical behavior that subjects them to blackmail. [Author's note: In one of my lives, I was a candidate for a Texas statewide elected position, as well as a local Texas county position, so I have been exposed to politicians at various levels.]

Author of *F.D.R.: My Exploited Father-In-Law*, Curtis B. Dall, who was married at one time to the president's daughter, Anna, was a close witness to the machinations and political happenings during almost all of President Roosevelt's administration. After the divorce in 1935 until 1943, he was often a visitor to the White House and was in a distinct position to observe first-hand the arena of politics during those years.

He developed a rather caustic and negative view of at least some politicians at the highest level of American political life. He maintained that some politicians through their legislative agendas were able to recompense themselves and their backers handsomely.

Dall believed that only a small group of individuals managed to pick and back candidates from each party to ensure that, in the end, their interests would be supported by the eventual victor. His opinion was that to become a "statesman," one must, of course, have "backers," but that also, a candidate must possess" ... great personal ambition and perchance, to be *vulnerable to blackmail* for some past occurrences." (Dall: 23).

This was a sad commentary indeed for the political arena in the 1930s and 1940s. Perhaps 80 to 90 years later, situations have not changed much in our political world, human nature being what it is.

Spingola weighs in on her opinion of the political arena:

> The bankers and their agents have co-opted, staffed and corrupted both parties. Sadly, both parties, infiltrated by strong influential personalities, have followed the same agenda, but from a diametrically different direction and the bankers fund both parties whose top echelon acquiesce and promote the industrialist's self-serving programs.

Despite the anti-war claim to the Democrats or the preventative war tactics of the Republicans, we are constantly involved in war, a cover for the corporations to seize valuable assets, transfer wealth or subdue dissenting populations. All of these warfare objectives create massive debts and the ultimate destruction of the U.S. economy. (Spingola *Imperialism:* 647).

A principal influence on the powerful of the world is noted by Knuth when he says, "The biographies of the House of Rothschild record that men of influence and statesman in almost every country of the world were in their pay... A large part of the profligate nobility (elitists) of all Europe was deeply indebted to them." (Knuth: 70). Perhaps, in "following the money" in world history, the actions and positions of politicians could be explained by what Knuth puts forth in the following quote:

It is reasonable to suppose that the immensity of the Rothschild fortune has taken it more or less out of the scope of the present heads of the House of Rothschild and that it is merged in the general conduct of the financial, commercial and political control of the world by the City (the London financial center). (Knuth: 70).

The connection between the rulers, politicians, money and warfare was described by Andrew Carnegie in his writings first published in 1886:

Perhaps the Democracy is soon to awaken to the truth that these vast accumulations of debt have the real source in the rule of monarchs and courts, whose jealousies and dynastic ambitions, stimulated by the great military classes always created by them, produce the wars or continued preparations for wars which eat up the people's substance and add to their burdens year after year. A nation with a large standing army and navy is bound to make wars."[14]

A distinguished and generous philanthropist throughout his life,

Andrew Carnegie was a very celebrated and well-known American. His Carnegie Steel Company was bought out by John Pierpoint Morgan in 1901 for $225,000,000.

The ever observant and candid Vincent Vickers wrote about politicians and the reality of their world:

> Under our existing parliamentary system, the first consideration of any self-respecting and duly elected government is to remain in office. The party can count on the whole-hearted support of that undeniable 'cheque-book influence' which banking, finance and big-business leaders have at their disposal and which they can at all times exert, possesses in itself an electoral advantage which renders true statesmanship in our political leaders almost impossible. (Vickers: 7).

This is truth revealed as to the world of politics and its connection with bankers and big business money.

In 2017, an outpouring of tragic revelations of harassment of both men and women by rich and powerful Hollywood figures extended even into the hallowed halls of our Congress and Senate. Writer and researcher, Kelleigh Nelson, summarizes the scandals in Congress thusly:

> Americans who actually pay attention realize that we have only one party in Congress, and the two sides collude together to protect each other and grow rich off the American taxpayer. Neither one of them is truly any better than the other, and none will risk outing the perverts because then they become the enemy of the good ole' boys network.[15]

Not far from the truth. That is why many Americans have become independents.

My efforts toward accountability will be reflected in the truths I have uncovered via exhaustive research to tell the true stories, not the revisionist ones, so that we may hold our elected officials to the truth when future conflicts send the patriots of America into harm's way. Perhaps our politicians come under too much control of monied interests? My own limited personal experience is that the favor of politicians is often sought by businesspeople by offering politicians "special deals." Those special deals, after a comparison of their net worth pre- and post- "public service," often reflect increases that are undeniably far and beyond any savings that would have been possible given their government salaries.

I have a final note as I close this section on elitism. On a small piece of paper, I have a quote from an unknown, but wise American, Texas Guinan. The quote reads, "A politician is a fellow who will lay down your life for his country."

Elitists: Lawyers

> "A dozen men with machine guns are no match for a single lawyer with a briefcase." – *The Godfather,* Mario Puzo

Admittedly, this quote is from popular culture and is fictional. I have nothing against lawyers, especially because I have had lawyers in my family. Byron Clark, my great-grandfather from Plattsmouth, Nebraska, who lived from 1847 to 1936, was once the general solicitor for Burlington Lines West, a railroad, in Omaha. His obituary included a description of him as "… one of the best-known lawyers in the middle west." My father, too, was a licensed attorney who was employed at an Army post legal office. At one time prior to my upcoming medical retirement from the Army in 1968, I took under serious consideration attending a law school. Therefore, it is not my desire to take aim at lawyers as a career field, only to relate the significant involvement of many lawyers who were influential at critical junctures of American history.

However, my research has come across many examples of

significant political influence exercised by lawyers. Some exercised their power through fee-based services and their capacity as lawyers, and some through high-ranking political positions. William Nelson Cromwell was intimately involved in the Panama Canal. Allen and John Foster Dulles, lawyers in Cromwell's New York firm (Sullivan & Cromwell), wielded extensive sway in many arenas of public life internationally. John Foster Dulles was an American negotiator at the Versailles Treaty talks after WWI, and he is followed in future chapters between the world wars as well as his during his time as Secretary of State in the Eisenhower presidency.

Stephen Kinzer in *Overthrow* wrote of perhaps the most powerful lawyer in U.S. history, John Foster Dulles:

> As the twentieth century progressed, titans of industry and their advocates went a step beyond influencing policymakers; they 'became' the policymakers. The figure who most perfectly embodied this merging of political and economic interests was John Foster Dulles, who spent decades working for some of the world's most powerful corporations and then became secretary of state. It was Dulles who ordered the 1953 coup in Iran, which was intended in part to make the Middle East safe for American oil companies. A year later he ordered another coup, in Guatemala, where a nationalist government had challenged the power of United Fruit, a company his old law firm represented. (Kinzer: 4).

Curtis Dall, mentioned earlier as President Franklin D Roosevelt's son-in-law, once engaged in a personal conversation with Felix Frankfurter, then a law professor at Harvard Law School. Dall wrote that Frankfurter at one time had written, "The real rulers in Washington are invisible and exercise power from behind the scenes." (Dall: 67).

Buckminster Fuller in *Critical Path* ascribes to Wall Street lawyers significant influence over the recruitment and administration of

Dwight Eisenhower. After World War II, "The Wall Street lawyers' grand strategists saw this as a time for breaking through the New Deal's hold on government, an event which, up to that time seemed impossible." The lawyers approached Eisenhower, and in the new affluent post-war American economy, persuaded Eisenhower to run as a Republican because, "...the new affluent majority would elect a Republican."

They convinced him that the New Deal was socialistic and anathema to America's free enterprise tradition. Upon his election, "...they instructed him to break loose all the economic controls of the New Deal." Buckminster writes that these "strategists" arranged to place John Foster Dulles as Secretary of State to counter Soviet influence, and to appoint his fellow lawyer brother, Allen Dulles, as head of, "...a new brand of absolutely invisible, U.S.A.-financed, capitalistic, welfare department, the CIA, established ostensibly to cold-war-cope with the secret-agent operations of our enemies." (Fuller: 102,103). For those of us schooled on the threat after WWII of a newly strong USSR and the imposition of the Iron Curtain and the enslavement of many people, these were worthy goals on their surface.

[Author's note: In my Vietnam War covert assignment in Army Special Forces as a Military Intelligence officer, I spent one month in the fall of 1966 in Saigon, debriefing Inchin Hai Lam, a "defector" from Cambodia, in fifteen separate meetings. Inchin spoke very well, or reasonably well, seven languages. He was a highly intelligent individual. He related to me his attendance in Moscow at the Patrice Lumumba University, where outstanding young people from all over the world were brought to be schooled to return to their home countries to foster and foment revolutionary conditions to install Communist/socialistic regimes. (Clark *Wounded:* 128).]

Fuller again describes how Wall Street lawyers during the term of President Eisenhower supported "foreign aid," and had bill riders attached that required monies to be spent through American companies in the undeveloped countries, if the companies had operations in those countries. (Fuller: 105). This provided jobs for Americans, obviously a worthy goal. The same lawyers established government policies that moved many corporations out of the country. (Fuller: 105). In 2017 and into 2018 it appears that new tax laws are encouraging repatriation of monies of overseas American entities back into the country.

American corporations eventually reaped great profits from enormous war orders and, of course, if prices were raised in the 1950s (as they were), this elevated the net worth of the CEOs and other executives. (Fuller: 103). Possibly even the fees charged by corporate attorneys?

The motto of the Army's Rangers is "Rangers Lead the Way." Perhaps at times in American history, it could be said that "Lawyers Lead the Way," but, this minimizes the patriotic accomplishments of celebrated Ranger heroes of America. Your author is not Ranger-qualified.

An exhaustive study of the powerful Sullivan & Cromwell law firm is embodied in the book, *A Law unto Itself The Untold Story of the Law Firm Sullivan & Cromwell: 100 Years of Creating Power and Wealth,* authored by Lisagor and Lipsius. Informational snippets and tidbits derived from this book are quoted in a very abbreviated fashion, but with pages noted. All the notes relate to clients of the firm or to involvement by partners of the firm. "In 1906 Cromwell attracted as a client one of the most notorious railroad robber barons, E. H. Harriman. Described by President Theodore Roosevelt as a 'malefactor of great wealth' and an 'enemy of the Republic.'" (35).

In the structuring of the new entity, U.S. Steel, "Three hundred insiders, including Cromwell got $200 million of the new company's stock for $25 million." (35). "The only way around Columbia's obstinacy (related to a Panama Canal) ...was a revolution in Panama." (47). Regarding a rebellion by Liberals in Cuba during WWI and the sugar plantation owners, "Dulles's overriding concern was not the Liberals but American property interest in territory controlled by the Liberals." (67). During WWI John Foster Dulles and his firm, "...willingly helped the company try to evade the Alien Property Custodian (legalities)." (68). "Dulles wanted to avoid State Department scrutiny of whether the German factories were producing military hardware in violation of the Versailles Treaty." (92). "He wasted no time neutralizing the department (State) by ingratiating himself with its loan supervisors, starting with Robert E. Olds, the undersecretary. Using the Council on Foreign Relations a prestigious New York club of businessmen and academics interest in foreign policy, Dulles invited Olds to a dinner in New York. Within three years, Olds had joined Sullivan & Cromwell as a partner to head the Paris office." (92,93).

More anecdotes about this prestigious law firm found in this book:

> The relationship between (German) Schacht and Dulles grew in the 1930s to a close collaboration. Schacht recognized the value of an American with his own reasons to promote German interests, and he used Dulles and Sullivan & Cromwell from the time the Nazis took power to the Second World War. (122).

Three days after Dulles and Schacht's dinner meeting, Sullivan and Cromwell mounted a campaign to unseat the management of the Allied Chemical and Dye Corporation, which had defied the German-led chemical cartel and secretly built a nitrogen factory in Hopewell, Virginia. It more than quintupled American nitrate exports from 28,630 tons in 1930 to 285,000 tons in 1933 and infuriated Allied's major stockholder, Solvay & Cie., the Belgian company that also owned part of the cartel leader, the notorious German I. G. Farbenindustrie. (I.G. Farben later ran part of the Auschwitz concentration camp as a private chemical factory)." (124). "Sullivan & Cromwell thrived on its cartels in collusion with the new Nazi regime." (125). "Dulles worked with the company (INCO) throughout the interwar period, resisting Canadian and British government efforts to curtail the shipment of nickel for military use." (126). "Still, as part of his responsibilities at Sullivan

& Cromwell, Allen Dulles continued to do business with the Germans. In 1937 he joined the Board of Directors of J. Henry Schroeder Bank, the American subsidiary of the London bank that *Time* magazine in 1939 called 'an economic booster of the Rome-Berlin Axis.'" (139). There is more, but one must read the entire book to get the complete picture. I guess memories are short due to the high-level government positions attained by the Dulles brothers in the Eisenhower administration after they had padded their assets through their legal work.

Lawyers are a segment of our society that attracts some of the best and brightest minds produced in America. They also are responsible for America being a society ruled under law, comprising fairness and justice. I wish only to relate some of those instances I have researched wherein sometimes these great minds are put at the disposal of individuals and groups and corporations, who worked to use every possible lever of political power to enrich themselves at the expense of the gullible and uninformed masses.

Elitists: Masons

Originally it was my intention to research and report on Freemasonry, but I've decided to leave this topic to others to explore as to the myriad of conspiratorial activities that are written about Masons by many authors. The direct connection about Masons in wars is very complicated.

This is my bottom line on Freemasonry. Many of my closest and best friends and relatives are Masons. They are all fine gentlemen, who love with dedication our country. Never would I desire to cast aspersions on Freemasonry overall.

However, I believe it necessary to make some simplistic and generalized comments about what my research has found. There are three basic areas of Freemasonry. Full disclosure by me is that I'm not a Mason, nor was I ever, with no negativity reflected in my decision not to become a Mason.

The three groupings are the standard lodges in Europe, the standard "blue" lodges in the United States, which I perceived to be very philanthropically-oriented as witnessed especially by the Shriner Hospital and "non-standard" or rogue lodges, whose existence and purposes become somewhat murkier and more mysterious.

When I have found references to Freemasonry relative to machinations and conspiracies within Freemasonry, a search of the author sometimes brings forth many writings published about the author relative to his own credibility and charging him with "misinformation."

There is copious literature relative to the involvement of Freemasonry in the conspiracy theory of history. They are combined with many organizations and groups supposedly responsible for the conspiracy theory of history. Others are Jews, international bankers, Jesuits, and the Vatican, among others. If, in fact, one of these entities is attacked, fairly or unfairly, that entity will be quick to develop their counterattacks to disabuse those who believe them to be guilty as charged. It remains far and above my humble position to attribute any overall blame to any of the groups.

As for Masons, they cannot but expect negative attention when as a group "with secrets," which they admit, it gets garbled with charges that they are a "secret" organization. If there is a "conspiracy," which I believe exists, most probably certain high-ranking individuals in all the groups are a part of it, but that is hidden from the lower levels of their individuals.

Leo Lyon Zagami is quoted in his *Confessions of an Illuminati* as saying, "True speculative Freemasonry (as opposed to occult or *fringe* Freemasonry), has nothing to do with such deviated and dark practices." (Zagami: 52). Zagami deals extensively in his book with the seamier side of the world today, whose subject I have addressed in the chapter on spiritual warfare.

Zagami writes to contrast and compare speculative Masonry with Jesuits and his belief is that both are opponents of the New World Order, but unfortunately are adversaries with each other, but believes both are subject to manipulations from a higher level. (Zagami: 52,53).

There appears to be controversy even among different lodges in Freemasonry. For example, Zagami writes:

> In fact, the so-called regular lodges of Freemasonry operating under the United Grand Lodge of England, UGLE, (like the Italian-speaking *Italia* Lodge in London), do not allow 'Masonic Brothers' from a non-recognized Masonic Obedience (as the Grand Lodges and Grand Orients of Freemasonry are called), that do not share treaties of Amity and Solidarity with each other under the supreme patronage of the UGLE.

Author Nesta Webster's 1921 book makes it very clear, although she writes extensively in a negative fashion about the French Freemason lodges being intimately involved with the Illuminati in carrying out the French Revolution of 1789. She writes that:

> ...as I have always clearly differentiated between British and Continental masonry, showing the former to be an honourable association not only hostile to subversive doctrines but a strong supporter of law, order, and religion. (Webster N.: Author's note).

Author Zagami is controversial, but his writings are expansive. His inclusion in my bibliography is due to its being a treasure trove of information on many disputed, yet compelling, subjects.

An American Mason friend of mine sent me the following:

> Mason lodges represent different agendas in different regions in the world. Usually, it is the wealthy vs. the

middle-class with economic objects or goals. It's money, power, or territory. Masons in Europe would be those that have the power and influence to pull the political or economic strings from behind the curtain. They have the power and do not want anyone to know it.

My conclusions on Freemasonry can be quite simply stated: An overwhelming majority of members of U.S. "Blue" lodges are philanthropically-oriented and extraordinary American patriots!

Chapter 10:

Media and Propaganda

"True and unbiased news-the highest original moral concept ever developed in America and given the world." — Kent Cooper

"The supreme freedom is the freedom of the people to know the truth. For the peace and prosperity of the world it is more important for the public to know the liberal truth than the reactionary truth. Perhaps some day all of us will be strong enough to stand the real truth." — Henry A. Wallace, former vice president of the United States (*New York Times*, Jan. 7, 1947).

Media

An absolute gem of a book published in 1942 has become a gold mine of background for this section on media. Please have your blood pressure instrument beside you because your blood, as did mine, will boil when you read what Kent Cooper wrote in *Barriers Down*. Kent Cooper was at date of publication of the book the General Manager of the Associated Press, a U.S.-based co-operative news-gathering association that, under the crusade of Cooper, broke the monopoly of dissemination of news enjoyed by three European news agencies since the nineteenth century.

In 1942, Kent Cooper, General Manager of the Associated Press, sought a new agreement with Reuters. Through the previous years he had been stymied in freely providing news to outlets such as in South America due to a monopoly. He discovered that all news in or out of the Far East or the Empire of Britain was controlled by Reuters and the rest of the world was divided between Havas of France and the Wolff agency of Germany. (Cooper: Back flyleaf).

These three European news agencies took on the names of their founders. In modern-day times news agencies collect and send out news to print media outlets. The original customers of the above Big Three were banks and businesses who were solely interested in equity prices and pronouncements and information concerning commercial and trade activities. They charged their customers high prices and it was quite lucrative for them. They basically possessed a monopoly on business news until the arrival of the telegraph. (Cooper: 6).

Havas claimed its origination in 1835. Reuter started in Germany in the 1840s, but, became an operation of real significance, when a move was made to London in 1851. Wolff of Germany became successful also at approximately the same time frame.

Cooper wrote:

> From these beginnings there arose the first, the greatest and the most powerful international monopoly of the 19th century. Its potentialities and its activities, viewed in the liberal spirit of 1942, were astounding. When Reuter, Havas and Wolff pooled their resources, established complete news agency control of international news and allotted to themselves the news agency exploitation in all the countries of the world, they brought under their control the power to decide what the people of each nation would be allowed to know of the peoples of other nations and what shade of meaning the news was to be presented....The mighty foreign propaganda carried on through these channels in the last hundred years has been one of the causes of wars that never has been uncovered. (Cooper: 8).

Allow me to repeat: "...HAS BEEN ONE OF THE CAUSES OF WARS THAT HAS NEVER BEEN UNCOVERED." Let that sink in.

Cooper correctly stated, "There can be no permanent peace unless men of all lands can have truthful, unbiased news of each other which shall be freely available at the source to all who seek it there, wherever that may be." (Cooper: 9)

It is obvious that the European agencies described herein were sometimes subject to the influence of governments, banking interests, and arms makers.

Cooper wrote, that after the beginning of the 20th century, international bankers under the leadership of the Rothschilds, were inclined to acquire interest in all these three agencies. The bankers were significant customers without a doubt and even without controlling financial interest, exercised influence surpassed only by the respective governments. (Cooper: 22).

My extensive research has brought me to the conclusion that at the least some, if not the majority, of history and news has been rewritten, obscured, manipulated, and interpreted to serve certain purposes. Arthur R. Thompson's book titled *To the Victor Go the Myths & Monuments* is most telling to uphold the theory. He quotes George Orwell author of *1984* and *Animal Farm*: "The most effective way to destroy people is to deny and obliterate their own understanding of their history." (439). He also quotes Cicero: "To be ignorant of what occurred before you were born is to always remain a child." (443.)

The "Secret Elite" are well-documented by authors Quigley, Docherty, and Macgregor in future chapters. Docherty and MacGregor wrote; "The Secret Elite dictated the writing and teaching of history, from the ivory towers of academia down to the smallest of schools. They carefully controlled the publication of official government papers, the selection of documents for inclusion in the official version of the history of the First World War and refused access to any evidence that might betray their covert existence. Incriminating documents were burned, removed from official records, shredded, falsified or deliberately rewritten, so that what remained for genuine researchers, and historians was carefully selected material." (Docherty: 15).

Thompson penned in his beginning message that he eventually came to the realization that the "history" we read may be distorted by an author's bias or to serve a purpose for a specific underlying agenda.

In his book, author Search wrote:

> With the control of business the money interest controlled the advertising put into the newspapers. When they could not own the paper, they could and most always would, control and influence their editorial policy, and worst of all, prohibit anything even of news value being printed that might tend to cast the reflection or doubts on their nefarious and inhuman grasp on the money and commerce of the nation. (Search: 111).

In 1939, F. Yeats-Brown (an editorial writer himself) wrote *European Jungle* and therein gave a very succinct and thought-provoking overview of newspapers. He wrote that newspapers without advertising are unprofitable. He quoted the then late Lord Riddell, who "...once told me with a chuckle that advertisers prefer a newspaper with no opinions at all, written for readers with a tidy allowance of cash but a slender allowance of brains." Yeats-Brown arrived at the conclusion that "big business" ran the newspapers. (Yeats-Brown: 14).

He believed that authoritarian rulers seldom sought loans. The financier wants change and active financial and trade markets with a need for capital, meaning bank loans. He maintained that the average newspaper reader will read the news that is reported reflective of the owners and supporters of the newspapers, *i.e.* the "rich" men.

Allow me to return to *Merchants of Death* by Engelbrecht and Hannigan, who wrote in their 1934 book that arms merchants could not neglect the powerful press, which sometimes they bought and owned, or at least in which they maintained a controlling interest. The same press individuals, managers or owners, will be placed on arms company boards. (Engelbrecht: 145).

In 1905, Russia needed French bank loans. There was massive corruption then and later in Russia with its "scandals, mutinies, and revolutions," all of which would have scared off French investors. Arms merchant M. Schneider had retained members of the press, and the stories were written to withhold bad Russian news. (Engelbrecht: 136).

Could this have been a not-so-long ago censored or "fake news," apparently also prevalent in our own day? The *Columbia Journalism Review* included an article in which the author quoted a Thomas Jefferson 1807 letter to one John Norvell: "It is a melancholy truth, that a suppression of the press could not more compleately (*sic*) deprive the nation of its benefits, than is done by its abandoned prostitution to falsehood," the sitting president wrote and continued with, "Nothing can now be believed which is seen in a newspaper. Truth itself becomes suspicious by being put into that polluted vehicle." In the article, Alexis de Tocqueville is quoted as saying, "His concerns... (were about) active manipulation of the truth for political ends."[1] Some things, like human nature and "cupidity," never change. This certainly rings true in an era of so-called "fake news."

Several sources have come to my attention that indicate that what we read, see, and hear is now under the control of just six media entities: Comcast, the Walt Disney Company, News Corporation, Time Warner, Viacom. And CBS Corporation.[2] Could it be possible that what the masses are being fed, may be a party line orchestrated by the "powers that be?" Perhaps even coordinated by some of the "usual suspects" documented in these writings?

With a chance encounter in around 2006 in a Dallas post office, it was my pleasure to become acquainted with a Korean War veteran by the name of Robert Ampudia Whitt. He had been an executive in Latin America in the newsmagazine publishing business for many years. The view from a man in the media trenches follows.

In his book *Expat,* he expresses his opinion about the media with which he was experienced. He believed in some parts of Latin America the government is antagonistic to any media reports that write honestly about governmental affairs. The editorial content of private media magazines is not manipulatable by governments, so those media were constant targets of intimidation. There were some that were secretly mouthpieces for their governments.

With his personal experiences brought to bear, he wrote in 2007 that in the United States there is, "... political media bias by major newspapers and periodical publications, (who) use every scheme and trick to influence the American people with deliberate partisanship, but without overt sponsorship from the government, political party, or individuals. The U.S. politicians happily go along with the printed bias that has been purposely leaked and abetted by lobbyists and others with vested interests." (Whitt: 24). One may assume that news and editorials bear the stamp of the philosophies and political leanings of the owners.

I rest my media case with examples as far back as 1807 up to the present!

Propaganda

> Definition: "Any association, systematic scheme, or concerted movement for the propagation of a particular doctrine or practice." — *Oxford English Dictionary.*

The term propaganda was not in extensive use prior to World War I. The term originated in 1622 by Pope Gregory XV to counter the worldwide spread of Protestantism. He formed the Office for the Propagation of the Faith (*Congregatio de propaganda fide),* established, and understandably so, to further Catholic missionary efforts. Subsequent to the several centuries-long original meaning of the term in the Pope's original usage, propaganda later was defined as materials that denoted "lies, half-truths, selective history or any of the other tricks that we associate with 'propaganda' now." (Bernays: 9).

Beginning in 1915, propaganda became a staple for governments, when they began concerted and organized efforts, to incite among their people through use of every means of media with the aim to inform and bring their populations to agreement in the conduct of warfare. (Bernays: 11).

Edward Bernays' *Propaganda* (1928) had in its Introduction (2005 edition) by Mark Crispin Miller the following description of Bernays' work; "His vision seems quite modest. The world introduced by 'public relations' will be but 'a smoothly functioning society,' where all of us are guided imperceptibly throughout our lives by a benign elite of rational manipulators." (Bernays: 16)

Bernays in his own words describes this vision in what cannot at all be defined as "modest":

> We are governed, our minds molded, our taste formed, our ideas suggested, largely by men we have never heard of. This is a logical result of the way in which our democratic society is organized. Vast numbers of human beings must cooperate in this manner if they are to live together as a smoothly functioning society. Our invisible governors are, in many cases, unaware of the identity of their fellow members in the inner cabinet....Whatever attitude one chooses toward this condition, it remains a fact that in almost every act of our daily lives, whether in the sphere of politics or business, in our social conduct or ethical thinking, we are dominated by the relatively small number of persons...who understand the mental processes and psychosocial patterns of the masses. It is they who pull the wires which control the public mind, who harness old social forces and contrive new ways to bind and guide the world. (Bernays: 28,29).

I do not know about you, but this is an earthshaking and

monumental statement from a man, who had incredible and far-reaching influence on the propagation and expansion of propaganda, which assuredly has not been to the advantage of humanity, as witnessed by the number of wars we have experienced and the state of the culture and civilization today!

This lays the groundwork for an understanding by the ones, who fight, suffer, and die in wars, to comprehend how management of ideas, purposes, and causes are communicated to us by the "elite" and the "manipulators." Knowing that propaganda is utilized to form the opinions of the people for purposes dictated by the "elite," is power and strength for the courage to question what we are told! It is power to question what we've been told all through history as to why governments have made decisions to carry out national policy, especially as it relates to those of us, who carry out those policies through military means.

The sophisticated and scientific employment of the techniques of propaganda appear to have had a beginning prior to World War I in Great Britain to derive support for a war against Germany. It was centered in an organization called Wellington House, which by 1921 became the Tavistock House of Human Relations. (Coleman *Tavistock:* Foreword).

Author John Coleman, previously introduced, goes into extensive detail in the formulation and ensuing movement of this propaganda machine. He relates that this British entity is responsible for the psychological manipulation techniques utilized for decades to effect what the establishments desire to accomplish. This quote is repeated from chapter three due to its significance. Major General John Rawlings Reese, one of the leaders of the Institute, explained their methodology in 1954:

> Their job is to apply the advanced techniques of psychological warfare as we know them to whole population groups that will grow ever larger, so that whole populations may be more easily controlled. In a world driven completely mad, groups of Tavistock psychologists

linked to each other, capable of influencing the political and governmental field must be arbiters, the power cabal. (Coleman *Tavistock:* 145).

If anyone is still on the fence regarding whether or not to lend credence to "conspiracies" and "elites" and profits by any means, open another can of beer or mix another martini or head on out to the local watering hole, but whatever you do, do not leave your comfort zone.

Coleman's book on the Tavistock Institute was published in 2005, and of course, propaganda will be utilized to dispute John Coleman's mere existence, much less credibility and accurate research. However, I can personally verify, as I have said before, he is a real person because I talked to him by phone. Either he has a vivid imagination, has made everything up, or he is to be accepted as informed and credible. I choose the latter. His catalogue of published books is extensive.

The original major propagators of propaganda utilized for World War I were Walter Lippman and Edward Bernays. (Coleman *Tavistock: i*).

Walter Hurt wrote *The Truth About the Jews* in 1922. In this book, he included his opinion on a variety of topics. Witness what he said about propaganda which I believe is very compelling. He quoted a *Saturday Evening Post* editorial of some unknown date:

> Propaganda is a slow poison, based on international envy, malice, ignorance, and hate. It has been an affair of government, directed by rulers and diplomats, iterated and reiterated by press and platform, and finally parroted by every fathead and bullhead until the national psychology is saturated with it. Its aim may be disguised as concern for the safety of the nation or cloaked under a desire to save an erring sister country, but the purpose of propaganda always is to foster hate and its end is war. (Hurt: 32).

He quoted another *Post* editorial from 1922 or before:

> The world needs new leaders, men who will plan as patiently and directly for peace as its old ones planned patiently and directly for war.... Only by peace can the world be saved morally and economically. The first step toward it is a stoppage of the propaganda that engenders hate and leads to talk of war...The world needs a new psychology and even more a new morality-- a morality that will brand the man who foments hate between nations, whether he be king, statesman, journalist, or demagogue, as a dangerous criminal. (Hurt: 187).

Hurt wrote this almost 100 years ago. With the dawn of the nuclear age, stronger and more deadly weapons, and rogue nations with nuclear bombs, what the world always needs is new leaders. This especially holds true in those nations with dictators and religious/political theocratic leaders, who can only be changed from within or through economic strangling.

This chapter is closed out with a final comment by Edward Bernays, who, by the way, is the nephew of Sigmund Freud, if that adds some special import to the influences he may have encountered and what he writes; "Propaganda will never die out. Intelligent men must realize that propaganda is the modern instrument by which they can fight for productive ends and help to bring order out of chaos." (Bernays: 168). The questions that follow for caring citizens are first, what are appropriate, fair, and just "productive ends" and secondly, what "order" should be sought, New World or God's?

SECTION III:

RELIGION – GOD AND WAR

Chapter 11:

Protestant Reformation and Religious Wars

Overview

It is with the utmost "fear and trembling" that I undertake writing about "religion." Allow me to state up front that writing about Protestants, Anglicans, Catholics, Jews, or Muslims in no way necessarily relates to individual current adherents of any of the four major faith groups, nor to their modern-day faith expressions, and assuredly not to their dogma or theology. In the case of "religious" Jews and to those, who identify themselves as Jews by whatever identification other than their faith group, since Jews are most controversial, I will go outside strictly religious factors in my coverage of them. The subjects I cover relate to the institutions and entities in a larger view in past and present historical contexts. Official histories and individual members of the four faiths will dispute some of what I write, however, it is illuminating and educative to indicate different opinions that I've discovered in the literature I have studied.

Protestant Reformation

Any discussion of warfare and casualties must begin in 1517, when Martin Luther triggered the Protestant Reformation. The movement proved to be a distinct threat to the Roman Catholic Church, headquartered with power for hundreds of years in the Vatican in Rome.

One rendering of the causes of the Reformation is expressed by author Hurt, who maintains the view that it was based originally on an "economic revolt," rather than a moral one, but decidedly evolved to a vicious and horrendous blight on humanity, when religious causes became predominant. He writes that Pope Leo X required massive financial resources for the rebuilding of St.

Peter's Cathedral in Rome. The sale of papal indulgences was undertaken as a fund-raiser. Germany's Archbishop Albert in whose diocese was Wittenberg, the home of Martin Luther, began very devotedly to undertake these commission sales, perhaps due to his own debt owed to the banker family of the Fuggers in Augsburg. (Hurt: 226,227).

Martin Luther, possibly having been thwarted in his own designs and supposed personal ambition to become the Pope himself, seized on the financial drain to coffers of German princes and bankers with the movement of monies to Italy and out of Germany, to begin his movement culminating in the Protestant Reformation. (Hurt: 227). It had always been my opinion that it was primarily theological, but, perhaps, the sale of indulgences was a trigger. For whatever the obviously much broader reasoning of Martin Luther to affect the schism from Roman Catholicism, this epic event in 1517 has caused incredible conflict and bloodshed. When one truly studies history and focuses on religious wars, it becomes immensely disheartening and manifestly saddening due to its horror. I cannot but believe that our Creator looked with great sadness on what his humanity brought and perpetrated on each other, but this was a major example of "spiritual warfare."

A very cursory rendering of the cataclysmic and truly earth-shaking event in Europe of Luther's break from the Roman Catholic Church is merited. My summary of some of the major events coincident with the religious wars is derived from David J.B. Trim's article in the May-June 2010 issue of *Liberty Magazine*. The larger reference for the article is footnoted.[1]

Beginning in the 1520s there was ongoing bloody fighting throughout Europe that was essentially religious in nature with a few socio-economic causes. In central and southern Europe Christians fought Muslims and in central and northwestern Europe what could be termed "confessional" wars were between newly-bred Protestants and Catholics. Trim defines them as, "The division between Protestant and Catholic caused or intensified numerous conflicts, resulting in some of the longest lasting, bloodiest, and most bitterly contested and destructive wars in history." (Trim: 1).

Germany:

In Germany from 1524 to 1525, peasants were motivated by one Thomas Muntzer, originally a disciple of Martin Luther, but distinctly extreme and fanatical. He eventually was banished. The then-named Peasants' War was not only about religion, but about socioeconomic elements. Luther was not supportive of this uprising, which became the first post-Reformation war. In 1534 and 1535, another conflict began between Protestants and Catholic armies. After this, the conflicts were decidedly religious only. (Trim: 1).

Another Example in Germany:

In 1531, German Lutheran princes and cities formed protective alliances against the Emperor Charles V. This Protestant movement expanded utilizing force and by 1546 full warfare broke out between the opposing religious bodies. "Confessional" wars were caused and sustained due to religion. After the 1555 Treaty of Augsburg the city-states or ruling princes in any given geographic locale established one faith or the other as the established one and conflicting persons either changed faith or were required to depart. It was unchallenged until the beginning of the 1618 Thirty Years' War. (Trim: 2).

Switzerland:

In this country, Huldrych Zwingli carried on the Protestant revolts where Protestant cantons fought Catholic cantons. Zwingli was in the thick of the fighting for his ideals and he died in the second war called Kappel. Armies in Bern and Zurich prevailed to preserve Protestantism. (Trim: 2).

Reform Protestantism:

A brand of very strict Protestantism evolved in Geneva, Switzerland in the 1540s. It was "Calvinism," (fellow adherents were Puritans in England and North America, Huguenots in France, and Presbyterians in Scotland). This movement brought on more and territorially-expanded religious wars. It was sometimes termed Reform. Calvinists were adamantly opposed to the Papacy. The militancy of Calvinists did not support the somewhat amicable peace established in Germany. In the 90 years after 1560 the militancy of the Calvinists/Reformists was significantly responsible for; "...the extraordinary extent, duration, bitterness, and bloodiness of the wars that raged across France, the Low Countries, the British Isles, and Germany." (Trim: 3).

France:

The Reformed Church members in France were called Huguenots, who were a minority surrounded by a Catholic majority. There were nine civil wars over forty years. The original horrendous calamity was suffered by the Huguenots in France when 3,000 of them were massacred in Paris in August 1572, and close to 7,000 more in other outlying areas of France.[2] In later engagements, English, German, Scottish, Dutch, and Swiss troops helped the Huguenots and Spanish, Italian, German, and Swiss troops aided joined the Catholics.

Netherlands:

Between 1567-1648 the Dutch fought Spain. Many of the Dutch were Calvinists, but included on their side Lutherans, Anabaptists, a few Jews, and even some Catholics. This conflict also had its political and economic aspects. This conflict was unique in that the protagonists agreed on everything except religion. Spain was very adamant in its demands on behalf of their Catholic faith and their only allowance was a time frame in which rebellious Protestants must depart the Netherlands. Eventually the Reformed Church became essentially the state church of the Netherlands. The cross currents of religious alliances in Europe brought England, Scotland, France and the Protestant German princes to support

208

the Dutch and when these groups were at peace with Spain, volunteer fighters of English, Scottish, and Huguenot backgrounds came to assist the Dutch. (Trim: 3).

The Thirty Years' War, 1618-1648:

Bohemian Calvinists were persecuted by the reign of Ferdinand II, archduke of Austria, Holy Roman Empire, and elector of Bohemia. The Calvinists invited a Calvinist German prince to replace Ferdinand, whom they considered toppled. The Jesuit influence raised its head in this conflict in that Ferdinand II had been schooled by Jesuits and he was of the conviction that by military warfare he could overturn the Lutheran Reformation. Another member of royalty in Europe, Sebastian I of Portugal also was trained by Jesuits. Both these rulers were opposed to any balance with anyone who was against Catholicism, an "enemy" of their faith. Ferdinand's approach brought on what can be called "Europe's tragedy."[3]

Ferdinand's militancy in support of his Catholic faith brought on this war. Eventually it spread to encompass the Lutheran kingdoms of Denmark-Norway and Sweden and brought the Spanish and Dutch conflict into its umbrella. Amazingly enough, Catholic France entered the war on the Protestant side in the early 1630s bringing the political rivalry of France and the Hapsburgs into the equation as a feature of rivalries of empires into the equation. However, it was begun strictly as a religious conflict and Trim wrote the following; "However, this was both started and prolonged by confessional rivalry; and confessional hatred helped make it so destructive of both human life and property that it was probably the greatest disaster to affect Europe between the Black Death and the First World War." The result in 1648 through the Peace of Westphalia brought the decision that sovereign units of rule would henceforth be responsible for any future persecution of "dissenters and dissidents" upon their own prerogatives. (Trim: 4).

Chapter 12:

Protestantism – Anglicans, Pilgrims, Puritans, Congregationalists, and Unitarians

[Author's note: In the interest of full disclosure, I worship in the Anglican tradition, having been Christened in the Episcopal denomination as an infant.]

As a matter of record, the 1215 Magna Carta, signed by King John, set an initial precedent that the English church is separate from the government. After Martin Luther's break with Roman Catholicism in 1517 it was not until 1536 that Henry VIII dismantled the Catholic abbeys and monasteries throughout his domain. An Anglican website posts the following:

> There is a public perception, especially in the United States, that Henry VIII created the Anglican church in anger over the Pope's refusal to grant his divorce, but the historical record indicates that Henry spent most of his reign challenging the authority of Rome, and that the divorce issue was just one of a series of acts that collectively split the English church from the Roman church in much the same way that the Orthodox Church had split off five hundred years before.[1]

Obviously, the public perception is that the break with Rome was all due to the King's desire for divorce, however, there were other issues. He had passed in 1534 the Act of Supremacy in Parliament based upon a nationalism concept beginning to emerge in Henry's latching on to the theory of divine right of kings. In 1533 Thomas Cranmer had become Henry's Archbishop of Canterbury, but when Catholic Mary Tudor (Henry's daughter by his Catholic first wife Catherine) became queen, she had Cranmer burned at the stake in Oxford in 1556.[2]

Henry VIII's member of the King's Council, Thomas Cromwell, oversaw a period of extraordinary horror against the Pope and the Catholic Church. Cromwell replaced Thomas More, who had been the Chancellor to Henry VIII. Cromwell went on the attack against Catholic monks in the abbeys and monasteries. Henry VIII assaulted many he considered heretics in his realm. Cromwell oversaw this effort, noting a situation characterized by "... destroying beautiful abbeys, taking away their valuables, tearing the lead off the roofs and pulling down the bells to sell them to the highest bidders."[3]

Many "heretics" were killed. An uprising to the king's authority was met with severe consequences (i.e., beheadings). Some 616 abbeys were confiscated by King Henry. As expected, the new property wealth went to the king and his elitists.[4]

Mary Tudor was the queen of England for five years from 1553-1558. She was called "Bloody Mary" because under her reign Protestants were persecuted and 300 of them were burned at the stake as heretics. She was intent in turning the country back to the Catholic religion of her mother, the Spaniard Catherine of Aragon, Henry's VIII's first wife.[5] Elizabeth, the daughter of Ann Boleyn, Henry's second wife, became Queen Elizabeth in 1558, when Mary died.

From 1560 to 1573 during the reign of Protestant (Anglican) Queen Elizabeth I, an extraordinary conflict arose in Scotland, beginning with a civil war started by the Presbyterians to combat Catholic oppression, followed by three English invasions of Scotland, which ultimately established a Protestant government. Elizabeth's military forces fought Spain from 1585-1603 in the Netherlands, France, Spain, Portugal, Ireland, the Caribbean, and South America during that period. This was highlighted by the English defeat of the Spanish Armada in 1588. (Trim: 4).

When Elizabeth died in 1603, the Tudor line of succession died with her and the Stuart line began with Scotsman James I, who brought the three British kingdoms together. He made peace with

Spain, but his son Charles I started up the warring again in 1625. England separated herself and stayed out of the Thirty Years' War, but the royal religious policy grated on the Reformed Protestants of both England and Scotland and on Ireland's majority Catholics. (Trim: 4)

The internal dissension between Reformed Protestants and Anglicans caused civil wars in Britain from 1641-1651. There were massacres and atrocities in all of England to include Ireland during this time. Dedicated Calvinist Oliver Cromwell, a Puritan, led the Puritan Revolution, which overthrew the monarchy and set up a short-lived British republic.[6]

The Reformation brought on between the 1520s until about 1650 a series of horrendous and bloody wars in the Christian nations of Europe — France, Spain, Portugal, Austria, Sweden, the Dutch Republic and Britain.

Protestants in Early America

Huguenots:

In a reference for the early Huguenots, who migrated to Florida, there is a fascinating tidbit of history that relates to the time in April 1517 when Martin Luther, then a Catholic priest, entered a small German town and observed that an agent of the Pope had before him a long line of individuals, who were receiving instruments, called Indulgences, for which they paid, that provided the purchaser and his relatives-both dead and alive, absolution from any punishment for past or future sins. Martin Luther was driven to write his 95 Theses, which these sales indicated, were reflective of a violation of the Catholic doctrine.

From this epochal encounter emanated the Protestant Reformation and one of the Protestant groups that was formed in France was the Huguenots. By the 1560s a group of Huguenots left France for a region of Florida north of what is now the city of St. Augustine. (Surprised that there was a history of European colonization in what became America prior to the English settlement at Jamestown in 1607?) This Protestant colony was considered by Philip II of Spain as a trespass on land which the Holy Church had bequeathed to the Spanish Crown. Besides the obvious incursion into Spanish territory, the Huguenots were considered heretics by the Spaniards because they adhered to a faith that was in opposition to Catholicism. An expedition under a very cold-blooded commander, Pedro Menendez, was sent to remove them. In September 1565 the Spaniards massacred the French Huguenots.[7] (The site of their fort has been restored and was visited by your author). Violence was carried into the New World by the atrocities and casualties caused by religious differences.

Other Huguenots (French Protestant refugees) were more successful in settling Virginia on land provided by the Virginia colony. In 1700, the Virginia General Assembly established the King William Parish, which allowed the Huguenots to have their own church in which to worship, and they settled on both sides of the James River.

Anglicans:

The Anglican faith was originally established as a distinct part of the Jamestown colony in Virginia in 1607 and an Anglican minister was a part of the early colony. A tradition in Europe of churches working directly with the government had been normal in Europe for many hundreds of years. This concept carried over into early Virginia and Virginia's ruling elite worked in total affiliation with the Anglican churches in Virginia.

The Virginia General Assembly required that office-holders be Anglicans. Taxes were levied to pay the clergy salaries and support the actual church buildings. In their favor, the local parishes oversaw support of orphans and the poor in their communities.

Religious diversity was introduced when immigrants of other faith

214

traditions settled in Virginia. A break from control and involvement of the Anglican church influence in the government represented one of the causes behind the separation from Great Britain. The Evangelical movement and the rationalism of the Enlightenment set roots in the colonies. Thomas Jefferson in 1786 wrote for the Virginia Assembly his Statute for Religious Freedom. This established for the first time in history a new way for individuals to live in a society and not be controlled by a central church authority.[8]

Pilgrims, Puritans, Congregationalists, and Unitarians in New England:

I took a memorable and educational trip to Massachusetts several years ago. In Quincy, Massachusetts, I visited the crypts in the Unitarian Church, where President John Adams and his son, President John Quincy Adams, were interred with their wives. Noted on my tour in Lexington, Concord, and Plymouth were more solid stone church buildings that were Unitarian, and Congregational churches were also within close proximity.

My curiosity was aroused and finally satisfied at Plymouth, Massachusetts. Up the hill from the landing place of the original Pilgrims was a town square. A venerable stone church stood on the supposed site of the original Pilgrim church built in 1622. It was marked as Unitarian denomination. On the same square was the white frame Church of the Pilgrimage. Finding the doors locked I walked across the square to the church offices, where I met the Rev. Gary Marks, who was most generous and gracious in time given to us to take us for a tour of his church and to help me understand the religious history of New England, the heritage of the Pilgrims, the Puritans, Congregationalism, and Unitarianism.

Marks' "The Church of the Pilgrimage in Town Square, Plymouth, Massachusetts, continues to carry on the faith and understanding of church government of the Pilgrim fathers and mothers." At Scrooby, England, in 1606, there began a "Separatist" movement of Christians following the effort of other European Protestants to reform the way in which they worshiped. By separating from the Church of England, they also separated themselves from the England, which they loved very much. The Plymouth church, which I visited with the pastor, considers itself in the succession of the original "owning the Covenant" tradition back to 1606. This early Pilgrim church was forced to move to Leyden, Holland, from which in 1620 the original Pilgrim group sailed to America and into Cape Cod, eventually landing at Plymouth.[9]

In 1630, Puritans settled in Boston and Salem, Massachusetts. This group never officially broke away from the Anglican Church of England. The Puritans believed the Church of England should be purged of any Catholic influence. Pilgrims and Puritans basically merged to establish the "Congregational" denomination. The Pilgrim tradition comprised the roots of what was to become the American democracy. Therefore, it is of the utmost value in its importance to the later United States of America. The following is a good description of how the Pilgrims governed themselves:

> The Pilgrim Church was composed of free people who ordered their own affairs. Each member had an equal vote in important matters affecting the church. This meant, of course, that the governance of the church was determined by democratic principles.... They desired to be independent of any ecclesiastical hierarchy and the imposition of forms of worship contained, for instance, in The Prayer Book of the Church of England... They drew up and signed the famed Mayflower Compact as a basic document which would govern both themselves and those 'strangers' who arrived with them and were not members of their congregation [10]

The outgrowth of this faith tradition is "Congregationalism," because each congregation controls itself without any outside interference from a higher body or authority.

The original concept of the Pilgrims' religious experience existed in the original Plymouth church and congregation in the Trinitarian tradition (belief in a Triune God, the Father, the Son, Jesus the Christ, and the Holy Spirit) until 1801. On January 1, 1800 a new minister was selected for the church. He was the Rev. James Kendall. He became known to many in the congregation as a "liberal preacher," whose theology reflected Unitarianism. In Plymouth, as in many other communities of New England, when the conflict developed theologically between Unitarians and Trinitarians, a vote was held and by a simple majority, the building and its furnishings and records went to the majority. Often the Trinitarians were compelled to accept being evicted and moved to begin anew in maintaining their traditional "Congregationalism" in a totally new physical location within the community. The web site of the Church of the Pilgrimage indicates that they are wedded to Trinitarianism and their separation from Unitarian tendencies in 1801 "...was an act of restoring confidence in the insights of those who first 'made covenant' in the hamlet of Scrooby in 1606, adhered to that covenant in Amsterdam and Leyden, and secured its perpetuation in new Plimouth from sixteen twenty until this very day." This congregation became a member in 1957 of the United Church of Christ.

Our guide and tutor, the Reverend Gary Marks, the 30th pastor of the Church of the Pilgrimage wrote:

> We have freely joined ourselves by a covenant of God into a church, into a community of the gospel, to walk in God's ways made known, or to be made known to us, according to our best efforts. We commit ourselves in generosity in service and mission, God assisting us.[11]

The other church edifice on that Plymouth Town Square as of 1961 became a member of the Unitarian Universalist Association. This church expresses itself in this manner on a plaque:

> The church of Scrooby Leyden and the Mayflower gathered on this hillside in 1620 has ever since preserved unbroken records and maintained a continuous ministry its first covenant being still the basis of its fellowship. In reverent

memory of its Pilgrim founders this fifth meeting-house was erected A. D. MDCCCXCVII. (1897).[12]

Discontented with my understanding of this rift/schism in the New England churches my study led me to some references. In the 1630s some 20,000 English Puritans migrated to New England and formed local parish congregations. Puritans rejected any ecclesiastical or civil body control over the local church. It was the Puritan John Winthrop who wrote about walking in "the Liberty of the Gospel' and for the Puritan churches becoming," ... a shining example of justice, peace and good order, that 'city set upon a hill' of Jesus' teaching." The Puritans sought to establish churches based on the Biblical pattern of liberty.[13]

I have always wondered how the break from these original stirring principles of faith evolved. Many second-generation New Englanders were hesitant to publicly confess their transgressions and need for a "conversion experience." By the mid-17th century, while the original generation was still living, membership began to be allowed for adults that did not believe it necessary to have been "regenerated," which is presumably what is spoken of today in Evangelical circles as being "Born Again." The heart of the Unitarian controversy became:

> The division-between those who believe that there were certain dramatic and specific and steps to love and faith in Christian life and those who awaited a slow and individualistic development of mature love and trust-would more than a century later, be at the heart of the arguments in the Unitarian controversy.[14]

The spiritual division attained an economic dimension when an early New England businessman rebelled against the Puritan laws that controlled such things as the profit that traders were allowed to achieve in their business transactions. There was a distinct belief that people were not to take advantage of others in the Puritan ethic. "By end of the century (17th) Puritan authority had lost its power to do more than utter ineffective admonitions against uncontrolled capitalistic behavior." By 1699, "… A group of Boston merchants, led by John Leverett and William and Thomas Brattle, issued a manifesto calling for the organization of the new church along 'broad and Catholick' lines." The power of this group of businesspeople was manifested when layman Leverett, replaced the conservative minister Increase Mather as the President of Harvard College in 1707." (Thus passed the original religious principles behind the founding of Harvard).[15]

The Great Awakenings begun in 1734 placed some brakes on the movement toward more liberal doctrinal theology. However, Boston minister Charles Chauncy, "deplored the excessive emotionalism, even hysteria, evoked in revival services, which did not consistently lead to a life of good works." (He surely would have been most critical of the happenings at 21st century athletic events all over the globe!). Criticism of the Trinity and other orthodox doctrines became commonplace. Chauncy advocated that "the use of reason was a better means of religious growth." (With all of the "unreasonable people" I have encountered in my life, I would take issue with Chauncy). Despite the deep theological divide that was developing in American religious expression, both sides united in support of the American Revolution.[16]

By the end of the 18th century, the following passage reflects the key factor I believe in – the deep and massive divide we are witnessing in our public life in America and our civil and political condition. According to *The Quiet Radical: The Biography of Samuel Longfellow* by Joseph C. Abdo, the religious liberals in our land can be characterized as follows:

> They rejected as unbiblical the traditionally held Calvinist doctrines of original sin, total depravity, predestination and the Trinity. They adopted positive doctrines of the nature of humanity and the possibility of continuing moral spiritual and intellectual growth. (81).

In 1805, a liberal named Henry Ware, was appointed professor to the vacant Hollis Chair of Divinity at Harvard. The Calvinists lost. Therefore, a new training school for ministers in the Calvinist tradition was established as the Andover Theological Seminary in 1808. The final rift occurred in the middle 1800s. Eventually, some 250 of New England's original parish churches formally took the name Unitarian, having been in fact Unitarian already for fifty or seventy-five years, as had occurred in Plymouth in 1801.[17]

A non-official web site in an article titled "Unitarianism in New England" had this quote at its head: "'Unitarian' means belief in a single God rather than a 'trinitarian' or triune 'God in three persons.'" (Not too difficult to differentiate Unitarians from orthodox Christians, especially Evangelicals, is it? Each to his own belief. I cast no aspersions on this denomination. They are free to believe what they will. That is part of the freedom of religion in America which we patriots have served for 250 years). The Unitarian Universalists are a product of a development spiritually that may be defined as *Deism*, "the belief that *God was truly understood through the power of Reason and Experience...Unitarian Universalists* promote peace, tolerance, religious freedom, democracy, assistance to the disadvantaged, and all persons' right to search for *religious fulfillment in their own way.*"[18]

Chapter 13:

Catholicism

Overview

The source for the following information regarding the Jesuits is the book *The Jesuits* (1987) by a laicized former Jesuit priest, Malachi Martin. His credibility and veracity are attested to by this review in the *World Economic Review:* "A Vatican insider for many years, Martin... opens up one of the strangest and most lethal deceptions since the Trojan horse... The most chilling and controversial portrait of the Society of Jesus in over three hundred years."

Basque Ignatius of Loyola, basically an unknown personage, founded the Jesuits in 1540. Their service to the Papacy and the Papacy's Roman Catholic Church, much less to mankind overall is immeasurable. Martin writes, "...the Society has withstood every test of time and circumstance except one: the perversion of the role, rule, and spirit he assigned it." (Martin *Jesuits*: 26). Eighteenth-century German theorist Norvalis wrote:

> ... never before in the course of the world's history had such a Society appeared. The old Roman Senate itself did not lay schemes for world domination with greater certainty of success. Their history is replete with 38 canonized Saints, 134 holy men declared 'Blessed,' 36 already declared 'Venerable,' and 115 considered to be 'Servants of God.' (Martin *Jesuits*: 27).

Their first mission was to counter Martin Luther's Reformation, Calvin, and Henry VIII of England. "They infiltrated hostile territories in disguise and moved around underground... That Church (Catholic) is a hierarchy of bishops in communion with that Bishop in Rome... Any other church institution is rank heresy, the child of Satan..." (Martin *Jesuits*: 28). Thus go many people of other faiths through the centuries!

Jesuits were educators without peer, educators of, "Voltaire, Luis Bunuel, Fidel Castro, and Alfred Hitchcock." (Martin *Jesuits*: 29). (To this list of well-known luminaries must be added your humble, non-luminary author for ninth and tenth grade at Gonzaga College High School, Washington D.C.). They were the first missionaries to go to "Kambaluc, Cathay, Sarkand, Shrinagar, (and many other exotic locales unknown except by atlas)... Mount Everest." The first even to Tibet. From their origin, they truly lived and died for the Pope because, "...he represented Peter the Apostle who represented the Christ they believed was Savior." (Martin *Jesuits*: 30).

By the mid-1700s, Jesuits were integral to all alliances of a political nature in Europe, "... an individual post with every government, an advisory capacity with every great man and each powerful woman...the list of history's greats frequented by Jesuits stretches on for pages... Oliver Cromwell, Philip II of Spain, Louis XIV of France, Catherine the Great, Cardinal Richelieu, Queen Christina of Sweden, Mary Queen of Scots, Napoleon, Washington, Garibaldi, Mussolini, Chiang Kai-shek..." (Martin *Jesuits*: 31).

The Jesuit Father General is called "The Black Pope." In 1773, Pope Clement XIV abolished the Society of Jesus. 41 years later in 1814, Pope Pius VII brought them back into existence." (Martin *Jesuits*: 30,31).

Throughout their fabled history, Jesuits were "expelled and banned from various countries -- France, Germany, Austria, England, Belgium, Mexico, Sweden, Switzerland." The expulsions from those countries was an indication that the government "was determined to eliminate the authority and jurisdiction of the Roman Pope." (Martin *Jesuits*: 33).

The vow Jesuits took was one of absolute obedience. They were begun as a military organization as Soldiers of Christ, their dual purposes were, "…to propagate the religious doctrine and the moral law of the Roman Catholic Church and to defend the rights and prerogatives of that same Roman Pope." (Martin *Jesuits*: 41).

Rare, but regular, occasions existed wherein the Society of Jesus crossed the line between its spiritual mission to propagate the faith and to take advantage of its extraordinary influence among powerful individuals to cross over into political activity. (Martin *Jesuits*: 35).

We depart the strategic history of the Jesuits to address the tactical aspects of the life and experiences of a German aristocrat, who left the Jesuits after 14 years and wrote two volumes of books. Many insults were cast upon Jesuits throughout history. However, addressed will be some specific examples of involvement by Jesuits in what *Webster's Third New International Dictionary* defines as, "…one given to intrigue or equivocation; a crafty person." In its definition of the Jesuits, Dornseif's Dictionary calls out, "…two-faced, false, insidious, disassembling, perfidious… insincere, dishonorable, dishonest, untruthful." (Hoensbroech: 28). Strong terms indeed and definitely contrasted to the warm-hearted, giving, generous, and intellectual Jesuit Fathers and scholastics with whom your author was acquainted as his educators at Gonzaga in 1956-1958.

Count Paul Von Hoensbroech, Former Jesuit

In 1911, this German count wrote about his experiences as a Jesuit from 1878-1892 and obviously left the Order very disenchanted. He wrote, "What I state is my opinion of the Jesuit Order,… I belonged to the Order long enough not to need the judgment of others when I write against Jesuits and their system." (Hoensbroech: I-*xiv*).

He wrote this about his faith:

> Catholicism abounds in heights, depths, grandeurs, and elevations, mountain summits whence may be seen

religious and mystical vistas into metaphysical domains of fantastic beauty. Such are the Catholic doctrines concerning God, Salvation, and the Sacraments, which, in spite of their objective untruth, captivate the mind and heart like beautiful legends and symbolic pictures. (I-12).

The count assuredly strayed far from his origins and long-time family tradition of the Catholic faith. He recalled how his mother was totally consumed by all the trappings of her Catholic faith, medals, lives of saints, miraculous remedies of water/oils, "pious observances--sacraments, prayers, masses, meditations, novenas, fasts, and penances." Her Ultramontanism (total control by Rome) caused her to be both anti-Protestant and anti-Prussian. (I-13-15).

The count wrote about how Jesuits began to influence completely and totally every element of the life of his parents. At age 12 he was sent to a Jesuit school. The Jesuits were expelled from Germany in 1872. At the writing of his book, he said the Jesuits educated the children of the nobility and those of influence. He relates that, "... the first law known to a Jesuit is obedience -- *i.e.* the interest of the Order." (Hoensbroech: I-12). He joined the Jesuits at age 28 after completing legal studies and practicing law for two years.

Hoensbroech's volume 2 was found in a search.[1] Quotes from this volume will be referenced by page number. I cannot paraphrase adequately the more salient passages from this volume and therefore must quote his writings directly:

> From what has been and must still be said I have not the least doubt that the Order has secret statutes, which it guards carefully. The Jesuit Order merits the designation 'secret society' more than any other association....The monita privata Societatis Jesu (Secret Instructions of the Society of Jesus) first appeared in print at Cracow in 1612...directly after its appearance, the General of the Order, Mutius Vitelleschi, twice (in 1616 and 1617) instructed the German Jesuit, Gretser,...to refute it. (II-7).

The count relates that numerous copies of this document have been discovered through the years. (II-9). He asked rhetorically, "How may rich widows be kept well disposed toward the Society of Jesus?" He indicates Jesuits were appointed as confessors and spiritual guides, were involved in household affairs and in constant requests for donations. These observations were from the experience of his own family and relatives. He maintained, from his own time as a Jesuit, Jesuits were hard at work obtaining money from wives and widows "under the mask of piety (confession and exercises) and indicated it was a worldwide and ancient malpractice of Jesuit confessors and spiritual guides." (II-11).

> Its blind obedience, its 'Statement of Conscience,' its system of espionage and leveling, training to denunciation, its misuse of confession, and many other peculiarities, are immoral institutions which Catholic Christianity should repudiate, and in former times would doubtless have been repudiated. (II-424). The more recent founders of orders, St. Dominic and St. Francis, did not introduce into their foundations intellectual and religious slavery and bondage, enveloped in a garb of religious Christianity. (II-424).

He believed that Ignatius Loyola, although assuredly a saint, nevertheless was focused on "temporal success, power, and influence over other men." (II-424, 425).

The Reformation was introducing a new outlook on the world in which the Pope-God of the Middle Ages, the sovereign Lord of the whole world, was no longer to be in that position of power. (II-427, 428). The Jesuits were to be the "shock troopers," an auxiliary military unit to re-establish the ultramontane system, "with its secular and political kernel disguised under a garb of religion." (II-428). He continues, "Doubtless the counter-Reformation was in the main the work of the Jesuit Order, but for that reason it also bears the stamp of its spirit and is characterized by measures of violence, even by blood and iron." (II-430). The count wrote that the political thrust of the Order brought about its suppression by Pope Clement XIV. The Order had its issues of being thwarted by the Pope, when its special issues raised their heads, followed by irreverence toward bishops and cardinals. (II-430, 431).

The Order enjoyed many successes in its political efforts as attested to the multitudes of European courts, where for many years all these courts were subject to the Jesuits. The Jesuit confessors of the German Emperor and the French, Spanish, and Portuguese kings in the sixteenth and seventeenth centuries wielded incredible influence by means of a variety of intrigues.

Hoensbroech also said:

> ...continuously for several centuries, they have caused disturbance, confusion and breaches of peace; they have increased the outward splendor and glory of the Order and filled its coffers, but they cannot point to a single political action with an effect on the present and future, nor a single far-reaching successful undertaking in the domain of universal politics. (II-432).

> The Jesuit has become a popular, indispensable spiritual director in the families of the upper classes, above all with the women. In this position the most secretive activity becomes easy and safe for him. (II-443).

> Unfalsified history represents it as an organization injurious to religion, politics, society and civilization, which endeavors with inconsiderate egotism to make mankind serviceable to its selfish ends, and is directed towards their selfish ends... (II-444, 445).

> The Jesuit Order is an international organization which most profoundly and skillfully, in hundreds of disguises, excavates religion and State, knowledge, and civilization in order to fill the gap with its own spirit. And this spirit is a spirit of lust and power, of lying and deceit, of immoderate

self-seeking, of greed for the possessions of mankind, and even more for their freedom and independence-the spirit of irreligion and anti-Christianity. (II-446).

The Count became a Protestant, but even of that faith walk, there were imperfections. He said:

> ...The Prussian State Church is a very imperfect human institution which, both inwardly and outwardly, has lost much of its religious Christian character, and assumed instead that of bureaucratic formalism combined with dependence on State and Court. (II-452).

He had issues with both Catholicism and his Prussian brand of Protestantism:

> The 'religious' Head of the State Church,...Is the lord of the land, who at the same time is head of the Army and Navy, and commander of such and such foreign regiments; the dignitaries of the State Church (the Head of the Consistory, the consistories, General Superintendents, Superintendents, pastors), or state officials in the pay of the state... The whole system of court chaplains is-to speak openly for once, a system of court flunkeyism--far removed from the point of view of Christian Religion. (II-453).

Between his Catholic and Protestant experiences, he got "the big picture," when he maintained sincere and simple religion will be truly successful only as it adheres to the model followed by Christ and the Apostles as depicted in the Bible. (II-454). He was an equal opportunity observer of what he believed to be the inadequacies of both Catholicism and Prussian Protestantism.

His belief can be summarized with this phrase: "The light which has dawned on individual Catholics must dawn on all." (II-427).

[Author's note: I would express that this final statement is the essence of what is needed in Christendom today. "Light" is needed, not legalism and the "prosperity and social Gospel" that are so prevalent in so many proclamations from pulpits, both Protestant and Catholic.]

Historical Jesuits

On a tactical level an extraordinary resource came to my attention, a book titled *The Secret History of the Jesuits* by Edmund Paris, a Frenchman. (1983). I will reference the page only for Paris' writings.

Again, I indicate the precarious position in which I place myself in bringing into the open the research I have discovered about the Jesuits and their involvement in history. But I am reminded of Ephesians 4:25 (LASB), "Wherefore putting away lying, speak every man truth..." I do not necessarily subscribe in any form or fashion to all the barbs and diatribes addressed to Roman Catholicism and especially the Jesuits. As I have written, there are many of my fellow Christians who worship in the Roman Catholic tradition, who share my Trinitarian beliefs, that Jesus is the Son of God, crucified and resurrected so that we can have forgiveness of our sins and a pathway to eternal life, based on faith and not works! What I am writing is a history of the Jesuits.

However, from Paris' extensive historical research, he maintains and, "... boldly exposes the Vatican's involvement in world politics, intrigues, and the fomenting of wars throughout history." (Paris: Back cover). It would be intellectually dishonest not to include the research I have studied because much of it relates to warfare and casualties and assumption or maintenance of power and in this case religious power.

Paris' book is meticulously researched and noted. As the individual political and warfare periods are considered in this book and in my future writings, the Jesuits will be included wherein they are referenced in different historical periods. The previous information by Malachi Martin and Count Paul Van Hoensbroech definitively laid the groundwork for the credibility of significant influence by

Jesuits in matters of state and religion throughout the past five hundred years.

Paris quotes the temperament of Jesuits as, "A mixture of piety and diplomacy, asceticism, and worldly wisdom, mysticism, and cold calculation as was Loyola's character, so is the trademark of this Order."[2] Loyola's personal history includes, "In April 1527, the Inquisition placed Ignatius in prison to try him on the grounds of heresy." He was released and although forbidden to hold meetings, he again began to do so.[3] He is renowned for his textbook of the "Spiritual Exercises," a small book which addressed his goal:

> ... To raise a man to a certain ideal is to become master of his imagination... (imbuing) into him spiritual forces which he would find very difficult to eliminate later, forces more lasting than all the best principles and doctrines; these forces can come up again to the surface, sometimes after years of not even mentioning them, and become so imperative that the will finds itself unable to oppose any obstacle, and has to follow their irresistible impulse.[4]

[Author's note: Upon the completion of my marching in President John F. Kennedy's 1961 Inaugural Parade as a member of West Point's Corps of Cadets, my roommate Bob McGrath and I went to my former high school, Gonzaga, to visit with my former headmaster, Jesuit priest Anthony I. McHale. He recommended I read the "Spiritual Exercises." Never did.]

Paris believed that the Jesuits early on began, "... To concentrate on the souls of man, especially among ruling classes. Politics are their main field of action." Two methods were employed, "to be the confessors of the mighty and those in high places and the education of their children." (Paris: 33,34).

The Jesuits were selected by the Pope to have secret supporting groups to influence civil society. "Many important people were connected in that way with the Society: the emperors Ferdinand II and Ferdinand III, Sigismond III, king of Poland, who had officially belonged to the Company; Cardinal Infant, a duke of Savoy. And these were not the least useful."[5] Paris wrote that Jesuits lead political parties, serve as officials, and generals. (Paris: 41).

In Italy in 1561, the Calvinist Waldenses religious group were persecuted as heretics by Emmanuel Philibert of Savoy at the instigation of the Jesuit Possevino in Portugal:[6]

> Under the first king of the house of Braganza, Father Fernandez was a member of the government and, under the minority of Alphonse VI, the counselor most heeded by the regent Queen Louise. Father de Ville was successful in overthrowing Alphonse VI in 1667, and Father Emmanuel Fernandez was made a deputy to the 'Cortes' in 1667 by the new King Peter II... Not only were they spiritual advisers to all the royal family, but the king and his minister consulted them in all important circumstances.[7]

> During the seventeenth century, they are all-powerful in Spain, among the high classes and at Court. Even Father Neidhart, former German cavalry officer, fully governed the kingdom as Counselor of State, prime minister and Grand Inquisitor... In Spain as in Portugal, the kingdom's ruin coincided with the rise of the Order...[8]

The main areas for the struggle between Catholicism and Protestantism were in central Europe: France, Holland, Germany, and Poland.[9]

> The Catholic cause could hope for a real success only if the fathers were able to influence and guide the princes, at all times and in all circumstances. The confessionals offered the Jesuits the means to secure a lasting political influence, therefore an effectual action.[10]

The power of the Jesuits to combat Protestantism by controlling the rulers is reflected here: "The Jesuit Mayrhofer of Ingolstadt taught in his 'Preachers Mirror:' We will not be judged if we demand the killing of Protestants, any more than we would by asking for the death penalty on thieves, murderers, counterfeiters and revolutionaries."[11]

As for Albert V of Bavaria, one author characterized his attitude as follows:

> As soon as the Fathers arrived in Bavaria, his attitude towards Protestants and those favorable to them became more severe. From 1563 on, he piteously expelled all recalcitrance, and had no mercy for the Anabaptists who had to suffer drownings, fire, prison, and chains, all of which were praised by the Jesuit Agricola.[12]

In 1617, the archduke Ferdinand was crowned king of Bohemia by the Emperor. "Influenced by his Jesuit confessor Viller, Ferdinand started at once to combat Protestantism in his new kingdom. This signaled the start of that bloody war of religion which, for the next thirty years, kept Europe in suspense." (Paris: 50).

Even after the thirty years war had ended with peace so that the German Protestants could have the same rights in their lands as the Catholics, the Jesuits in vain attempted to continue the bloodshed.[13]

> Any plan forged in Rome, or by other foreign powers against Protestantism in Switzerland was assured of the Jesuits' full support...In 1620 they were successful in making the Catholic population of the Veltlin rise against the Protestants and they slaughtered six hundred. The Pope gave indulgence to all those who took part in that horrible deed.[14]

I do not know about you, but I am overwhelmed with sadness for the persecution of those who desired religious freedom. However, my pride swells for my United States of America in adopting the

First Amendment to our Constitution. Our founders knew Europe's history of religious oppression and we were not going to condone all the atrocities, killings, and wars to continue. Bravo to my land!

The Constitution was passed by the Congress on September 25, 1789, and was ratified on December 15, 1791. The document contains ten amendments that form the Bill of Rights. The first amendment in the Bill of Rights expresses: "Congress shall make no law respecting an establishment of religion, or prohibiting the free exercise thereof..."

One website gives the following context regarding the Switzerland aftermath:

> When the order was restored in 1814, the Jesuits were invited to return to Lucerne by the Canton authorities. They were reluctant at first because of strong opposition from radical anti-Catholicism, and when they finally did return in 1844, they encountered a serious political situation in the country that led to a civil war, the Sonderbund War. That war was lost by the Catholic cantons, and in December of 1847, the Jesuits were expelled from the country and Switzerland introduced an article into its constitution prohibiting forever the presence of Jesuits in Switzerland. This prohibition contradicting freedom of religion prevented Switzerland from entering the European Union until in 1973 a slim majority of 54.9% voted to amend the Constitution to permit the Jesuits back in.[15]

Author H. Boehmer wrote in 1910, as of the 19th century, "The Jesuits were entirely responsible for Poland's annihilation...The decadence of the Polish State had started before they came on the scene. But they undoubtedly hastened the kingdom's decomposition."[16]

In Russia in 1586, the Jesuits succeeded in pitting Poles against the Russian Czar Boris Godounov. (Paris: 57). Machinations at this time caused Russian Orthodox members to massacre several hundred Poles. Poland once even had a Jesuit King, Jean Casimir (1649), a sovereign, who had been a Jesuit previously.[17]

In the Scandinavian countries, a Lutheran king, Jean III Wasa (secretly in favor of Catholicism), married a Catholic Polish princess in 1568. In 1574, Jesuits on the surface became Lutherans, while secretly proselyting for Catholicism. King Jean III was converted to Catholicism and his son, the future Polish King Sigismond III was educated by Jesuits. Jean III's Polish wife died and he remarried a Swedish Lutheran. The Jesuits were removed from Sweden. (Paris: 59).

Once Elizabeth I became the Queen of England, the Jesuits, supported by Philip II of Spain, endeavored to have Elizabeth replaced by the Catholic Scot Mary Stuart. They worked diligently to oppose Elizabeth and the Anglican Church and to turn King James of Scotland to their cause. Constant intrigue caused several Jesuits, such as Fathers Campion and Garrett, to be hung. (Paris: 61). By 1688, another effort in England resulted in prison or eviction and failure.[18]

In France, the Order found resistance although they had curried favor at the Court and amongst the upper classes. Bally wrote that on December 1554 the Faculty of Theology decreed, "... this society appears to be extremely dangerous regarding the faith, she is an enemy of the Church's peace, fatal to the monastic state and seems to have been born to bring ruin rather than edification."[19]

The Saint Bartholomew massacre in 1572, when thousands of French Huguenot Protestants were massacred in Paris and in provinces of France, marked much religious strife. France had suffered through three French Wars of Religion with the opposing peace having been signed on August 5, 1570. The Jesuits were involved in assassinations in the late 1500s in France.[20]

France was a classic example wherein Jesuit confessors utilized "laxism," in which they allowed penance for moral failures, especially of the adultery of King Louis XIV. Eventually all members of the royal family and the King's court had Jesuit confessors. In 1681 Jesuits convinced Louis XIV to begin again persecution of Protestants. On October 17, 1685 the King oversaw a new edict to announce as "outlaws" all who did not become Catholics. It was especially brutal for Protestants. (Paris: 67,68). There is no other way in all honesty and candor, but to acknowledge Jesuits carried out in France most successfully and loyally their mission to oppress and abuse Protestants.

The result for France was devastating. 400,000 French Protestants left and gifted their francs and abilities to other countries. Soon after this debacle Jesuits were banned from many countries. (Paris: 69).

In Paraguay there was a classic example of total control of the Guarani Indians by the Jesuits. (Paris: 82).

A modern-day Jesuit, F. Charmot, S. J. wrote what defines the obedience of the Jesuits; "He (the Jesuit) will not forget that the characteristic virtue of the Company is total obedience of the action, the will, and even the judgment..." The superiors were to be bound to the Father General and he to the Pope. They were by education to ensure the primacy of Catholicism.[21]

An explanation for a type of control Jesuit confessors could have over their penitents related to the belief that they were more lenient with those confessing to them, than other Orders or the secular clergy. (Paris: 91). This observation could perhaps be the principal explanation for why the Jesuits held so much influence over their penitents. It is perhaps analogous to a child asking permission from the more lenient parent.

Boehmer wrote:

> We can understand easily why this clever leniency made them such successful confessors. This is how they won the favor of the nobles and higher-ups of the world who always

needed the condescension of their confessors more than the mass of ordinary sinners.[22]

In the 17th century, the Jesuits achieved remarkable political influence, sometimes even assuming political responsibilities and state positions.[23] Boehmer indicates that the morals and politics carried on by Jesuits even pours over to condoning assassinations by "tyrants," who did not toe the religious line.[24]

The Jesuits made good use of their proximity to those whose souls they were winning as they also won over many economic and financial opportunities especially in Mexico and Paraguay. Pierre Dominique relates that; "Bishop Palofox, sent as an apostolic visitor by Pope Innocent VIII, wrote to him in 1647, 'all the wealth of South America is in the hands of the Jesuits.'"[25]

By the middle of the eighteenth century, the Jesuits had already undergone banishment thirty times since they were founded. (Paris: 98).

With Jesuit control of Paraguay, previously noted, in 1750 they led the Guaranis in a guerrilla war against the Portuguese on behalf of the Spaniards. (Paris: 98).

The multitudinous indictments of the methods of Jesuits in many countries finally caused Pope Clement XIII, elected in 1758, by 1769 had decided to suppress the Jesuits. The day before the action was to be taken, the Pope became ill and cried out; "I am dying... It is a very dangerous thing to attack the Jesuits."[26] In 1773 Pope Clement XIV signed a Dissolution of the Jesuits and the Order's general was actually placed in prison. (Paris: 100, 101). As horrendous as it appears, the Jesuits must be suspected!

Here is another testimony:

> 'Pope Ganganelli did not survive long after the Jesuits' suppression,' said Scipion de Ricci, 'the account of his illness and death, sent to the Court of Madrid by the

Minister for Spain in Rome, proved that he had been poisoned; as far as we know, no inquiry was held concerning this event by the cardinals, nor the new pontiff. The perpetrator of that abominable deed was then able to escape the judgment of the world, but he will not be able to escape God's judgment.'[27]

Baron de Ponnat wrote; "We can positively affirm that, on the 22nd of September 1774, Pope Clement XIV died by poisoning."[28]

They were banished from Russia, where they had insinuated themselves as educators by working against the Greek (Orthodox) religion.[29]

By 1814, Pope Pius VII reestablished the Order. Afterwards there were again many banishments or suppressions: Portugal, Spain, Switzerland, Germany, France, Guatemala, Mexico, Brazil, Ecuador, Colombia, and Costa Rica.[30]

Even in the United States, which offered the Jesuits religious freedom, both John Adams and Thomas Jefferson looked on the Jesuits with much disdain.[31]

This quote relates to the period after the French Revolution of 1848:

> The Society of Jesus was literally master of France for eighteen years...She enriched herself, multiplied her establishments and spread her influence. Her action was felt in all the important events of that time especially in the expedition to Mexico (1863) and the declaration of war in 1870 (against Germany).[32]

The Crimean War had its origins in a religious dispute between Catholics and Greek Orthodox. The Crimean War was described as "bloody battles, deadly epidemics and inhuman suffering [that] cost France one hundred thousand dead."[33] Monsignor Sibour, Archbishop of Paris, then said, "The Crimean War, between

France and Russia, is not a political war, but a holy war; ... it is not a state fighting another state, people fighting in other people, but singularly a war of religion, a Crusade..."[34]

Regarding the expedition to Mexico in 1863, author Paris writes that Mexico, (after the Benito Juarez successful revolution) was to become an empire, offered to Maximillian, archduke of Austria, a strong Catholic stronghold, so that Mexico would block the Protestant United States from the Catholic influence in South America. (Paris: 114). M. Albert Bayet wrote, "The war's aim is to establish a Catholic Empire in Mexico and curtail the peoples' right to self- rule; ... it tends especially to serve Catholic interests."[35]

M. Gaston Bally wrote; "(this) war of 1870, which history proved to be the work of the Jesuits..."[36]

In 1927, Louis Roguelin wrote, "Under the cover of the Jesuits...These evil men who have made the Gospel into a spectacle of tears and blood and remain the worst enemies of democracy and freedom of thought,... penetrate everywhere, set up 'informing' as a system of government..."[37]

Aftermath – Jesuits:

The number of expulsions of the Jesuit order through history is ... fifty-six. Author Paris reports that at least as of 1983 when the Pope conducts a mass, beside him is always his Jesuit confessor. (Paris: 273). It is very painful to have had to write this ignominious history of the Society of Jesus, but to be true to myself and what I've discovered in my research it was necessary to be done! As of the time of this writing, the Pope is a Jesuit.

The Catholic Church in the United States of America

Catholics originally were not allowed in the Virginia colony, which had been established by the Church of England, nor in New England which had been established by Calvinists, nor in the Dutch colony of New York or the Swedish colony in Delaware.

Thomas Dongan in 1683 was appointed by English King James II as governor of New York and religious liberty was achieved by all faiths for a time. The Jesuits established a Catholic chapel in New York City and began education at a Latin school in 1685. In 1700 Catholics again suffered oppression in New York.

In 1634, a Catholic colony was established in Maryland by Cecil Calvert. Jesuit priests accompanied Catholics settlers. Catholics permitted religious freedoms to others, but their own freedom suffered until after the Revolutionary War. Three Catholics signed the declaration of independence and the articles of Confederation: Thomas Fitzsimmons, Daniel Carroll, and Charles Carroll of Carrollton. One member of the distinguished Carroll family, Father John Carroll, eventually was consecrated in 1790 as Catholic Bishop in the United States. Bishop Carroll was ordained in England and eventually became an Archbishop. He founded Georgetown University and in 1801, when the Jesuits were restored, he asked them to oversee that school. Archbishop Carroll is considered the principal leader and founder of Catholicism in the United States. Catholics proved their loyalty to the United States in the Revolutionary Army and Navy. Many of the priests in America had come from France after their revolution.[38]

Chapter 14:

Judaism

Overview

The major difference, as I see it, between Christianity and the following definition of Judaism in the Life Application Study Bible (King James Version) is that Christians believe the Messiah came 2000 years ago and the Jews believe the Messiah has not yet arrived! We share together a system of moral laws and the United States of America has its founding and underlying roots in the Judeo-Christian ethic.

> Judaism is not about being second-rate or easy. Divinely designed, it was the best religion, expressing true worship and devotion to God. The commandments, the rituals, and the prophets described God's promises and revealed the way to forgiveness and salvation. Then Christ came, fulfilling the Law and the Prophets, conquering sin, and freely providing eternal life.[1]

In this chapter, it is my belief that it is important to define the term "Semite" to understand the perceived meaning of "anti-Semitic," which is a term typically understood to relate only to Jews. Definitionally, it really relates to a much larger group to include Palestinians in Israel's West Bank. To be accurate, it also includes the inhabitants of the Arabian Peninsula. Of course, by the very mentioning of this distinction, probably I will be called anti-Semitic in certain circles.

> *Semite*, person speaking one of a group of related languages, presumably derived from a common language, Semitic (see Semitic languages). The term came to include Arabs, Akkadians, Canaanites, some Ethiopians, and Aramaean tribes including Hebrews. Mesopotamia, the

western coast of the Mediterranean, the Arabian Peninsula, and the Horn of Africa have all been proposed as possible sites for the prehistoric origins of Semitic-speaking peoples, but no location has been definitively established.

By 2500 BCE, Semitic-speaking people had become widely dispersed throughout western Asia. In Phoenicia they became seafarers. In Mesopotamia they blended with the civilization of Sumer. The Hebrews settled with other Semitic-speaking peoples in Palestine."[2]

In all respects, after my research on this subject, the terms "anti-Semite" and "anti-Semitic" are tossed about rather loosely, and candidly, the terms are also very limited in scope. Following my research for this work, the larger question comes to mind. Do the terms relate to Palestinians, Arabs, Abrahamic Jews, Orthodox or Reform Jews, Jewish citizens of Israel, atheistic Bolsheviks and Communists of Jewish heritage? Or do the terms relate to citizens of any country worldwide, who happen to identify themselves as Jews due to heritage, blood line from mother only, or genealogy?

My own pursuit in the study of Jews begins with an examination of Abrahamic Judaism. A citizen of Israel gifted me a copy of *The Torah* (the first five books of the Old Testament) after an incredible visit I once made to the ancient land of Israel. It is important to begin my study of Jews by beginning with the Judaism of Abraham. The foundation of the Judeo-Christian ethic is found in the teachings of the Torah. In a capsule my text of the Torah indicates: "Some people gain authority and use it to make the world better. Others become strong and rich only to swell their egos." The full text follows:

In his most exalted state of mind, a person can realize that the true essence of all his earthly endeavors is his service of God, and that plows and fences can dull the spirituality and blind them to the purpose of his mission. For example, we are all familiar with sad tales of idealists who long to improve the world--only to fall in love with power and

240

forget why they sought it. Some people gain authority and use it to make the world better and accumulate money that they contribute to important causes. Others become strong and rich only to swell their egos and gratify their desires. Or let us imagine that we could make a wish and improve people's lives. How would we do it? Some would give them homes and bulging bank accounts; others would give them knowledge and morality. (Scherman: *xxiv*).

This passage reflects very succinctly the ultimate thrust of this "Cupidity" section and differentiations of individuals and their motivations.

One segmentation categorizes Jews into four arenas: 1. Citizens of Israel, who are Jews by nationality; 2. Jews, who are faithful to their religion, focus on the Torah, the first five books of the Hebrew Bible (the Old Testament to Christians), who are Jews by their religion; 3. Individuals, who are Jews by descent, blood, or whose mothers are Jewish, who are considered members of the Jewish race; 4. There is questionable speculation relative to a fourth category of Jews who, allegedly in some circles, are descended from the Khazars of Asia. (Koestler: *The Thirteenth Tribe*).

An American by citizenship or a Jew by race or nationality may be either religious or an atheist. The defining factor for members of any race, nationality, or religion relates to true expression of a life based upon character, i.e. not lying, cheating, or stealing, and being a person of integrity who demonstrates ethical and moral behavior.

People who are religious, and perhaps even those who engage in philanthropic activities, are not necessarily people of true outstanding character. An outer facade may be a cover for a life based upon deception that reflects truly low character in the pursuit of actions wherein reflection of cupidity is their life's expression.

My work is reflective of research and extensive review of many resources. Much of my research and review denotes dealings, actions, and transactions reflecting the concept of "laying up of treasures on earth," which are not transferable upon one's demise. One's balance sheet upon death remains only records of the past on spreadsheets. Also, the grave dimensions for all of us will be roughly the same basic size. Historically, the tombstone or mausoleum is the only differentiator between the wealthy, acclaimed, celebrity, and plain inhabitants of earth.

Both Gentiles and Jews may be people of character, or people in pursuit of a reflection of cupidity. Much literature consists of enumeration of the lives of Jews and their politics. Several authors in my bibliography write in detail about Jews. My work will reflect, where applicable, Jews in financial institutions, politics, and movements such as international financing, Bolshevism, Communism, and Zionism (political Semitism).

It is critical to differentiate between the categories of Jews. I have toward Israel as a country a decided bias in favor of the creation of Israel as a state and therefore Jews as a nationality. I have a definite and abiding respect for Jews who are faithful to the precepts and teachings embodied in the Torah, of which I, too, am a student.

In relating the discoveries from my research, I will express the opinions of others toward Jews, some of whom would be considered "anti-Semitic," (especially by the Jewish Anti-Defamation League), whether there is negativity toward the Jews as a nationality, or Judaism as a religion (which is especially abhorrent to me), or Jews as a member of a race. It is intellectually honest and fair to attack the positions of individuals, rather than the individuals themselves.

If the identification of a person as a Jew relates to behavior that is not that of outstanding and honorable character, then it is not anti-Semitic, just as it would not be anti-American to refer to a person of dubious or low character as an American or Christian because that is what they identify with based on nationality or religious belief.

Extensive references to Jews appear in many arenas of this book because Jews are prevalent in many arenas of society. Although a minority in population worldwide, collectively they are possessed of incredible talent and success, especially in business and financial circles. The extensive articles and references to Jews throughout history, their exiles, the Holocaust, and the ill will directed towards them are explained in many ways, many of which are not always understandable. However, the more I studied these opinion pieces, I realized that many opinions I read may have been due to jealousy. Therefore, when I indicate that a person is a Jew, it is not reflective of anti-Semitism, nor is it to be considered judgmental. It is strictly for demographic identification purposes.

One of my favorite historical characters of all time is Winston Churchill. On February 8, 1920, the *Illustrated Sunday Herald* carried an article titled "Zionism versus Bolshevism: A Struggle for the Soul of the Jewish People," in which he describes his beliefs:

> The conflict between good and evil which proceeds unceasingly in the breast of man nowhere reaches such an intensity as in the Jewish race. The dual nature of mankind is nowhere more strongly or more terribly exemplified. We owe to the Jews in the Christian revelation a system of ethics which, even if it were entirely separated from the supernatural, would be incomparably the most precious possession of mankind, worth in fact the fruits of all other wisdom and learning put together. On that system and by that faith there is been built out of the wreck of the Roman Empire the whole of our existing civilization.

Churchill reflected that he perceives the Jewish of the world as belonging within three political groupings. The first two are contributory to a "high degree" of humanity, but the third, he says is "absolutely destructive." The first grouping relates to a definition of "national" Jews, those regarding themselves as loyal citizens of a certain country foremost, in which they practice faithfully their own religion. The second group contains the "political Zionists," those desiring their own homeland in Palestine. With the Balfour Declaration the full support of British policy was supportive of this endeavor. The third group are the "International Jews." From this third grouping Churchill demonstrates their involvement in the Bolshevik Revolution in Russia, which he describes as being primarily led by this third class of mostly atheistic Jews. He relates that this is a malevolent movement seeking an equality of humankind that is practically unachievable, was responsible for every insurrectionary movement of the nineteenth century, and, as of his writing in 1920 had total control of the massive land mass of Russia. (Churchill Article: 5,6).

The "International Jews," not discussed by Churchill, relate to the abundant examples found relative to this group (and the New York Gentile bankers) being involved in international finance, typically financing both sides in conflicts. There is disputed literature relative to Jews being descended from those in the Caucasus area north of Turkey, who made a political decision and choice centuries ago, to adopt Judaism instead of Christianity or Islam, two other major factions vying for power in those centuries. They are called "Khazars." Arthur Koestler presents evidence to support his thesis that the Jews of eastern Europe are descended from the Khazar-Turkish group, rather than the Semitic group from ancient Abrahamic history. (Koestler: 199). One opinion is that the Ashkenazi Jews are the descendants of the Khazars.[3] However, a scientific study disputes that the Ashkenazi Jews are descended from the Khazars.[4]

Various authors reflect their considered opinions as to the definition of Jews. In 1915, future Associate Justice of the U.S. Supreme Court Louis Brandeis, said in a speech that, "Councils of Rabbis and others have undertaken at times to prescribe by definition that only those shall be deemed Jews, who professedly adhere to the Orthodox or Reformed faith." Brandeis broadens it to "Jewish blood" and writes, "When those of Jewish blood exhibit moral or intellectual superiority, genius or special talent, we feel pride in them, even if they have abjured the faith like Spinoza, Marx, Disraeli or Heine. Despite the meditations of pundits or the decrees of council, our own instincts and acts, and those of others, have defined for us the term Jew."[5]

Brandeis is distinctly a "political Zionist," supporting a homeland for the Jews in Palestine,[6] a concept originally proposed by Theodore Herzl in 1896.[7] Herzl was the founder in adopting a public position for the establishment of a homeland for the Jews. He was originally spurned for financing by wealthy Jews such as Baron Hirsch and Baron Rothschild. His original plan was to procure Palestine by obtaining enough money to be contributed by Jewish financiers to offer to the Sultan of the Ottoman Empire to purchase the land. The Sultan turned him down. He was first offered Uganda as a homeland.[8] His efforts found final fruition in the establishment of the nation of Israel in 1948.

It is evident with Jews that there is a dichotomy, believed in some circles, between prosperity and persecution. Author Yeats-Brown (a journalist with extensive military and travel background), is of the opinion: "The Jews have been treated abominably in many countries indeed in *all* countries, at some time or other, except China or India, where they do not seem to prosper. Wherever they have prospered, they have been persecuted." (Yeats-Brown: 175). History is replete with banishments of Jews.

Author Walter Hurt (a Gentile) wrote, "... the Jew is hated because of superior knowledge *that gives him a decided economic advantage*." Hurt explains that the general opinion is that the Jews have been massacred and banished for religious reasons, but, that it is very significant that these travesties are followed by seizure of the wealth and properties. (Hurt: 26).

In Hurt's opinion, "Christians (excepting Armenians), seeing themselves economically outstripped by the Jew, kill and rob him when unrestrained; elsewhere they persecute him in other and permissible ways." He also writes; "It is the immemorial practice of all races, when sufficiently powerful physically, to make war, under various pretenses, on any people that surpasses them in economic ability." (Hurt: 29).

Gentile author Hurt's book could be described as an apologetic and booster in its simplest terms to Jews, but to his opinions I ascribe much credibility. He writes that the Jews have always been persecuted even by fellow Semites, the Arabs. They have suffered immeasurably. The religious argument that the Jews are responsible for the crucifixion of the Christ, is a long-held spurious reason. (Hurt: 42,43).

Hurt's rendition of the Jews' economic advantage being due to "superior knowledge," may have an interesting footnote in financial history as related by author Werner Sombart. Sombart saw a translated "Report of the French Ambassador" in the Hague, Netherlands, written in 1698. The report indicates that the Jews on the Amsterdam Stock Exchange were very successful because they gather on the Christian Sabbath and share financial information gleaned by their rabbis in their synagogues on the Jewish Sabbath, the day before. The information is utilized by Jewish stockbrokers and agents the following trading day. (Sombart: 172,173).[9] Perhaps the need to institute prosecution for instances of "insider trading" had its originations in this historical example.

Sombart covers extensively the evolution of the Jews in their acquisition of power and influence in commerce and trade. They had extensive experience as providers to the military, what we would term today the "quartermaster" or "logistics" units. (Sombart: 50-53).

Significant Jewish influence has been in the financial arena. Hurt wrote in 1922, "Robbed the world over with ruthless hand, and deprived to all possible extent of the privilege of acquiring wealth, today he holds the treasure keys of every land. And whoever masters the world's finances is potential master of that world itself." (Hurt: 40). Anti-Semitism (as defined about "financier"

Jews) is correlated with this financial power. (Hurt: 51). Hurt wrote that many fear the economic competition of Jews. (Hurt: 145). Hurt (arguably) places the blame for starting wars on Gentile governments. (Hurt: 206). Your author believes that starting wars is an equal opportunity situation.

Sombart makes the case that the incredible influence in finance of the Jews originated in their being the treasurers and money lenders on behalf of European royalty. The English Cromwell-era Long Parliament brought migration of rich Jews to England in the mid-1660s. The German Ashkenazi Jews, less wealthy than the Spanish Sephardic Jews, began to arrive in England. In France Jews began to be prominent financially in the nineteenth century with the Rothschilds, the Helphens, the Foulds, the Cerfbeers, the Du Ponts, the Godchaux, the Dalemberts, the Pereires and others. In the 17ᵗʰ and 18ᵗʰ centuries many Jews, due to extensive exclusion, became "crypto-Jews," the forced "converts" to Christianity. In Germany, Jews had privileged positions as "Court Jews." (Sombart: 53-58).

A very close and valued friend of mine was Jewish by birth and background and was a convert in later life to Christianity. He was very learned and scholarly. My friend's writing capsulizes much of what I have written in this chapter and ties together several important factors. What follows is his input to me about Jewish financiers to conclude my chapters on Cupidity. It is very compelling and brings my writing up to date to current machinations of the Jewish (by blood) financiers.

Gentile and Jewish Financiers

[Author's note: The following information was derived from several conversations over the past three years with this close friend of mine, who is now deceased.]

The most powerful factor throughout my study and review of major world history as it relates to warfare is the continual and all-pervasive involvement of "international financiers," a cabal of international/globalist financiers. The world of global banking transcends any single sectarian group. Gentile and Jewish bankers alike share responsibility for the financing of conflicts to obtain bank loan fees. The American Morgan, Aldrich, Harriman, and Rockefeller families are more numerous and had a greater impact beginning with World War I. Prominent Jewish family names throughout history include the Rothschilds, the Warburgs, and the Schiffs. The disproportionate (to the population) representation of the Jewish (who can be included in this "Cupidity" chapter), reflects quite candidly the disproportionate giftings of talents and skills amongst the Jews.

According to my dear, valued and highly respected friend Dr. Elliott Snyder:

> The facts of banking in the Middle Ages point to religious prohibition against lending by the Catholic Church and Islam, therefore Jews became financiers. The Knight Templars' persecution by Philip IV of France on October 13, 1307, follows the same pattern as with other princes against the Jewish financiers, who were persecuted by the princes seeking to nullify their debts. The Rothschilds were originally a response to a series of European princes first welcoming Jewish bankers, then borrowing from them to finance wars, then expelling the Jewish to nullify their indebtedness. Jews have had the need to be able to transport wealth owing to centuries of nominal Christian/Gentile persecution. Rothschild (and therefore Jewish) transnational finance permitted the Jewish bankers to counter-game the gentile princes of Europe. The common diaspora Jewish people failed to benefit from the enterprise of the Jewish money lenders. On the contrary, they were persecuted and exiled as objects of general pogroms, promulgated to serve the financial interests of the princes and to provide a scapegoat for whatever were the problems being experienced by the prince's gentile subjects.

In a more recent conversation with my now deceased friend, Dr. Elliott Snyder, he provided me with more information relating back to my chapter on "Spiritual Warfare":

> Singling out the Jewish bankers misses the idea that in running his kingdom, Satan is both an equal opportunity and merit-based employer. The disproportionate (to population) representation of Jews among Lucifer's servants, simply reflects (again) their disproportionate giftings of talents and skills. Just as Jews represented nearly 1/3 of the German Nobel Prize winners in the sciences before 1933, despite their representing less than 1% of the German population follows from the same logic. Most Jewish people (and non-Jewish people) never benefitted from the schemes of the clever and wealthy few (both Gentile and Jewish) other than to become the victims of further pogroms (for the Jews), inspired by the envy of the princes and transmitted to the people. One way to unify a kingdom is to identify the scapegoat upon which to heap blame for the problems of the prince. Labeling the Jews of whatever stripe still falls within the false narrative of The Protocols of the Elders of Zion.

Dr. Arnold G. Fructenbaum wrote an article entitled "Zionism - What It Is and What It Is Not." He maintains that the PROTOCOLS OF THE ELDERS OF ZION were "actually a Russian forgery by a group of anti-Semites who were attempting to propagate the theory of a worldwide Jewish conspiracy. It purports to be the record or 'protocols' of Jewish elders who came together to develop a program for world domination, but it has been proved to be a Russian forgery by Czarists who were trying to propagandize the masses against the communists. From this came the popular view that communism was a Jewish conspiracy."[10]

Although I accept that the Protocols were not written by Jews as a means for world domination, thereby supporting the conspiracy theory of history or the End Times Prophecies, there is a larger importance to this population. The outline of the methodology promoted in the Protocols, upon serious reflection and examination, is assuredly a game plan being carried out by perhaps a sinister and hidden group of powers and individuals directed by an evil and dominating influence. I will state unequivocally that my candidate is Satan! One needs only to study the Protocols and connect the dots to be able to attribute it to a Luciferian scheme.

According to my friend Dr. Snyder again:

> The establishment of a State of Israel is God-ordained. Israel has to be regathered 'in a day' in order for the redemption of Israel via the Tribulation to be possible. There are any number of prophecy events that require Israel's regathering in unbelief. Are some of the funds to finance the repeated purchase of Jewish lands from the Turkish absentee landlords gained by wicked devices by Rothschilds? Yes! Recall their obtaining information on Wellington's victory over Napoleon, transmitting part publicly to crash the London market only to swoop in Soros-style to buy British government bonds in the midst of the false panic, only to profit when the rest of the message was transmitted!

Jews in America

Several years ago, I visited the Touro Synagogue in Newport, Rhode Island. It is a National Historic Site and not a place of worship anymore. The web site for Touro reflects a recap of Jewish migration to America:

> Their beliefs had gotten them expelled from England in 1290 and cast out from Spain in 1492. The forced conversions, torture and expulsions of the Inquisition sometimes caused them to change their names and hide the religion, but never to forget who they were.[10]

Israel in Prophecy

Personally, I am of the opinion that, despite centuries of persecution, intense current hatred by Arabs, and others, especially those adhering strictly to the teachings of the Islamic Koran, and widespread current opposition to the Jews of Israel by the United Nations Human Rights Council,[12] the Jewish nation will prevail and will continue to exist!

In the vein of a continuation of the effort to "connect the dots," it will take some effort, if one is not already versed in Biblical prophecy, to discover the prevalence, much less importance in history of Israel, for its being the focal point in the End Times for the culmination of history. In a study of Biblical prophecy (Old and New Testaments) one will discover the prophecies centered in Jerusalem of the final seven years of history, titled the Great Tribulation, when, unfortunately, due to rampant evil in the world (well documented in this book), God simplistically "pulls the plug," if you will in the vernacular, upon humanity's earthly existence by the physical return to earth of Jesus, the Messiah, of two major religions.

The *Prophecy Study Bible* says that:

> The ultimate deception of the End Times will involve the worldwide worship of the Antichrist. But the Antichrist will not rise to power alone. His success will result from a worldwide spiritual deception perpetrated by the False Prophet. This prophet's ability to perform miraculous signs will enable him to convince the public that the Antichrist is the leader for whom they have been searching. (*PSB:* 386).[13]

Recall previous references to the writings of Francis A. Schaeffer laying the groundwork for a worldwide dictator:

> Israel has always been a troubled people, her existence threatened, her survival hanging by the slenderest of

threads. Surrounded by hostile neighbors, who have sworn themselves to her destruction, she is presently beset by malicious media, greedy politicians, manipulators, and opportunists, and holds onto life with the most tenuous grasp... The book of Revelation states that at least fifty percent of earth's population will die during these seven years of the Tribulation Rev. 6:8, 9:15-18. Only Israel is promised survival. Other nations may survive, in reduced capacity, but only Israel has been promised continued existence. (*PSB:* 936).[14]

The footnotes for Revelation 18:5-8 in the *Prophecy Study Bible* say:

The righteous God of the universe has not overlooked the sins of the power brokers who have used commerce and government for centuries to live luxuriously at the expense of others. The commercial, social and political systems of the Antichrist will receive double judgment for their sins. (*PSB:* 1394).

Perhaps today's acolytes (from Greek *akolouthos* or "follower") on my list of "Usual Suspects" should consider changing the leaders whom they follow.

One of the most controversial and sensational prophecies relate to the Battle of Armageddon, to be conducted in northern Israel on a vast plain just north of Megiddo, west of the Sea of Galilee. The battle will be fought in the final period of the Tribulation. In Revelation 16:12 it is written, "...the waters of the Euphrates will be dried up to prepare the way for a military invasion of Israel by the kings of the East..."

John F. Walvoord wrote, "At the beginning of the Great Tribulation, through satanic deception and power, a world government is formed, with the ruler of the ten nations of the revived Roman Empire becoming a dictator over the entire globe." (cf Rev. 13:7). The world government is confronted by armies of the world. The Holy Land is to be the site of the final conflict. The place is the Mount of Megiddo, known in Aramaic as Armageddon. There is to be a worldwide earthquake and the cities of the world will be destroyed. (*PSB*: 1392).[15] For the world not to be totally wiped out, the Messiah returns to earth at Jerusalem's Mount of Olives (just up the hill from the Garden of Gethsemane and just east of the Temple Mount, whereon today is situated the Muslim Dome of the Rock). This momentous occasion in Biblical history is the precursor to the Millenial Kingdom.

The KING OF KINGS AND LORD OF LORDS returns to reclaim His territory and "Check Mate" becomes the final move on the board of history and Satan is vanquished!

Israel is important!

SECTION IV:

AMERICA'S WARS – MONEY AND BLOODSHED

Chapter 15:

American Revolutionary War (1775-1783)

Most Americans are aware of the adage, "Been there, done that." This applies to me for my "pilgrimages" to the sacred grounds of the history of our great land of America. It has been my privilege to walk with adequate mobility on my shrapnel-scarred legs through Jamestown; Plymouth; colonial Williamsburg; the church in Richmond, Virginia wherein Patrick Henry proclaimed his "Give Me Liberty or Give Me Death" speech; Boston's Common, Faneuil Hall, and Old North Church, where were lit the lanterns indicating the British route to Lexington and Concord (and both those villages also); Bunker/Breed's Hill; taken a seat in George Washington's pew in Christ Church, Alexandria, Virginia; Independence Hall in Philadelphia; battlefields of Bennington, Vermont, Fort Ticonderoga and Saratoga; and viewed from the raised overlook platform the surrender field at Yorktown and pictured my ancestor, Corporal Joseph Higdon, in the ranks of the American forces in formation accepting the surrender. All were indelibly imprinted in the deep recesses of my mind.

Causes

There were many causes for the American Revolution. Since the beginning of the American Revolution to today's endless conflicts, especially against the war on terror, there are always two facets. First, there is that which is pursued by the Main Street Media and reported to a typically uncaring, distracted, and uninformed American population. The second, hidden from public view, portrays the true reasons for conflict. "If you want the truth, follow the money," the ages-old reasons for conflict, typically portrayed in reasoning and rhetoric more easily grasped by the masses. Great Britain had spent a fortune defending the colonies from Native American Indians, as well as defending against the French, during the seven-year French and Indian War. Another cause for the American Revolution was the westward expansion of the poor colonists into territories in search of free lands to settle and the passage of laws by Great Britain (Proclamation of 1763) to prohibit this movement. Many colonists had fought in the French and Indian War and felt entitled to reap some of the benefits. These territories were Indian lands and the constant pushing of the frontiers westward provoked Indian attacks. Great Britain's war debt accumulation and Parliament's attempt to mandate that the colonists pay for these conflicts on the American continent were two principal causes for the revolution. Following the money motivation caused Great Britain to enact laws and impose taxes and fees that would principally benefit the Mother Country for financing debt and enriching the British treasury to the detriment of the colonists who were taxed without representation, which became a major rallying cry for rebellion. (Jess Johnson).

Since the beginning of the American Revolution to today's endless conflicts, especially the war on terror, (or more appropriately termed the war on Islamist Jihadist Terrorism), there are always two parts. The first, pursued by the Main Street Media, is as presented to an uninformed American citizenry. The second part, hidden behind the veil of secrecy and deception is the truth of most conflicts, "If you want the truth, follow the money." (Jess Johnson).

The growing separation from England began to reflect the development of a separate American culture, economy, government, and political system. A major impact on the colonies was the religious movement known as the Reverend Jonathan Edwards-inspired Great Awakening (1726-1750), which caused many colonists to acquire a deep-seated belief in their worth individually, pride in from whence the country had evolved from the days of the Pilgrims and Puritans immigrating for religious freedoms, and a deepening of spiritual convictions, underlying a new spiritual dimension that laid the groundwork morally and spiritually for the American Revolution. The ministry of George Whitfield also made a great impact on the spirituality of many colonists. His final sermon in 1770 before his death was to 6000 people in Exeter, New Hampshire several hundred feet from my preparatory school, the Phillips Exeter Academy.

The below conversation possibly engaged in by Samuel Adams is related in one of author's references and, of course, as being so far in the distant past, there can be no distinct and specific historical accuracy to it, but it speaks well to an initial attitude by a Founding Father in 1780 with a Frenchman, Marquis de Chastellux. The final response of the Marquis will be the omega of this chapter. (Preston: 390).

> "You were right," said Chastellux. "When a people say, 'We want to be free,' it is difficult to prove that they are in the wrong. You are a noble people. It is just that your commerce should be unhampered.
>
> "But, sir," cried Adams, "it is not alone for that! Not alone for commerce. We are not looking for great wealth, but for liberty. America is the sweet asylum of free souls. They come here who wish to escape persecution, tyranny, who wish to live according to their ideas. It is a basis of equality and love."
>
> "I agree with you so far," said the marquis, "but let us speak of the future."
>
> "The future will be the same."

To be continued.

Historical Prelude

Some of the roots of the colonies must reflect to the English conflict between the united courtiers and cavaliers under Charles I and the Puritans under Cromwell in the middle-1600s Civil War. The English commoners, desirous of departing from the oppression of the feudal periods, were becoming informed and began to be finally aware of the bondage imposed by their privileged elitists (especially regarding freedom of expression in worship). "With prayer, and fasting, and hymn, they drew the sword in defense of equal rights for all." The Roundheads swept to victory over Cromwell's Cavaliers, but all was lost in the dustbins of history when Charles II assumed again the throne. The Puritans were again placed under the control of the oppressive elitists. Many of our original immigrants were the pioneers to America after this time. They came to America and endured extraordinary hardships, but America began to be a republic where equality of all under the law began to be the norm. (Abbott: 18). Our pioneers endured the insecurity of uprooting to a new land and off they came to the New World, America, with all its attendant challenges to body and soul. A new experiment for people was to be undertaken. Education would be widely extended, and privilege of class was abolished so that all classes could be elevated to the highest positions. (Abbott: 19).

The Mayflower Compact was drafted and signed shortly after the Pilgrims, the original group of Puritans migrating to the New World, arrived at Cape Cod in Massachusetts and even before they went ashore at Plymouth. Harkening back to Old Testament phraseology this document may truly be considered the "Genesis" of our American Republic. The Compact was signed "in the name of God." In 1802 John Quincy Adams said of the Compact, "Here was a unanimous and personal assent by all the individuals of the community to the association *by which they became a nation.*" (Marsh: 21-22).

William Bradford was elected Governor in 1621 and served until 1657. The character of this early leader of what was to become America was expressed by Cotton Mather thusly, "But the Hebrew he most of all studied. Because, he said, he would see with his own eyes the ancient Oracles of God in their native beauty...But the crown of all was, his holy, prayerful, watchful, and fruitful walk with God, wherein he was very exemplary." Author Marsh wrote, "They made of their commonwealth a place where initiative lay within themselves, and not with landlords, nobility or kings."

(Marsh: 23). These original colonists laid the groundwork and the foundation for a new system of governing that had no prior equal. It was a system of life in unequivocal terms one centered on God with complete fidelity.

As one recounting indicated, "...they left behind them their native land, its history, and its throne; its Church, its gold, its worldly cheer;" (Marsh: 24). They looked forward to reaping the benefits of this new land, but the control by their native land, England, slowly began to assert itself.

The elitists of the privileged aristocracy of England, accustomed to trampling upon the rights of the common man, began to recognize the growth in America of riches and power and proceeded to impose a yoke of tyranny on the colonies. They began to look with disfavor upon the American colonists, possibly due to jealousy due to the contrast of their own system. Determined as they were to exert the typical points of pressure on their American subjects, partially freed from the class of privilege in England, they were met with resistance by the people of this new land, who had become accustomed to living a new way of life, without the boot of the sovereigns of the old empires. The governors of the colonies were the nobility of England and they enjoyed the perks of position and prestige. This did not set well with the roughhewn and independent residents of the colonies across the Atlantic, who sought to self-rule. (Abbott: 19).

The demands for more self-government were generally denied due to the belief they would lead to independence eventually. The Tories were the "loyalists" amenable to British rule and the Whigs were the "patriots." The American Tories believed originally that peaceful measures could be pursued to forestall independence, but the American Whigs stood on the belief that only an Armed British force could protect the loyalists. (Van Doren: 8).

Causes

Little has ever been known about some of the conditions evident in the colonies upon the onset of the Revolutionary War. The war could be termed the first American Civil War due to the division of the colonies between loyalists and patriots and the ensuing attacks, plundering, and guerilla warfare conducted between the two protagonists. Also, there had developed a significant underground economy based upon corruption and smuggling of goods into the colonies, evading fees and taxes imposed by the British. This financial situation really became a prime mover for the Revolution on a coequal basis for the more well-known causes to be served such as freedom and enlightenment.

Beginning in 1651, the British imposed a series of Acts (the Navigation Acts) upon Colonial America that became onerous and oppressive. A delineation and description of them would drag this chapter out interminably so only the very significant ones will be mentioned.

From 1754 to 1763, the British fought the French in what was called the French and Indian War or the Seven Years' War. The British prevailed, but the war cost money and the powers that be in Britain prevailed upon various and sundry methods to cause the colonists to foot the bill. The colonial trade was very profitable for the Crown. By 1770, the trade figures had reached 2,800,000 pounds. The Crown was pleased with these additions to its coffers. When the war was concluded, it was said, "The war had brought glory to the generals, death to the privates, wealth for the merchants, unemployment for the poor." (Zinn: 59). What else was new after the captains and the kings depart? Just the residue for those who got caught in the cross fires! Immediately afterward the British imposed an Act which forbade the colonists to settle west of the Appalachian Mountains. This war expanded the British Empire.

The Quartering Act of 1765 placed a mandate on the colonies to save the Crown money wherein the colonies basically had to provide room and board to the occupying British "redcoats."
The Stamp Act of 1765 was not on the books long, but its revenue-enhancement for Britain placed stamps to be purchased

and placed on 55 public documents. The previous taxes were viewed by the colonists as related to trade, but this new one infringed on the rights of the colonists and it caused the formation of the Sons of Liberty, a somewhat underground and secret assemblage of patriots to begin the long march to independence.

A classic example of smuggling in the colonies occurred on June 9, 1768, in Boston Harbor, and of all people to be involved in illicit smuggling was one of the fathers of the revolution, John Hancock. Hancock's name would boldly appear with the eventual signatures on the Declaration of Independence. However, on that evening, his ship, the *Liberty,* contained a cargo of wine smuggled into Boston. The sloop and cargo were owned no less by the above-named John Hancock, who was in his own right an "elitist" in the colonies, as defined by position and wealth.

Soon upon his landing, customs officials descended upon the ship, charging a violation of the trade laws and a demand to turn over his ship to the authorities. The British position was that any wine desired for consumption by the colonists should be transported by British ships so that Britishers would reap the profits. The next morning Hancock at the lead of a group of locals returned to the sloop and after a confrontation with the British officials, who were caused to evacuate and repair to a local tavern, additional threats to the other customs officials caused them to evacuate to Castle William in Boston Harbor, the British fort. On October 1, several months later after requests for assistance from the British authorities, two regiments of redcoats marched into Boston and camped on the Boston Common. In their off-duty time these troops were not as well-disciplined as they were on the parade field and caused significant discord in the community reflected in carousing, drinking, raping, and pillaging. Seeds of significant discontent and anger began to come upon Bostonians. (Preston: 2-8).

Since the middle 1750s, another colonist destined to be the money man for the colonies was Robert Morris, whose smuggling endeavors were by means of his ships traversing the seas to the

Dutch West Indies to load cargoes of tea that were brought back to the colonies as illegal cargoes, evading the British customs fees. Smuggling of tea, possibly to be termed the "brew of revolution" was so pervasive that these cargoes far surpassed those that were conveyed legally. (Dolin: 61). Navigation Acts were passed to curtail the illegal traffic.

One Samuel Adams, cousin of John Adams, a Bostonian of limited business success, took it upon himself to turn to radical measures to begin to fire up the populace and strive for separation and independence from the mother country. He was a leader of the Sons of Liberty. The twin motivations of greed and freedom were motivators, but for Samuel Adams it was very purely altruistic to seek freedom and independence.

A supposed innocent encounter on the street of Boston on March 2, 1770, had an immense consequence on the road to independence. A British soldier was passing by a ropemaker's place of business and the rope maker offered the red coat some additional work. Amazingly enough the redcoats quartered in the city moonlighted by obtaining additional income and working for the colonists from time to time in a variety of endeavors. The rope maker offered him only work cleaning the privy. The incensed soldier began to yell out insults on the street. Eventually other redcoats and colonists began to rumble in the streets. This confrontation eventually ended up in the Boston Massacre. Three days later March 5, 1770 a group of young boys began to taunt soldiers with snowballs. An ongoing complaint by Bostonians maintained that the redcoats were taking jobs that they needed themselves. A street fight began, and British soldiers fired upon Bostonians, killing five of them. The most celebrated of them was Crispus Attucks, an African-American and escaped slave. Discord descended again upon Boston. The soldiers and customs agents evacuated to Castle William. (Preston: 7-9).

One of the major precipitating causes of the war were the Townshend Acts which were passed in June 1767, imposing taxes on tea, glass, paper, lead, and paint imported into the colonies.

They were repealed in March 1770, but tea continued to be taxed at a lower rate. Most of the tea consumed in the colonies was still obtained from smugglers. In May 1773, Parliament passed the Tea Act and it essentially consisted of a bailout of a business that had an immense influence on the British economy. This was the British East India Company, which, as a giant business entity had a monopoly on the China trade and basically controlled India. The smugglers significantly decreased the British East India Company's profits and its lower business viability multiplied damagingly through the entire British economy. To maintain the Company, the Parliament devised a scheme to bypass American tea merchants and sell directly to the colonists at reduced prices, ensuring that the twenty million pounds of tea inventory could be moved from British warehouses into the American markets thereby underselling the Dutch tea. This constituted a significant financial threat to the American merchants much less the tea smugglers. Propaganda began to run its course to raise the specter of additional commodities being foisted upon the colonists under the control of the British East India Company. (Dolin 66-69).

A modest amount of "cupidity" was exhibited in the emotional outburst of John Hancock, probably still in the smuggling business. Boston warehouses were already overflowing with smuggled tea and new supplies introduced at lower prices would be disastrous, so what could the reputable merchants of Boston do, but protest ever so vehemently and keep the waters of discontent boiling? It was not a stretch to withhold this bit of economic intelligence from the great masses of Boston, now being stirred up to further frenzied attitudes and actions. (Preston: 23). Perhaps this was an instance of stirring a populace up to action based on propaganda?

Most American school children with even a modicum of knowledge of history know of the Boston Tea Party. This knowledge is possibly not so much as to its causes or implications, but instead due to the drama of the "Indians" carrying out the deed of dumping tea from three ships into Boston Harbor on the night of December 16, 1773. The Port of Boston was shut down and a demand was made for payment of the lost cargo. (Preston: 24-26).

The First Continental Congress met on September 5, 1774, and it was attended by Samuel Adams, John Adams, Patrick Henry, and George Washington, a patrician Virginian – genteel, wealthy, and constrained to still support conciliation with England. However, the fires of inflammatory rhetoric began to win the day, and on October 27, 1774, the Congress closed just as Governor Gage was bombarding Boston. The peace had been broken! (Preston: 26-35).

Amidst all the turmoil and increasing pressure on the colonies perpetrated by imperial Great Britain with the various and sundry laws, acts, pronouncements, fees, and taxes little attention has been paid to one that probably was the one of most consequence, but, since it related to the arena of finance and currency, it has been misunderstood by the masses and therefore has received scant attention, but stands tall in importance as to the cause of the Revolution. It was the 1751 Currency Act, which originally applied only to the New England colonies.

In 1763, Benjamin Franklin paid a visit to London, and presumably was dismayed to view the slums of that metropolis. (Goodson: 57). When he was questioned about the prosperity of the Colonies, he answered, "That is simple. It is only because in the Colonies we issue our own money. It is called colonial scrip, and we issue it in the proportion to the demand of trade and industry." (Owen: 98). This was something that could not be sanctioned by the Bank of England, because in the following year Parliament passed the 1764 Currency Act which banned the opportunity for the colonists to mint coins or issue any official money by colonial governments. The colonies must now use only English money.

The result of this act was that now money in the colonies was based on debt. "Benjamin Franklin stated in 1 year from that date the Colonies were filled with the unemployed, because when England exchanged with them, she gave the Colonies only half as many units of payment in borrowed money…as they had in scrip. Accordingly, their circulating medium was reduced 50 percent, and everyone became unemployed. The poor houses became filled, according to Benjamin Franklin's own statement." Benjamin Franklin said this was the real underlying cause of the Revolutionary War. He claimed the colonies would have paid the tea taxes. But this currency manipulation caused the colonies massive financial and economic damage. (Owen: 99).

Could this have been the smoking gun that ignited the spark for the revolution? Perhaps future causes of wars should analyze the financial manipulations of the central bankers. By 1773, restrictions were lifted and the legislatures of the colonies were allowed to print currencies to be used as legal tender.

In 1729, Benjamin Franklin published a pamphlet titled *A Modest Enquiry into the Nature and Necessity of a Paper Currency*. He was considered the father of colonial paper money. He knew well his subject. Once war was declared, Congress issued Continental dollars and this medium depreciated quickly. The depreciation was aided by England's printing of counterfeit currency.

Our Founding Fathers recognized that absent financial independence and independent government from within the colonies that other freedoms would all be lost. Then came another struggle to separate from the oppressive British.

In England, the Colonies began to be looked upon with disfavor due to the increase of wealth and power they had begun to achieve. The colonists had begun to live a new life separate from the oppression of the mother country. Control was exercised by the Crown through the appointment of governors and judges, mainly individuals in the privileged aristocratic classes from England. (Abbott: 19).

During September and October of 1774, the colonists began to take the first steps toward deciding whether to separate from Britain by convening the First Continental Congress in

Philadelphia. On the military front, the colonists began to prepare for a war.

BATTLE JOINED!

The stage was set. Grievances were multitudinous. The colonists had had all they could stomach.

Lieutenant General Dave Palmer, former Superintendent of the United States Military Academy, in his book *George Washington's Military Genius*, identified the background for the development of the strategy of the war initiated in the Colonies in 1775. Our Colonies were identified with a population of only two and a half million inhabitants spread over eleven hundred miles from Savannah to Boston. Twenty per cent were black. Some whites had several years of indentured service. They hugged the coastal areas for the most part and trade out of seaports was the principal commercial endeavor. Believe it or not, it is startling that only four cities had more than ten thousand people. These were Boston, New York, Philadelphia, and Charleston. (Palmer *Genius*: 26-29). There was only one very strategic location in the entire expanse of the colonies and that was at West Point on the Hudson River north of New York City. This military fortification would figure later in the most celebrated example of treason by Benedict Arnold. The Hudson River basically was a natural dividing line between the northern and southern colonies.

In European armies, the officer corps was typically from the aristocratic classes, but the armies, "...filled their ranks by scouring the social gutters for human flotsam." The American Continental army would consist of members dedicated to the purposes of freedom or those who had some financial reason for the revolution such as members of guilds or landowners. Our people were accustomed to the terrain and geography and the right to bear arms was unquestioned. Messages typically were sent by ship back and forth to London. Messages were difficult even within the Colonies due to a primitive road system, which left much to be desired, but allowed the patriot communication system to be better than that of England. We were an agricultural country not a manufacturing one. Another deterrent to development of any industry was the Iron Act of 1750, which prohibited new foundries. (Palmer *Genius:* 29-31).

On April 18, 1775, British General Thomas Gage sent his troops from Boston to capture the militia supplies stored at Concord upon information provided by one of those "loyalists," Benjamin Church, a disloyal patriot, who was a paid informant of the British. Church was a member of Massachusetts' congress and was considered to have been of dubious loyalty to the patriot cause. (Van Doren: 19). This was a major challenge of the patriots, to know whom to trust. Another purpose for the march on Lexington was that two rather renowned patriots were staying at the Lexington home of the Reverend Jonas Clark. The British wished to apprehend the reverend's guests, Samuel Adams and John Hancock, and take them to London for hanging. (Preston: 37). By the time the militia gathered on the Lexington Green to confront the redcoats, Adams and Hancock were long gone. We all know about the first skirmish at Lexington and "The Shot Heard Round the World" at Concord. The British were soundly routed and headed in defeat back to Boston, chased by militia from behind every hiding place on the road. Church was in frequent contact thereafter with Gage and gave him intelligence on the Bunker Hill plans of the patriots as early as May 1775 just as the Continental Congress had begun meeting in Philadelphia. He was eventually discovered, jailed, and upon being freed, disappeared, but his wife was given a pension upon her move to England. (Van Doren: 23). The British paid off one way or the other their spies during the war.

There was a major significance to the fighting at Lexington and Concord. The world has never been the same since April 19, 1775. It represented the "...voice of the common man demanding his political and economic rights as he had never dared demand them before;" (Preston: 39). It was the first successful breakthrough in throwing off the feudalism of the empires of the old Europe. The war for our independence had begun! It was time to throw off the yoke of the belief in England that the colonies existed only to benefit the home country.

In May of 1775, the Second Continental Congress met and constituted the government for the Colonies until the termination of the Revolution.

It was not long before the British realized they were in for a hard fight and their army was not up to the task. Within England and Ireland, the American patriots found great support. The British decided they would hire mercenaries from the German principality of Hesse, the infamous "Hessians." It was written about the Hessians, "These mercenaries fought only for cash and plunder, cared nothing for England and cared a great deal for whiskey and loose American ladies." (Preston: 66).

On July 2, 1776, it became official. We declared our independence and the Declaration of Independence represented our *Exodus* from the tyranny and bondage of Great Britain. It mirrored those long before Hebrews beginning their exodus from Egypt to the Promised Land. Prior to this the colonists had been fighting a war that was defending us against the intolerable acts and laws placed on us by Great Britain. The Declaration of Independence signified offensive action by declaring our freedom. Every society through the millennia has exhibited the division of classes based on wealth and power so the expression of "all men are created equal" was not pleasing necessarily even to our own privileged classes in America, but it was a clarion call that something new was now to be witnessed on planet earth, something never evident previously. Author Daniel Marsh claimed, "The Declaration says to all humanity that there is but one family picnicking on this right little, tight little playground of ours called the earth. Adam, or cave man, ... it does not matter-the blood of the first man is in all our veins. And the Declaration of Independence is the Call of the Blood." (Marsh: 35). Throughout the two centuries and a half since 1776 there has been much blood spilled due to tyranny and the machinations of the subjects enumerated in the previous chapters of this book. But, if the doctrine of this incredible Declaration of Independence were to be followed, then governments must be the servants of the people and not the other way around.

Despite protestations to the contrary, the recognition of the grand Creator of all, God, had three references: First, "the laws of Nature and of Nature's God;" second, "We hold these truths to be self-evident, that all men...are endowed by their Creator with inherent and inalienable Rights (amended to read 'certain unalienable Rights);" and third, "to the Supreme Judge of the world for the rectitude of our intentions." Try as many may to dispute it, our Nation was founded upon a belief in a Supreme Being. The record is accurate and unmistakable!

Marsh wrote, "The draft closed with these words of total dedication: 'And, for the support of this Declaration, we mutually pledge to each other our lives, our Fortunes, and our sacred Honor.'" A later amendment by Congress added, "with a firm reliance on the protection of divine Providence." (Marsh: 36).

Thousands of "platitudes" have been written and expounded upon as to the greatness of our land, founded upon the original principle that people are born and should remain free. Many economic, political, and self-aggrandizement purposes have been exhibited to nullify these principles throughout history. However venal and self-serving have been the purposes that have caused the bloodshed and suffering of the flower of the youth of America and other lands, always there remains that grand and abiding and elevated purpose for which the Declaration of Independence remains as a beacon for us and for the world. Why else have so many always wanted to immigrate to these shores? In his First Inaugural Address on March 4, 1801, Thomas Jefferson, the author of the Declaration, said, "...should we wander from [the Founding Principles] ... let us hasten to retrace our steps and to regain the road which alone leads to peace, liberty, and safety." We have available the beacon of freedom. Let it not be extinguished!

From 1776 until the signing of the treaty in 1783, well-known are the commentaries of the battles and struggles and bloodshed and suffering that covered our paths to freedom and independence. There were Bunker/Breeds Hill, Boston, Ticonderoga, Saratoga, Valley Forge, Eutaw Springs, South Carolina (where one of my ancestors fought), and finally Yorktown, where another of my ancestors, Joseph Higdon, was a soldier. With the Higdon legacy, your author qualified for membership in the Sons of the American Revolution.

But little known are the amplified side stories of Benedict Arnold, the cast of characters and conflicts representing our First Civil War of both patriots and loyalists, the contrast of lives of the combatants and the congressmen, the casualties, the consequences, the aftermath to include our Constitution, the establishment of the First National Bank, George Washington's Farewell Address, and two wars closely following the culmination of our revolution.

The Man without a Country

One of my favorite authors of history is Lieutenant General Dave Palmer, who also penned *George Washington and Benedict Arnold a Tale of Two Patriots*. Benedict Arnold began as a patriot in no uncertain terms. Upon the convening of the Continental Congress in 1774, Arnold was one of the leading citizens of Connecticut and a staunch member of the Sons of Liberty. When George Washington and Benedict Arnold crossed paths at the First Continental Congress, this would be the first of an intermingling of their lives throughout the war. There were many festive social events in the Philadelphia of that period. One young resident, Peggy, was but fourteen years of age. The daughter of the prominent Judge Edward Shippen, Peggy worked her feminine charms on both Washington and Arnold. (Palmer *Patriots:* 7).

Upon the death of his father Benedict Arnold was saddled with much family debt, a condition which spurred him to succeed, beginning with a career as a shipowner. He joined the Masons, which attracted many outstanding citizens because it became a stepping stone to many contacts of influence in his community. George Washington also was a distinguished member of Freemasonry. Eventually Arnold became quite wealthy in his hometown of New Haven, Connecticut. Immediately after Lexington and Concord Arnold and other patriots were marching to Boston. As Palmer wrote, "Benedict Arnold, resplendent and proud in his new uniform, an eager if neophyte warrior off to adventures unknown. A patriot destined for fame—and infamy." (Palmer *Patriots*: 74). Famous as a patriot, Arnold became a war hero at Ticonderoga, Canada, Lake Champlain, and Saratoga.

Arnold's odyssey to infamy was comprised of bitter disappointments upon being passed over for major commands, death of a wife, charges of financial mismanagement and malfeasance in command, surrounded by enemies, crippling wounds, illnesses, and remarriage to the previously-mentioned Peggy Shippen, the daughter of a Quaker Tory in Philadelphia. There is no questioning about the battlefield bravery of Benedict Arnold. However, eventually he went down in history as the most celebrated traitor of the American Revolution. Possibly a major part of Arnold's road to treachery was marriage to the Tory, Peggy Shippen, after he became the patriot governor of Philadelphia upon the departure of the British general, Henry Clinton. In this command, he was continually dogged by charges that may or may not in all cases have been merited.

When the British occupied Philadelphia, Peggy became acquainted with British officer, John Andre and supposedly began constant correspondence with him. Meanwhile, General Arnold was being accused of improprieties as governor and too much fraternizing with Tories. (Preston: 397). Arnold married Peggy on April 8, 1779.
Palmer related that Arnold had always been driven by avarice, but now it was turned to vengeance. On May 10, 1779, a spy reported to the new British head of spies, John Andre, that a Major General Benedict Arnold was prepared to become a turncoat. (Palmer *Patriots*: 301). As the plot unfolded, Arnold requested a generous payment to turn over to the British the plans for West Point,

where he would eventually became the Commanding Officer on August 3, 1780. He took up residence at the Robinson House across the Hudson from West Point, ensuring a faster escape route to British lines were he to be discovered. Eventually Arnold and Andre began to consummate their plans to overtake the strategic fortress of West Point with a meeting on September 22, 1780. Andre was to depart the area on a British warship that was bombarded, and Andre was now left only with a horse to escape. Arnold had given Andre a safe conduct pass. On his way to the British lines, Andre was stopped by patriot soldiers, searched, and discovered with the plans for West Point in his possession. As fate would have it, General Washington was almost at Arnold's quarters when Arnold received a dispatch indicating the capture of Andre. Arnold departed just prior to Washington's arrival. (Palmer *Patriots*: Chapter 20). Arnold soon donned the uniform of a British officer. Andre was hanged as a spy. Arnold attacked Richmond, Virginia leading British troops. His treachery was complete! Eventually he was granted a pension in England, moved to New Brunswick, Canada, then back to England, where he died in debt in June 1801. General Palmer closed this chapter of the treason of Benedict Arnold with these words, "The lives of George Washington and Benedict Arnold bear profound witness to the proposition that character is destiny." (Palmer *Patriots*: 395).

The First Civil War

Political disagreements turned into a civil war. The British began to treat localities and individuals who were not in rebellion separately from the patriots. This magnified the internal turmoil. The Tories, loyal to the Crown, began a significant clash across the Colonies with the patriots (the Whigs). A major contributing factor to the conflicts began when the British King proclaimed that it was incumbent upon the loyalists, with an order, "to aid and assist in putting down the rebellion." This became an official sanctioning, once the war commenced and it was beyond political disagreement. It required the loyalists to adhere to the "lawful" government of the Crown by violent means if necessary. The violence was evident on both sides. (Van Doren: 11).

The patriots believed the Declaration of Independence dictated that they had established a legitimate government. The American patriots began to hound and harass the British loyalists and perpetrate much more severe penalties and actions against the loyalists, with "fines, imprisonments, banishments, confiscations, and—later—even death sentences against the loyalists as the patriots themselves might expect if they should be defeated." (Van Doren: 12). The loyalists began to migrate to Boston, New York, and Halifax. New York City became the headquarters for clandestine activities against the patriots. (Van Doren: 13).

There were frequent instances of Americans being bribed by the British. Patriots had to be aware of not only the British military, but also the civilian loyalists who went so far as raise militias to fight the rebels. Individuals in high level diplomatic positions, supposedly loyal to the patriots, were turned and bribed as traitors to spy for the British. (Van Doren: 61).

The British began to enlist members of some American Indian tribes into militias soon after patriot efforts were made to keep them all neutral, however they succeeded only with the Tuscarora and Oneida. The British won the favor of the Mohawk, Onondaga, Cayuga, and Seneca tribes, somewhat due to appreciation that the British, after the French and Indian War, kept the colonists from migrating west of the Appalachians. Loyalists on the frontier, along with their native confederates, made raids on patriot areas that exhibited the savagery that was then typical of the American Indians in that they killed not only patriot soldiers, but also women and children. (Van Doren: 122). Loyalists who acted against the patriots were offered the plunder they could appropriate. (Van Doren: 237).

In 1777, all of the above horror had been authorized by the British War Office, when Henry Hamilton, royal governor of the Northwest Territories, had been ordered to war upon the patriot border settlements. Partial motivation was to contain the Americans from encroachments in areas settled by French, who might then attack the British. The "war" was described as follows:

"Slash, torture, wreck!... Burn the villages. Destroy the crops. Kill men, women and children indiscriminately." The Indians, as mentioned above, became co-conspirators with generous offers to include rum. Massacres were the order of the day (and night). "It was a reign of terror. It was a reign of axes, of children with their arms and legs cut off. Hamilton's program included the annihilation of every white family on the Ohio that was not Tory." (Preston: 273). So transpired the inhuman atrocities of the "civilized" minions of the powerful British Empire. Humanity committed many more atrocities; however, these are all your author can stomach at this sitting.

The most committed and cruel loyalists existed in the form of the Associated Loyalists, presided over by their president, William Franklin. Throughout 1781, they indulged in horrendous guerilla warfare in Connecticut and New Jersey, typically with many civilians as victims. (Van Doren: 430).

The British consistently sought to turn the patriots from their cause and though there were successes, in the main, the entreaties to turn against their fellow patriots were met with disdain and denial. "Desertion or treachery, the patriots were told, would bring them lasting honour and immediate rewards instead of the uncertainty and poverty they had otherwise to face." Van Doren wrote the real struggle of the patriots was not just in armed combat, but through the undercover operatives of the Crown. (Van Doren: 435).

After the war began, the patriots began their fight against the loyalists. The Sons of Liberty began invading the homes of loyalists to commandeer any weapons and ammunition available. It was reported by author John Hyde Preston that, "These liberty-loving vandals broke into the richest houses, stole all the silver, burned libraries, pricked servants with stolen bayonets, molested women, smashed everything that would break, rubbed dirt and dung into rugs, and sometimes shaved protesting heads." (Preston: 50). Apparently once a war is declared, animal instincts explode to the surface on both sides. Loyalists became cowed, and their numbers decreased appreciably with time. John Adams was to have declared that most of the patriots were mired in debt, to the loyalists. (Preston: 51).

The loyalists might have totaled as much as 40% of the population. Arithmetic analysis of the population and this loyalist number dictated that the base for the potential patriot combatants was only 535,000. The middle ground of individuals neither loyalist nor patriots, the "fair weather" patriots, probably numbered 25%. George Washington's base of potential soldiers, therefore, was only 225,000, and not more than 25,000 were counted in its highest number. Yet George Washington, the cunning and accomplished and magnificent leader he was, prevailed to win out over a seemingly invincible British Army! This was not all Washington and the Continental Army had to fight!

As horrendous as warfare of and by itself is with its horror and blood and suffering, the conditions for the non-combatants, the merchants and the political leaders were not too shabby. While the rank and file at Valley Forge went without "uniforms, underwear, shoes, stockings, trousers, coats, hats, blankets, and beds," the farmers in the environs of Philadelphia, most of whom were Quakers, brought the British quartered in Philadelphia much of their meat and supplies, paid for in gold, much more lucratively than being paid for with Continentals. (Preston: 258-259). [Author's note: Their bank accounts and gold stock were supposedly intact at the end of the war when they reaped the benefits of freedom achieved by our long-suffering patriot soldiers].

While the soldiers were freezing and losing legs due to frostbite at Valley Forge, it was said that, "Profiteering ran riot. Huge shiploads of shoes and clothing were captured by the agile privateers, but fat speculators hid them in their cellars to rot, waiting for prices to go soaring up. Hogsheads of boots mildewed in American harbors while the soldiers wrapped their feet and legs in sacks." (Preston: 258). There will be a special corner or space in hell for those businessmen!

The politicians were guilty of, "intrigue, hollow promises, official abracadabra," much less the jockeying for position and favor and power. The health conditions amongst the soldiers were appalling, with pneumonia and smallpox rampant. (Preston: 259). The Congressmen, probably comfortably ensconced in their warm lodging, no doubt partied every night, flirting with the local belles. Meanwhile, Washington originally quartered 10,000 men at Valley Forge. Is it too hard to believe that 3,000 deserted to the British, and that on February 5, 1778, Washington reported that 3,989 men presented unfit for duty due to a lack of shoes and clothes? (Preston: 260). Should I ask how many politicians and merchants were unfit for duty each day only because of too much wine the preceding night?

At Christmas of 1778, General Washington traveled to Philadelphia, and after having personally witnessed the privation and suffering of his army patriots, he was appalled at the contrasts evident among the civilians enjoying the pleasures of Philadelphia. It was reported that:

> He looked on in sickness and anger. The rich patriots entertained at banquets that cost enough to keep a whole regiment in food and clothes for a month. Most of the members of the Congress indulged in so much good cheer in the evenings that their hangovers kept them from beginning work before noon of the next day. (Preston: 361).

Case made!

Foreign Involvement

The most obvious and important foreign involvement during the revolution emanated from France, perpetual enemy and economic competitor to England on the high seas of the world. The major reason France eventually supported us was that, if America made peace with the British, it would upset the European balance of power, which was a constant foreign policy challenge of all European countries. Originally Louis XVI was opposed to the success of our battle for independence because he was concerned our success might be an example for his subjects, who might seek to emulate our new Republic as a model of a freer government. However, he realized that without foreign assistance our rebellion might be crushed by the British, creating a massive military presence right across the narrow channel between the two countries. He feared us and the British. He also was very protective of his sugar trade in the West Indies. (Preston: 286).

On the battlefields of America, the tide only began to turn with the victories by General Washington at Trenton and Princeton between December 26, 1776, and January 23, 1777. In early 1777, France began surreptitiously to provide rifles and ammunition to the Americans utilizing a "cutout" operation ostensibly established as an export firm in France. The company was called Hortalez & Company, presided over by a shadowy character under the *nom de guerre* of De Beaumarchais. (Preston: 164).

It is relevant at this stage to discuss the military genius of General George Washington, the American Commander in Chief. He truly possessed superior strategic judgment, shrewdness, cleverness, and common sense. Palmer defines the evolution of his phases of military prowess as consisting of the appropriate degree of audacity, caution, decisiveness, and steadfastness as was required for the situations and timing of the military operations. (Palmer *Genius:* 226). The military achievements of the patriot forces represented the turning points that derived the support of France, a country most eager to recoup some of its prestige after the loss of the Seven Years War.

Two very important contributions were made by France. One was the Frenchman, the Marquis de Lafayette, who became an instant Washington protégé, confidant, and extraordinary combat leader for the Americans. The other French "donation" to the American cause manifested itself in the form of Baron von Steuben, who became the American Army drillmaster at Valley Forge. Steuben had served in the Prussian Army in the service of Frederick the Great. Although unknown at the time, the Baron's compensation was in French gold. (Preston: 262).

The victory at Saratoga in October of 1777 served as the final signal to France that they could now openly embrace an alliance with the new nation. On May 6, 1778 at Valley Forge a celebration for the soldiers was the order of the day. It was the day the official alliance with France was announced. The formal Treaty of Alliance and the Treaty of Amity and Commerce had been consummated on February 6, 1778, when the alliance became official. As momentous as was this declaration of support by France, it was a full year before it became more complete as to be expressed in specific military support. (Preston: 290). Comte de Rochambeau arrived in Newport, Rhode Island, in 1780. Notwithstanding the delays of military involvement by the French Army and Navy, they finally combined forces with the Americans to achieve victory at Yorktown in October of 1781 when the French fleet trapped General Cornwallis. Although the British held Charleston and New York City for two more years, the war had been won!

Micah 4:3 (KJV):

> And he shall judge among many people, and rebuke strong nations afar off: and they shall beat their swords into plowshares, and their spears into pruninghooks: nation shall not lift up a sword against nation, neither shall they learn war any more. [Author's note: It was the beginning of many more wars.]

My ancestor, Joseph Higdon, served as a corporal and private of cavalry in the Virginia Militia (serving at the Surrender of Cornwallis at Yorktown), and also in a second enlistment in the Continental Army. At time of enlistment, he was a resident of Montgomery County, Maryland, once the county of residence of family members. Imagine through eleven generations back to

Corporal Higdon, the connection to the same Maryland County?

Another ancestor, Isham Davis, from South Carolina, served the patriot cause at the Battle of Eutaw Springs in the Carolinas. Presumably, both, upon mustering out, took their muskets with them, and went back to working the land with their plowshares!

Our emissary to France was Benjamin Franklin, diplomat extraordinaire, whose charm and enchantment of the ladies of the court served us well as our representative to encourage support from the French. His success as a diplomat in representing the new United States proved to be a major factor in achieving eventually the essential political and military support of France. (Preston: 288). With the entry of France on our side and eventually that of Spain and Holland, the war had now expanded to be considered a global conflict. (Palmer *Genius*: 225).

Author Arthur R. Thompson renders another side to the sterling qualities of our otherwise esteemed American in Paris. Even at his then age of seventy during his diplomatic service Franklin was known to have a distinct weakness related to women and their allure. John Adams, upon his visit to Paris, became outraged at what he perceived as scandalous behavior by Franklin. Arthur Lee, the American Commissioner in Paris, charged that Franklin should be recalled and accused Franklin "of drunkenness, whoring, and accepting bribes." As is now understood, scant evidence existed of those bribery charges. (Thompson: 94).

Thompson relates that he has extensively read books on leadership, and only one mentioned a weakness as related to fulfillment of appetites, in this case, those of a sexual nature, ever discussed in those books. In Thompson's ponderings, an implication exists that those in positions of influence, dominance, and control, or maybe as a result of those positions, are those who seem to possess that significant weakness. Thompson indicates that, during our American Revolution, this purported characteristic might have applied to Franklin, Jefferson, and possibly, just once, for Alexander Hamilton. (Thompson: 94).

These observations lend themselves to an interesting comment related to the extraordinary instances of "cupidity" and treasonous activities so prevalent throughout history. Were some individuals subject to blackmail, or just succumbing to, and indulging in, their lusts as personified by David with Bathsheba? Thus, too, are the frailties of many.

Notwithstanding the reports of human frailties of Benjamin Franklin, he performed yeoman service to the cause of our freedom. As early as November of 1775, he and Thomas Jefferson were appointed by the Continental Congress to represent America in Europe to obtain support. That was under the auspices of the Secret Committee of Correspondence, by whose name itself indicated the necessity of being very confidential so as not to have its efforts revealed to the British. Franklin became the preeminent diplomat in attempts to derive both French and Spanish support.

Spain had its own New World colonies and an independent America was considered a threat to Spain, since it might raise sympathy by their own colonies to do likewise. But Spain entered the war, not as a direct ally of America, but rather in alliance with the French by means of a treaty against Britain. Early in the war, the Dutch Republic served as an arms merchant, supplying weapons to our revolutionary forces. When France and Spain combined forces against Great Britain, the Dutch were officially neutral. Therefore, their ports remained open and unblockaded by the British, and they continued as a weapons supplier. When discovered in 1780, the Dutch effectively became our ally by the British declaration of war against the Dutch.[1]

Finance

Since the late 1700s, history is rampant and continuous relating to the influence in financial circles of the "Rothschilds." The original founder of the Rothschild banking dynasties was Mayer Amschel Rothschild. Presumably, as referenced in the *Jewish Encyclopedia,* it was not until 1785 that Mayer became an agent of William IX, Landgrave of Hesse-Cassel. (Vol. 10, 490). This encyclopedia entry further states that Mayer, who upon the death of his father in 1785, "had inherited the largest private fortune in Europe, derived mainly from the hire of troops to the British government for the putti down of the Revolution in the United States." These troops were the infamous "Hessians."

Robert Morris and Haym Solomon raised funds to support the Army in the field, but corruption was widespread and somehow much of it ended in private pockets. (Preston: 381). Robert Morris borrowed twenty thousand dollars in cash from Comte de Rochambeau, the French Army commander in America. France sent six million livres in gold. Efforts were underway to obtain funds from Amsterdam bankers. (Preston: 447).

Robert Morris was a distinguished American born in Liverpool, England in 1734. He became a pillar of the Philadelphia community by the early 1770s through leadership in a shipping firm. Morris became a Pennsylvania delegate to the Continental Congress, however he did not sign the Declaration of Independence until August 2, 1776, due to a hesitation based on a desire for negotiating with the British. He was indispensable to the patriot cause and basically became the chief financial officer for the new nation. He established the first national bank. His own fortune was used to assist the payment of cash and buy supplies for the Army. He helped establish the American Navy. As dedicated as he was to the public cause of the Revolution, he still maintained a private life wherein he profited from a trading empire based on outfitting privateers to attack British ships. After the war Morris became involved in the China trade, but a series of bad investments landed him in debtor's prison in 1798 for three and a half years, an unfitting end to a patriot, who performed exceptional service to the patriot cause. (Dolin: Varied references).

Haym Salomon was born Jewish in Poland in 1740 and migrated to America in 1772. He founded a brokerage company, and when the Revolution broke out, despite having many loyalist clients, he became a patriot and joined the New York chapter of the "Sons of

Liberty." When the British took over the city on September 15, 1776, many patriots were jailed to include Salomon. After escape from a second imprisonment, he moved to Philadelphia and quickly built up another fortune. He made personal loans to government officials. Salomon was hailed as a faithful patriot who raised funds for the American cause. His imprisonment had caused extensive health issues and he died in 1785 in bankruptcy! The nation prior to the Constitution being adopted in 1789 had no authority to raise funds by taxation and only obtained monies by import duties. The United States had massive debts. The main priority was to provide pensions for wounded veterans rather than financiers such as Morris and Salomon.[2]

Buckminster Fuller studied foreign investments in America, and he discovered that even though the British government had lost the American Revolution in the war, their own British (East India Company-advised) very quickly invested in ventures in the new United States. (Fuller: 104).

Soldiers' Blood:

Doctor Benjamin Rush of Philadelphia commented that it was "a proposition long since established in Europe, that a greater proportion of men perish with sickness in all armies than fall by the sword." That assuredly was borne out with our soldiers in the Revolution. Cox enumerated that, "Smallpox, scurvy, dysentery, a variety of disorders called putrid fevers (probably typhus and typhoid), and pulmonary and respiratory diseases were facts of military life." Dr. Rush in his *Directions for Preserving the Health of Soldiers* described that some of the conditions were derived from lack of sanitation and the closeness of the troops to each other. Other causes for the troops related to conditions, "malnourished, poorly clothed, and often forced to sleep on wet ground without blankets or straw." (Cox: 119-120). Physician James Thacher wrote in his memoir that "fully 70,000 men had died during the war in battle and from disease, making the ratio of deaths from disease about nine times those on the battlefield, and his figures became entrenched in histories of the war." (Cox:

134). Author Cox cites some reports that indicated total American deaths at approximately 25,000, with about 7,000 of those being from combat wounds and the remainder from diseases and illnesses. Cox studied pension claims and found reports of deaths in units of twenty five out of sixty and sixteen out of thirty succumbed to illnesses. (Cox: 135). Is it any wonder that our line company combatants had to deal with post traumatic stressors upon their return home after the war?

Baron Friedrich von Steuben was a professional soldier that provided instruction to our Army at Valley Forge in many arenas beside just drilling. He wrote a manual titled *Regulation* and noted the critical importance of separating the kitchens from the latrines, these from the living areas (tents), cleanliness, and airing out of the bedding. Hygiene was not to be neglected. (Cox: 138). Doctor Lewis Beebe was unable to adequately describe his chagrin at the conditions he found in a patriot encampment near Lake Champlain. He wrote, "Language cannot describe nor imagination paint, the scenes of misery and distress the Soldiery endure." The wounded were frequently transported in carts which did not provide smooth rides. They often did not even have blankets. In the winter of 1777 to 1778, Army surgeon James Tilton wrote that the patients in the hospitals, "SUFFERED AND DIED IN A MANNER THAT WAS TRULY SHOCKING TO HUMANITY." (Cox: 148). The conclusion is that this was another major challenge for Washington.

Conditions at Fort Ticonderoga were described as follows:

> There was no food and sick, starved men went down in the snow and the lean timber wolves came and snarled around them and tore away their flesh before they were quite dead. Then famine and disease began to thin further the ranks at Ticonderoga. Whole companies, racked by raging fevers, lay on the stone floors of the fort with old shreds of blankets wrapped around them, and cursed Wayne (Anthony) and God indiscriminately... They died by the dozen, clutching their blankets helplessly for more warmth,

and then got packed out in the snow, like so many cold-storage hogs, awaiting burial when spring should thaw the ground. (Preston: 176). [Author's note: Graphic depiction of conditions for our patriots!].

Desertions were understandable, especially when soldiers received letters documenting the privations suffered with their families back home, without food and firewood. "The war profiteers reclined in their luxury and grew fat. The heads of state blew off steam and guzzled public funds-while the army rotted slowly away in hunger and filth and disease." (Preston: 182). Dr. Albigence Waldo capsuled it all, "Poor food...Vomit half my time...hunger and filthiness...There comes a soldier, his bare feet are seen thro' his worn-out Shoes, his legs nearly naked from the tattered remnants of an only pair of stockings...He comes, & cries...I am sick, my feet lame, my legs are sore." (Preston: 183). Little can we possibly even imagine what sacrifices were made to bring forth our freedoms and our peace and our standard of living today in America! But, the latest dance craze, scandal in Hollywood, or state of undress of some starlet or celebrity consumes so many!

Our deaths were estimated at 25,000, as were our wounded.

Propaganda

Before the modern-day master propagandist Edward Bernays was even born, the Revolutionary War had its examples of successful "propaganda." After the March 5, 1770, firing on a crowd by British soldiers produced five dead Bostonians, Paul Revere, later to become famous for his Midnight Ride, engraved a depiction of the incident and called it "a massacre." That it was, but it also began to stir up the population with disdain for the British to add fuel to the fires of all the financial and economic machinations of the British Crown against the Colonies in America. The British utilized the same methodology. Witness the 1774 print in Great Britain showing a government official in America being abused with "tarring and feathering," apparently a standard technique of harassment, but it served its purpose in Britain to personify the ingratitude of the Colonists to the magnificence of the Crown's rule.[3]

Samuel Adams accomplished success as a propagandist in an exemplary fashion. It was he, who recognized early in the struggle, that, as important as were the true political reasons for the rebellion, the people had to be influenced and this was accomplished by a swaying of the emotions, a more preeminent human motivator than the thought process of the mind. (Miller: 112).

The preeminent propagandist on the patriot side during the Revolution was none other than Thomas Paine, who migrated to the Colonies after being discovered in 1773 in London by Benjamin Franklin. Franklin had been impressed by Paine's intellect and his editorial and writing skills in a small newspaper. Very quickly Paine became the best-known and acclaimed writer of the Revolution, writing and printing *Common Sense,* which made the case for the oppression placed on the little people of the Colonies by the rich and powerful British Empire. Paine's writings became very popular. An opinion was expressed that, prior to Paine's writings, the overbearing tendency of Britain was admittedly a form of tyranny, but the fires of the Revolution reached the common man with Paine's stirring up of emotions. (Preston: 87). His writings cannot be considered propaganda as such, but anything that stimulates emotions could be viewed as a subset of propaganda. Indeed, propaganda in other wars was much more inflammatory and much less factual.

Aftermath and Consequences:

The official conclusion of the Revolutionary War came on September 3, 1783, with the signing of the Peace Treaty of Paris, wherein the signators were Great Britain and the United States and its allies, France and Spain.

The terms of the treaty recognized the independence of the United States, our territory was established as from the Great

Lakes and Canada south to Florida, which was granted to Spain, and all the way west to the Mississippi River, and all prisoners of war (30,000 Brits) were released.

As many as 100,000 loyalists migrated to Canada. The British government made payments to many of these loyalists for their dedication to the Crown. Little has ever been known about this civil war during our Revolution. Author Van Doren capsulizes a contrast between the loyalists and the patriots, "The truth is that no loyalist even approached Franklin in intellectual distinction and political understanding, or Washington for power and dignity of command, or Jefferson as a master of written elegance." The loyalists never truly grasped the depth and fervor of the patriots. (Van Doren: 434). Through it all we had prevailed.

A most moving note of the aftermath of our military victory occurred at Fraunces Tavern in New York City on December 4, 1783, when General George Washington made his farewell to his officer corps. He said, "With a heart full of love and gratitude, I now take leave of you, most devoutly wishing that your later days may be as prosperous and happy as your former ones have been glorious and honorable." (Preston: 489). The camaraderie and embraces shared in this setting of men who had prevailed against the mighty Army of the British Empire can only be evident amongst comrades at arms who serve together in mortal combat.

In Annapolis on December 23, 1783, Washington officially resigned his commission before Congress prior to departing with three aides for Mount Vernon. He arrived on Christmas Day as a marvelous gift to Martha, the children, the staff, and the workers. The next day, donning civilian clothes for the first time in eight years, he rode to the Alexandria turnpike with the aides, who now could celebrate their own homecomings. (Preston: 490). This chapter closed the life of this hero of the Revolution. The unfolding of events that would again bring him to the service of his country waited on the horizon.

The major consequence of the war was to bring immediacy to the necessity of organizing a structure and a new government that recognized the rights of the thirteen states, but that also could provide unity of purpose, strength, and action for issues of national importance and foreign relations.

The French Revolution in 1789 presented the first major foreign policy challenge because we felt a distinct loyalty and affinity for France. The violent aspects of that Revolution caused significant divisions in our own country with President John Adams breaking ties with France and almost coming to a war and President Thomas Jefferson, a Francophile, overseeing peace with France, but remaining neutral in the newest adversarial relationship between France and Britain. In 1803, Jefferson purchased the Louisiana Territory from France for only fifteen million dollars, which eventually allowed us to expand our United States from the Mississippi River all the way to the west coast.

The example of our success had given heart to France and later throughout Latin America to other people likewise to seek their own liberties and self-government.

The Constitution of the United States of America

Conditions in America after the war were not all that positive. Admittedly, good (patriots) had prevailed over bad (loyalists, Indians, and the British), but we needed to cobble together a country, which was beset and besieged by innumerable and almost insurmountable challenges.

Major conditions existed internally to disrupt our fulfillment of all the Revolution's causes and purposes. There was rampant lawlessness, a disastrous financial condition, there was no responsiveness from the states with requests for a national government to raise revenue, the army went without pay, disunity was the order of the day, and there was not a national structure for successful business or commerce to be conducted. The new nation began to meet as a Constitutional Convention on May 25, 1787. (Marsh: 41).

Benjamin Franklin and George Washington again lent their enormous prestige and wisdom to the proceedings with Washington elected president of the convention. They labored with the utmost discretion and secrecy (unlike all the modern-day leaks in our public and governmental arenas). Massive compromises needed to be made to weigh and balance all the varied interests of the large and small states. Eventually a document was agreed upon and required nine of the thirteen states for ratification. George Washington commented on the last day of the Convention, "Should the states reject this excellent Constitution, the probability is that an opportunity will never again offer to cancel another in peace-the next will be drawn in blood." Eventually after eighteen months eleven of the thirteen states ratified the Constitution. Rhode Island and North Carolina signed on after Washington's inaugural. (Marsh: 45).

Our Constitution begins with the following words: "We, the People." It was ours. We had fought, bled, and died to bring it to life. A true nation had come forth, one that never before, nor since, had been in existence. Some of the essential elements of the document were, "...that in order to enjoy freedom under *any* form of government the powers of that government had to be balanced and divided, and that every person connected with the government must be effectively checked and restrained by others." (Marsh: 47). Our Constitution is the oldest written Constitution anywhere and our Republic is the most senior government existing under the written definition as elucidated in our Constitution. It is our *book of the law*. The Ten Commandments with their "Thou shalt not's" to individuals closely parallel the first ten amendments to our Constitution, which comprise our Bill of Rights with its "Thou shalt nots" directed at our government to protect our citizens. (Marsh: vii).

Illuminism

Little known to anyone is a movement termed Illuminism, which raised its ugly head in the horror of the French Revolution, in direct contrast to the true illuminating purposes for good and light brought forth in our American Revolution. The Jacobins were part of a movement in France that was also revolutionary, but in a movement directly antithetical to the revolutionary movement in the United States, which was based on freeing the people. The movement in America in opposition to our Constitution and the presidency of George Washington had its beginnings in the original Illuminati founded on May 1, 1776, just before our Declaration of Independence was signed. The Illuminist movement, based upon the Illuminati precepts and movements toward control and conspiracy, had its moments in America. (Thompson: 63). It goes beyond the scope of this work to reflect in detail upon its origins and involvement in stirring up discord in the United States.

Several Illuminati groups were founded in America prior to 1785. Some of their lodges purported to be members of the Masonic orders, but Freemasons in America disputed their claims of affiliation. (Thompson: 22).

No less a respected American personage than George Washington wrote from Mount Vernon on October 24, 1798, "It was not my intention to doubt that, the Doctrines of the Illuminati, and principles of Jacobinism had not spread in the United States. On the contrary, no one is more truly satisfied of this fact than am I."

Two More Wars

It was not possible for America not to "learn war any more" due to the next attacks on our country. In the late 1700s our new republic began to experience our first experience with the Islamists/Muslims of the four Muslim Barbary Coast states: Algiers, Tunis, Tripoli and Morocco. We were struggling to develop internationally, so we could begin to prosper commercially. Our ships began to be attacked by Ottoman Empire piracy wherein our crews were taken into captivity until ransoms were paid. It was the adage, "follow the money." Typically, the ransoms were paid rather than fight. When John Adams and Thomas Jefferson visited the office in London of the Tripoli's representative, they were confronted with a demand to pay him a bribe and to his country to stop the depredations of these outlaws. The ambassador from Tripoli invoked religious grounds from the Koran to justify their actions. We continued to pay these tributes. In 1802 Jefferson decided to pursue military efforts to curtail these actions. We stood up to these pirates and a Marine expedition to Tripoli resulted in a victory. It was not until 1815 before there were treaties that ceased these payments. This was called the First Barbary War.[4]

When the United States prevailed against the British in the War of 1812, it represented the solidification of our position of power and respect to be derived finally from all the European powers.

Recounting by only a paragraph above the significance of the War of 1812 does not render justice to a signal event of that war and that occurred in Baltimore Harbor on September 14, 1814, when the British bombarded Fort McHenry. No visitor to Fort McHenry can be anything but totally in awe when the briefing on the bombardment is complete and the curtain is drawn to the right with the magnificent national colors, the Flag of the United States of America since June 14, 1777, waving in all its storied glory over Fort McHenry.

Francis Scott Key of Frederick, Maryland, witnessed the shells falling on the Fort from a British ship in the harbor. On the morning he penned those immortal words, which have become our *Star-Spangled Banner*, the national anthem of our native land, he witnessed the flag, damaged as it was from shell holes in the massive bombardment, still waving over the Fort. (Marsh: 71).

Author Marsh writes most eloquently relative to the nationalism and patriotism embodied in those immortal words of our anthem. He says, "...nationalism-patriotism-is one of the noblest of man's sentiments, and one of the most sovereign instincts of a good man." (Marsh: 74). There are those who would proclaim our anthem as antiquated and glorifying of strife. However, it only reflects an event of extraordinary valor of Americans in the fort.

The Fort McHenry Commanding Officer, George Armistead, suffered after the bombardment, evidencing one of the first instances of what would later become termed Post Traumatic Stress. He died at age 38.

Marsh believes that our anthem is a national psalm, as were the psalms of David. Patriotism to the old prophets of Israel was much more than strictly an uplifting of emotion, yet, as I pen this writing, I have just returned from my July 2, 2017, worship service during which, as I sang the anthem, tears wet my eyes. So for me, it was an emotional time.

Marsh quotes Sir Walter Scott (whose home in Scotland I have visited) in his *Lay of the Last Minstrel:*

>Breathes there the man, with soul so dead
>Who never to himself hath said,
>This is my own, my native land!

This will remain our native land only and so long as the globalists are unsuccessful in uniting us under the banner of one great big joyous family who gather around campfires to sing *Kumbaya* together!

Our national colors are the symbol of our individual rights embodied in our Declaration of Independence and preserved for us in the Constitution of the United States. (Marsh: 77). And "O long may it wave O'er the land of the free & the home of the brave!" Because of the brave!

Soldiers' Blood – The War of 1812:

Our casualties were estimated to be approximately as follows: 15,000 Killed in Action and 4,505 Wounded in Action.

The First Bank of the United States

The aftermath of our American Revolution cannot be complete

without some discussion of the establishment of our First Bank of the United States, which was chartered in 1791 for twenty years. It was capitalized in the amount of ten million dollars with the United States owning 20%. Then began the controversy wherein there was major foreign ownership of 70 per cent by Europeans.[5]

Differing opinions existed as to its constitutionality as expressed by Alexander Hamilton, Washington's first Secretary of the Treasury, and Thomas Jefferson. It was chartered in 1791, principally at the insistence of its merits by Alexander Hamilton. It was significantly controversial, and the Second Bank was not extended by President Andrew Jackson. The controversy of a central national bank has drawn significant interest after our Federal Reserve was founded in 1913.

The Enduring Legacy of George Washington

Rabbi Jonathan Cahn in his book *The Harbinger* wrote about Inaugural Day for George Washington. Across the street from the New York Stock Exchange, arguably the center of the world's financial system, George Washington on April 30, 1789, took the oath of office as our first president, establishing a new chapter in his service to the United States. These are some of his words that day:

> No people can be bound to acknowledge and adore the Invisible Hand which conducts the affairs of men more than those of the United States…It would be peculiarly improper to omit in this first official act my fervent supplications to that Almighty Being who rules over the universe, who presides in the council of nations, …that His benediction may consecrate to the liberties and happiness of the people of the United States a Government instituted by themselves for these essential purposes.

Our first president possessed a distinct and abiding faith in the Creator, our God of the universe. Immediately after his swearing-in, Washington led the leaders of our country to a little chapel not far away in New York City. It was St. Paul's Chapel. His presidency began in a prayer service to consecrate our future and our new Republic. He spoke these words:

> The propitious smiles of Heaven can never be expected on a nation that disregards the eternal rules of order and right which Heaven itself hath ordained.

Perhaps our country has in fact disregarded those eternal rules of order and right mentioned by President Washington. You see St. Paul's Chapel is right across from Ground Zero, the site of the horrendous terrorist attack on September 11, 2001, two hundred years later. Despite the proximity to the Twin Towers, which collapsed, this chapel remained undamaged! Perhaps it was a recipient of "The propitious smiles of Heaven?"

Our Christian Bible tells the stories of many prophets, but one would not be in error to name George Washington a major American Prophet and to claim his *Farewell Address* as the greatest of his prophecies. A study of these words could lead a reader to conclude that this was the last will and Testament of the Father of our Country. He said, "Of all the dispositions and habits which lead to political prosperity, Religion and morality are indispensable supports." He proclaimed that neither reputation nor life itself is secure when "people fail to be religious, fully and sincerely." (Marsh: 64).

Our land, blessed with resources, personal freedoms, and a magnificent Constitution, is built foundationally upon the strength and religious faith of this greatest and noblest of all Americans!

The previous conversation between Adams and Castellux concluded as follows, with this commentary by Castellux:

> 'I should love to believe that, sir. But it is my unhappy fate to be a skeptic. The inequality of fortunes will increase, and your government is founded upon the complete equality of its citizens, upon the right of votes for all. Will there not be

in that a source of contradiction?'

'No, no, no!' Mr. Adams said.

'But I fear it,' insisted Chastellux. 'You have changed government, not human nature. A poor man by the side of a rich one will suddenly become a criminal. Which evil will win? Aristocracy or anarchy?'

'Oh, no, no, no! shouted Mr. Adams, trembling.' (Preston: 390-391).

A scant few years later, the French would confront anarchy rising up against the aristocracy, but America had its *Exodus*, we were into the new promised land of a representative republic. But as Benjamin Franklin said, "Can we keep it?"

In 1897, Rudyard Kipling wrote:

"The tumult and the shouting dies; The captains and The Kings depart; still stands thine ancient sacrifice, An Humble and a contrite heart. Lord God of hosts, be With us yet, lest we forget-lest we forget."

Collect for Independence Day:

Almighty God, who hast given us this good land for our heritage; We humbly beseech thee that we may always prove ourselves a people mindful of thy favor and glad to do thy will. Bless our land with honourable industry, sound learning, and pure manners. Save us from violence, discord, and confusion; from pride and arrogancy, and from every evil way. Defend our liberties, and fashion into one united people the multitudes brought hither out of many kindreds and tongues. Endue with the spirit of wisdom those to whom in thy Name we entrust the authority of government, that there may be justice and peace at home, and that, through obedience to thy law, we may show forth thy praise among the nations of the earth. In the time of prosperity, fill our hearts with thankfulness, and in the day of trouble, suffer not our trust in thee to fail; all which we ask through Jesus Christ our Lord. Amen. (*Book of Common Prayer* of the Protestant Episcopal Church in the United States of America p. 36).

Chapter 16:

The Civil War (1861-1865)

In fulfillment of my interest in the details of the Civil War history, I have visited the following battlefields: Antietam; Gettysburg; Bull Run; Ball's Bluff; Fredericksburg; Pea Ridge, Arkansas; Hampton Roads; Glorieta Pass, New Mexico; Chancellorsville; Vicksburg; Port Hudson, Louisiana; Chickamauga; Chattanooga; Monocacy, Maryland; Winchester; the Wilderness; and Lookout Mountain.

There was nothing civil about this war!

Per the foreword by David Aiken:

> According to the sources used by Graham, the death of the American Republic, that shining light to oppressed humanity everywhere, was not caused by slavery. Nor was the death caused by unfair tariffs, or even by states asserting the right of succession. No, the great American experiment in constitutional government by the consent of the governed was ruined by a plot to gain control of banking and currency----the love of money, the root of all evil according to St. Paul. Blood money. (Graham: 12).

> We have here, simply the repetition of that great conflict, which for ages has agitated our globe-the conflict between aristocratic usurpation and popular rights...There are many in the North, who are in cordial sympathy with the slaveholding aristocracy, and who would gladly see their principals triumphant over this whole land.... The disposition on the part of the rich to trample upon the poor, and of the strong to crush the weak, is alike execrable in its initial origin and in all its manifestations...The rebels having failed to carry their point at the ballot-box have appealed to the sword. (Abbott: *iii-vi).*

The fatal wound that robbed the Republic of its life was neither slavery, nor tariffs, not even secession. It was money, money bathed in the blood of American soldiers, both North and South. (Graham: 11).

Prelude: Roots of the Conflict

America's Civil War is generally considered to be that of freedom versus slavery. As important as the slavery issue was to the war's origins, there were decided economic and political issues that were also the causes of the war.

The roots of the discord which culminated in the horrific War Between the States began as early as the writing of the Declaration of Independence in 1776. Thomas Jefferson originally included in his draft of the Declaration of Independence the following passage relating to slavery:

> He has waged cruel war against human nature itself, violating its most sacred rights of life and liberty in the persons of a distant people who never offended him, captivating and carrying them into slavery in another hemisphere or incur miserable death in their transportation thither...

The final phraseology only included King George's "incitement of domestic insurrection among us." Later, Jefferson blamed the removal of the passage on delegates from South Carolina and Georgia and Northern delegates who represented merchants who were at the time actively involved in the Trans-Atlantic slave trade.[1]

Upon the signing of the Constitution there was allowed a twenty-year grace period until 1808 to allow the continued movement of new slaves into the country. (Dye: 8).

The beginnings of slavery in the American colonies began in the mid-1600s when planters moved to the Carolinas from the Caribbean and brought their slaves with them. The Dutch were the original slave traders. Originally, English indentured servants worked the lands, but by the time the colonists acquired extensive lands from the Indian tribes, more workers were required. By 1710, the slavery system was firmly established.[2]

By the time of the 1787 Constitutional Convention, slavery was well-established in the United States. The 1790 census reflected 3.8 million persons, 18% (700,000) were slaves. Many original U.S. men of note such as John Jay, Oliver Ellsworth one of the signers the Constitution and Patrick Henry were opposed to slavery.[3] At the time of the Constitutional Convention, it was accepted as fact that slave labor was essential to the success of the agricultural industry of the South. Probably, even this early, there were murmurings of the South forming their own nation, if slavery were to be abolished. In favor of Southern congressional representation in the Congress, slaves were counted as three-fifths of a person.[4] As a consequence the congressional delegation of the South counted 20 additional congressmen due to the slave population. (Dye: 7).

Some additional background for the roots of the disorder underlying the Civil War relate to the national bank experiences of the country. The first National Bank of the United States was formed just after the Revolutionary War primarily due to the support of Alexander Hamilton. The first and the second U.S. Banks had European investors. President Andrew Jackson, a decided populist, determined that the Second Bank of the United States was a federal monopoly and he decided not to renew its chapter, claiming it was, "...a den of vipers and thieves."[5] Both had European stockholders, so foreigners had a financial interest in the prosperity or lack thereof of the United States.[6]

Presidential Assassinations

In the decades leading up to the outbreak of hostilities between the North and the South, a significant, but little-known phenomenon occurred related to successful presidential assassinations and other unsuccessful probable attempts. A sidelight on history relates to the time when two former presidents who were intimately involved in the Declaration of Independence exactly 50 years previously, Thomas Jefferson and John Adams, both died peacefully on the same day on July 4, 1826, within hours of each other. (Dye: 5). Lives of other presidents were not so peaceful due to the continued conflict of slavery in the nation. By 1820, the Congress passed an act in which the slave trade was considered "piracy." (Dye: 13). John Jay, the first Chief Justice of the Supreme Court, wrote on November 17, 1819 that slavery should not be allowed in any new states to be admitted to the Union. (Dye: 14).

Missouri was admitted as a slave state in 1820, and Arkansas and Florida allowed slavery. By 1830, Southerner John C. Calhoun, vice president under John Quincy Adams, began to advocate the political principle of States Rights. The effort was being proposed that States Rights would become preeminent to the Union. (Dye: 18). John C. Calhoun was its principal adherent and termed by author Dye as "heresy." (Dye: 21). By 1832, Calhoun was committed to secession or nullification, and the effort began as early as November of 1832. One of the arguments he used was the detriment to the South of the tariff which it was argued was only for the benefit of northern manufacturers. In 1833, President Andrew Jackson was adamantly opposed to this effort. (Dye: 25). The States Rights movement for the time being was dead in the water.

After this proclamation by Jackson, the assertion was met with expected negativity by Calhoun, by his calling of Jackson a "tyrant and despot" and better men than he had been hung. (Dye: 27). Author John Smith Dye, writing in 1864, said, "In fact, it was no uncommon thing at that time to hear threats against the President's life. The corrupting influence of the money power of the United States Bank joined hands with the slave power, although from very different motives. (Dye: 27).

On January 30, 1835, an Englishmen by birth and house painter by work attempted an assassination of President Jackson. Assassin Lawrence upon examination by two physicians, claimed Jackson was a "tyrant." (Dye: 29). Perhaps the assassin derived that term from Calhoun's verbiage?

By 1836, Mexico, who controlled Texas, abolished slavery. Many supporters of slavery moved into Texas and a war ensued, won by Texas. (Dye: 34).

The duo of William Henry Harrison, the hero of the Battle of Tippecanoe, and John Tyler won the 1840 election. Harrison was opposed to slavery. (Dye: 35). A delegation of Southerners approached Tyler and determined that he would support introduction of Texas as a slave state. (Dye: 36). Harrison was inaugurated on March 4, became ill on March 26, and died on April 4, 1841, a mere thirty-one days into his term.

Author Dye began an intensive study of the death and claimed that Harrison had died of arsenic poisoning, although the official cause was pneumonia, supposedly contracted days after his exposure to bad weather in his inaugural. (Dye: 40). Perhaps this was one of the first "conspiracy theories" expressed in American history. John Tyler became president. His cabinet members, except for one member, were all from the slave states. (Dye: 45). Secession raised its head again and it was proposed that Texas be admitted as a slave state or the Union would be broken. Another war was started on May 13, 1846, between Texas and Mexico soon after Texas was annexed as a slave state. (Dye: 47).

Zachary Taylor, the hero of the Battle of Buena Vista in the Mexican War, became president in 1849. He suppressed a planned incursion into Cuba that was predicated on its allowing slavery. California was seeking entry to the Union and its Constitution forbade slavery. President Zachary Taylor was obviously not a friend of the pro-slavery forces. Amazingly Zachary Taylor on July 4, 1850, became sick with the same symptoms to which Harrison had succumbed. (Dye: 54). Taylor served one year and four months into his term. Perhaps he too was poisoned?

Author Abbott, also writing during the war in 1864 his Volume 1 of the *History of the Civil War*, wrote that James Buchanan was a decided candidate of the slaveholders. (Abbott: 40). Buchanan was inaugurated president March 4, 1857. The pro-slavers were intent upon Buchanan staffing his cabinet with pro-slavers and pro-secession individuals. He originally was opposed to the individuals from the pro-slavery faction to be in his cabinet. (Dye: 91). Another conspiracy raised its ugly head. Before his inauguration on February 22, 1857, Buchanan attended a dinner party at the National Hotel in Washington where 38 attendees died presumably from arsenic poisoning. Buchanan became ill, but survived. (McCarty: 60). This episode convinced Buchanan to support Kansas entering the Union as a slave state. Much blood was shed in Kansas. (Dye: 99). The conflict in Kansas really reflected the beginning of the Civil War, not the firing on Fort Sumter.

Conspiracies

The close call on Buchanan's life was probably instrumental in bringing him around to a strong position supporting the slavers so that between the election of Abraham Lincoln and his inauguration on March 4, 1861, a significant degree of treachery was present amongst the members of Buchanan's cabinet.

Another significant but little-known series of events began to occur during the administration of Buchanan. A "secret" organization, the Knights of the Golden Circle, formed in 1858 to advance the southern causes and for the eventual purpose of supporting military operations into Mexico and eventually the Caribbean Islands and Central America, in order to bring those areas into the fold to allow slavery. (Keehn: 1).[7] There was originally a somewhat tacit approval by President Buchanan of a military filibuster into Mexico when he spent a quarter of his December 1859 annual message describing the horrendous conditions existing in Mexico between "liberals" led by Benito

Juarez and the "conservatives" led by wealthy Mexicans and the Catholic clergy. (Keehn: 19). Buchanan requested authority to establish military outposts in Mexico in the northern states of Sonora and Chihuahua. (Keehn: 32). Promises were made to the mercenaries for land in Mexico and a piece of the riches from the Sonora mines. (Keehn: 37).

In early March of 1860, thousands of Knights descended on Gonzalez, Texas, ready to begin an expedition into Mexico. Texas Governor Sam Houston had requested federal funds for an expedition into Mexico, but the Buchanan administration declined the request, whereupon Houston dropped the idea of an "invasion." It was recognized that the Knight's mission was to occupy Mexico and "Americanize" it and the national administration only wanted Mexico to be kept as an independent republic. (Keehn: 41-42).

In the summer of 1860, the Knights remained committed to achieving a conquest of Mexico and carving it up into a multitude of states of the Union, all supportive of slavery. (Keehn: 55). Knights leader George Bickley continued to advocate for an invasion of Mexico and continued military preparations were in effect in south Texas. However, Juarez's forces began to obtain the upper hand against their opponents and they no longer were supportive of any military help from the Knights. (Keehn: 60). The Knights evolved to being supportive of secession and offered a military resource to southern governors. A report from an "informer" to U.S. Army Colonel Joseph K. Mansfield in Texas related that the outgoing Buchanan secretaries of war and treasury, John Floyd and Howell Cobb, were members of the Knights. This informer related that members of Buchanan's cabinet were to be treasonous in allowing control of federal military posts by southern factions. (Keehn: 70). Members of the Knights became the nucleus of the armed factions in the south called Minute Men. (Keehn: 78).

By October 20, 1860, Lincoln became aware of plans for his assassination were he to be elected president. (Keehn: 87).

Secretary of War Floyd began to implement his nefarious schemes and actions to assist the South in its preparations for secession. He arranged for arms shipments to be sent to southern bases so that they would be readily seized by southern sympathizers. He appointed known southern adherents on active duty in senior commanding positions in the Army to include a West Point Superintendent Major P.G. T. Beauregard, who immediately suggested to cadets from southern states the advisability of resignations to join southern forces. (Keehn: 91). Winfield Scott, general-in-chief of the U.S. Army, warned President Buchanan in late October 1860 of the plans afoot to commandeer nine posts in the south. Buchanan ignored the warnings. (Keehn: 92). Floyd attempted to divert heavy guns to southern posts. Discovered for his treasonous actions, he resigned on December 29, 1860, but the damage to the military capability of the north and the buildup of the southern capabilities had been accomplished. Takeover of more than twenty federal arsenals and posts in the south was accomplished both before and after secession by some of the states. Knights of the Golden Circle were very much parties to these moves. (Keehn: 95, 99). Floyd further performed admirably his own part in treason when he ensured that federal troops were disbursed far afield in western posts, was "negligent" in that 1200 cannon were seized in southern posts, and ordered thousands of weapons from arsenals in Springfield, Massachusetts and Watervliet, New York to southern arsenals He arranged for sale to the south before his resignation of U.S. muskets worth $12 each for only $2.50. (Abbott: 43). General Twiggs in command of the Army in Texas surrendered without a fight. (Dye: 111).

Other disloyal members of Buchanan's cabinet were involved in the chicanery. Secretary of the Treasury Howell Cobb, a slaveholder from Georgia, accomplished his mission and it was reported that as much as six million dollars was missing from the treasury upon his resignation to join the Confederacy. (Abbott: 42). Secretary of the Interior Jacob Thompson, slaveholder from Mississippi, played his part in the conspiracy. When Fort Sumter in South Carolina was placed under siege and a ship was dispatched in relief of the starving garrison, Thompson alerted the conspirators in Charleston and the ship was repulsed by shore batteries. He later admitted his disloyalty in his official position. (Abbott: 43).

Navy Secretary Isaac Toucey, a northerner from Connecticut, but sympathetic to the South, dispatched naval ships to various overseas ports. (Abbott: 45). President Buchanan was either clueless, or powerless, or acquiescing as these actions were carried out by his cabinet members. By this time individuals sympathetic to slavery had plotted and planned to control the reins of power in the federal government and they had succeeded. (Abbott: 55).

In early 1861, the Knights began a plot to seize the District of Columbia, Washington. The plot was discovered and foiled by Colonel Charles Stone. Lincoln continued to receive death threats. At this exact time, John Wilkes Booth, on his acting circuit, was becoming more pronounced in his expression of sympathies for the South. (Keehn: 110).

The conspiracy of historic proportions continued as it recruited twenty men to assassinate President-elect Abraham Lincoln on February 22, 1861, as he was to pass through Baltimore by train. Alerted to a planned Baltimore assassination by Knights members, Lincoln surreptitiously passed at night through Baltimore on February 23, 1861, averting the assassination and proceeded on to Washington. (Keehn: 112). Suffice it to say in conclusion regarding the Knights of the Golden Circle, they were an integral element in the effort to accomplish secession and will return later in our commentary as individual sympathizers probably related to the deceit and disloyalty of John Wilkes Booth.

Causes: Overview

Our ancestors left societies in Europe where they were downtrodden by the privileged classes, to live in a representative republic, wherein all are presumably protected under laws which favors no one (although this is an imperfect assumption), should be able to make as much money as one can honestly desire, to enjoy as many comforts as one can endure, and appropriate all the learning desired. These were universally accepted in the United States and today are the foundations of our country and its precepts.

However, in the South, the privileged class of slave-holders took over the reins of power with ever-increasing prosperity. (Abbott: 23). The bottom line is that, notwithstanding protestations by the South regarding States Rights, it was down at its core about slavery, an abhorrent practice. Other nations by these times had banned slavery, and it was time for the United States to cease the practice. (Abbott: 25).

The challenge, as expressed by the author Abbott in 1864, held that "It is impossible that two such antagonistic systems as democratic equality and aristocratic privileges should live in peace under the same government or even side-by-side." (Abbott: 21). For all time, this is the eternal conflict, that of equal rights and responsibilities.

The conditions, separations, and antagonisms between Northern and Southern senators was expressed thusly by the Honorable Iverson (Georgia) on the floor of the United States Senate on December 5, 1860: "Sir, disguise the fact as you will, there is an enmity between the Northern and the southern people, which is deep and enduring, and you never can eradicate it-never. Look at the spectacle exhibited on this floor. How is it? There are the Northern senators on that side; here the Southern senators on this side. How much social intercourse is there between us? You sit upon your side, silent and gloomy. We sit upon ours, with knit brows and portentous scowls. Here are two hostile bodies on this floor; and it is but a type of the feeling which exists between the two sectors. We are enemies as if we were hostile states. We have not lived in peace. We are not living in peace. It is not expected that we shall ever live in peace." (Abbott: 22).

Economic conflict that had lasted for decades was a major cause of the Civil War. (Griffin *Creature*: 369). For humans to kill each other in warfare, the emotional aspect of hatred had to be instilled, so both sides commenced to inculcate this attitude in their populations. Of course, once again, the elitists would sit in their paneled offices and comfortable places while the rank-and-file commoners shed blood on the battlefields!

Causes: Northern Perspective

Senator Garrett Davis of Kentucky said, "the cotton states, by their slave labor have become wealthy and many of their planters have princely revenues-$50,000-$100,000 a year. This wealth has begot pride, and insolence, and ambition, and these points of the southern character have been displayed most insultingly in the halls of Congress. As a class, the wealthy cotton growers are insolent, they are proud, they are domineering, they are ambitious. They have monopolized the government in its honors, for 40 or 50 years with few interruptions. When they saw the scepter about to depart from them in the election of Lincoln, sooner than give up office and the spoils of office, they determined in their mad and wicked ambition to disrupt the old Confederation and erect a new one wherein they would have undisputed power. Nine out of ten of the Northern people were sound upon the subject. They were opposed to the extension of slavery, and I do not condemn them for that; but they were willing to accord to the slaveholders all their constitutional rights. (Abbott: 22).

The privileged few in the South were accumulating wealth on the backs of the slaves. The common man, who would eventually shed his blood for the southern cause, was not in the greatest economic and financial position. There was a constant push by the slaveholders to extend slavery to new U.S. territories. If slavery were to have been extended to new states, more privileged few would have enjoyed the luxuries gained from the backs of the slave laborers, who would have worked the field. (Abbott: 20).

Americans had fled the same conditions in Europe where serfdom was systemic, to populate this new frontier and break the shackles of the tyranny of the European elitist classes. The living of the American dream meant then and means today that under our laws, all, both rich and poor, are entitled to equal rights, born to mansion or log cabin, and common man and owner's child have equal opportunity to advance and prosper.

In Abbott's own words:

> There will always be an aristocracy. There will always be some wiser, better, nobler than others... They are not in transmitted titles and ribbons, and the musty records of a dead ancestry, but in their own heroic achievements.

> But it is impossible to respect an aristocracy founded on the most sordid and vulgar claim earth has ever known- that of owning slaves; - an aristocracy which can sell child from the mother, and scourge the back of the maiden, and a wrench from the worker-woman her dollar, and sell female virtue and loveliness at auction; an aristocracy whose only appropriate crest is a trembling Negro. (Abbott: 54).

> The only nobility America can recognize, is the nobility of achievement and worth... It is this spirit only which develops the whole latent talent of the nation. It is this principle which has enabled the United States to make such giant strides, spreading such marvelous thrift and energy over the free North; and it is the absence of this spirit, which has spread such dilapidation and decay over the enslaved South. (Abbott: 55).

Causes: Southern Perspective

A case can be argued and made that tariffs, supported by the industrial North, were part and parcel of the underlying causes of the Civil War. Upon the election of Andrew Jackson taxes on imports were raised to such an extent that a recession was caused in the South. A compromise was achieved, and tariffs were decreased. In South Carolina, a crisis that threatened secession as early as this time in the history of our nation developed. This cause eventually did not carry weight, because by 1857 only a limited quantity of products had an ad valorem tax. (Graham: 43).

Southerners constantly supported new states being admitted to the Union that permitted slavery to be expanded because the slave owners of the South knew that their primary crops, exports of tobacco and coffee, were eroding their acreage and they needed new land to continue their livelihoods. (Colby: 710).

Senator Wigfall, a Texan in the Senate, said, "... We say that our slaves are our *property*. We say that it is the duty of every government to protect its property everywhere. For 20 years, the slave trade was kept open by the Constitution; and if that was not a clear recognition of the right to trafficking human flesh, and buy and sell men and women, then I would like to know what would be." (Abbott: 26). Senator Hunter of Virginia proposed changes to the Constitution that would permanently impose slavery on our country.

Vigilante committees were established in the South and mail was searched. Shades of the Gestapo in Germany! The free slaves were told to leave the South. Unfortunately, many Christian ministers in the South spoke not against slavery. Also, unfortunately, there were untold number of women slaves in the South in whose veins coursed the blood of their white masters. (Abbott: 33).

The election of Abraham Lincoln as president was a major immediate cause for the rebellion to begin to take effect and become a serious issue in the nation.

The Honorable John C. Calhoun, previously noted, was a member of the House of Representatives. As early as the War of 1812, he had been quoted as saying, "It is through our association with that party (Democrat), in the middle and western states, that we hold power. But, when we cease thus to control this nation, through a disjointed democracy, or any material obstacle in that party which shall tend to throw us out of rule and control, we shall then resort to the dissolution of the union." (Abbott: 35).

For vote count, a compromise in the Constitution for the southern states had been allowed, wherein five slaves to three white men were counted for congressional representation. This provided extraordinary extra voting strength to the southern delegations. When the tide was turning toward more free states, they realized they were close to being outvoted. (Abbott: 36).

The South (5 million strong) desired that the North (20 million strong) bend to the wishes of the slaveholders. The demands of the South made peace impossible. (Abbott: 37).

When Lincoln campaigned against three other candidates for the presidency he said unequivocally, "Slavery and oppression must cease or American liberty must perish." He maintained slavery could be allowed where it was present, but he would not support any extension. (Abbott: 39).

Both protagonists had depended upon each other for trade. The South bought the north's manufactured products and sold its cotton to the north as well as to Europe. When Europe sold products competitive with the North at lower prices to the South, the north's market share suffered so their solution was to pass legislation that placed tariffs on manufactured goods prior to the Civil War. The South then was required to pay the higher northern prices. European demand for the South's cotton was lessened and the situation seriously impaired their economy. (Griffin *Creature*: 375). Abolition of slavery meant their economy would collapse.

Supposedly, an overwhelming majority of Southerners did not even own slaves, but the argument for them to take up arms in the struggle boiled down to a deep-seated belief in slaves as property and States Rights. Some Southerners favored a gradual end to slavery to allow the economy to adjust to the change.

Foreign Involvement

At the beginning of Lincoln's administration, relations with England and France left much to be desired. In October 1861, the collective fleets of France, England, and Spain began preparations to invade Mexico for the payment of bank debts to French lenders. The Russian czar as well as Denmark, Sweden, Switzerland, and Italy were friendly to the United States. (Emerson: 867). England allowed southern privateers to use its ports, the only foreign power to do so. (Emerson: 868). The combined invasion fleet attacked Veracruz, Mexico, in 1862.

In 1864, a meeting was held in London that was attended by representatives of the Catholic Church: Frenchman Baron James de Rothschild III, a Mr. Davidson who represented the English House of Rothschild in Mexico, Englishman Lord Lionel Nathan Rothschild, and the French ambassador. The purpose of the meeting was to obtain a loan from the Rothschilds for continuation of the war in Mexico, guaranteed by the large Catholic landholdings in Mexico. A Jesuit, Father Fisher, made the case for the loan. The subject of the Monroe doctrine was discussed, but, shelved as not applicable due to the Civil War. It was the opinion of the French ambassador that the United States would soon become two countries. (Messervy: 24-25). Father Fisher claimed that the Confederate States of America would be a firm ally of a government led by a European to be installed in Mexico. (Messervy: 26). Possibly behind the financial arrangement was the suggestion of military support of the South by the French, if the Confederacy would offer up Louisiana and Texas. (Cherep-Spiridovich: 172). Before the Civil War, the invading European powers no doubt looked with great interest as to the potential of an invasion of Mexico by the Knights of the Golden Circle.

The European powers were supportive of the Civil War in America because that would break the Republic into two nations, both much weaker than the one, enabling Europeans to recognize Latin America with no fear of the Monroe Doctrine becoming operative. With France in Mexico, England moved troops on the Canadian border in the north. (Griffin *Creature*: 377).

Russian Tsar Alexander, threatened by France and England with the breakup of his empire, decided to throw his weight and support behind the United States. This was accomplished by deployment of two Russian fleets, one to San Francisco on October 12, 1863, and another one to New York on September 24, 1863. (Knuth: 90). With this new threat to their designs in the Western Hemisphere, France and England got the message and remained officially neutral. This factor could have been the decidedly positive factor in negating this threat to the north. (Griffin *Creature*: 378).

Eventually, the motivation of the North to carry on the fight to preserve the Union was predicated upon the "propaganda" argument that it was a battle for freedom of the slaves, not that of "preserving" the Union. (Griffin *Creature*: 379). This argument carried weight in the European capital cities. Despite quietly siding politically with one or the other protagonist, Europe officially remained neutral without overtly aiding either side.

By 1862, the American Civil War had major economic ramifications for England in that English exports to the United States were substantially reduced. The Union blockade cut down on cotton imports, but trade with France increased to make up the difference. (Emerson: 892).

Causes: Banking and Currency Considerations

Money makes the world go 'round, and financing wars costs massive amounts of money. Little cause is lent to the money cause of the Civil War because it has been vastly overshadowed, and almost totally covered in history books, by slavery and Union issues. This slant might have occurred because slavery and union issues may be much more comprehensible than money and currency and banking to the general reading public.

Money and currency machinations underlying the causes of the

314

Civil War may actually have been a major cause of the war. To lend credibility to this thesis, one must perhaps ascribe this approach to a "conspiracy," which automatically comes into abuse because naturally dots for something hidden cannot be connected. However, per Graham, "There is actually such a judicial standard for proving up conspiracy in civil litigation," once aptly expressed as follows: (Graham: 29).

> Conspirators do not make minutes of their machinations, progress and objectives. Seldom, therefore, can conspiracy be proved by other than circumstantial evidence. It is only by summing the results, with such evidence as may be of the progress thereof by the participants, that the victim can ever make a case of conspiracy. If in the end there is a completed structure of result, the frame of which has been furnished piecemeal by several individuals, the parts when brought together showing adaptation to each other and fitness for the end accomplished, it is at least reasonable to infer concert in both planning and fabrication.[8]

Despite the attempt by the North to finance the war independently, the final outcome for both North and South is reflected in these words: "Furthermore, the financial needs of the United States and the Confederacy imparted significant political power to an elite group of London-based financiers who became intimately involved in American foreign relations during this period." (Sexton: 1).

Author Des Griffin reported that:

> The establishment *Times* of London stated: 'If that mischievous financial policy which had its origin in the North American Republic [i.e. honest Constitutionally-authorized *no debt* money] should become indurated down to a fixture, then that government will furnish its own money without cost. It will pay off its debts and be without a debt to the international bankers. It will become prosperous beyond precedent in the history of the civilized

governments of the world. The brains and wealth of all countries will go to North America. That government must be destroyed or it will destroy every monarchy on the globe.' (Griffin *Descent*: 34).

Self-financing of a nation and especially of a war was anathema to the governing and especially the banking classes.

Union Financing

Recall that the United States by 1861 did not have a national Bank. Throughout the European societies national banks were a means by which control could be exercised via control of banking and currency to be able to expand and contract money supply. In the United States this power eventually was accomplished by the establishment of the Federal Reserve in 1913. However, in 1861, the United States did not suffer under this onerous and devastating financial control. France and England were officially neutral, but if the United States could be split into two countries (again the unspoken political desires maintained within the two countries), South America colonization could be revived. With the cause of the North eventually gravitating with the Emancipation Proclamation being that of freedom instead of quelling an overt rebellion, contemplated financial aid to the South evaporated.

The Union began financing the war with the use of "Greenbacks," American money, United States Treasury notes. This financing was carried out without the use of gold. During these horrendous four years, Congress eventually passed a variety of measures that allowed foreigners to buy money at prices which had suffered depreciation and by various machinations by the end of the war turned the financing into indebtedness. (Hobart: 48).

However, at the war's beginning, President Lincoln's use of these "Greenbacks" meant that the North was able to pay its bills without resorting to the usurious rates offered by London or New York banks. Obviously, private bankers, being deprived of profitable and protected government loans, were deeply disdainful of President Lincoln. (Engdahl *Gods of Money:* 15). The final amount financed through "Greenbacks" was $432 million. The government (i.e., politicians) had their non-interest paying money, but the banks were out of the equation. Bankers missed the profiting from the interest on their loans to the government [my definition of "blood money"] so presumably their lobbying brought Secretary of the Treasury Salmon Chase eventually to the decision to utilize government bonds as security for bank notes. (Griffin *Creature*: 385).

It is important to note that the final effect that began in the mid-1850s of the financial power of the international bankers was centered in Europe. It is expressed by author Carroll Quigley as to their goal (and to a degree successful possibly even into the 21st century):

> ...to form all these (financial institutions) into a single financial system on an international scale which manipulated the quantity and flow of money so they will able to influence, if not control governments on one side and industries on the other. (Quigley *Tragedy:* 51).

The combinations thereof looked in defiance and distinct negativity at what President Lincoln was accomplishing without their assistance.

Northerner August Belmont was a German-American politician, financier, foreign diplomat, and chairman of the Democratic National Committee before the Civil War and all the way through the war. He was born in Germany and eventually settled in America, involved with the Rothschild banking interests. After the panic of 1837, he exercised his banking acumen to assist in restoring the financial solidity of the Rothschild family's financial interests in his newly adopted country.

Banker J.P. Morgan was halted from lending to the North because the South pulled their northern deposits. However, under Philadelphia banker Jay Cooke's management, the Union sold war bonds, but "...German–Jewish bankers on Wall Street raised loans from numerous Union sympathizers in Germany." (Chernow: 13).

Eventually the banking lobbyists in Europe and the United States managed to push through their interests (perhaps with sufficient political contributions) so that on February 25, 1863, the National Banking Act was passed, which established nationally-chartered banks. It was explained as a method to create a market for the government bonds, which led to money being available to meet the military needs of the war. The bankers were pleased because they again made money off the new system. (Griffin: 387). This Act gave bankers control to issue money and therefore a virtual lock on substantial profits to be derived. (Sutton: *Federal Reserve:* 38).

The establishment of the National Banking Act drew attention from European banking interests. On June 25, 1863, after the Act had been in effect for four months, the following messages were found, presumably stating an accurate opinion of a member of the London Rothschild operation to a banker in New York. The Rothschild reply was in response to an original letter from United States Senator John Sherman, who wrote the letter to ensure that the London Rothschild banking interests were informed about the recently enacted national banking act. (Sutton *Federal Reserve*: 38). The original letter from the Senator to the Rothschilds describing the new act has apparently not been found. Obviously, it could have been "fake news." The correspondence is quoted by Sutton from his original source.[9]

As a follow-up to Sherman's letter, a letter signed "Rothschild brothers" was sent June 25, 1863, to Messrs. Ikleheimer, Morton and Vandergould at No. 3, Wall St., New York. The Rothschild letter stated that the Act was originally devised by the British Bankers Association and recommended to their friends in the North. The letter quoted, "… [the Act] would prove highly profitable to the banking fraternity."

The Rothschild letter quotes that Senator Sherman wrote: "The tremendous advantages that capital derives from the system will bear its burden without complaint, and perhaps without even suspecting that the system is inimical to their interests."

The sentiments expressed to the Rothschilds by Senator Sherman was considered credible enough to derive a response. Senator Sherman was one of many "elitists" who harbored a rather low opinion of the "masses" who were not informed of the "science of money."

The response from the Wall Street lawyers back to the Rothschilds on July 6, 1863, described in detail the financial details of the Act, and that Sherman was an ambitious member of Congress. The profits were of such a nature for a national bank that the gross earnings of the bank amount to from 28% to 33.5%. By the way, the lawyer letter declared that the recipients were to consider the imparted information to be confidential. (See note 9 reference). No knowledge is public in my research as to whether the Rothschild interests invested in any national bank directly, or perhaps indirectly through Belmont.

President Lincoln vetoed a bill which would have required Southern cotton to be used to pay off southern debt, much of which had been bought by the Rothschilds at a discount as engineered by August Belmont. (Griffin *Creature*: 391).

In summary, for the North, the issue at its heart was not about slavery or freedom, but really about the economic bones of contention; destroying the North, monopolies of the banks, and the expansion of European powers once again into Latin America while the United States was distracted by the Civil War. A national banking system resulted after war bonds, taxes, and greenbacks could not pay the bills.

The Union from the beginning of the war was concerned that Britain might support the South for three reasons: a need for Southern cotton (for their textile mills), a policy of sympathy for the original threat of the South politically (one of self-determination), and thirdly and very discerningly, an attempt to weaken a very strong competitor. (Sexton: 82). Secretary of State William H. Seward made it very clear to the United States Minister to London, Charles Francis Adams, to communicate that enmity between United States and Britain might occur if Britain recognized the South. (Sexton: 83).

August Belmont was sent on a secret mission to London by Secretary Chase to obtain a bank loan for the Union. Naturally, Belmont, the Rothschild representative in the United States, favored the Rothschilds as the loan agent. "The largest and most influential bank in the world, the Rothschilds had a history of assisting governments in their hour of need." (Sexton: 83). When bankers lent to the government, collateral of taxes of the citizens was a far superior promise to pay than individual or corporate security. Belmont was unsuccessful in obtaining any loans in Britain. Queen Victoria on May 13, 1861, had declared Britain officially neutral, the position that they held to throughout the war. (Sexton: 87).

A young Rothschild, Salomon, the third son of Baron James, was sent to review the financial situation in America. Salomon ended up becoming enamored with the South, but, not the North. He wrote back to his family on April 28, 1861, that Europe should recognize the South, and perhaps that influence would cause the Civil War to cease. (Wilson: 185). In conclusion, regarding Rothschild financing, the Rothschilds bought into neither Belmont's nor Salomon's arguments.

Belmont and the Rothschilds were not held in the greatest esteem in all quarters in the United States. Take this opinion stated in an 1864 *Chicago Tribune* article: "Will we have a dishonorable peace in order to enrich Belmont, the Rothschilds and the whole tribe of Jews..., who have been buying up Confederate bonds, or an honorable peace won by Grant and Sherman at the cannon's mouth?" (Ferguson: 115). Apparently at this time in the Civil War there was extensive public disdain for the international financiers, many of whom were members of the Jewish race, not religion! An unnamed politician's vehement opposition to Belmont was expressed as follows:

> The agent of the Rothschilds is the chief manager of the Democratic Party! ... There is not a people or government in Christendom in which the paws, or fangs, or claws of the Rothschilds are not plunged to the very heart of the treasury... and they would like to do the same here... We [Americans] did not want to borrow from the Rothschilds and the Jews have got mad and have been mad ever since. (Wilson: 186).[10]

Niall Ferguson, an exhaustive chronicler of the Rothschild family, maintains the Rothschilds had been in a quandary at the beginning of the Civil War due to loans to the North for railroads and exporting cotton and tobacco from the South. (Ferguson: 92).

In the London Baring Brothers Bank, some benefit accrued to the North in that the bank arranged for funds for the North's purchase of arms. The head man at Baring's, Thomas Baring, a member of Parliament, supported the Union. (Sexton: 90). But, no direct loan from Baring's was evident. Barings facilitated funds to Union agents for the acquisition of 150,000 weapons (small arms) in Europe. Eventually the Union efforts procured a grand total of 1,165,000 weapons. Eventually by 1863, Union weapons were produced by Union suppliers. (Sexton: 105).

Somewhat surreptitiously, Liverpool shipbuilders produced two ships for the South (the *Florida* and the *Alabama).* (Sexton: 107). Eventual pressure from the North on Britain and reminder of their supposed neutrality curtailed further shipbuilding for the South. (Sexton: 112).
The selling of Union bonds through the efforts of Jay Cooke was relatively successful through the spring of 1863. A second attempt to obtain bank loans from Britain was unsuccessful. (Sexton: 114). In the end, the Union never obtained bank loans from Europe. (Sexton: 131).

The Morrell Tariff (custom duties to fund the war) was very

distasteful to Britain. Eventually conflicts between the North and Great Britain constantly fueled flames of war that were ready to be ignited. When the British ship, the *Trent*, had been boarded by a U.S. Navy ship and two Southerners, James Mason and John Slidell, were apprehended, Britain demanded the release and an apology. This incident brought the nations close to war and caused a financial panic. (Sexton: 96). The Southerners were freed, and an apology followed. (Sexton: 100).

American banker, George Peabody and London (whose firm eventually became J.P. Morgan) was instrumental in providing influential Britons to be courted by Union representatives. Peabody marketed an unknown quantity, although at least some, Union bonds. (Sexton: 103).

The primary impact of the diplomatic efforts of the North in Europe, although it received no direct loans, was that it ensured the South did not receive recognition.

Confederacy Financing:

Soon after his inauguration on March 4, 1861, President Lincoln instructed his Navy to blockade Southern ports into which goods were being transported in great quantities from Europe. (Griffin, Des: 35). When Lincoln became president, the House of Rothschild through its own and other London banks were the principal lenders for the Southern cotton business. (Engdahl *Gods of Money:* 14).[11]

The South had its own financial genius to counter the North's Belmont in Judah Benjamin, born in St. Croix, the Virgin Islands in 1811. As a young boy, he and his British parents departed to begin residence in the United States. Benjamin became a New Orleans lawyer and eventually a U.S. senator, only the second person of the Jewish race to become a U.S. senator. Benjamin served the Confederacy beside his fellow former Senator Jefferson Davis as, successively, attorney general, secretary of war and secretary of state. It appears he was connected to John Surratt, one of the collaborators in Lincoln's assassination.[12]

Immediately after the beginning of the conflict, the South sent their representatives to Europe seeking political recognition as a new nation. The South believed that their cotton would be a powerful incentive (Abbott: 157). One avenue that was a success for the South was in obtaining 130,000 rifles for the most part from the London Armory, which played both sides by supplying arms also to the North. (Sexton: 142).

After the controversial apprehension by a Union vessel of the British sloop, the *Trent*, and eventual release of the two Southern emissaries to Great Britain and France on November 8, 1861, full diplomatic recognition of the South was postponed by Great Britain and France and they officially remained neutral as indicated previously. However, Great Britain allowed southern privateers to use its ports. (Emerson: 867).

At the beginning of the war, the powerful aristocracy of England was not only tied economically to the South to the cotton trade, but were favorable to the South for the economic reason that a breakup of the Union would mean the United States would no longer be a rival on the high seas, being the economic arena believed to be the sole preserve of Great Britain. (Cincinnatus: 34). This was another indicator of the economic competition present in the overall conditions of the war.

The Confederacy's most lethal weapons that preyed on northern ships, the *Alabama* and the *Florida* were clandestinely produced in Great Britain as previously reported, the *Alabama* at Laird's shipyard in Birkenhead. (Emerson: 914-915). The Confederate ships were highly successful, capturing 261 vessels, basically scuttling the North's commerce on the seas. After the war the United States went to arbitration to recover monetary damages from the British collaboration. Great Britain ended up paying 3,100,000 pounds as damages. (Emerson: 917).

Several sources report that one John Slidell, a former Louisiana senator, who served beside Judah Benjamin, and also one of the southern envoys detained in the *Trent* affair, was the Confederate representative in France. He befriended Emile Erlanger, a financier very close to Napoleon III. As it progressed, the financial tie became closer personally when Erlanger married Slidell's daughter a year after the consummation of an eventual three-million-pound loan for the South. (Sexton: 163).

The South made this 1863 loan despite its having significant financial disadvantages, because the South was desperate for funds to finance the war. The Erlanger firm was not a top-tier European firm, but nonetheless the loan was hopefully a signal of acceptance of legitimacy of the South and consequently possibly would serve a diplomatic purpose to derive British and French re-examination of recognition of the Confederacy. The loan was offered in London through J. H. Schroeder and Company. (Sexton: 165). One of my sources, *War! War! War!* quotes from Burton J. Hendrick's book, *Statesmen of the Lost Cause*, that Erlanger profited more from the loan than did the Confederacy.

Part of the terms to repay the bonds was to deliver cotton to the investors, but for this to succeed, steamers had to evade the Union blockade of Southern ports. (Sexton: 166) This was no small impediment to ensure its success.

On March 16, 1863, W.W. Murphy, the Consul General of the United States in Frankfurt, Germany wrote a letter published in *Harper's Weekly* on April 30, 1863, indicating that the German branch of the Rothschild family, M. A. VON ROTHSCHILD & Son was opposed to slavery and supported the Union. Murphy related that, "a converted Jew, ERLANGER, has taken the rebel loan of 3 million pounds, and lives in this city; and Baron Rothschild informed me that all Germany condemned this active lending money to establish a slaveholding government, and that so great was public opinion against it that ERLANGER & CO. dare not offer it on the Frankfurt Bourse." Murphy goes on to express a very signal opinion, "I further know that the Jews rejoice to think that none of their sect would be guilty of lending money for the purpose above named; but it was left, they say for apostate Jews to do it." The orthodox Jews, by religion, held in contempt Jews who had left the religious faith.

Once the Emancipation Proclamation was signed by Lincoln, the purpose for the war turned to slavery versus anti-slavery. Although previously there had been sympathy amongst many quarters of the political and business communities of Britain to support the Confederacy, Britain, a nation that had outlawed slavery years before, now began to withdraw any support for the South.

The Erlanger bonds began to depreciate especially after the Union victory at Gettysburg in July of 1863. The British welcome mat for Southern agents was withdrawn due to this financial situation. (Sexton: 175).

Private British interests showed extensive support for blockade-running with British-built ships to continue to obtain cotton from the South so that the British textile mills could continue operations, thereby maintaining worker employment. (Sexton: 181). Eventually the British operation did not succeed, and the South attempted to move the ship-building effort to France, but Union people discovered the clandestine effort and it too was shut down. Napoleon III was on shaky grounds due to his venture in Mexico and, unwilling to antagonize the North, he withdrew his tacit approval of the effort. (Sexton: 184). All avenues of European support eventually collapsed for the Confederacy.

In the end, none of the giants of the European financial markets, "... The Barings, Rothschilds, Peabody, Hope and Co.-were prepared to jeopardize the historic relations with the U.S. government and northern states and railroads in order to advance funds to a slaveholding Republic, ..." (Sexton: 187).

At the end of the war, Judah Benjamin escaped capture and eventually reached England, where he became an attorney. He eventually died and was buried in Paris, where his wife and children had resided for many years during the time when he was serving the South and living in Richmond.

Battle Joined!

The merchants of death began the Civil War ready to reap their ill-gotten gains. One Philip S. Justice, a gun maker and dealer, produced 4,000 defective rifles and the Union government declined to pay their $20 price each. (Engelbrecht: 58). There were extensive abuses by the arms merchants, who sold rifles to the Union that was it discovered could have been manufactured with better quality at half the cost. (Engelbrecht: 59).

A name eventually of ultimate prominence in Wall Street was John Pierpoint Morgan, in his mid-20s at the onset of the war. Recognizing the profits to be made, he partnered in a scheme termed the "Hall Carbine" debacle. Supposedly, Morgan was the financial backer for the purchase from the government on May 20, 1861 of 5000 obsolete guns at $3.00 each, determined to be unsafe. After the purchase, they were marketed back to the government by Morgan at $22 per gun being described as "new carbines" in perfect condition. It was a fraud and a blight upon banker Morgan. When fired, Union soldiers "shot off their own thumbs." After a lawsuit, Morgan retrieved his full price. (Engelbrecht: 60-61).

J.P. Morgan was quite an enterprising entrepreneur. So as not to be unavailable to continue profiting from wartime business, he paid $300 for a replacement to fill his draft responsibility, when he was called up after Gettysburg. During the Civil War, many socially and financially prominent sons of the North bought draft replacements, so they did not serve the cause. This was partially the cause of serious draft riots in July of 1863. (Chernow: 22).

Rank-and-file Northerners by the thousands became cannon fodder, while young industrialists like Andrew Carnegie, Philip Armour, James Hill, John D. Rockefeller, Jay Gould, Jim Fisk, and J.P. Morgan, all in their draft-age twenties and all destined to become luminaries in American business history, managed to buy replacements for their numbers in the draft lottery for only $300. (Colby: 89).

The North did not have a monopoly on elitists evading the privilege of serving their cause. The law in the South allowed exemption from military service for one slaveholder for each 20 slaves. Of course, the plantation owners and their sons were necessary for the oversight of the plantations while thousands of the commoners of the South performed their rebel yell and were taken apart by musketry and cannon metal while the elitists sipped their mint juleps on their porches! (Acemoglu: 354).

The DuPont Dynasty did its part by providing gunpowder to the Union from its plants in Delaware. According to Stuart, "In terms of the present dollar's buying power, DuPont made tens of millions of dollars from their contracts during the Civil War." (89). Throughout the war, DuPont continued to raise prices. (Stuart: 91). Wars are very profitable for businesses that achieve government contracts, but, are not so profitable for the families that lose their children and for the wounded from the war.

Soldiers' Blood:

During the war, 2,213,363 individuals served in the Union forces. 140,414 battle deaths and 224,097 other deaths occurred (mainly by diseases), and 281,881 non-mortal wounds were incurred.[13] Estimates of the Confederate combat deaths ranged from 74,000 to 94,000, along with 225,000 other deaths. On September 17, 1862, the bloodiest day in American wars, the Battle of Antietam resulted in 23,000 casualties. Over three days, the Battle of Gettysburg resulted in close to 50,000 casualties.

In Gettysburg after the battle, more than 20,000 Union and Confederate soldiers were left on the battlefield. The 2,390 residents of the town did all they could to help the wounded. The battlefield had 163,000 combatants and one third were killed or wounded. On July 4, Lee's defeated army worked its way back to the South with a 17-mile wagon train transporting the wounded. "In their thousands, the men of Lee and Meade-those beardless youths who had faced each other at Little Round Top, Culp's Hill, the Peach Orchard, Seminary Ridge, the Devil's Den-lay motionless on and under the silent countryside, by the roads, on the farms, and among the barns, the fences, the pastures, and the trees...Mutely, they seemed pleading for tranquility, and that the soil which their common blood had so enriched send forth gardens, and orchards, that these in their blooms and fruits might speak of some future peace and understanding among men." (Musmanno: 8).

The heart of Abraham Lincoln as commander-in-chief of the Union forces was best expressed in his emotion for a family that suffered greatly in this war. The ravages of war were expressed so eloquently by him:

> I have been shown in the files of the war department a statement of the Adjutant General of Massachusetts, that you are the mother of five sons, who have died gloriously on the field of battle. I feel how weak and fruitless must be any words of mine which attempt to beguile you from the grief of a loss so overwhelming. But I cannot refrain from tendering to you the consolation that may be found in the thanks of the Republic they died to save. I pray that our Heavenly Father may assuage the anguish of your bereavement, and leave you only the cherished memory of the loved and lost, and the solemn pride that must be yours, to have laid so costly a sacrifice upon the altar of freedom.[14]

Personally, I would have lost peace had I bought my way out of the draft to serve this cause. Mrs. Bixby surely never overcame her grief.

In the aftermath of one battle in West Virginia, the casualties were described in the following way:

Around was a sickening sight. Along the brink of that bluff lay ten bodies, stiffening in their own gore, and every contortion which their death-anguish had produced. Others were gasping in the last agonies, and still others were writhing with horrible, but not mortal wounds, surrounded by the soldiers whom they really believed to be about to plunge the bayonets to their hearts. The scene afforded a ghastly realization of the horrible nature of this fraternal struggle. All these men were Americans-men who had once been proud to claim each other as countrymen. (Abbott: 162).

One poor fellow was shot through the bowels. The ground was soaked with his blood. The stranger asked him if anything could be done to render him more comfortable; he only whispered, 'I'm so cold.' He lingered nearly an hour in terrible agony. Another young man, just developing into vigorous manhood, had been shot through the head by a large mini ball. The skull was shockingly fractured. His brains were protruding from the bullet-hole, and lay spread on the grass by his head. He was still living! ...And then the poor Georgian lay, gasping in the untold and unimaginable agonies of that fearful death for more than an hour....Near him lay a Virginian, shot through the mouth, and already stiffening...The ball struck the tip of the nose, cutting that off, cut his upper lip, knocking out his teeth, passed through the head, and came out at the back of the neck. The expression of his ghastly face was awful beyond description. And near him lay another, with a ball through the right eye, which had passed out to the back part of the head. The glassy eyes of the dead were all open; some seemed still gasping, with open mouths; all were smeared in their own blood, and cold and clammy with the dews of death upon them...All around the field lay men with wounds in the leg or arms, or face, groaning with pain, and trembling less the barbarous foes they expected to find in the troops, should commence mangling them at once. Words can hardly express their astonishment when the men gently removed them to a little knoll, laid them all together, and formed a circle of bayonets around them to keep off the curious crowd, till they could be removed to the hospitals and cared for by the surgeons. (Abbott: 162, 163).

There was a terrible moral in that group on the knoll; the dead, the dying, the wounded, protected by the very men they had been fighting, and who were as ready then as they had ever been to defend by their strong arms every right these self-made enemies of theirs had ever enjoyed.... The wound on the battlefield removes all differences; in the hospital all are alike the objects of a common humanity that left none beyond its limits." (Abbott: 163).

Chivalry and compassion among combatants! Surely there were instances of the same moral behavior by soldiers of the South in overseeing the Union wounded. Unfortunately, soldiers of both sides were guilty of atrocities on the battlefields.

In the same action, two West Pointers crossed paths again, General Garnett of the South was killed and his body was prepared for burial by Major Love, his roommate for four years at the Academy. (Abbott: 164).

During my service as the director of the National Cemetery System of the Department of Veterans Affairs for eighteen months from 1991 to 1993, it was my responsibility to visit 85 of the then 115 national cemeteries overseen by the Department of Veterans Affairs. The most graphic example of the horrors of the prisoner of war camps witnessed by me was the one at Salisbury, North Carolina. (Holt: 321).

Upon my visit to Salisbury, I observed a huge expanse of ground covered by mowed green grass, and was informed that this was the mass gravesite of Union prisoners who died of illness and lack of food in the camp.

Historians agreed that prison conditions were horrifying on both sides. Politicians on both sides provoked their citizens to stories of the POW camps and the atrocities prevalent therein. In the winter of 1864 to 1865, the conditions were harsh at the Salisbury prison camp. "The records (at Salisbury) indicate that 11,700 men are buried in 18 trenches, each about 240 feet long, ...These men perished at the prison during 1864 and 1865." (Holt: 322).

All were "unknowns" to include Robert Livingstone, the son of Dr. David Livingstone, the well-known missionary to Africa. Robert died on December 5, 1864. (Holt: 322). The death rate here was only exceeded by that at the infamous Andersonville, Georgia prison.

In the northern POW camp at Camp Douglas, in Chicago, Illinois, there were reports of its own share of horrendous conditions concerning Confederate POWs, which were estimated to account for 23% of the population. George Levy, author of *To Die in Chicago*, observed that "the atrocities that occurred in [Douglas] were even more heinous than those at Andersonville." Deaths were due to "...typhoid, diphtheria, smallpox, cholera, tuberculosis, dysentery and measles..." Some of the dead were disposed of in Lake Michigan. The physical consequences of the War Between the States were harsh indeed. "But this is the history of war. The enemy must be dehumanized to salve the consciences of those in control."[15]

A very poignant relating of a touching story about Lincoln and the war casualties is related in Musmanno's book, *The Glory & The Dream*. The incident itself probably has a basis in fact (as many specific names are mentioned), but the discourses themselves had to have been speculative. Lincoln had been to Gettysburg and spoken those memorable words on those hallowed and blood-soaked grounds. He was disposed to take walks around the Capitol and found himself one day before the entrance to a military hospital on the Potomac River. He was as always deep in thought as the president, but, "A sense of utter shame and mortification assailed him. What were his frustrations, his own afflictions, compared to the pains of wounded and shattered soldiers? What a politician did, or what an editor wrote, were as nothing. *Here* was the heartbeat of the Nation." Of course, the hospital commander Colonel Brockton offered a guard to accompany the illustrious visitor. The president demurred and requested he visit by himself. (Musmanno: 43).

It was a three-story building with one thousand beds of men wounded in action. "With each encounter his heart grew heavier, and more humble. How insignificant, how puny, was all against this vast catastrophe, this chaos of shattered bodies, of perforated lungs, of disfigured faces and amputated limbs." Eventually on the third floor in a large room he came upon the Blind Soldier's Ward, wherein were forty men, all twenty-three or under in age. Obviously, none could recognize him and when asked his name, he replied simply, "Lincoln." Of the 2,300,000 Union soldiers, seventy per cent were less than twenty-three in age. He asked if they had any issues the War Department might address. One answered, "Well, the only complaint I got is that I can't see." A wave of laughter filled the room. "And then, as he pictured the greed and selfishness of those who caused the war, and of those who would not end it, he added simply: 'But there are many running this war on both sides, who although they have eyes, see less than you do, my boy.'" As they began discussing the various Lincolns whom they had known, eventually one by the name of Corporal Miller said he had heard President Lincoln at the Gettysburg Cemetery. He commented on how wonderful and moving it was. (Musmanno: 47).

Miller inquired about requesting that a hospital orderly obtain a copy of the speech to have it read. Still not revealing his identity, the president asked if he might just recite it as he recollected the words. The men all gathered to hear it spoken by their visitor. Perhaps this vision was brought to their minds:

> The cemetery at Gettysburg, with its white headstones marching on to eternity. They see the gathering hosts of the living, massing in a great semicircle about a platform,

where sit the leaders of the Nation...Deep lines are carven in his [Lincoln's] features, to hold within them, seemingly all the sorrows of mankind. He opens his lips and speaks: "Four score and seven years ago our fathers brought forth on this continent, a new nation, conceived in liberty, and dedicated to the proposition that all men are created equal..."

President Abraham Lincoln completed his recitation of his comments originally delivered, put on his hat, and left quietly. Soon Corporal Miller, who was at Gettysburg and heard the Gettysburg Address, cries out, "My God! Boys! Boys! I remember that voice. My God! Boys! That *was* Lincoln!"

Perhaps it was visits to military hospitals and letters to mothers and widows that motivated Lincoln to conclude his Second Inaugural Address (which could be described as a *Gospel* of Americanism) with these words:

> With malice toward none; with charity for all; with firmness in the right, as God gives us to see the right, let us strive on to finish the work we are in; to bind up the Nation's wounds; to care for him who shall have borne the battle, and for his widow, and his orphan-to do all which may achieve and cherish a just and lasting peace, among ourselves, and with all nations.

These words above reflect the mission of the Department of Veterans Affairs of the United States of America. It was my pleasure to have served my fellow veterans in this Department for thirteen years. The words also reflect a magnificent tribute to the heart of Lincoln. They reflect a magnanimity toward the South that would be prevalent at the end of the war. It amazes me that the conspiracy to kill him could have been based on a perceived animosity toward the South. As we proceed in the story it is distinctly probable that there were the typical financial motivations found throughout history as to the motivations for the assassination.

Assassination of a President

History is replete with many stories of President Lincoln's assassination in Ford's Theatre and the intensive manhunt that ended in the shooting of the assassin John Wilkes Booth. However, there is possibly an alternative ending to the story of what happened to Booth.

The granddaughter of John Wilkes Booth, Izola Forrester, accomplished extensive research on her grandfather, and maintains that her grandfather did not die in that farm house barn as history has led us to believe. She traced Booth through multitudes of interviews and correspondence to travels among other places to the Royal Hotel in Montréal, which was a sanctuary during the Civil War for Confederates who would escape captivity and sought return to their homeland. The South maintained in Canada during the war a "secret cabinet" involved in clandestine operations against the North. (Forrester: 206-207).

She discovered that Booth had made what was then a secret trip to England and Paris. She quotes a *New York Times* article of July 12, 1936, in which Booth purportedly was sent by Confederate President Jefferson Davis to France in early 1865 in one final effort to obtain support from Emperor Napoleon III in trade for total control of the South's cotton. (Forrester: 215).
The uniform of a Southern colonel was found in his trunk at the National Hotel, where he resided in Washington. (Forrester: 206). Forrester said her mother showed her a picture of her grandfather in uniform with other Confederates to include Judah P. Benjamin, the Confederate Secretary of State. (Forrester: 345). This connects Booth perhaps to a widespread plot encompassing more than just Booth.

Booth's original plan was to kidnap President Lincoln so that he would become a hostage for the freeing of Southern prisoners held in the North. (Forrester: 207). The end of the war caused Booth to change his plans.

In 1902, Forrester visited in New York City an old family friend, John Matthews, who had been a member of the cast at Ford's theater, the scene of the assassination. Matthews had been arrested for involvement in the case, but, proven innocent. Matthews wrote and corroborated the account that Booth's original plan had been to kidnap Lincoln. Matthews claimed a letter he received from Booth indicated that it was Booth's belief that the war had been "upon southern rights and institutions." (Forrester: 228).

The manhunt to track down Booth after the assassination was extensive. A healthy reward was offered for the capture of Booth and any conspirators. The soldier that supposedly shot Booth, as the story has been reported, received a reward. (Forrester: 294).

One of the most credible sources interviewed by Izola Forrester was General James R. O'Beirne, who, by October 1908, was a judge in New York City. Judge Byrne was exceedingly well-versed in all aspects of the Booth case, since in 1865, he had been Provost Marshal in Washington of the civil and military police and had been in charge of Booth's pursuit, which consisted of a contingent of 1600 cavalrymen. Forrester never revealed to him during the course of their conversation that she was related to Booth. He told her, "I can tell you something that has never been published on this case, and never even mentioned, something you will never find on any record. There were three men in that barn and one of them escaped...It was never brought out in the testimony that there was another exit from the barn, but there was." She continued the conversation and the judge concluded, "We were all pledged to secrecy in those days. It was not safe to tell anything. Everyone was after a share of the reward. I received $2000 myself." The Judge said he intended to write his story someday and asked Forrester not to use what he said. He did not live to tell his story. Forrester concluded from this that her grandfather had been the escapee! (Forrester: 302-305).

Her investigation of the eventual culmination of the life of her grandfather John Wilkes Booth after the assassination and his potential escape, took her to Forestville, northern California, in the Russian River area, where she met an Elisha Shortridge, who amazingly enough, declared himself the grandson of Richard Garrett, on whose farm Booth supposedly had been shot and killed. Shortridge said the actual one killed in the Garrett barn was a Confederate soldier. He corroborated that he had heard one got away from the barn. Nearby where she had met Shortridge in a cemetery called Shiloh, the tombstones listed names of Southerners, who had refused to pledge allegiance to the Union after the war. Shortridge said they were all members of the secretive Knights of the Golden Circle. (Forrester: 459-470).

Forrester's conclusion, after chasing down other reports, was most probably that her father had lived out his final days in Asia, but the value of the comments of Shortridge gave plausibility to the theory that her father had not died in the Garrett barn.

John Wilkes Booth had a significant connection with the Knights of the Golden Circle, within which he became a leader. The group itself went somewhat into oblivion officially in 1863, but Booth called upon many of its former members in planning for his elimination of President Lincoln. (Keehn: 2).

One final historical footnote on the treachery of John Wilkes Booth unfolded in May 1934, in Ottawa, Canada, when Gerald G. McGeer, a former mayor of Vancouver, testified before a Canadian House of Commons committee on banking and commerce. McGeer testified that Booth was an agent compensated to plan and conduct a kidnapping and hold Lincoln as a hostage. McGeer explained that his examination of the evidence after the assassination collected by the Secret Service indicated to him the theory that the plot originated in Toronto and Montréal by a group that represented international financiers, whose money-making machinations were dashed when President Lincoln planned only a national program of debt.[16]

Plausibility for this theory advanced by McGeer holds some weight because in his 1864 political campaign Lincoln expounded upon his philosophy that his plan upon election was to finance the U.S. government with a national currency, thereby curtailing a major source of profitability for international bankers, who had opposed Lincoln's "greenback" financing methodology.[17]

Consequences

The self-financing of the war at its beginning had been anathema to the Wall Street and international financiers with whom author Hobart described thusly, "These were the Wall Street bankers-the internal foes of human liberty, the vampires of civilization, the merciless, pitiless leeches upon the efforts of labor." (Hobart: 52). These banking interest lobbyists had descended upon the capitol and arranged that the debt to the United States could be paid by an issuance of $150 million in 1862. The bankers however placed an "Exception Clause" in the bill that mandated that importers had to purchase gold to pay their import fees, a machination typically understood only by the bankers. (Hobart: 55).

Author Hobart writes (corroborated by other sources), at the end of the war an enormous crime had been perpetrated on our country. With all the various and sundry efforts of the bankers and their lobbying of the politicians, Hobart analyzed and wrote that, what transpired eventually in the financial condition of the country, after manipulation of the price of gold (which caused depreciation of the original "greenbacks"), was now, "...the legalized privilege of every foreign, lord, prince, and money monger of Europe to come into our country and buy up our money at thirty-five cents on the dollar and convert it into a bonded debt against us of one hundred cents on the dollar. Appalling crime." (Hobart: 56).

The bottom line and consequences of all this manipulation by the bankers was that immense profits were made by foreign and U.S. bankers. Finally, while the draftees in the North, some taking the place of the "rich boys" previously described, and the "good ole boys of the South returned to bury their dead (if they were found), searched for those missing in action, and licked their physical and emotional wounds for decades, the banking elitists lined their pockets with the wealth of America causing our debts to mount up.

Foreign capitalists worked the exact techniques of finance, made their profits and our new national government was in enormous debt. (Hobart: 57).

Incredibly, it was under an outstanding, but hapless, military hero, President Ulysses S. Grant, who presided over an administration in which "$450,000,000 'Exception Clause' greenbacks were converted into $1,640,000 of bonded indebtedness." (Hobart: 58).

Many of the bonds issued during the war were in the possession of Junius Morgan (J.P. Morgan's father) and James Rothschild. Grant had reassured payment of the bonds in the Civil War in gold. Grant won his stand, but just barely. It was discovered that the previously-mentioned August Belmont, a secret owner of the *New York World* newspaper, had been involved in political chicanery and confusion was rampant as these financial shenanigans were being carried out. When his connection with the Rothschilds became well known, Belmont was discredited, and the Rothschild interests became merged with the House of Morgan (draft-dodger J.P. Morgan's bank). (Graham: 53).

Author John Remington Graham describes what the War Between the States really reflected, "Pseudo-religious fanaticism, raw greed and corruption, political folly, unwholesome ambition, and cultural misunderstanding were abundant in those days." (Graham: 17). The eternal state of humanity when our lesser angels and the forces of darkness become preeminent!

A major consequence of the war produced a distinct division of the United States between the monied interest of the East Coast and their connection with internationalist bankers and the farming interests of the South and the West. (Engdahl *Gods:* 17).

The Civil War represented the beginning of warfare on a scale that caused immense future devastation. The instruments of warfare began to develop to such an extent that massive counts of the dead and horrendous wounds became the order of each day of future battles. Divisions in the war produced political divisions wherein it was 1928 before the South voted Republican and the West did not support Democrats until 1932. (Quigley *Tragedy:* 70).

In some ways, the South has never really recovered economically due to the demise of the South's financial base, albeit based on the odious slave labor. General Robert E Lee was brought up on a charge of sedition, which was quashed by General U.S. Grant. President Andrew Johnson on December 25, 1868, declared amnesty to all former Confederates.

Cavalryman Brigadier General J. O. Shelby, who commanded several hundred of his Southerners, went to Mexico after a review of his division 50 miles to the southeast of Dallas, Texas. There, he proclaimed that he preferred, "...exile to submission, death to dishonor." Emperor Maximilian, the "puppet monarch" of Mexico, refused Shelby's offer of the military support of his disaffected troops. By two years later, Shelby and most of his men had returned to the United States. Very tellingly, to put all the pain and sacrifice of the troops who fought the bloody battles into total worthlessness, Shelby in the 1890s stated that Southern emotions over slavery produced irresponsibility and concluded, "I now see I was so myself."[18]

Here ends the most horrendous episode of the flower of our Nation's youth and their blood being expended in satisfaction of bloodied money!

Chapter 17:

The Spanish-American War (1898) –
The Beginnings of American Imperialism

[Author's note: The principal reference for this chapter is the book *The Martial Spirit* by Walter Millis, originally published in 1931.]

The following letter dated November 19, 1897, from Theodore Roosevelt to William W. Kimball, clearly shows Roosevelt's attitude at the time:

> I would regard war with Spain from two viewpoints...second...and especially the benefit done our military forces by trying both the Navy and Army in actual practice...I would hope the force would have some fighting to do. It would be a great lesson, and we would profit by it. (Brands: 157).

Prelude to the War

In February of 1895, Americans became aware of a third rebellion which had begun in Cuba wherein two entire provinces were subject to martial law imposed by the ruling power of Spain, which had controlled Cuba and Puerto Rico in our hemisphere and the Philippines in the Far East for three centuries. The large Cuban populations in New Orleans and other American seaports received this news with great delight. It was a fascinating time in America, thirty years after our Civil War, a time in which we had furthered and completed the conquest of our West and had made tremendous strides toward our industrial revolution with its attendant exports' potential. The three centuries of Indian Wars were finished, and this rendered only modest "practice" for our Army. It was a period in which Big Business in our land as defined significantly by Wall Street and its financial and investment entities began to flex political muscles. It was a time witnessing the evolution of labor unions, anarchism, and militias firing on our citizens. Our foreign policy was virtually non-existent. The Army was very small, and the "glories" of war were only experienced in the recent Indian Wars. However, the Navy had become upgraded with an updated fleet.

There was discussion of a canal in Nicaragua, so the Caribbean Basin became more vital. A financial crisis had occurred two years previously. Even with that decline in business activity, our business interests were beginning to awaken to the prospects of becoming a competitive influence in world trade and markets. "For the nation to continue its rise to wealth, it needed foreign markets. They would not be found in Europe, where governments, like that of the United States, protected domestic industries behind high tariff walls." (Kinzer: 34). Although, typically, the owner class, financiers, and elites were doing well financially, conditions were not quite as positive for rank and file Americans at the working-class level. "By 1893, one of every six American workers was unemployed, and many of the rest lived on subsistence wages. Plummeting agricultural prices in the 1890s killed off a whole generation of small farmers." (Kinzer: 34). These market and employment issues brought forth a desire to acquire more overseas customers and to locate more natural resources. It was an economic situation of over-production. We produced more than we could consume internally. A class struggle was part and parcel of the silver question and populism was beginning to evolve under William Jennings Bryan.

With Cuba so close to us, it was eminently important to pay at least modest attention to what might be described as "...a simple case of an oppressed people rising spontaneously to free itself of an alien tyranny." (Millis: 10). Spain had lost its New World Empire in the early 1800s with the uprising begun by Simon Bolivar. Amazingly enough, no less an eminent statesman as former president Thomas Jefferson, as early as 1823 spoke of a possible annexation of Cuba. Cuban freedom seekers always harbored a belief that we might assist them in seeking their freedom. A majority of the Cubans were descendants of African slaves who, with the poor whites in the mountains, were allowed no self-governance by the Spaniards.

We had spread our eagle's wings in the Mexican-American War in 1848, and with California in the Union, we looked westward across the Pacific Ocean. Hawaii came up in our visions. Japan was visited by Commodore Perry. 1895 became a period of heightened enthusiasm for an expanded empire. Decades previously in 1848, a former Spanish officer, General Narciso Lopez, had established residency in New York. It was the period of emotion and belief in our "Manifest Destiny." By 1850, an attempt was begun by Lopez to enlist American volunteers, promised bonuses and land grants, to assist Cubans to seek their freedom. It was unsuccessful. When he tried again in 1851, he again was so unsuccessful, as to lose his own life. (Millis: 11). Support in our South was evident, perhaps to bring in another slave-owning state. Democratic politicians based in the South supported Cuban annexation to add to slave territories.

In 1860, the Democratic Party wrote in its platform a plank to annex Cuba peacefully. Our country's abolition of slavery with the Civil War ending took away the original Lopez motivations to overthrow Spanish rule, but in 1868, a ten-year-long limited rebellion began, backed by small farmers and members of the skilled worker class. The ensuing severe Spanish efforts to clamp down on the insurrection, mainly centered in the mountainous east was not viewed favorably by Americans, but the "profits" to be made by running guns into the island was found attractive by some soldiers of fortune. (Millis: 13-14).

As a nation, we remained basically uninvolved until in 1873, an American-flagged ship filled with probable Cubans intent on an expedition backing Cuban freedom was run down by a Spanish boat and we protested, followed by cries for the necessity of war to right this wrong by Spain. By two years later, Hamilton Fish, Secretary of State, warned Spain of potential intervention, if Spain could not obtain control of their Cuban colony. A new Spanish

Army general took command in Cuba and the island settled down without oppression by the Spanish authorities. Slavery was abolished in 1886.

American and European financing entered the economy primarily for the sugar industry. While conditions were calm in Cuba itself, Millis wrote, "For the insurrection of 1895 was made in the United States, the work of *emigres* who had no real stake in the island, who had dissociated themselves from its life, and many of whom had scarcely even set foot upon its soil during the whole period in which they were laboring to involve it again in civil war. It was these men----the unemployed generals of the Ten Years' War, the professional enthusiasts of liberty, and the agitators who had made a place for themselves in the emigrant colonies---who kept the passions of the earlier struggle alive, and abroad perfected the technique of insurrection until conditions made it possible for them to import it once more into Cuba." (Millis: 16). Alfred Thayer Mahan, eminent American historian, geo-strategist and author, wrote in his 1897 work, *The Interest of America in Sea Power, Present and Future,* that control of Cuba was critical to military strategic purposes in the Caribbean. He specifically wrote of the country's three natural harbors, Havana, Santiago, and Cienfuegos, all important for naval operations. (Spingola *Seizure: 154).*

In the timeframe of 1890 to 1900, the United States was in a mood of intense discontent for several reasons: farmers in an uproar, businesses in monopoly growth, labor being run over in a roughshod manner, and a financial situation overseen by Wall Street, which was committed to defense of the gold standard, thereby maintaining low price levels. Obviously, the national economic grievances needed to be addressed. A foreign policy crossroads as a distraction was addressed with the uproar in Cuba, just a short distance from Florida. It provided just the propitious opportunity for America to flex new muscles outside our homeland and Senator Henry Cabot Lodge and Theodore Roosevelt took full advantage of the situation. (Quigley *Tragedy*: 75). In this decade the economy admittedly had boomed at least for big business such as the DuPont Company of Delaware, but the average American had become poorer. (Colby: 123).

In 1880, Harvard graduated a student by the name of Theodore Roosevelt, who eventually played a key role not only in Cuba, but in the strengthening of our naval forces. In 1889, a little-known event happened in Samoa where German war vessels faced off against an American naval squadron and the sirens of war with Germany had a brief blaring. Awakened in the United States were the enticements of commerce in far western Pacific areas. In 1890 we began to build our first battleships. Our Navy was on its way to prominence. In the fall of 1891, an incident occurred in Valparaiso, Chile in which American sailors on liberty from the U.S.S. Baltimore were attacked and two killed and several wounded. Cries for a war resounded anew throughout the land. Thankfully, the fires of bellicosity were extinguished by cooler heads. (Millis: 19). In 1893, a *coup d'état* came about in Hawaii and it was declared by economic powers as an American protectorate. We were casting acquisitive eyes toward the western reaches of the Pacific.

In 1891, a New York Cuban, Jose Julian Marti, began an organizational effort to bind together the American Cubans and the Caribbean countries into a newly revived effort for revolution. Our financial catastrophe of 1893 caused an economic crash in Cuba. A republic was declared in Hawaii, and Theodore Roosevelt supported annexation of Hawaii. (Millis: 24). In 1894, tariffs were imposed on Cuban sugar and Cuba fell apart, allowing the perfect opportunity for Marti to make a serious move to begin another attempt at freeing Cuba from Spain's yoke. American arms interests sold ammunition and rifles to the insurgents. But our authorities learned of this latest effort, and three steamers destined for Cuba were intercepted. An uprising in Cuba was set for February 24, 1895, anyway.

Meanwhile back on the home front, the gold reserve was dwindling and to the front lines galloped the cavalry to save the day, with its profits to be made by J. Pierpont Morgan, the Wall

Street financier, who fashioned the Morgan-Belmont arrangement to sell bonds to save the gold reserve. On February 20, 1895, the bankers offered their bonds for sale (of course, with a generous profit in commissions) and the gold reserve was saved. William Jennings Bryan proclaimed on the floor of the House of Representatives, "We cannot afford to put ourselves in the hands of the Rothschilds!" About this time editorial comments were being made toward, "...the annexation of Hawaii, the undivided control of the Nicaragua Canal, the acquisition of a strong naval station in the West Indies, and the emphatic assertion of certain principles regarding European interference in the affairs of Central and South America would form a very moderate and reasonable American policy." (Millis: 26).

On March 12, 1895, the insurrection had not been gaining traction, but in the Caribbean a Spanish gunboat fired upon and gave chase to an American freighter. Millis wrote, "The flag had been outraged, and our new martial ardor awoke in an outburst of fury." (Millis: 28). The *New York Tribune* in what would become a common journalistic outcry proclaimed, "...the outrage would not have been more flagrant if [the Spanish gunboat] had entered the harbor of New York and bombarded the City Hall...Several American cruisers ought to be sent to Cuban waters without delay..." (Millis: 28). The *New York Sun*, "...advised editorially that 'peremptory orders' be given to our naval officers 'that the next shot fired by a Spanish warship on a vessel flying the Stars and Stripes shall be followed by a broadside from an American cruiser. The rule in such cases should be to strike first and explain afterwards.'" (Millis: 29).

Politicians made calls to have Cuba become an American colony. Naturally, for those who would fight the war there would be more skin in the game than those in the protection of New York editorial board rooms or the privileged sanctuaries of the Senate and House. It always works out that way! The cries for war against Spain began in many quarters. Americans in some protected quarters were eager for a war!

Rebel leader Jose Marti was killed soon after landing in Cuba on May 19, 1895. The rebellion was supported by the always active Cubans of New York and the cigar-makers of Ybor City, Florida. A guerrilla war was instigated in a method of economic terrorism, whereby the sugar cane crops were destroyed, and the populace had a choice of joining the rebels or starving in the cities. For the next three years numerous attempts were made to supply arms and ammunition to the island. The "Merchants of Death" were pleased to be a part of this endeavor. The revived navy and its leaders, intent on trying out their new ships and their firepower, were a force for involvement in Cuba and a strong propaganda effort was ongoing, but the reports of the horrors of desolation propagated by the rebels gave hesitation to some Americans, recollecting we were only thirty years past the savagery of our own rebellion.

The leader of the rebellion, Maximo Gomez, underwent a tactic of burning the cane fields owned by American citizens. Meanwhile on the home front on September 6, 1895, a supposedly innocuous happening in New York occurred, which was later to have much broader consequences. William Randolph Hearst consummated a purchase of the *New York Morning Journal.* Concurrently, an event which involved Great Britain and a boundary dispute in Venezuela in which we had voiced an opinion and had awaited six months for an official response, when, in coming, angered us immensely, bringing, if you can imagine, a chance of war with Great Britain! Our future president and "hero" of San Juan Hill, Teddy Roosevelt, was ready to support a war with Great Britain and wrote to his friend Senator Henry Cabot Lodge that perhaps a war would allow us to take Canada. Britain turned to threats on their own front in Europe with Germany and the threats between us over Venezuela were placed on the back burner, but the flames of war were stoked anew by the press and the passions of exertion of national patriotic ardor.

Into 1896, after a period, the Cuban insurgency increased in the damage it perpetrated on the country and especially on the innocent bystanders, the common people, who lost their livelihoods and their lives. But, so are the "unintended," but always prevalent consequences of warfare at any level. American newspapers began to send to Havana correspondents who, with their primarily naturalized Cuban-born citizens of the U.S. as interpreters, began to be drum-beaters supporting the rebels. Now began the dramatic and sometimes exaggerated stories emanating from the New York newspapers, led by the soon-to-be famous Hearst ready to make a name for himself, plus a profit from enhanced sales brought by sensational headlines. Millis described it thusly, "...the American people were brought to look upon Cuba as a tortured land, where a decadent tyranny, unable to crush out the heroic aspirations of the populace, was endeavoring to drown them in torrents of blood. It shocked us profoundly---and it was extremely good reading." (Millis: 43).

Navy Captain Alfred Thayer Mahan oversaw the Naval War College and wrote *The Influence of Sea Power Upon History* in which he contended that no country had ever become a powerful nation without dominance in overseas markets and ability to obtain foreign natural resources. He argued that a strong navy with overseas bases as supply points was necessary to ensure opening for expanded trade and capital investments. He advocated building a canal in Central America and establishing Caribbean and Pacific bases to facilitate commerce for America. He said, "The growing production of the country demands it." (Kinzer: 33). These ideas were music to the ears of many political and business leaders.

Causes of the War

In early 1896, we began to be serious to recognize the importance of the "defense" of the country (against which "invaders" it was not described) and this sentiment became so prevalent, surely enhanced by the armament and ship builder lobbyists (although they were not termed that until later in our history), that bills began to be introduced for more weapons and ships. No less an eminent being than Senator Henry Cabot Lodge, a political compatriot of Theodore Roosevelt, spoke about issues other than the oppression in Cuba. He spoke of the other considerations always just under the surface of all conflicts, when he boldly and candidly proclaimed, "Our immediate pecuniary interests in the island are great. They are being destroyed. Free Cuba would mean a great market for the United States; it would mean an opportunity for American capital invited there by signal exemptions; it would mean an opportunity for the development of that splendid island...But we have also a broader political interest in the fate of Cuba...She lies right athwart the line which leads to the Nicaraguan Canal." (Millis: 47). Evident with this Senator, the characteristics of candor and explicitness were not always so prevalent with later political leaders of our country. Senator Lodge was defined by Ferdinand Lundberg as one of the politicians supported by John D. Rockefeller to be proponents of the war as were other members of the elite in the country to include the Rockefeller-Stillman National City Bank axis of influence. (Lundberg: 62).

House member, Charles A. Boutelle of Maine, evidenced a most practical nature when he declared, "Somebody says, 'Oh, Spain don't amount to much anyhow. We can lick her easy.' How many lives do you want to sacrifice to do it?" (Millis: 49). He asked the key question that should be asked prior to sending our young men and women into harm's way. Some more incisive terms were used by some politicians to ask whether we were being motivated in those times by greed or humanitarianism in our approach to Cuba. One even brought up hypocrisy. At least there were some politicians who did not go with the prevailing flow of bellicosity. On April 6, 1896, a Senate vote passed that documented our neutrality, but that also indicated that we desired the Spaniards to provide independence to Cuba. In April of 1896, the Spanish captured a schooner that was intent upon supporting the rebels. A journalist aboard was decidedly an American. Support for his American citizenship was called forth. The crew was spared, but the situation dragged on for two years and kept burning the embers of the fires of war. The press constantly wrote of the likelihood of a war that would be finished in a short period of time completed by naval activity only. The country was alive with promoting a strong foreign policy, harkening back to the Monroe Doctrine relative to our hemisphere.

J. P. Morgan, Andrew Carnegie, and other prominent business tycoons publicly expressed disdain for the war, but as Ferdinand Lundberg described it, the major elitist families typically united in efforts personally benefitting them. Privately, they were interested in capitalizing on the natural resources of Cuba. According to Lundberg, "Senator Joseph B. Fraker and Representative Joseph Bailey, both in time disclosed as outright hirelings of the Standard Oil Company, daily, while the decision hung in the balance, demanded a declaration of war." (Lundberg: 62). In later wars, the Morgan bankers overcame their disdain for wars and were eager to finance them.

The 1896 election pitted Republican William McKinley, a promoter of tariffs, against the Democrat nominee William Jennings Bryan, a proponent of the Populist position on free silver. McKinley was supported by preeminent Ohio businessman and John D. Rockefeller compatriot Mark Hanna, promoter of the gold standard. Once McKinley was elected, Cuba moved up on the list of priorities for attention once again. Some opinions were expressed, that due to home front dissatisfaction with economic challenges, especially after his bruising presidential race, McKinley felt that an international effort with a conflict would be a worthy national unifying cause. (Quigley: 75). Attempts were made to urge President Cleveland on the eve of the end of his term to declare war, but he wisely demurred. Congressman said they had the constitutional right to declare wars. The president agreed, but he also rightly pointed out that he was Commander-in-Chief and would not call up the army. By this time Spain was faced with another simmering revolution in the Philippines.

An intense journalistic competition with negative consequences had developed in New York City between the newspapers of Joseph Pulitzer and William Randolph Hearst. Each publisher was bent on selling newspapers notwithstanding whether there was total credibility to that which was reported. Necessarily the stories, whether truthful or exaggerative of the truth, had their impact on popular opinion. A free press is important for a country, but much more important is a press that reports truthfully. Propaganda's value to stir up attitudes toward a perceived enemy became immensely successful. These attitudes were utilized again to great effect against Germany in World War I, and were perfected as a science by a nephew of Sigmund Freud, one Edward Bernays, who will be discussed in future writings. The Spanish recognized that they could lose Cuba.

Upon the ascendancy of McKinley to president on March 4, 1897, there was a modest desire to keep us out of war, but the clamoring for war never totally went underground. The jingoists pushed for dispatching battleships to Cuba in response to the latest report of some outrage or other, real or manufactured. Newspapers in the U.S. reported famines all-prevalent in Cuba. The Spaniards attempted to move the populations into cities and therein provide support in food and housing, however, there was at least one report of the rebels destroying crops established to support the non-rebel inhabitants.

Papers relayed exorbitant reports of many deaths, but they were later repudiated. Catastrophic conditions were reported with few to zero attempts to dampen exaggerations that were once again copiously published. The appointment in April of that year of the dynamic Theodore Roosevelt to the powerful position of Assistant Secretary of the Navy went modestly unnoticed in political circles.

Roosevelt left no one with any doubts that he was to be a political appointee with a bent towards extreme martial activism. Upon extensive study of Roosevelt's attitude and actions related to Cuba and the Philippines, it would not be a stretch to believe that wars were glorious for Roosevelt. For the men in the field, they are far from being glorious. McKinley preferred peace and no war, but the die was cast in the country, and he was prompted to deliver to Spain an ultimatum that, if unanswered, would demand our intervention.

The Spanish military leader in Cuba, General Valeriano Weyler y Nicolau, was on the verge of winning against the rebels with the support of Spain's conservative government led by Spanish Premier Antonio Canovas del Castillo. This new direction toward a possible victory, which would preclude the intervention by America, was thwarted by the assassination of Canovas by an Italian anarchist, an event representing the first of many future changes of political direction due to the assassination of leading figures. Roosevelt drove onward and upward with a desire for a foreign policy expressed to President McKinley that encompassed containing the Japanese and capturing Manila, the principal city of the Philippines. The Cuban rebels began to promise land redistribution which would be a decided threat to the American business entities, who had millions invested in Cuba, especially in agriculture. (Kinzer: 36).

Smoking Gun!

[Author's note: The following continuation of excerpts of the Roosevelt letter of November 19, 1897, is very telling of the attitude of the future president relative to our sending our military into combat.]

> ... I am not the boss of this Government; ... from my own standpoint, however, and speaking purely privately, I believe that war will have to, or at least ought to, come sooner or later; and I think we should prepare for it well in advance. I should have the Asiatic squadron in shape to move on Manila at once...

On October 8, 1997, the U.S.S. *Maine*, a 300-foot-long, 6,682-ton armored cruiser with ten mounted guns, was ordered closer to Cuba with positioning at Port Royal, South Carolina. The perceived rationale was to be ready if there were "anti-American disturbances" in Cuba. This repositioning of an American man-of-war would have earth-shaking repercussions. Another supposedly innocent occurrence was the appointment of Commodore George Dewey on October 21, 1897, to command the Navy's Asiatic

Squadron. This appointment was instigated solely upon the instigation of Roosevelt without the cognizance of the Secretary of the Navy himself, John D. Long. It was done in secret always with Roosevelt's purpose of having Dewey positioned to fight the Spaniards at Manila. Dewey began research on the Philippines. Commodore Dewey took command of the American fleet at a city in Japan that would later be of significant historical importance, Nagasaki.

Diplomatically, the Spanish proposed a degree of autonomy for Cuba that perhaps might be acceptable to defuse the movement toward a war, but by this time the pacification efforts by a new Spanish commander were unsuccessful and the people's food challenge had gotten worse. On December 6, 1897, President McKinley's annual message to Congress contained elements of recognition of the dire humanitarian conditions within Cuba, but he was still decidedly against intervention, and for allowing further time for Spain to end the war. However, he left open the potential of our intervening with force. At this exact time the *Maine* was ordered to Key West, Florida, one step closer to its destiny and important part in the war. Conditions in Cuba worsened, and it was suggested by the State Department that perhaps alleviation of the reports of starvation could be countered by the dispatch of Clara Barton and the Red Cross to Cuba. The United States did begin a relief effort to the people of Cuba and contributions of food, money, and clothing began. It was a humanitarian intervention. Unfortunately and inexplicably, our Consul-General in Cuba, Fitzhugh Lee, was given authority by use of the coded message, "Two dollars," concurrently to be able to order the *Maine* to steam to Havana.

On January 12, 1898, there was supposedly an assault by unarmed Spanish Army officers on Havana newspaper offices due to some unflattering writings about Army conduct. No Americans were involved. The U.S. Consul-General Fitzhugh Lee jumped on these events to sound the alarm at the State Department. Our press printed "war extras." Ten days later President McKinley ordered the *Maine* to Havana as a reflection and signal that there was such a lack of danger in Havana that the Navy could even send there a warship on a visit. Its arrival in Havana harbor and its initial stay occurred uneventfully. Reciprocal protocol visits were exchanged along with modest gifts by the respective dignitaries. It appeared there was no danger to Americans or their property, but the Spaniards, fearing some accident that might precipitate hostilities, were on edge at the very presence of this American ship.

The Spanish minister in Washington, Señor Enrique Depuy de Lome, who had served successively for three years, had written a letter in December of 1897 that was unflattering of President McKinley's annual message with words such as, "... McKinley is, weak and a bidder for the admiration of the crowd, besides being a common politician..." (Millis: 98). The letter was apparently intercepted at the Havana post office the following February, and leaked publicly soon thereafter. He was forced to resign, and of course, the flames that had been fanned by those desiring a war were immediately doused.

In the Far East, our Navy's secret mission to move toward Manila began at Yokohama via Hong Kong. The Cuban insurgents were burning US-owned crops and dynamiting trains. The *Maine* had quietly been moored in Havana harbor for three weeks. The famine was horrendous, but American supplies had been arriving. For the captain of the *Maine*, Charles D. Sigsbee, the evening of February 15, 1898, began uneventfully. It was a typical hot tropical night. In Asia, Commodore Dewey was steaming toward the Philippines. With the food situation improving, one of the primary causes of the Cuban insurgents was in the process of being quelled.

Twenty minutes after the bugle player blew taps, the silence of the night and the wardrooms was ended with an explosion on the *Maine*. An apparent contradiction to its having been an act of war by the Spanish, some wounded were taken aboard a Spanish man-of-war. Everyone (i.e., Washington officialdom, the members of the press corps, and newspaper editors) was aroused and incensed. It was war at last! The forward ammunition magazines had exploded, many sailors in their hammocks below decks were dead, and other crew members were floating in the water. The ship sunk slowly to the bottom of the harbor.

American Consul-General Fitzhugh Lee proceeded toward the harbor, but first stopped at Captain-General Ramon Blanco y Erenas' palace. He found Gov. Blanco tearing profusely and obviously experiencing sincere regret and anguish. Lee then went to visit Captain Sigsbee, who had been taken to the Ward Line steam ship *City of Washington*, where some of the wounded sailors had been placed on mattresses. There had been 350 officers and men on the *Maine* and 252 were dead and eight others were wounded severely. The city went into mourning and Captain-General Blanco called on Sigsbee at the Inglaterra Hotel to offer his deep and sincere condolences. Our 260 dead were buried in the Colon Cemetery (in plots dedicated forever to the United States).

The fires of war began to burn out of control. For three years the groundwork had been being laid to be consummated in this fashion. "Whether consciously or unconsciously they had one by one been assembled, by the patriots and the politicians, by personal ambition and partisan rivalries, by the gentlemen who had talked war on Capitol Hill because it was politic and the gentlemen who had printed inflammatory sensations because they were lucrative … but between them all they had carefully prepared the train which could lead nowhere save to war." (Millis: 107).

Senator Henry Cabot Lodge, already described as a close friend of Theodore Roosevelt, expressed his thoughts, "We have a record of conquest, colonization, and expansion unequalled by any people in the nineteenth century. We are not to be curbed now." (Colby: 125).[1] He was ready for other people to go to war to satisfy his political aims! Senator Nelson Aldrich, a Rockefeller relative, was also eager to send other people into a fray, when he "demanded a 'bitter conquest' for 'industrial supremacy' in their

world." (Colby: 124).[2]
Originally the blame was said to have been accidental, and probably not to be blamed on a plot. Reporters at Mr. Hearst's *Journal* newspaper in New York fired up the emotions of their readership by proposing that the Spanish had blown up the *Maine*. The report was accompanied by a drawing indicating a torpedo placed under the ship had been detonated from the harbor's edge. Mr. Pulitzer jumped on the crisis bandwagon and sent a tug to Havana. The *Journal* sold 1 million copies. Public opinion was dramatically formed for this war by the newspapers with large print headlines, "We Have Got to Fight. Must Declare for War. Crisis is at Hand Spanish Treachery." It was termed "Yellow Journalism." The media fanned the flames.

Volunteers came forth ready to fight. The Navy promptly sent a court of inquiry to the disaster scene. Secretary of the Navy John D. Long initially proposed two theories, one, an accident, and, the other, a deliberately-designed attack. Our government was being led to war much more slowly than our media, which was whipping up war fever. *Evening Post* Editor E. L. Godkin wrote of the *World* and the *Journal:*

> Nothing so disgraceful as the behaviour of these two newspapers in the past week has ever been known in the history of journalism. Gross misrepresentation of facts, deliberate invention of tales calculated to excite the public, and wanton recklessness in the construction of headlines which outdid even these inventions have combined to make the issues of the most widely circulated newspapers firebrands scattered broadcast throughout the community. (Millis: 110).

In one week, the *World* sold 5,000,000 copies.

The Navy court was moving toward the conclusion that the explosion was externally generated. On the afternoon of Friday, February 25, the Navy secretary decided he needed a solid night of sleep and left the Navy Department in the capable, but, as it evolved, aggressive and ambitious hands of Assistant Secretary Theodore Roosevelt. Overnight Roosevelt issued all sorts of orders to the Navy to bring it to a state of preparation for war! A wire was sent and signed by Roosevelt in just those hours in which he had the reins of power from the Navy, that contained the following orders to Commodore Dewey, "Secret and confidential…. In the event of declaration of war on Spain, your duty will be to see that the Spanish squadron does not leave the Asiatic coast, and then offensive operations in Philippine Islands." (Millis: 112). Roosevelt had set upon a course that would lead to a condition of implementation of American imperialism.

Spain was prepared to fight a war and even to lose Cuba, but they desired to preserve their dynasty. We were not yet prepared, barring undeniable blame upon Spain for the loss of the *Maine*, to go to war. Many in the Washington corridors of power were most reluctant to go to war. Back and forth began an analysis of the real ramifications of going to war and its justification. Much revolved around thoughts of negligence by Spain, if a harbor mine exploded the *Maine*, or the exercise by a junior Spanish officer of the calamity, or even blame to be attributed to the rebels, who had the most to gain from a war. The bottom line became that Spain could only escape culpability, if the cause of the explosion was due to an accident on board the *Maine*. President McKinley was in a highly tenuous position.

On March 6, he moved closer to a decision on the crisis by inviting Congressman Joe Cannon, chairman of the House Appropriations Committee, to the White House. The President asked him to introduce an appropriations bill for $50 million for "defense." It was voted on unanimously by both legislative houses on March 9. Mr. Godkin went back to his condemnations of the all-pervasive journalism rampant in the major dailies, profiting from ever-higher circulations.

The president gave only $16 million to the Army and it was designated for coastal fortifications (as if there was a threat of a Spanish warship bombardment). The Navy fared much better, gaining $30 million. Facing this threat of upgrades of the American forces, the admiral of the main Spanish squadron decided to resign because he faced 3 to 1 odds in the superiority of the naval force he would face. So much for commitment to the national security interests of your native land once the guns began to be fired!

In the Philippines in the fall of 1896, another active rebellion had begun. It was equated by many Americans as analogous to the one in Cuba against Spanish rule. The representative of the Philippine insurrection, a Mr. F. Agoncilla, called upon our consul in Hong Kong in November of 1897 to inquire about the purchase of 20,000 weapons. Our Manila Consul, Oscar Williams, began to report the existence of atrocities perpetrated by the Spanish against the "guerrillas." American economic and business interests began to raise their heads attentively as Commodore Dewey wrote, "...what we all want is Chinese trade and we are gradually getting more and more of it." (Millis: 122). Those comments were all it took for our business heads to cast glances longingly to the Far East. Germany and Russia also were making their moves into China.

Senator Redfield Proctor of Vermont visited Cuba and reported the perilous condition of the Cubans. This began to turn the tide toward war, jumped upon by the secular press, and amazingly enough, also by the religious press.

President McKinley was committed to peace, but, looming before him was the specter of the Democrats and populists who were committed to a war. In Madrid Stewart Woodford, our minister to Spain, on March 17 concluded after all his diplomatic efforts with Spain, that Cuba under the U.S. flag was the only viable alternative. The shadow of the final report of the cause of the destruction of the *Maine*, being attributed to an external explosion, was beginning to abate as the report became more imminent. It was evident that what was needed was for Spain to allow the native Cubans to leave the sequestered towns to return home to farm their fields to alleviate the rampant starvation evident throughout the island. The Spaniards would not accede to our demands. The diplomatic back and forth was like a ball being tossed back and forth.

Naturally, the pulse had to be taken of the titans of American business such as William Rockefeller, Thomas Ryan, John Jacob Astor, and J.P. Morgan. March 15, 1898, a representative from the federal government reported back they were "militant" and reflected very warlike attitudes at this stage. One year later John D. Rockefeller was reported to have proclaimed, "Dependent solely upon local business we should have failed years ago. We were forced to extend our markets and to seek for export trade." (Colby: 126).[3]

On March 28, the final *Maine* report was sent to Congress. The report concluded that an explosion caused by a submarine mine was responsible, but no responsible party was named. "Whether or not the findings were correct has never been established; for the destruction of the *Maine* remains to this day a mystery." (Millis: 127). Later investigations concluded the possibility that the explosion was caused internally.

Millis further wrote, "Yet in the 30 years that have elapsed since the catastrophe occurred, no shred of positive evidence has ever come to light that a mine existed." (Millis: 128). In 1911 the *Maine* was brought up from its watery grave and it was then decided that some type of explosive was placed outside the hull. After the original report of 1898, the U.S. believed that Spain should turn over Cuba to us and we would solve its challenges. The moneylenders were prepared to get their piece of the financial action by offering to the Cuban junta based in New York $.20 on the dollar for $10 million par value of Cuban Republic bonds. The junta would take no less than twice that.

The final proposal of Spain was not acceptable to us. Mr. Woodford cabled Washington that Spain realized Cuba was lost to them. The only hope was their recognition of this without a war. Eventually the diplomatic efforts had run their course and the inevitable began to be carried out on April 4 when American ships were ordered to Havana to evacuate American citizens and lower the flag still flying on the mast of the *Maine*. [Author's note: The mast of the *Maine* is prominently displayed as a Memorial at Arlington National Cemetery just across the roadway from the amphitheater.] Spain was finally ready to meet our requirements for Cuba, but it was all too late. The newspapers, of course, were ready and their editions began to report military preparations to stir the pot!

The Spaniards finally completely capitulated to all our demands. However, we were on a runaway train and Congress basically ignored this final Spanish offer, after President McKinley sent on April 11 his message to Congress. The president traced for the Congress all the negatives, to include the damage to American trade interests (of course, the business lobby must be heard and mollified). After all, their lobbyists contributed heavily to politicians even back then. The President requested Congress to "authorize and empower" him to terminate the hostilities between Spain and the insurrectionists, to establish a secure government, and to use military and naval forces to accomplish these objectives. As almost an afterthought in the message, he did mention the final Spanish offer to terminate the fighting. But conditions had become such after the arduous course of previous events up to that time that most of America was ready for a war. Some still harbored negative attitudes toward members of the U.S.-based Cubans. Teddy Roosevelt's diary entries at the time were very negative of the president.

European Positions

The Pope had attempted to forestall hostilities amongst several European countries, the leaders of which were endeavoring to cobble together an alliance to oppose the United States. But England was in favor of the position and motivation of the United States. An element of support for Spain appeared from the position of the Vatican and those countries that were also Catholic, as was Spain. The hostilities escalated very quickly to an

American victory before an opposing alliance could be accomplished. Germany's major motive to form an alliance very well could have been dictated due to British Admiral Chichester's blocking of German warships bent on opposing Admiral Dewey in the Philippines. (Steed: 130-132).

War at Last!

Patriotic songs began to be sung in the halls of Congress and the jingoism began. Of course, bellicosity and bombastic barrages of cries for war were safe for them. It would be for our troops to carry out the orders and suffer on the battlefields with the shedding of their blood.

On April 20, 1898, President McKinley signed the war resolution. It had passed overwhelmingly in the house by 310-6, but the vote was closer (42-35) in the Senate, the more august and deliberative legislative branch. An American student of the war later expressed that "the particular form of intervention in 1898 was unfortunate, irregular, precipitate, and unjust to Spain. The same ends-peace in Cuba and justice to all people concerned-in themselves good, could have been achieved by peaceful means safer for the wider interests of humanity." (Millis: 144). Of course, one of the results of a country going to war would be that there would be those seeking contracts to profit from the war. War profiting escalated to even greater heights in World War I. On April 22nd, war began with a blockade of Havana.

During the Cuban rebellion against the Spanish, the U.S. Remington Company had sold high quality weapons and ammunition to the Cubans. The Spaniards also desired purchases from Remington, but the company was occupied with orders from the Russians. A secret agreement between Russia and Spain enabled Russia to forego immediate supplying of cartridges for them in favor of supplies to the Spanish so that the Spanish military response to the insurrectionists would not be impeded. (Engelbrecht: 48). The ever-present Sir Basil Zaharoff received commissions on $25,000,000 of arms purchased by Spain for their

wars in both Cuba and the Philippines. (Engelbrecht: 100).
Another "Merchant of Death" that received massive orders during the war was the DuPont Company of Delaware. Whereas in 1898 they had been producing only 3,000 pounds daily of brown prismatic powder, they geared up immediately (working their employees 18-hour days) to fill government orders for 20,000 pounds per day. (Colby: 128). In four months, DuPont provided 2.2 million pounds of brown prismatic powder invoiced to the government at a charge of 33 cents a pound. This became a classic example of "fraud" and "extortion" because it cost the company only 8 cents per pound to produce. (Colby: 129).[4]

This was Teddy Roosevelt's moment when he would resign from the Navy Department and organize a volunteer cavalry unit. Common lore entails that he recruited his "Rough Riders" in the bar at the Menger Hotel adjacent to the Alamo in San Antonio, Texas. [Author's note: The bar capitalizes on that note of historical significance by displaying many photos and artifacts.] Theodore Roosevelt eventually rode the fame of his "Rough Riders," and their celebrated charge up San Juan Hill in the war, to become Vice President upon McKinley's reelection in 1900 and then President upon McKinley's assassination in 1901. An ascent politically from Navy assistant secretary to New York Governor to Vice President to President occurred all within three years! No time was wasted in transmitting orders for Commodore Dewey to rid the Philippines of the Spaniards. The groundwork for this very mission had been laid previously by Roosevelt. The ultimate jingoism, "Remember the *Maine*, to Hell with Spain," was born.

Immediate thoughts by Army General Nelson Miles, as concerned about his troops as is any good leader, related to the risks of yellow fever for our combatants. This was the beginning recognition of what would comprise the cause of many of our casualties for this war. (Millis: 154). There would be more to be sure.

Amazingly enough, but most enlightening to this West Point graduate, was the sentiment being expressed by some in the

National Guard, who felt it to be an untenable situation to be commanded by West Pointers in Regular Army units. Because, as one writer said, "West Pointers have seen fit to introduce a class feeling – no, I will go farther and say a caste feeling – between themselves and noncommissioned officers and privates that is unpleasant in the extreme." (Millis: 155). Of course, this was written by a National Guard officer accustomed to the social aspects and camaraderie evident at the time in their hometown units. Soon it became dictated that any full-strength guard regiments would not have any West Pointer officers assigned. This meant that these units would have no leaders who actually had trained full-time for war. In fact, it was said, "... there must be, the legislators insisted, no 'West Point martinets.' Perhaps it made little difference, since the West Point martinets were as scarce as they were later to prove valuable." (Millis: 157).

It is fairly illuminating to report that the best-known National Guard unit nationwide was the New York City Seventh Regiment, which, "...numbered in its ranks the sons of many wealthy and socially prominent New York families." The colonel commanding that regiment proclaimed they were prepared to serve their nation at this time of peril, but they would not volunteer to be integrated into the regular Army. "Thus it was that the crack Regiment of New York State maintained its dignity – and remained at home when it came to fighting." (Millis: 159). At least one elitist New Yorker, John Jacob Astor, fulfilled part of his patriotic duty by outfitting an artillery battery, named the Astor Battalion, which was deployed to Manila. The obituary of General Peyton C. March, a West Pointer and eventual Army Chief of Staff, indicated that he commanded this battery in the Philippines as a first lieutenant. Astor paid for the guns and ammunition, which came from overseas. He served as a volunteer in the Army as a staff officer during the campaign in Santiago, Cuba. He died in the sinking of the Titanic, which struck an iceberg in 1912 off the coast of Newfoundland.

There was no secrecy for our military. The term "embedding" by journalists, which became a regular occurrence in our much later two Gulf wars, was then modest, contrasted to involvement by the press in this war, which assigned its reporters everywhere amongst our military for their preparations. There were no issues about security. There was no secrecy. All our movements were reported extensively in the then media journals.

As is always the case, once the bugles are blown to announce the "Charge!" command, the battle flags are unfurled, and the young patriots go off to shed their blood while the war profiteers begin to raise their well-coiffed heads to ensure their profits. Sometimes patriotism inspires deplorable situations. Navy Secretary Long wrote, "Congressman Bowman calls (on Navy Secretary Long) with a delegation of Pennsylvanians to urge the use of anthracite, instead of bituminous coal on board ships. It is interesting to note how every section of the country, although all are patriotic, has an eye on the main chance." (Millis: 164).

The situation for some businesspeople was reflected as follows: "...but after all, when the politicians and editors were making such a good thing out of the war, one can scarcely blame the business men if they saw no reason why they should not do likewise." (Millis: 164).

On the Spanish side, "...but the spirit of resistance was dead in them at the start; and the war was over before it begun – except for the unfortunate soldiers and seamen who were to be sacrificed to the exigencies of statesmanship and politics." (Millis: 169). These words capsulize the final results of the causes of this conflict. The U.S. won, of course. We "won" Cuba, Puerto Rico, Guam and the Philippines. As to the Philippines, Roosevelt had plotted and planned all along to take Manila, even months before the formal declaration of war. Even the President realized our venture into the Pacific would promote our Chinese business. Mr. John Bartlett, our Minister to Siam, now Thailand, related, "It is of the greatest importance that the United States should take the Philippine Islands. Their value is not realized at home. They are richer and far larger than Cuba, and in the hands of a strong power would be the key to the Far East." Could this key be financial profits rather than relieving the besieged masses of the yoke of tyranny? (Millis: 182).

When the first casualties began to be reported from the fighting in Cuba, Americans began to realize that the red on the flags they proudly waved, and the bunting draped everywhere, was also to be reflected in the blood shed by our military as hostilities began on May 11.

Author Colby wrote, "The Spanish-American War had begun, but it was actually a war against indigenous revolutions in overseas lands that American capitalists wanted and Spanish colonialists were unable to defend." (Colby: 126).

Seacoast dwellers descended upon the Navy Department to have their fiefdoms protected, among them Jekyll Island, playground of the rich in Georgia (later to be the site of the conference to establish our Federal Reserve). All the rich and powerful wanted their seaside properties protected from the potential of Spanish bombardments. George B. Cortelyou, President McKinley's secretary, wrote in his diary on May 15, "Added to these things is the struggle for place among the ambitious gentlemen who desire to serve their country in high-salaried and high-titled positions." (Millis: 212).

Unfortunately, some of those National Guardsmen, who held such great disdain for the West Point "martinets", were described thusly, "The National Guard officers were incompetent. They had little idea of how to care for the health and comfort of their men, while their ignorance on the conduct of troops in the field was all-embracing." (Millis: 214). When we went to war, the regular Army numbered only 28,000. Improper political favors and involvement were a regular happening.

Once Commodore Dewey succeeded in the Philippines, which had become that much more important to us because it had become known that Germany also had its imperialistic eyes on its treasures, a change of attitude in the United States to this faraway archipelago was becoming manifestly evident (to satisfy our "Manifest Destiny.") The *Chicago Times-Herald* reported, "The belief was general that we had acquired through the unavoidable exigencies of war something we did not want. But all this has changed. We find that we want the Philippines....The commercial and industrial interests of America, learning that the islands lie in the gateway of the vast and undeveloped markets of the Orient, say, 'Keep the Philippines.'" Surprise! Surprise! Surprise! Case closed as to the decided economic pressures to expand our sphere of influence!

Another interesting contrast in leadership and motivation was made in Cuba between Army General William R. Shafter and Lieutenant Colonel Teddy Roosevelt, who, as indicated previously, vaulted into the presidency because of his success at San Juan Hill. As an aside, General John J. Pershing, West Point class of 1886 served with the Buffalo Soldier 10th Cavalry, another unit to charge at Kettle Hill and San Juan Hill. General Shafter was one of those rare generals, "... for whom bloodshed is a necessary evil rather than a desired end; unlike Colonel Roosevelt, he regarded it as his business not to achieve personal glory by fighting successful battles, but to secure the larger purposes of battle... with the greatest economy of life." (Millis: 321). He obviously cared for his troops.

Puerto Rico was an entirely different situation. In 1897, Puerto Rico had accepted an offer of autonomy from Spain and was on its path to home rule when, on May 12, 1898, an American fleet entered waters outside San Juan and began firing on the Spanish positions. On July 25 American sailors and Marines made an amphibious landing on the southwestern coast. We now added Puerto Rico to our control. Our casualties were light: 9 dead and 46 wounded. Spanish and Puerto Rican losses, killed, wounded, and captured, totaled 450 military and civilians. (Kinzer: 46).

Meanwhile back across the Pacific, Philippine Consul Oscar F. Williams wrote to the State Department about, "... the 'fabulous natural and productive wealth of these islands,'..." and he urged that, "Those who come early will reap great rewards and serve patriotic purpose at the same time." (Millis: 330). Sounds like the carpetbaggers after the Civil War. Because of our success in the Philippines, relations began to be strained with Germany because concurrently it was also attempting to establish itself in Asia.

An interesting footnote portending the rise in power and imperial designs of Germany, which we would be fighting twenty years later, is a scantly-known anecdote of history that about his time, 1897-1906, there were prepared in Germany, upon the order of Germany's Emperor Kaiser Wilhelm II, military plans to invade the United States. As sensational as this appears, the plans were not discovered until 1970 when the plans were found by archivists of military history. During that time frame, and because of the Spanish-American War, Germany was being denied its own designs of building a naval base in Cuba and expanding its power into the Pacific. The plans were never carried out.[5]

The quick Philippines "victory" by Dewey in April 1898 was followed by an attempt by the original Filipino rebels to establish an independent Republic of the Philippines. That would not stand with our politicians and business interests who had designs on the commercial opportunities in Asia. The United States moved immediately to exert total military control over the 7,000 islands. Emilio Aguinaldo, the rebel leader, had led the insurrection to free his people from Spain and now was confronted with the new threat posed by an acquisitive United States. However, he took the bold move on January 23, 1899 to declare a constitutional Republic. It was followed by a declaration of war on America. (Kinzer: 48).

Supporters of our imposing our sovereignty on the Philippines were quoted as feeling that "...that possession of the archipelago would bring in incalculable commercial and strategic advantages." (Kinzer: 49). The advantages eventually came to fruition, but beginning in February 1899 it would take another war, one perhaps to be termed the "Philippines-American War," which was to last several years and was noted significantly by reports of horrendous atrocities by both sides. It ended only when, by a subterfuge on March 23, 1901 by Filipinos opposed to Aguinaldo, he was captured. (Kinzer: 51). West Point General John J. Pershing served in the Philippine-American War from 1899 to 1903, and was recognized belatedly with the Distinguished Service Cross for his heroism.

Aguinaldo surrendered and urged all his rebel elements to do likewise. A dissident unit attacked our troops on the island of Samar in an action described as barbaric. This led to our own very brutal response. The *New York Post* reported that our troops, "...have been pursuing a policy of wholesale and deliberate murder." (Kinzer: 54). Both sides perpetrated horrendous acts. By now the President was Theodore Roosevelt (after McKinley's assassination) and he assigned his former "partner in political machinations," Senator Henry Cabot Lodge, to investigate the allegations of harsh conduct by our military. No major consequences ensued. Future American General Douglas MacArthur, West Point Class of 1903, served his first assignment with the Seventh Cavalry Regiment in the Philippines from 1903 to 1904.

On July 4, 1902, President Roosevelt announced that hostilities finally were over. This "war after the war," lasted three and a half years, significantly longer than the much better-known warfare in Cuba, and undeniably, not as well-documented perhaps as a result of the public relations stories of the Battle of San Juan Hill!

Soldiers' Blood:

According to Office of the Secretary of Defense, our total military casualties in the 1898 war (Cuba and Puerto Rico) amounted to 385 killed, 1662 wounded, and 2061 other deaths principally by disease (typhoid and yellow fevers). Many of our military succumbed to disease upon return to the United States. The *Baltimore Sun* on March 24, 1898, reported horrendous deaths under the policy of bringing the rural Cubans into the cities to withdraw partisan support for the rebels. Deaths under the

Spanish regime were variously reported, but always over 200,000! Reports of Spanish military casualties were not as precise as ours, but approximately at least 10,000 were killed in combat and 50,000 from disease in Cuba.

To General Leonard Wood, who had served with the Rough Riders and was an ex-army contract surgeon, fell the assignment of assuming the occupation of Santiago. What he and his staff discovered (from Hermann Hagedorn's book titled *Leonard Wood*) were, "At every turn, emaciated, 'ghastly-looking' people dragged aimlessly in search of a patch of shade. All about, 'poisoning the air with foul exhalations,' lay the rotting carcasses of dead animals piled among heaps of decomposing garbage, dung, and filth." Refugees from the surrounding area had streamed in to Santiago and were able to subsist only on raw fruit and foul water. Hundreds of dead remained unburied, while the number of dead increased each day by 200 souls, before Wood took control and lowered the rate to the mid-thirties each day. The dead were piled up on the outskirts and burned. (Musicant: 38, 39).

The scene at Camp Wicoff, a "hospital" built on Long Island, which became another place for our men to die upon their return from Cuba, was described as follows: "There wasn't an ample supply of potable water, and almost no food. An article in the *New York Sun* reported, 'There are no board floors in (the tents), but strips of canvas are spread on the ground and the men lie on them with their own uniforms for pillows and army blankets for covering. The men are all pale and wasted. In one tent, two men burst out crying when a reporter asked them if they were getting enough to eat.'...Food rations arrived slowly, some filled with worms. Medical supplies were in short supply, and sanitation was almost non-existent....*The East Hampton Star* wrote: 'There must be a screw loose somewhere when Uncle Sam's soldiers, backed by a country of unlimited resources, are...compelled to depend upon charity for food.'"[6] It is not known whether William Randolph Heart and Joseph Pulitzer covered these conditions in their newspapers for their returning troops as diligently as they covered sending them off to fight!

A report on the action and casualties for Cuba would be incomplete without commenting upon the Buffalo Soldiers, Americans of black heritage. A Colonel Charles Greenleaf was the commanding officer of the hospital at Siboney, and he needed volunteers to help with the in-country Cuba casualties from yellow fever. General Shafter requested volunteers. According to one account, "Eight different regimental commanders ignored the call for volunteers," but on July 16th, to a man, "...the Buffalo Soldiers of the 24th Regular Infantry..., stepped forward to render their services... For six weeks they performed the job no other soldiers would volunteer to do. Only 24 among their ranks escaped sickness during their tenure at the hospital, and 31 men of the regiment died."[7] *Leslie's Weekly*, on November 3, 1898, reported "There was not one Negro who stayed behind. (It was) as fine a bit of heroism as was developed in the whole war."[8]

The government was well-furnished by DuPont with ample supplies of brown prismatic powder, which was supposedly transported efficiently to the battle front, but our troops were not so efficiently outfitted in other needed supplies. The situation was described as follows:

> The cavalry had no horses, the horses had no saddles, and the infantry had no shoes. Sometimes the men had no food and sometimes what food they had killed them. Rations put in tin cans gave whole companies ptomaine poisoning. Troops in the tropical heat of Cuba found themselves clad in woolen uniforms...For every man killed in action, thirteen died of disease. (Colby: 129).

As to be expected, some companies with government contracts got fat on profits and our troops suffered, while some bureaucrats added to their pension longevity without managing efficiently.
There were casualties even on the home front when DuPont explosions killed six of their own employees, toiling away for their wages of 18 cents per hour. (Colby: 129).

With the personal experience of having been treated so well for fifteen months from 1967 to 1968 by many Army nurses at Brooke General Hospital at Fort Sam Houston, Texas, it was a privilege to discover that during the Spanish-American War "1500 women served from Cuba to Puerto Rico, in the Philippine Islands, and on a Naval Hospital ship." Unfortunately, fifteen of them died of Typhoid Fever contracted from their patients during the Spanish-American War. General George M. Sternberg served as Surgeon General during the war and wrote in his 1899 Annual Report, "American women may feel proud of the record made by these nurses in 1898-99, for every medical officer with whom they served has testified to their intelligence, and skill, their earnestness, devotion and self-sacrifice." An Army Nurse Corps was established in 1901.[9]

The war in the Philippines conducted to pacify the Filipinos, who desired their independence from the Spaniards, as well as the United States, turned out to be very bloody. It consisted of two phases. The first lasted from 1898 until 1902 and the statistics indicate that 4,196 American soldiers were killed (ten times the casualty rate in Cuba) and the count of the wounded totaled 2,930. At least sixteen thousand guerilla warriors died, as well as upwards of twenty thousand civilians. Many other civilians succumbed to cholera. But now America had a major footprint in Asia! It only took pain and suffering for almost forty thousand Filipino families in our new commercial and naval base in the Philippines!

Little known was another conflict in the Philippines which involved the United States forces fighting what was called the Moro Rebellion from 1899 to 1913. The religious/political movement of Islam in the Philippines had begun many centuries in advance with the Arab traders who came to the Philippines. The Moros began fighting the Spanish, the Americans, and eventually the Philippine government, even up to the current day to overturn any foreign rule but their own. In the struggle against the Moros, the United States casualties totaled 130 killed and 270 wounded, and after pacification of the Philippines in 1902, our military units included members of the Philippine Scouts and Constabulary, who suffered deaths and wounding.

The Islamic State-affiliated Maute group in May 2017 began a serious incursion into Marawi City in the Philippines. It has been intense urban fighting.[10] The Islamists continue their efforts to impose Islam by violence.

Consequences

The final consequences of the Spanish-American War were specifically that we controlled Cuba, and took Puerto Rico, the Philippines and Guam. We had flexed our muscles of war just as had the great powers of Europe. We bested one of those powers. President McKinley justified one day to a group that we must keep the Philippines. One of the alternatives that we declined to pursue was to "... turn them over to France or Germany – our commercial rivals in the Orient – that would be bad business and discreditable."
Originally our purpose was to assist Cuban and Filipino patriots desirous of breaking the shackles of Spanish colonialism. However, instead of the patriots being aided in achievement of their independence, which would have been a lofty goal indeed, they became somewhat the "first" colonies of the United States, under the guise of "protecting" them. This led to our pattern of becoming involved in "overthrowing" governments, arguably, in some quarters, to "protect American interests." (Kinzer: 3).
Lundberg also reported after the war that the Rockefeller-Stillman National City Bank obtained the financial opportunity to be the banker of choice for branches in Cuba and the Philippines. Wall Streeters had visions of the riches in mineral wealth of South America. Control of the Caribbean and an Isthmus Canal was integral to these goals. (Lundberg: 62). The Cubans expected freedom from foreign control, but we oversaw the government in such a manner that our business interests were protected from expropriation and barriers to trade.

The Du Ponts raked in over $500,000 in profits from what was termed by Secretary of State John Hays as "a splendid little war." (Colby: 129).

Author Leland Hamilton Jenks wrote in his book *Our Cuban Colony: A Study in Sugar* that the United Fruit Company in 1901 purchased large parcels of Cuban property to plant cane and bananas. (Spingola *Seizure:* 165*).*[11] It became a very lucrative and prosperous investment for the capitalist risk-takers. Obviously, as a positive outcome to be sure, this provided employment opportunities for the Cubans, who had survived the Spanish domination.

A variety of references reported that we were quick to begin to exploit the great amounts of mineral resources in the Philippines. Eventually we imported Chinese workers as a less costly source of labor. (Spingola *Seizure: 213).*[12]

After this war and the loss of much of the Spanish colonial empire, the relatively large Spanish Army began to establish its power base in Spain proper and across from Gibraltar in Morocco, Africa. (Quigley *Tragedy*: 588).

Perhaps, for this war and others in which we would be engaged in the future, the question comes down to this: Whether or not we are to go to war and risk the treasure and blood and tears of our young combatants for our true "national security" purposes, or to achieve economic or financial gain typically enjoyed by only the "privileged" few.

Aftermath:

Our economy recovered due to the opening of new markets overseas that enabled expansion of opportunities for capital investment and product exports. (Colby: 127).

The *Army and Navy Journal* of March 26, 1904, reported that in Panama, revolutionaries were outfitted with "thousands of rifles suspiciously like the Mausers captured from the Spanish forces in

Cuba." (Engelbrecht: 64). The U.S. Secretary of War said that 21,154 rifles and carbines were captured from the Spanish in Cuba and Puerto Rico. One of the "Merchants of Death," Bannerman, bought 18,200 of them. Our Secretary of War was unable to connect the dots and was clueless as to whom Bannerman might have sold them. (Engelbrecht: 65). Perhaps this account was a harbinger of future pronouncements by politicians, who could not, or preferred not, to be on top of their game or who maybe really were part of "the game."

Cuba

In Cuba's "protectorate" period, legal fees were earned for the Sullivan & Cromwell firm in 1917 when John Foster Dulles, the principal of the New York-based law firm, became involved in Cuba's internal politics, by representing his clients, thirteen large Cuban sugar plantation owners with $170 million in cane fields. The owners were supportive of Cuban "liberals" (the "outs"), who occupied areas adjacent to their plantations. The "liberals" were intent upon overthrowing the duly-elected "conservative" government (the "ins"). The owners hired Dulles, who submitted a legal brief to the State Department, which attempted, of course, to make a case for a "stolen" or fraudulent election, however, the actual purpose was to support the plantation owners, who were most probably threatened by the dissidents. Ostensibly, Dulles' influence was not political, but rather strictly financial for his clients. The decision to remain in support of the conservative government and to decline to intervene this time in Cuba's internal politics, was made at the "top" by President Woodrow Wilson. Wilson, however, appeared to be sufficiently "moved" by the interests of the business people to send 1,600 American troops to Cuba for five years of "training," and incidentally to provide security for the American-owned interests. (Lisagor: 67).

It is probable that these troops were pleased to endure the heat of Cuba rather than the trench warfare beginning in France! This was just one instance in which the United States was to be involved in the unpredictability of Central and South America and thereby directly intervening when our American-owned businesses were in jeopardy. This was a classic example of the exertion of political influence on behalf of business interests with the use of our military as "hired guns." I make no judgment as to the worthiness or unworthiness of protection of American businesses abroad by use of our military, but would just like to ensure that examples such as these are, in fact, brought to light in explanation of how power is exerted through maneuvers "behind the scenes" at the highest economic, financial, legal and political levels.

By 1920 to 1921, the Cuban economy was devastated, and the aforementioned America's National City Bank, which held ninety percent of Cuba's bank deposits and basically had evolved to being Cuba's central bank, ended up owning twenty percent of Cuba's sugar mills through foreclosures. (Chernow: 237). This is an indicator of the close financial ties the New York money center banks derived after the immediate past military "excursion."

Through a connection in the 1920s with an eventual dictator, Gerardo Machado, Chase Manhattan Bank (to be involved many times in the future) got in on the action in Cuba. The relationship by the bank with this head of state was solidified by a personal loan to Machado of $200,000 and employment by the bank of his son-in-law. (Sampson *Lenders:* 62). Presumably, the son-in-law was well-qualified for his position, but this explains how business sometimes is done!

Our troops occupied Cuba until 1904, but returned in 1906, 1912, 1917, and 1920, to quell uprisings against U.S. economic policies. Opposition movements, especially among the unions, began in 1925, becoming communistic by 1930. Gerald Machado became a dictator and was overthrown in the 1930s by an army rebellion (assisted by the U.S.) led by Fulgencio Batista, who threw out the communists and accepted U.S. military advisors. By the 1950s, Cuba had a highly successful tourist industry (assuredly enriching Batista and his cronies), a part of which was overseen by gangsters. In 1952, he cancelled a congressional election, one of whose candidates was one Fidel Castro, whose revolution overthrew Batista in 1959. (Kinzer: 89). Our occupation of Cuba was useful to the Marxists historians as expressed here:

> Among the countries occupied by American troops…, the assessment of American empire is uniformly critical, predictably so in socialist Cuba, where Marxist historians have rewritten history to portray the two military occupations of the early twentieth century as examples of capitalist exploitation. (Langley: 218).

Puerto Rico

The new addition of Puerto Rico to America's empire ensured our ability to oversee protection of our Caribbean trade routes. The United States dominated the government of Puerto Rico for decades. "During the early years of the twentieth century, four American corporations gobbled up most of Puerto Rico's best land." (Kinzer: 92). Sugar became the major crop. Puerto Rico basically became our "colony" comprised of mostly poor people. However, economic improvement came to the island, and as of recently, they seem to be satisfied with a political system existing between statehood and independence. (Kinzer: 93). As of 2016, they were experiencing extraordinary stresses in their governmental finances.

In June of 1920, a unit of volunteer soldiers in Puerto Rico was named the 65th Infantry Regiment of the United States Army. Approximately 62,000 Puerto Ricans served in both WWII and the Korean War, many becoming wounded and receiving our Nation's highest decorations for valor.[13] Many of them are buried in our national cemetery at San Juan.

Philippines

American businessmen looked with greediness upon the opportunity to open markets to China. The United States was aware of the vacuum apparent in the Philippines and knew that

France and Germany had their eyes on the Philippines. Therefore, we posted tens of thousands of soldiers to the Philippines and were confronted with a type of warfare with which we were totally unfamiliar. The Filipinos, who had fought the Spaniards for their freedom, now had a new enemy to fight. And fight they did. According to one account, "They laid snares and booby traps, slit throats, set fires, administered poisons, and mutilated prisoners." Our forces sometimes responded with our own set of atrocities. (Kinzer: 50).

We oversaw political control and ignored local demand for independence until 1934, when we were prepared to grant the Philippines its independence. WWII intervened and the Philippines became the scenes of the historic attacks by the Japanese on Clark Air Base (where I spent one night on the way home to the United States from Vietnam in late June 1967), the Bataan Peninsula (with its horrendous ensuing Bataan Death March, many victims of which were my friends), and Corregidor, from which General Douglas MacArthur was spirited away to safety by U.S. Navy boats on March 16, 1942.

By 1945, the Philippines were eventually freed of the Japanese occupation when General MacArthur fulfilled his pledge to return. On July 4, 1946, they did eventually receive their freedom. The United States maintained two large military bases, Clark Air Force Base and Subic Bay Navy Base until 1992, when they were closed. As of 2016, China's efforts to establish airfields on atolls and islands nearer to the Philippines than mainland China were causing the Philippines to reconsider a closer military cooperation with the United States. America's Special Operations forces are also engaged in the Philippines to counter a troublesome operation by the Abu Sayyaf Islamist jihadists. Jihadists never give up a drive for supremacy.

During World War II, approximately 260,000 Filipinos were very active in guerilla operations against the Japanese invaders. Once the Japanese invaded the Philippines, they conducted a three-month battle against the American forces and Filipino allies and took 15,000 Americans and 60,000 Filipinos on the Bataan Death March.

United States

McKinley was reelected, then assassinated, Roosevelt became president, the Panama Canal was built, and our "police power" began to be exercised in the Caribbean. Russia and Japan fought it out several years later in the Russo–Japanese War from 1904 to 1905. America was an empire! Our power at the time was characterized as follows:

> And 30 years away there was America, rich, powerful, commanding a greater economic and perhaps political strength in the world than any nation which had ever gone before – aloof, untrammeled, admitting no restraints upon the uses to which power might be put. (Millis: 410).

Old and long-time European power Spain was vanquished and was finally pushed out of the western hemisphere. We pushed into the eastern hemisphere.

[Author's note: Within a few years of the end of the Spanish Empire my maternal grandfather, Placido de La Fuente, and his brother Marcelino, both bachelors, left the northern Spanish province of Asturias, seeking a better life and traveled to Veracruz, Mexico, before eventually residing in Mission, Texas along the Rio Grande River in South Texas, where my mother Amalia de La Fuente Clark resided in her youth. My mother's parents managed silent movie theatres in South Texas. My grandmother Isabel Nielsen played the piano during the shows.

Her father was Henry Nielsen, a German merchant in Matamoros, Texas, just across the Rio Grande from Brownsville, Texas. Her mother was Agathe nee Hagen, whose father was Hans Christian Hagen, German Royal Consul for Sweden and Norway. Their hometown was Flensburg, Germany. This German family history is an indicator of the depth of German business interests worldwide.

German business interests and the competition they represented to British business interests worldwide factored into causes of World War One.]

Chapter 18:

Banker, Oil, and Banana Wars – Central and South America

"I helped in the raping of half a dozen Central American republics for the benefit of Wall Street." – Major General Smedley D. Butler (USMC-Ret.), two-time Medal of Honor Recipient, in a 1931 speech before the American Legion (Butler: 5)

Monroe Doctrine (America's "Protectionism" of Latin America)

Most students of American history are aware of the Monroe Doctrine. Some history on the Doctrine and motivation for its declaration provides illumination into the invasion of Mexico from 1861 to 1862 by the French at a time when, due to our Civil War, we took no action to oppose France's hostile action by invoking the Monroe Doctrine.

On December 2, 1823, President James Monroe declared in his annual message to Congress that "... the American continents... are henceforth not to be considered as subjects for future colonization by any European powers." Necessity for this proclamation by the United States was twofold; one was due to Russian designs on territory, but more importantly, also to what was occurring in Central and South America. Many former Spanish colonies were revolting and there were moves by France and Spain to regain these possessions. Great Britain was in favor of the decline in Spanish colonialism, because it had inhibited Britain's trade.[1]

Research has once again uncovered the story behind the story of the rationale for the Monroe doctrine. Perhaps the first official pronouncement of why the Monroe doctrine was necessary relates to testimony by Senator Robert L. Owen on April 25, 1916, and it is included in the Congressional Record. Senator Owen spoke and entered the following remarks in his testimony:

> I wish to put in the RECORD the secret treaty of Verona of November 22, 1822, showing what this ancient conflict is between the rule of the few and the rule of the many. I wish to call the attention of the Senate to this treaty because it is the threat of this treaty which was the basis of the Monroe Doctrine. It throws a powerful white light upon the conflict between monarchial government and government by the people. The Holy Alliance under the influence of Metternich, the Premier of Austria in 1822, issued this remarkable secret document.[2]

Signed by Metternich of Austria, Chateaubriand of France, and both Bernstet and Nesselrode of Russia, this secret treaty was made in Verona, Italy, on November 22, 1822. Essentially, it was a call to arms against representative government by the people in favor of monarchies, who would maintain sovereignty over their people. They were in favor of suppressing the press, and in defending religion because it kept nations in "passive obedience," especially to the Pope with whose cooperation they were in gratitude, and they authorized annual payments by France to Spain and Portugal to end their war.[3]

Senator Owen said, "The Holy Alliance... had well laid plans also to destroy popular governments in the American colonies, which had revolted from Spain and Portugal in Central and South America under the successful example of the United States." Owen theorized that Thomas Jefferson and James Monroe proposed and brought to fruition the Monroe Doctrine so that the United States would consider it a hostile act, if any European power attempted to overpower any American Republic. He proclaimed that the ultimate purpose of the secret treaty of Verona was to support monarchical government of an elite versus governments of the people such as instituted in the United States.[4]

Foreign Involvement in Mexico (Rothschilds)

The N. M. Rothschild & Sons of London were instrumental in the development of Mexico business networks, especially mercury. After Mexico won its War of Independence in 1821, it needed foreign capital to continue its mining efforts, thus Mexico prevailed upon capitalists, mainly British, to finance its efforts for the next twenty years. The Rothschilds became heavily involved in Mexico in bond issues, the export of silver, quicksilver distribution, and real estate. The Texas Revolution in 1836 and the so-called Pastry War of 1837 with France brought about much turmoil throughout Mexico. Throughout all of this period until about 1850, the Rothschild representative in Mexico was Lionel Davidson, who maintained an ample production of mercury from the Mexico mines. The French branch of Rothschilds became involved in the El Boleo mines in Baja California.[5]

Roots of the Mexican-American War (1846 to 1848)

James K. Polk was inaugurated on March 4, 1845, and entered office with a decided attitude that the United States should expand its territory all the way to the Pacific Coast. After Texas won its independence in 1836, there was a move for it to join the Union, but Northerners were opposed to another slave state entering the Union. However, President Polk was in favor of Texas being admitted to the Union, which occurred on December 29, 1845. Even prior to Texas' statehood, Polk ordered American troops to Texas and they debarked at Corpus Christi in mid-June of 1845. (DeVoto: 14).

Throughout the period of the Republic of Texas from March 2, 1836, until statehood, the security of Texas had been in jeopardy. Mexico never recognized Texas' independence and constantly disputed boundaries. Texas claimed its boundary extended to the Rio Grande, but Mexico claimed it was marked by the Nueces, 120 miles north. The dispute undoubtedly may be considered at the center of the cause of the Mexican-American War. (DeVoto: 14).

Between the time of the Republic of Texas and its statehood, Texas was the site of extensive armed clashes: One with Comanche Indians,[6] a short 1842 unsuccessful Mexican incursion led by General Rafael Vazquez who was attempting to occupy San Antonio, as well as a later 1842 attack led by General Adrian Woll, which succeeded in capturing San Antonio also for a short period.[7]

The animosity between Mexico and its lost territory of Texas carried over to the national United States government. When Texas became a state on December 29, 1845, Mexico found this action intolerable and threatened war. President Polk coveted California and the other western Mexico territories. Polk supported the Texas position on the Rio Grande as the boundary between Texas and Mexico. (DeVoto: 5,14). [Author's note: I was born in McAllen, Texas, and my mother grew up in the Spanish-speaking side of the town of Mission, Texas, literally just hundreds of feet from the Rio Grande River.]

President Polk sent U.S. representative John Slidell to Mexico to negotiate for a payment of $30 million that would establish the boundary as the Rio Grande river and to purchase the New Mexico and Upper California lands. Mexico was unwilling to consider the offer (DeVoto: 108). Both sides sent troops into the disputed area. The specific incident that caused the U.S to declare war against Mexico occurred on April 25, 1846, when a small U.S. force of sixty dragoons under Captain Seth Thornton was attacked and overwhelmed by a vastly superior Mexican force of sixteen hundred cavalry. Sixteen Americans were killed and the rest were taken prisoner. This was the provocation that was sufficient to trigger the war against Mexico that would later be declared on May 13, 1846. (DeVoto: 129, 134).

The United States prevailed in the Mexican-American war, and on February 2, 1848, the Treaty of Guadalupe Hidalgo was inked, and all the U.S. demands were met. The Rio Grande River became the boundary, Mexico recognized the statehood of Texas, and for a payment of $15 million and forgiveness of prior debt, California and the remaining Mexican territories became a part of the U.S.[8]

An interesting tidbit from history is that gold was discovered in California on January 24, 1848, just nine days before the signing of the Treaty of Hidalgo. Obviously, the news did not reach Mexico in time to put off the signing. John Tiffany, writing in the 2001 March/April issue of the *Barnes Review*, theorizes that most of the payment went to the Rothschild bankers since Mexico was in debt to them.[9]

Soldier's Blood:

Mexican War Army battle deaths totaled 1,733, other deaths totaled 11,550, and those with non-mortal wounds totaled 4,152. Mexican casualties were estimated to total 25,000 killed or wounded between 1846 and 1848.[10]

Arms Merchants and Mexico

In the Mexican-American War, Alfred du Pont of the DuPont operation sold one million pounds of powder to the government. The company was confronted with orders for their powder from cutouts in Havana and from a joint Spanish and French entity that Du Pont deemed were being ordered for use by Santa Anna's Mexico. Du Pont declined filling the order because, although Du Pont was not supportive of efforts against Mexico, he was patriotic and would not sell his powder to our then enemy. (Engelbrecht: 29) and (Colby: 60).

After the Mexican-American War, DuPont kept its business vibrant as their powder was used in land clearing for stump removal, in William Astor's Oregon Fur company hunting, railroads, and mining. But in 1854, it got a new war in Crimea. As arms merchants are inclined to seek profits anywhere, they sold to both sides, England, France, and Turkey versus Russia. (Engelbrecht: 30).

The Mexican-American War brought new strength to the Colt Firearms company when General Zachary Taylor ordered 1,000 revolvers. (Engelbrecht: 41).

One major consequence of the Mexican-American War was that the United States' territory became substantially enhanced. Another major consequence resulted in heightened conflicts regarding slavery in the new areas.

Foreign Invasion of Mexico

Texans had set their sights on acquiring the four northern Mexico provinces of Nuevo Leon, Coahuila, Chihuahua, and Sonora since 1840. The Sonora province, housing the capital city of Guanajuato, was mineral rich to include silver and gold. Between 1849 and 1859, five different U.S.-based attempts to acquire control over the northern Mexican provinces occurred. (Keehn: 20).

By 1859, the population of Mexico was eight million and conditions there were horrific. Financial ruin through bankruptcy was eminent due to nonpayment of loans to English and other foreign banks. There were two main parties. The Conservative Party, controlling 90% of the land and 65% of the populace, consisted of wealthy Mexicans and the Catholic hierarchy. Benito Juarez's Liberal Party controlled other areas, such as the coast and ports. Their capital was Veracruz. The Liberal Party took the populist stand of disassembling the huge land ownership of the Catholic Church as well as that of the monied aristocracy. (Keehn: 19).

In 1859, the Knights of the Golden Circle (K.G.C.), an organization formed to proliferate slavery, were in the planning stages for an expedition into Mexico. These plans were discussed at a meeting of the Circle at the Greenbrier Resort in White Sulphur Springs, Virginia, in August of 1859. (Keehn: 23).[11] The K.G.C. published a sixty-page booklet, *Rules, Regulations and Principles of the American Legion of the K.G.C.*, which called for the "Americanization of Mexico" through an expedition into Mexico, and funds were raised for the operation. The participants were promised Mexican land. (Keehn: 27).[12] Another document, not public, was the *Degree Book* which documented a conquest of

Mexico. (Keehn: 27).[13] Mexico was just the starting point for a new empire planned to include Central America and the Caribbean. As is prominent in "secret" organizations, these lofty plans and goals were not disclosed to the lower level of K.G.C. members. (Keehn: 20). Other efforts were expressed to export slavery to Mexico and areas farther south.

Little known by many were the contents relative to Mexico in President James Buchanan's annual message to Congress in December of 1859. Due to arrests and murders of U.S. citizens, President Buchanan desired "peace and order" to be restored in Mexico and therefore he desired authorization for the United States to send military forces into Mexico! (Keehn: 32).[14] In a letter dated January 26, 1860, by K.G.C. leader Elkanah Bracken Greer, he indicated that this stand by the president was music to the ears of his organization. (Keehn: 34). Texas Governor Sam Houston was even considering moving into Mexico to establish a "protectorate." One of his justifications for this action was based upon Mexican bandits coming into Texas, as well as slaves escaping from Texas into Mexico. Houston had requested federal funding for the military expeditions. Houston's potential financial supporters were supposedly English capitalists who were supportive of the annexation by Texas of the northern Mexico provinces. (Keehn: 36-38). Perhaps they were interested in the silver mines? Or maybe they possessed altruistic motives of truly helping the downtrodden of Mexico?

By early 1860, there were designs on Mexico by the United States government, by Texas Governor Sam Houston, and by the K.G.C. By this time, liberal president Benito Juarez and most of his cabinet members had grown cold to mercenaries engaging in a military operation into Mexico. (Keehn: 38).

Thousands of Knights began to gather in Gonzalez, Texas on the Guadalupe River. Many traveled on to the Rio Grande border in South Texas. Buchanan refused federal funding for Sam Houston's plans and differentiated between his goal, which was to intervene only to assist Mexico as Republic, while both Texas and the K.G.C.

desired the route of annexation. (Keehn: 42).

Governor Sam Houston decided to forego any operation led by Texas and he ordered the Knights to disperse. The Knights did not initially forego their plans for Mexico even when Juarez apparently refused any further support. The Knights continued through September 1860 to muster its forces in Texas. (Keehn: 61). Military action by the K.G.C. was placed in the dustbins of history because by late 1860 it basically redirected to efforts to the coming secession of the South.

Benito Juarez and the Catholic Church

In June of 1856, Benito Juarez had been Mexico's Minister of Justice and under his direction he abolished special courts for the military and the clergy. He forced the Catholic Church to dispose of its property, but it was not to be seized by the government. He became essentially the vice president of Mexico. In January 1858, conservatives revolted and overthrew the presidency. Juarez retreated to Veracruz and created a new governmental structure wherein he had to battle the conservative element and the Catholic power structure, both united against him. He had placed all Catholic Church property under government control except structures specifically utilized for teaching and services. By January 1861 he returned to Mexico City and became officially and constitutionally the president.[15]

Invasion of Mexico in 1861

A little additional historical background is in order. In 1857, Liberal Benito Juarez, a Mexican reformist, pitted his forces against the Conservatives in Mexico and came out as the victor, albeit with war debts to foreign banks and the country's treasury was bare. Secretary of State William Henry Seward offered American loans to Juarez. The cost would be concessions for Mexican mines and a default would require that Baja California and other Mexican states would be turned over to America. These terms were turned down by Mexico and our own expenditures for our Civil War precluded our being able to make the loans anyway. On July 17, 1861, President Juarez told the Europeans (France, Great Britain, and Spain) that it would be necessary to forego interest payments for two years.[16] In a manner of speaking the collateral had been the country of Mexico itself.

The French, under the rule of Napoleon III, originally allied with Great Britain and Spain, invaded Mexico in January 1862, and captured Mexico City. Great Britain and Spain had signed an agreement to unite to invade Mexico to force payment of the loans, but quickly dropped their support when it became evident that France desired to conquer Mexico and not just demand payment of the loans. Abraham Lincoln's Union administration indicated disapproval of the invasion, but tacitly acquiesced to the takeover because of the desire to have France rebuff openings by the South to obtain French support in their cause.[17]

Again, another underlying case of economic determinism motivated Napoleon III. The silver mines of Mexico were a major motivation to invade Mexico.[18]

On May 5, 1862, the Mexican military, commanded by General Ignacio Zaragoza, defeated an "invading" French army in the Battle of Puebla, Mexico. Known as Cinco de Mayo, this day is celebrated as a holiday in Mexico, and many Mexican-Americans take special note of this day each year.

By June of 1863, President Benito Juarez's government was overthrown, and in the summer of 1864, Austrian Hapsburg Archduke Ferdinand Maximilian became the Emperor of Mexico by accepting an offer, through a political move, to forge an alliance by Napoleon III. [Author's note: Recall the precepts of the Treaty of Verona.] Although northern pressure during the French incursion was constantly present to address the issue, moderation by President Lincoln prevailed so as not to push France into the arms of the southerners.[19]

By 1863, there was a leak to the press that Napoleon's real

purpose other than the supposed financial one was to establish a strong Mexican government able to curtail "the growth and prestige of the United States."[20]

When Benito Juarez was in rebellion, he ordered from the arms merchant, Winchester Repeating Arms Company, 1000 rifles along with 500,000 rounds of ammunition. The Winchester representative, "Colonel" Tom Addis, delivered the rifles to Juarez and his demand for payment in silver was met. Maximilian attempted to take possession of the rifles and ammo, but to no avail. (Engelbrecht: 43).

By the time period from 1864 to 1867, the United States was able finally in the waning and end stages of our Civil War to focus our attention on the situation with Mexico. Toward the end of this time frame the Atlantic cable became operative thereby allowing interception of cable traffic. Mexico was still ruled by Maximilian up until 1867 and the French army remained just across the Texas border.[21]

After General Lee's surrender, Confederate General Slaughter crossed the border into Mexico and offered to the French commander Marshal Bazaine 25,000 Confederate troops. This attempt to support Maximilian and the French by former Confederates caused the North to support Benito Juarez. (Emerson: 937).

After the end of the Civil War, U.S. Generals Ulysses S. Grant and Philip H. Sheridan covertly gave support to Juarez's guerilla operations. In 1866, Napoleon III began to remove French troops from Mexico and without this support, Maximilian was captured and executed in 1867. Herein ended another European invasion of the Americas caused again by economic causes.[22]

Soldiers' Blood:

24,000 killed, one half on each side. More than 8,000 wounded on the Mexican side. Nowadays bankers restructure debts and do what is called "workouts" with the borrowers. This would have precluded all the blood that was shed! But, the French bankers surely pressured Napoleon III to assist militarily to obtain the repayments of Mexico's loans. Harken back to the "Cupidity" chapter. Some world events never change.

Emperor Maximilian's Reign

Napoleon III had offered the rule of Mexico in 1864 to Archduke Maximilian and he had his own motivation for Maximilian to assume this position of responsibility. Napoleon desired this position for Maximilian as compensation for Austria's previous loss of her Venetian provinces and to allow for a secret combination with Austria against Prussia. (Balance of power issues in Europe). Maximilian amazingly enough was to compensate France for the "privilege" of the gift of Mexico with the payment of 270 million francs. Naturally, Austria became indebted to London and Paris bankers, who were only too eager to lend for this enterprise on America's southern doorstep. On April 4, 1864, the United States refused to recognize this new monarchy. (Emerson: 926).

Maximilian attempted financial support by obtaining the properties of the Catholic Church in Mexico. However, he was denied any support for this effort in no uncertain terms by Pope Pius IX. (Emerson: 927). He was executed on June 19, 1867.

Author George P. Messervy wrote in 1921 *The Quickstep of an Emperor Maximilian of Mexico.* The work reflects the historical background for the evolution of the selection of Maximilian to become the Emperor of Mexico after the French invasion. Messervy makes his case that Maximilian was "...a 'dupe' of a band of desperate conspirators within the Church of Rome." (Messervy: 8). Messervy makes his case that Maximilian was used by Napoleon III, but the extension of the Roman Catholic Church in the Western Hemisphere was the underlying motivation for the elevation of Maximilian, a Roman Catholic Bourbon Prince. The Mexican Catholic clergy believed he was pledged to the Holy See to restore the confiscated property of the church. (Messervy: 9).

In 1866, the United States with the Civil War over insisted upon the provisions of the Monroe Doctrine again to be operative. The dictum by the United States led to an undermining of Maximilian and was added to all his other governing inadequacies. (Messervy: 11).

Mexico Post-Maximilian and French Invasion

Porfirio Diaz in 1877 began a reign as the president of Mexico that lasted until 1911. During this timeframe, Mexico originally achieved wealth, "...however, it was not distributed throughout the country: most of the profits went abroad or stayed in the hands of a very few wealthy Mexicans."[23] What else is new? The haves have more on the backs of the have nots!

Mexico's Oil Wars

In Diaz's longer-than-thirty-year rule, the business interests of Great Britain and the United States profited immensely due to extensive investments in Mexico's minerals, railroads, and oil wells.[24] The magnitude of these investments in Mexico between oilmen, bankers, and businessmen between 1900 to 1910 had increased by 100% to nearly $2 billion. This was reflected in American ownership of 43% of the property values of the country, 10% more than the Mexican nationals.[25] It is little wonder that American investors in Mexico had great interest and involvement in the various Mexican revolutions over the next few years.

Over the next few years, Mexico's history was in great turmoil and somewhat complicated. Oil in the Western Hemisphere became a competition between British and American interests. By 1910, British Lord Cowdray's Mexican Eagle Company owned more than 50% of Mexico's production in competition with Rockefeller's Standard Oil and other companies. In a conflict between President Porfirio Diaz of Mexico and the Rockefeller-controlled Pierce Waters Oil Company, the Rockefellers interest supported Francisco Madero in a 1911 revolution to overthrow the dictator President Porfirio Diaz. Then in 1913, British oil interests supported

Victoriano Huerta to overthrow Madero and kill him. Another coup began with the Rockefeller- Morgan interests financing Venustiano Carranza and Pancho Villa to overthrow Huerta. (Josephson *FDR*: 108).[26]

Carranza originally supported Madero and then fought against Huerta. He was opposed by rebels Pancho Villa and Emiliano Zapata, who continued their opposition to him. Carranza had significant conflicts and controversy with the United States over the April 1914 occupation of Veracruz, the March 1916 pursuit of Pancho Villa after his foray into New Mexico, and his 1918 effort to control the oil industry. He eventually was murdered in 1920.[27]

In February of 1912, Madero, who had sold his Mexican land to Rockefeller, staged his revolution against Diaz, and, of course, oil concessions for the Standard Oil Company were a factor. Then the British supported General Huerta's revolution over Madero. The U.S. did not recognize this new regime. (Josephson *Rockefeller*: 190).

The United States began to pressure Huerta with withdrawn American support because America believed him to be a pawn of Britain, who desired control of American oil wells in Mexico. It was the plan of the U.S. to support a new group of rebels.[28] President Woodrow Wilson ordered blockades of munitions and financial support to Mexico and allowed arms to reach Carranza and Villa. He ordered an American military and naval operation into Veracruz. American oil companies were in opposition to the British-supported Huerta and withheld tax payments and supported General Carranza financially.[29]

Tampico, Mexico, in 1914, was populated by a large foreign group and housed oil refineries and warehouses of Standard Oil Company and national petroleum. These interests felt protected by the U.S. Navy parked offshore. As result of a minor issue in Tampico and an apology unacceptable to the Navy's admiral, Americans decided to occupy Veracruz, being further justified after learning of an arms shipment arriving for Huerta's forces.

Seamen and Marines entered Veracruz in mid-April 1914 amid sporadic fire from the Mexican forces. (Langley: 91). The ship carrying the arms was boarded and it was discovered that the arms had been purchased in New York. The ship eventually delivered its weapons to another port for Huerta's people. Smedley Butler's Marines had landed in the port of Veracruz. American casualties were 17 killed and 63 wounded. (Langley: 92-95). The U.S. Army took over administration of Veracruz. By November 1914, Americans evacuated Veracruz. The then ongoing Mexican Civil War continued with Carranza going to Veracruz and Zapata and Villa occupying the capital. (Langley: 107).

In a 1919 Senate document, an American oilman Doheny reported that the U.S. had supported Carranza (with his own personal contribution of $100,000 cash to Carranza) while the British were in full support of Huerta.[30]

Carranza was eventually recognized as Mexico's president, then his administration became embroiled in World War I and German espionage. The revolutions in Mexico in 1915-1916 revealed involvement of financial interests in New York once again. A German espionage agent, Von Rintelen, was tried in a May 1917 trial in New York City for attempting to reroute ammunition shipments from the Allies in Europe to both Mexico and Japan.[31] In mid-1915, through Von Rintelen's advisor, Sommerfield, Guaranty Trust Company of New York was the conduit by which $380,000 of ammunition was purchased from the Western Cartridge Company of Alton, Illinois, and shipped to Pancho Villa. On January 10, 1916, Villa murdered at Santa Isabel seventeen American miners and on March 9, 1916, he crossed the U.S. border to Columbus, New Mexico, and killed eighteen more Americans. (Sutton *Bolshevik:* 52). General John Pershing chased Pancho Villa 350 miles with 10,000 troops back into Mexico in the Mexican Punitive Expedition. Unable to capture Villa, at least his revolutionaries were dispersed.

The Carranza government purchased and received shipment of

additional arms and ammunition from the American Gun Company over the objections of the American ambassador to Mexico, but, was overridden by Secretary of State Robert Lansing.[32]

District Attorney John A. Walls from Brownsville, Texas, testified before the 1919 Fall Committee that there was a link between Boslsheviks in the U.S., activity of German espionage, and the Carranza people in Mexico.[33] The Carranza revolution, which eventually reflected the first Soviet-style constitution in the world, written by Trotskyites, was therefore a product of Wall Street bankers and American politicians.[34] This support by U.S. Wall Streeters and business interests was just the beginning of their machinations through the 1920s and 1930s to support Bolsheviks, Communists, and Hitler.

Aftermath of Mexico's Oil Wars

The legacy of all the coups and revolutions of the decade beginning in 1910 in Mexico is captured by author Harvey O'Connor, who wrote about Mexico's nationalization of its own resources in 1938, which represented freedom from control by the Rockefeller Empire. O'Connor wrote:

> Behind nationalization in 1938 were twenty years of crude exploitation of the Nation's natural resources for the benefit of foreign capitalists, of brazen contempt for the government and people, of studied defiance of Mexico's constitutional laws, and efforts to impose taxation, of continued interference in internal politics, of incessant bribery and subordination of federal and state officials, of subsidies for armed uprisings and maintenance of 'white guard' armies in the oil region. (O'Connor: 314).

The history of Mexico during this period reflects undoubtedly a serious indictment of outside interference in Mexico all for domination of its oil riches. It laid the stage for the future vying of control between British and American empires for control of oil resources all over the globe.

Panama and the Panama Canal

In the 1913 congressional hearings, it was summarized that the Wall Street law firm of Sullivan & Cromwell had been involved in the Panama Canal controversy. The hearings consisted of testimony by Congressman Rainey that the November 1903 revolution on the Panama isthmus was brought about because the law firm, headed by William Nelson Cromwell, controlled the revolution and fostered and fomented it to separate Colombia from its province of Panama with a $40 million deal to acquire control of the Panama Canal.[35]

The story behind the above story relates to the above-mentioned Cromwell of the venerable New York law firm of Sullivan & Cromwell. There had been significant controversy about building a canal either across Nicaragua or Panama. Cromwell became the principal proponent of the Panama route. Theodore Roosevelt considered the canal a grand measure of his success. Ferdinand de Lesseps had succeeded in building the Suez Canal, but failed in a Panama Canal. The Paris-based New Panama Canal Company procured the legal expertise and connections of Cromwell to lobby for the United States to choose the Panama route. (Lisagor: 40).

It was Cromwell's charge (for which he would be amply remunerated for success) to convince the United States to take over the lease of his French client. Many Southern senators supported the Nicaragua route. Cromwell cultivated the support of President William McKinley and Republican Senator Mark Hanna of Ohio. Support from Hanna was cemented by a contribution of $60,000 from the account of the New Panama Canal Company to the Republican Party. Cromwell pointed out a German interest in the Canal project to a Paris delegation from the U.S. (Lisagor: 43). Competition with Germany was beginning to be evidenced years before WWI.

Back-and-forth negotiations about a price to be paid to France to ensure total U.S. control of the project ensued. A volcano explosion in Nicaragua swayed sentiment to Panama and the

Senate voted to support the Panama route. A major hurdle still standing was the approval of Colombia to endorse the sale of the lease to the United States. The Colombian Senate refused to ratify the U.S. treaty in favor of Panama. Cromwell decided that only a revolution in Panama to secede the province from Columbia would bring about the opportunity to make the Panama effort successful. Cromwell became the instigator and organizer of the revolution. Cromwell had gotten the ball rolling, but needed to escape the machinery moving the revolution forward and moved to Paris. Philippe Buneau-Varilla became the leader of the revolution. The bloodless coup occurred on November 3, 1903, with the help of U.S. Navy ships blocking the Panamanian harbor from Colombian forces. Within 72 hours, the United States recognized the new Republic of Panama. (Lisagor: 45-51).

As a result of all his efforts, attorney Cromwell became the most famous lawyer in America, but also prompted the Bar Association of Alabama to write a professional ethics standard of reform to counter Cromwell's use of "publicists, lobbying, and unlawyerly conduct in fighting for the Panama Canal." (Lisagor: 52).

Many of the above tactics continue in the world today when opportunities for profit or power are involved. Stay tuned for a return to prominence of other partners of the Sullivan & Cromwell law firm.

Overview: United States Military in Latin America

Author Lester Langley wrote that our incursions into Mexico, Central America, and the Caribbean, and their "civil wars, rebellions, [and] revolutions," constituted our definition of maintaining order in the countries to our south. However, he makes the case, except for the border problems fomented by the uprisings in Mexico and German outreach in World War I to ally with Mexico, that the other military actions had little to do with the actual national security of the United States. (Langley: xvi).

Much of the explanation for our military actions in the Caribbean and Central America undeniably related to elevating trade and protecting United States investments. Langley makes the case, that in the late 19th century, there was a clash in the United States of the "elites," who were facing violence, after our fast move toward industrialization and the final conquering of our West. He believes Theodore Roosevelt set the tone for the "banana wars." (Langley: xvii).

Author Ivan Musicant proposed that Theodore Roosevelt upheld a Corollary to the Monroe Doctrine invoking the authority of the United States in Latin America to utilize our military to involve ourselves in internal affairs of the countries when we believed "the political, economic, or social conditions" indicated necessary a force as a "protective" measure. This policy, from the American viewpoint, coined the term "dollar diplomacy," whereby American capital investments in these areas would be provided economic stability protected by the U.S. military. (Musicant: 3). The countries in a manner of speaking could be considered "vassals" of Big Brother to the north. As will be described below the biggest pushback began in Nicaragua in 1927.

One of Langley's references, Herbert Croly, believed that our actions in applying military force and interventions reflected, "the way to achieve political and social unity at home is to pursue a nationalistic and purposeful foreign policy."[36]

Cuba

In 1917, a typical conflict occurred in Cuba between liberals and conservatives. After a contested election, Liberal influence was exerted on the U.S. to claim electoral fraud. The Sullivan & Cromwell law firm of New York, representing American property interests, (thirteen clients who owned $170 million of sugar cane fields in Cuba), exerted their lobbying to support John Foster Dulles's position of support for the Liberals, not for their stated political issues, but in support of their clients. President Wilson sided with the establishment government, the Conservatives. The American owners, although originally disappointed, were indeed delighted when President Wilson ordered 1600 American troops back into Cuba, not departing for five years until 1922. The mission was defined as "military training." (Lisagor: 67).

Haiti and Dominican Republic (Hispaniola)

The Marines were utilized during the Haitian and Dominion actions during World War I in a last "banana war" in Nicaragua in the late 1920s. The U.S. maintained strategic goals in our incursions to defend the Panama Canal and Wall Street investments, but, also to police these countries and maintain order.

By 1907 in Hispaniola (Dominican Republic and Haiti), a new strongman named Ramon Caceres opened the country to foreigners, who immediately acquired large landholdings for growing sugar. He was assassinated in 1911. Hispaniola became somewhat an American "protectorate," because the United States appointed the custom collectors and American minister. These individuals stood practically alone in Hispaniola as examples of integrity and responsible civic duty performance in the country. Another rebellion caused the U.S. to send in Marines in 1913. In the Haitian Republic, Marines had been landed eight times between 1867 and 1900. Our policy with Dominican customs collections was to allocate 55% for claims from foreigners and 45% was paid to the politicians. (Langley 111-115). Public service in this country reaped huge rewards!

German influence began to appear in Haiti by 1897, and German migration began with intermarriages and business investments. (Langley: 117). After a 1902 northern Haiti revolt ensued (what else was new?), the senior U.S. Navy officer in the area proclaimed to Haitian rebels, "I am charged with the protection of British, French, German, Italian, Spanish, Russian, and Cuban interests. You are also informed that I am directed to prevent the bombardment of the city without due notice [and] to prevent any interference with commerce." (Langley: 118). Numerous naval records recorded this incident. This exchange confirmed suspicions that the U.S. military had a least a principal mission of protecting business interests in these "protectorates."

In 1910, the Taft administration became the middleman in Haiti in conflicts between French, German, and American bankers for control of the Banque Nationale and its control of government monies. A part of U.S. pressure on the Haiti banking system on behalf of American banks was motivated due to German influence. (Langley: 118). Constant political upheavals occurred with suspicions laid upon Germans, who had investments in Haiti. A small group of Marines in October 1914 removed gold bullion from the national bank for safekeeping in New York. (Langley: 119).

Marines and blue jackets landed again in 1915 in the middle of the recurrent bloodbaths inherent in Haiti. This occupation by the U.S. military lasted 19 years. (Langley: 123). Marine Smedley Butler was involved in this Marine operation also. There was recurring involvement by the U.S. military in the affairs of Haiti and the Dominican Republic during the time before and during World War I. Unfortunately, there were charges of misconduct by the Marines during the occupation of Santo Domingo toward the end of WWI. The senior responsible Marine shot himself in his cell, either with a secreted weapon, or one provided by another Marine to save him from trial. (Langley: 147).

By 1923, treaties had been signed in Central America, and it was decreed that future overthrows would be denied diplomatic recognition and denial of borrowing from American banks. (Langley: 169).

Honduras

The United Fruit Company had become involved in the banana industry in Honduras as early as 1910 when they financed a revolution in Honduras and received financial concessions for their banana business for 25 years. (McCann: 20). In 1924, a civil war broke out in Honduras and both Liberals and Conservatives desired support of fruit companies such as United Fruit. The banana-growing industry companies had survived with constant payoffs and bribes. (Langley: 170). During this timeframe Nicaragua and Honduras were in debt to European banks, but the

New York Morgan bank muscled into these countries to provide funds. (McCann: 19).

Nicaragua - The Last "Banana War"

In 1893, Nicaragua was led by Liberal General José Santos Zelaya, who proceeded in 1907 to attack and overwhelm Honduras. In 1909, a revolution against Zelaya began. U.S. Marines from Panama under the command of Major Smedley Butler were dispatched to Bluefields, Nicaragua to protect Americans and other foreigners from the advancing Zelaya forces, who were attempting to quell the uprising against him. Butler became basically a police chief of the community and was negative about what he perceived had become a mission of protecting American entrepreneurs and various and sundry Soldiers of Fortune. (Langley: 58).

Zelaya was forced out and Dr. José Madriz became Nicaragua's president and continued to fight the opposing rebels. Governments rose and toppled, and the U.S. eventually arranged for loans from American banks. Private investment depended on political stability in Nicaragua. Several American companies (i.e., Speyer and Company, Brown Brothers, and J. and W. Seligman) provided funds to Nicaragua. (Langley: 62). Nicaragua fell into crisis and the American-owned railway became threatened. The Marines under Smedley Butler again entered the country on August 15, 1912. During this operation the Marines suffered 37 casualties and Nicaragua suffered 1000 casualties in their Civil War. This began involvement by the U.S. in overcoming the European influence in Nicaragua. The U.S. involvement quieted Nicaragua down for 15 years. (Langley: 70).

The *Nation* magazine published a very telling report on the situation in Central America, and especially Nicaragua, in 1922. The magazine discussed a revolt staged in Nicaragua against the unpopular president, who supposedly was a puppet of the New York investment banking firm of Brown Brothers. The revolutionaries took over a fort overlooking Managua, the country's capital, and the U.S. Marine commander threatened an artillery bombardment unless the revolutionaries retreated. The article summarized this action as occurring typically in Latin America, "...where U.S. bankers ruled through puppet governments backed up by U.S. troops."[37]

There are, or were, twenty independent republics to the south of us. Five at least--Cuba, Panama, Haiti, Santo Domingo, and Nicaragua-- have already been reduced to the status of colonies with at most a degree of rather fictitious self-government. Four more-- Guatemala, Honduras, Costa Rica, and Peru-- appear to be in process of reduction to the same status. Mr. Hughes is not treating Mexico as a sovereign, independent state. How far is this to go? ... Is the United States to create a great empire in this hemisphere--an empire over which Congress and the American people exercise no authority, an empire ruled by a group of Wall Street bankers at whose disposal the State and Navy departments graciously place their resources? These are the questions which the people, the plain people whose sons die of tropic fever or of a patriot's bullet have a right to ask. [38]

In 1927, a rebel named Augusto Cesar Sandino began a revolt in Nicaragua under the ideology termed "war of national liberation." (Musicant: 3). A guerilla war was fought by Marines against his forces, called *Sandinistas,* for five years. Sandino led a movement to liberate his country from what he termed were "foreign invaders."

By 1933, after the election and inauguration of Liberal Dr. Juan Sacasa, the United States removed the Marines from Nicaragua. Renowned Marine "Chesty" Puller, of WWII fame, served in Nicaragua. [Author's note: General Puller's son served as a Marine in Vietnam and was severely wounded necessitating amputation of both legs above his knees and several fingers.] Several days after the election of Sacasa the Nicaraguan National Guard was placed under the command of Anastasio Somoza

Garcia. (Musicant: 357). President Sacasa began negotiations with Augusto Sandino and invited him to the capital in February 1934. On February 21, 1934, Sandino and several of his top compatriots, after a dinner with President Sacasa, were apprehended by Somoza's national guardsmen and machine-gunned to death. (Musicant: 359-361). By 1936, Somoza effected a resignation of Sacasa and Somoza became Nicaragua's new strong man dictator. He and his sons would rule Nicaragua until 1979.

Anastasio Somoza's sons, Luis and Anastasio Somoza Debayle, West Point class of 1946, followed him. Author Malachi Martin wrote, "Both Somoza's were backed by the United States, and each was always ready to bolster his regime with use of the remarkably brutal National Guard, a unit that would have given Hitler's elite corps a run for their money." (Martin: 53).

This was not the end of Sandino's influence. His efforts on behalf of his country were resurrected in 1961 with a new *Sandinista* revolution. In the 1970s a new *Sandinista* leader came to prominence in Nicaragua, Daniel Ortega y Saavedra, who led a successful military effort against Somoza. Ortega was defined very specifically by Martin as a "doctrinaire Marxist." (Martin: 54).

Ortega's forces triumphantly entered Managua on July 17, 1979 and Somoza was overthrown. The revolution to topple the Somoza regime was not without its casualties: 45,000 wounded, 40,000 children orphaned, and over 1,000,000 Nicaraguans left starving. (Martin: 62).

Enter Fidel Castro into the picture. Martin relates that the triumphant Marxist revolution in Nicaragua was the only victory for Castro's efforts to bring Marxism to Latin America since his support of three other movements, the Uruguayan Tupamaros, the Argentinian Montaneros, and the Puerto Rican Socialists were not successful.

The U.S. President Jimmy Carter was supportive of the new junta and American tax dollars began to flow to the new government.

Daniel Ortega came to the Rose Garden at the White House and posed with his new benefactor. Later in 1979, after Somoza had escaped to Paraguay, a squad of Ortega's supporters assassinated him and ensured his demise through 25 bullets into the former dictator. Opposition to the new *Sandinista* was solidified with the execution of 2000 and prison cells for 6,000 political enemies. (Martin: 62, 63).

Malachi Martin, a former Jesuit priest himself, relates that there was significant and powerful support of Jesuits and other Catholic priests in the revolution. He wrote, "In Nicaragua, the Jesuits aimed at establishing a Marxist system of government that would embrace the sociocultural and political and economic life of Nicaragua." (Martin: 51).

In Malachi Martin's obituary of August 9, 1999, he was described as a:

> ...writer, priest, [and] archaeologist,...[who] embarrassed a Roman Catholic church that he loved, but despised for what he regarded as the betrayal of its beliefs by the clergy....While in Rome, Martin became a close friend of the influential German Jesuit, Augustin Cardinal Bea, confessor to Pope Pius XII, confidant of Pope John XXII, and theological leader of progressive thinkers in the church. He became privy to the operation of the Vatican machine, working with three popes—above all, Paul VI.[37]

With this background, Martin established his insights into involvements by ordained Catholic priests in Ortega's eventual success.

In 1978, Martin related that:

> ...in the area that stretches from the southern borders of Texas down to the tip of South America, Jesuits and others were carrying on their own as creators and chief fomenters of a new outlook—'Liberation Theology,' they called it in a typically effective bid for romantic appeal—based on Marxist

revolutionary principles and aimed at establishing a Communist system of government. (Martin: 47).

This support of revolutions could not be accepted by Pope John Paul II, but the Jesuits, as they had been since their establishment early in the sixteenth century, were a power unto themselves and operated very independently. Martin, having been schooled and committed himself personally to the spiritual dimension of his church, defines very succinctly the official position of Roman Catholicism "...as the sole purpose of the Church in this world is to make sure that each individual has the means of reaching the eternal life of God after death. It is an exclusively otherworldly purpose." However, Martin relates concerning his own former Order of the Society of Jesus that, "For many Jesuits, on the other hand, the Church's centralized authority, the command structure through which it is exercised, and its purpose are all unacceptable today." (Martin: 15).

He maintained that the Society of Jesus substituted the message of eternal salvation through belief in God and His Son, Jesus the Christ, in favor of a current day salvation, "...for the liberation of one class of men and women in our society today: those millions who suffer from social, economic, and political injustice." (Martin: 15). On the surface, these are worthy goals indeed.

[Author's note of full disclosure: My high school education for ninth and ten grades (1956-1958) was in the Jesuit Gonzaga High School in Washington, D.C. The Jesuits were excellent educators and thinkers!]

Martin postulates that, as of his writing in 1987, that he believed the Jesuits were in:

> ...a willing alliance with Marxists in their class struggle. The aim of both is to establish a sociopolitical system affecting the economies of nations by a thorough-going redistribution of earth's resources and goods; and, in the

process, to alter the present governmental systems in vogue among nations. (Martin: 15).

Who can argue with lofty sounding goals to support the poor and the oppressed!

Several Catholic clerics took up this cause in Nicaragua. Jesuit priest Father Fernando Cardenal with the support of his Major and Minor Superiors in the Society of Jesus joined the *Sandinistas.* He went all out in attacking, "...the injustice perpetrated by rich capitalists on 'Christ's poor'." He engaged with the rebels early on when they were being trained by the Palestine Liberation Organization. (Martin: 55).

This movement was violently opposed to capitalism, especially as reflected in U.S. society. Several priests became original supporters of the movement and upon Ortega's victory took positions as cabinet members. As a footnote author Martin died under what some have termed "suspicious" circumstances.

Soldiers' Blood:

Deaths: 489
Wounded: 875

Aftermath of the Banana Wars

Perhaps the most believable summary and capsulation of our military involvement in the early 20th century was spoken in 1931 before an American Legion convention by retired Marine Major General Smedley D. Butler:

> I spent thirty-three years and four months in active military service, and during that period I spent most of my time being a high-class muscle man for Big Business, for Wall Street and the bankers. In short, I was a racketeer, a gangster for capitalism. I helped make Honduras right for the American fruit companies in 1903. I helped purify

Nicaragua for the International Banking House of Brown Brothers in 1902-1912. I helped make Mexico and especially Tampico safe for American oil interests in 1914. I brought light to the Dominican Republic for the American sugar interests in 1916. I helped make Haiti and Cuba a decent place for the National City Bank boys to collect revenues in. I helped in the raping of half a dozen Central American republics for the benefit of Wall Street. In China in 1927 I helped see to it that Standard Oil went on its way unmolested. Looking back on it, I might have given Al Capone a few hints. The best he could do was to operate his racket in three districts. I operated on three continents. (Butler: 5).

It is my inclination to accept the conclusion above spoken by a United States Marine, who was on the fields of mortal strife with his command of Marine units (with the admitted assistance of Army and Navy personnel), called to fulfill their missions under very dangerous and precarious conditions in uninviting climates and areas. He remains most credible with the two Medals of Honor he has received!

Conclusion

A major thesis of this entire work is a description of the acts of some "capitalists," who have been devoted to personal monetary enrichment and achievement of personal power at the expense of the wounds and deaths of millions of the "little people" all over the world. Many have been in my veteran circles to include myself.

In conclusion of this work, it must be stated that in no way do I advocate any system of government that is any better than the constitutional republic of my homeland, the United States of America. In no way do I advocate the disestablishment of the financial and economic free enterprise system that exists in American society. However, hopefully the case has been made, that throughout history the lusts, perversions, and selfishness of many people in positions of power politically, economically, socially, and financially have served their selfish ends at the expense of many others, utilizing misleading, and spurious justifications.

The history we have learned has, in some cases, been shallow and deceptive.

Just as many others, who have revealed truths or have brought attention to nefarious schemes and actions, have faced untimely demises, perhaps it may likewise be a danger to myself for my writings. I have brought forth what I have learned of international bankers, Jewish and Gentile, titans of industry, politicians, purveyors of weapons, lawyers, possible rogue elements in intelligence agencies, and various and sundry others, that are now termed by me the "usual suspects" consistently in machinations causing casualties. At my advanced age of middle eighth decade, I shall be ready for my final residence in Heaven whenever my Lord dictates.

Meanwhile, it is my fervent wish and desire that, before the bugles blow and the tocsin sounds, that there will be serious debate about any ventures to send the young men and women of any nation into harm's way. It is necessary to debate fully and openly what is the real reason we are called to arms. We must follow the money down whatever bloody trail it may lead!

[Author's note: Francisco Madero, one of Mexico's revolutionaries, and Pancho Villa were mentioned in this chapter. My family history has a related anecdote that my great-uncle, Marcelino De La Fuente, brother of my maternal grandfather, after migrating from Spain, originally settled in northern Mexico and was a retail merchant. During one of the raids of Pancho Villa's men, his store was ransacked. As an indicator of the closeness of South Texas to the history-makers of Mexico, Marcelino and my grandfather both eventually settled in a very small community south of Mission, Texas, named Madero, which was literally across the Rio Grande River from Mexico. My Godfather was a successful Mission merchant, C.G. De La Garza. My mother's childhood friends were all originally of Hispanic heritage.]

SECTION V:

CASUALTIES – HEALING AND TRIUMPH

Chapter 19:

A Spiritual Approach to Healing

Up to this point, this work has predominantly focused on bloodshed, but the casualties of war and cupidity also include the vast impact to the spirit and the soul. Based on my personal experience, all healing is rooted in deep spiritual faith.

Faith is the antidote to fear. Hope is the antidote to depression. "*Now faith is being sure of what we hope for and certain of what we do not see.*" Hebrews 11:1 (NIV). Faith is not belief alone, but it is the tangible foundation of belief. Faith is a gift of God; however, exercise of faith is our responsibility!

The following approaches to a spiritual treatment for PTSD reflect a methodology that was developed by a close friend of mine and retired psychiatrist, Dr. Elliott Snyder. Now deceased, Dr. Snyder served as a veteran caregiver in an Army medical facility and a Veterans Affairs Medical Center.

Spiritual Treatment for PTSD

Building up of our spiritual life, through the exercise of our faith is the global remedy for PTSD. Spiritual formation complements and amplifies the secular/medical/psychological treatments, which are designed to target specific symptoms such as insomnia, depression and irritability. Spiritual formation comes through the following of the faith disciplines of prayer, reading of Scripture and corporate involvement in a faith community, the church:

1. Reading of the Scriptures as they relate both generally and specifically to the symptoms.

2. Prayer: Petitions are our requests and needs brought before God. There are five petitions which are always appropriate to

bring before our God by requesting:

a) Forgiveness
b) Protection
c) Strength
d) Direction
e) Purpose

However, it is praise of God which brings His presence and power into our lives. This includes the power of His healing.

3. Community of faith: Worship in a family of believers or church home.

The patient with Post-Traumatic Stress may have medication prescribed which serves to alleviate some of the psychological and physical symptoms, rendering them more tolerable. The primary spiritual battle is necessarily addressed with spiritual methods! Psychologically, it is of benefit to employ Scripture to interrupt thoughts or feelings of fear and depression and some of these may be found in 2 Timothy 1:7, Psalms 23 & 27 (fear) and Psalms 13:22 (depression).

Once the primary problem is successfully addressed spiritually, acute symptoms diminish. Medication may become less necessary. The problem is that any hint of a God-centered approach or spiritual healing in VA or military clinical records may be met with disfavor by clinicians embracing standard (non-Biblical) medical therapies. But, troops, "drive on" to take care of yourselves.

A good first-step program of combined prayer, scripture and going to church (faith community) is basic, culturally acceptable and powerful. Great progress can be made through these measures alone. God honors and blesses those who diligently seek Him.

It is not the flashy interpersonal techniques, but simply the presence of God which delivers. As you make room for Him in your heart and invite Him to become the Lord of your life, He will come and "clean house." He will evict the enemy, renew your mind and transform your heart. As the Spirit of God grows within you, you will grow to experience spiritual fruit. This starts with love, joy and peace within; patience, kindness and goodness directed toward others; and meekness (strength under authority), temperance and faith in your relationship with the living God!

The simple three-step program is a cost effective, socio-biblio therapy in which God becomes the LORD who heals you and brings you into His Shalom, His peace and rest!

> *"Come to me, all you who are weary and burdened, and I will give you rest.* [29] *Take my yoke upon you and learn from me, for I am gentle and humble in heart, and you will find rest for your souls.* [30] *For my yoke is easy and my burden is light."* Matthew 11:28-30 (*Bible* NIV)

When we seek God diligently by reading, speaking and meditating on His word, Scripture; through prayer, including praise; and by regular fellowship with His people; then we are to experience His rest, His peace, His Shalom!

Choosing to Heal

My dear fellow warriors, the choice is yours. How far do you desire to advance up the hill occupied by the enemy in foxholes and in bunkers with machine guns with interlocking fields of fire? In today's warfare how far down the road will you take your convoy? How far into the wilds of the mountains of Afghanistan will you patrol? Of course, if you want the enemy to be defeated, with all their weapons on the ground, and being sent to the POW camp or detention center, you will want to destroy them and get all the way to the top of the hill to occupy the high ground and deep into the heart of the territory of the terrorists and insurgents.

This will require a disciplined, but sure, method for the formation of your spiritual life, as evidenced by this Scripture:

10Finally, be strong in the Lord and in his mighty power. 11Put on the full armor of God so that you can take your stand against the devil's schemes. 12For our struggle is not against flesh and blood, but against the rulers, against the authorities, against the powers of this dark world and against the spiritual forces of evil in the heavenly realms. 13Therefore put on the full armor of God, so that when the day of evil comes, you may be able to stand your ground, and after you have done everything, to stand. 14Stand firm then, with the belt of truth buckled around your waist, with the breastplate of righteousness in place, 15and with your feet fitted with the readiness that comes from the gospel of peace. 16In addition to all this, take up the shield of faith, with which you can extinguish all the flaming arrows of the evil one. 17Take the helmet of salvation and the sword of the Spirit, which is the word of God. 18And pray in the Spirit on all occasions with all kinds of prayers and requests. Ephesians 6:10-18 (NIV).

[Author's note: My lay ministry web site is www.combatfaith.com and I blog intermittently at www.combatfaith.blogspot.com.]

Community of Believers

An essential feature for healing from PTSD is to get connected with and rooted within a fellowship of believers, who love God and hold fast to His revealed Word. Such a community should not be centered on the treatment of wounded individuals, but rather upon God's Word and person!

The most important elements of spiritual formation are explained in PTSD 101, which describe the three practices which fulfill the requirement that the individual exercise his God-given faith and seek God diligently. Just the supernatural understanding of the spiritual war raging over every earthly battlefield is enough to grasp that the disciplined application of BASIC spiritual countermeasures is the most consistently and reliably effective! If one is a believer then the real healing issue is one related to spiritual warfare and if someone desires to explore some new and heavy spiritual issues, read on!

A key scripture that relates to our PTSD is Ephesians 6:12: "For we wrestle not against flesh and blood, but against principalities, against powers, against the rulers of the darkness of this world, against spiritual wickedness in high *places*." (PSB). This verse gets to the heart of the issue with which we are challenged.

The heart of the issue for those suffering from PTSD really relates to a spiritual healing process from what may be termed spiritual warfare against spiritual possession/ oppression. This always raises concerns and red flags of individuals and particularly secular medical/psychological who have not been exposed to and who are not accustomed to utilizing Biblical understanding of these supernatural methods of deliverance.

Be aware that there would be some concern that if anyone were to carry any discussion of demonic possession/oppression back to their treating physicians, either it would be taken as evidence of psychotic delusions or might at least be labeled as religiously supported cultish beliefs. Without participation in a faith community, which agrees with Ephesians 6:12, this information isolated from Biblical understanding might be misunderstood. So, sufferers, my fellow military warriors and veterans, use wisdom in to whom and how you speak about what is to follow. You know the old military "need to know" is operative. Secularists may not have a high enough "spiritual clearance" to grasp what we are going to get into for your healing.

[Author's note: PTSD is now commonly referred to simply as Post-Traumatic Stress (PTS).]

Now, let's address PTSD from the perspective of spiritual warfare. It is through the senses (eye gates, ear gates) that we experience the world. Satan puts before us "evidence" that overwhelms our senses and reason, breaching our defenses and penetrating our minds. From these mental strongholds, Satan's proxy "spirits" set up shop. Demons particularly seek a warm, moist body that they can inhabit. Without getting into a discussion of fallen angels vs. demons, let us just say that in the middle of battle trauma there are plenty of homeless spiritual entities looking for a place to dwell and do their mischief.

To maintain their new abode, these demons create thoughts which contradict God's word and raise doubts regarding God's sovereign reign over the soul of the person who is oppressed/possessed. This is what demons do in to avoid being evicted or cast out. Meanwhile, they create biological symptoms such as insomnia, irritability, anxiety, nightmares and flashbacks. This is not protective of their abode, but simply what demons do to people acting on behalf of the adversary of our soul. These conditions are what we face interminably upon our return from the battlefields and to our death unless we can understand what is happening to us.

Satan hates God and is jealous of man. Since the cross, he is a defeated foe, who is not yet fully subdued! He is unable to attack God directly, however, Satan is drawn to trouble those made in God's image. It is as though we have been created and given initial dominion over the earth as a lure to invite attack by the powers and principalities of Satan's kingdom. Satan hates all men, but more particularly people in God's kingdom and most particularly the God-man, Jesus Christ.

When we enter the battlefields of mortal battle against fleshly enemies, we enter arenas that open us up to experiences that bring on our issues we define as PTS (with the D in PTSD added for the Disorders that follow if we become dysfunctional in life with our families, work, or ourselves).

Those believers suffering from spiritual oppression should strive to make their body uninviting to demons. Recreational chemicals such as alcohol and drugs, put out the welcome mat for uninvited guests. A routine of prayer, reading and meditating upon Scripture and serving in a community of faith is basic spiritual hygiene. Reading Scripture aloud is particularly useful in overcoming the demonically-generated thoughts of doubt and unbelief as is group Bible study. Having praise music playing softly throughout the night may also be of benefit.

You have choices of bodies of worship (i.e., churches). Most churches are beyond their competence in specific application of what is needed to heal war veterans; however, participation in worship and fellowship with other believers as well as group Bible study is very important.

A more controversial and specific tactic is for the believer in the company of an intercessor (i.e., a trusted spiritually-mature person) to assume the authority delegated to us as Christ's deputies in binding the powers of Satan and his demons, breaking the power of any unwanted inhabitants and casting them to a high, hot, dry place where Jesus would have them go! Many may recall or have heard of the movie genre begun several decades ago related to exorcising of demons. The Roman Catholic Church is noted for this ministry. Protestant denominations term it deliverance.

The demons do not desire to depart the earthly, warm moist human body in which they have taken up residence or are bothering. This is not the same as praying that God come to our aid and remove the problem. This starts to get really heavy spiritually because it is far and beyond simple prayer to God, "Remove this problem." This procedure of spiritual warfare is done "eyes open" and speaking directly to the intruder, who has gained illicit influence over the mind and body of a member of God's Kingdom! An excellent web site for gaining an understanding of this process can be found at http://www.delmin.org, a ministry in Oklahoma City overseen by a former naval officer, Everett Cox, who is a personal friend of the author's.

This last part about spiritual warfare against demonic oppression is not accepted in the secular medical, psychological, and psychiatric community. Even many churches distance themselves doctrinally from this approach or consider it simply too "weird." But this approach, when accepted by a soldier with PTS, may prove helpful.

Simply, it is the presence of God which delivers.

[Author's note: I request that individuals involved in ministry direct themselves more to the body of my work in its entirety rather than picking apart portions of my content. This may also occur in personal attacks on some sources throughout my secular work due to disagreement with positions they have taken in fields outside those for which I have utilized them as a reference. Attacks based on the person are termed *ad hominem* rather than *ad rem* to the issue. Hopefully my detractors and critics will stick to the issues.]

My retired psychiatrist friend was blocked in both an Army Medical Center and my own VA Medical Center in his treatment method by being required to refrain from any mentioning of a Christian approach and praying for the Holy Spirit to engage in the healing process even when the patient acknowledged his Christian faith. My own experience at the Veterans Affairs Medical Center at which I was employed was an experience that I believe to be odious.

I volunteered in my own hospital's Mental Health Department to be a resource for veterans to be able to describe my healing process through my faith walk. I was categorically and unceremoniously denied. The VA chaplain at my Medical Center (the same chaplain who also rebuffed my psychiatrist friend) was outright hostile to me and a multi-wounded Marine from Khe Sanh in Vietnam, when we offered to visit with patients to explain how our faith healed us. My psychiatrist friend, Dr. Snyder, and I agree that the VA and military mental health approaches are purely a secular humanistic system, which has scant chance of real healing for our combat veterans. It is sad for me to say, but I must that many chaplains in the VA are just an auxiliary section for the Social Work Service. It is too late in life not to call attention to the failure of the government system to have any long-term real healing success with our veterans!]

Chapter 20:

My Personal Healing Story

"Allen's story has the potential to touch many lives. It is a message of struggle, perseverance, courage, and hope."

– **Ross Perot**, from his foreword in my book *Wounded Soldier, Healing Warrior*

Twenty-two years in active military service or in service to veterans in the Department of Veterans Affairs are a part of my life. I imagine I have heard the width and breadth of military experiences; the sheer terror when under fire, the sadness for those killed beside us, the regrets of the medics because not all were saved. Also, we recall the agony of the battlefield memories, the sleepless years, the triggers of war, wives talking about the weapons close at hand and the explosive tempers. There never seems to be any real lasting relief and many suffer until their deaths, albeit with counseling, psycho-therapy, group sessions and years of pills. Each of us has our own demons. In 1968, I had my own personal brush with Post-Traumatic Stress after losing both legs below the knees in a mortar attack on my Special Forces camp in Vietnam. I had been back eight months and was stressed out with fears of ever walking with artificial legs, of ability to have and raise children, and of having gainful employment upon my release from Brooke General Hospital amputee ward at Fort Sam Houston, Texas. I harbored anger and sadness.

Without sleep for four days, I had to be admitted to a closed psychiatric ward for fourteen weeks in duration and required individual psychotherapy for the next five years until 1973, but, by the grace and healing power of God and the love and caring of Jesus, I have needed neither anti-depressants nor a psychiatrist since then (more than forty years ago as of this writing).
Two elements are critical to our healing: Resiliency and identity.

Our resiliency is our ability to bounce back and recover from setbacks. We have two identities, one as a patriotic, loyal, and courageous warrior. The second, and more important, is our identity as a person of faith. My own identity is as a committed and faithful Christian. This identity is reflected in four ways: 1. We all have sinned and broken God's laws; 2. We deserve to be punished for our sins; 3. Jesus Christ died for our sins. He paid the penalty for all the guilt and sin we have committed and provided a gift to us. 4. We can only receive this gift by personal acceptance of Jesus as Savior.

Warfare of and by itself is an ultimate case of warfare of our soul and spirit, but we have the choice of allowing our healing to proceed through our religious/spiritual maturation. However, many of us turn instead to the abuse of substances to mask our problems. We succumb to the wrong choices to self-medication.

Ultimately our ability to be healed, if not at least being able to cope with our issues, will be based upon a spiritual healing. One of the most important things we must do is forgive ourselves and others for mistakes encountered in "the fog of war." We cannot even have a chance for healing unless we recall the issues from our military service (and before and after) that continue to be a burden to us. We must not harbor bitterness, anger, or unforgiveness to all others whose actions impacted our lives. We all have sins in our lives besides the "stupids" we committed. Unless we ask forgiveness for our sins through confession, we will not have our decks cleared to receive God's forgiveness and begin our opportunity for spiritual healing. In God's word it is written, "For if you forgive men when they sin against you, your heavenly Father will also forgive you. But if you do not forgive men their sins, your Father will not forgive your sins." Matthew 6:14-15. It is assured that I want my sins forgiven.

A method I use for the healing process is to audit three arenas of my life: Unhealed hurts, unmet needs, and unresolved issues. These elements are evident in all lives, but especially in those of us who have been to war. Once these are listed, then we must list in another column what it would take to heal the hurt, meet the need and resolve the issue. Then column three very simply is to pray that column two is satisfied. It is a simple method that can be a guide for all of us.

Jesus allowed me to be saved from my battlefield wounds to return and be able to live my life again. I now know that He was there and with me through all my recovery and rehabilitation which continues even today as I seek to follow Him in all my ways. I have accepted Him as Savior, and know I live only by the grace of God. The rest of the story: not only have I grown in my faith over the years, but also in my height from 5'9" to 6'2" with new artificial legs!

My peace and hope are found in Jesus Christ. Jesus offers all who believe/trust in Him forgiveness of sin and the gift of eternal life. The Bible says, "For God loved the world so much that he gave his only Son so that anyone who believes in him shall not perish but have eternal life." (John 3:16). "Believe in the Lord Jesus, and you will be saved." (Acts 16:31).

Trust/believe in Christ today and receive His peace. You can tell Him through a prayer like this:

> Dear Jesus,
>
> I know that I am a sinner and need Your forgiveness. I believe that You died on the cross to pay the penalty for my sin that You rose from the dead to give me the gift of eternal life. I now trust in You as my Savior. - AMEN

Learn more at www.combatfaith.com.

GOD BLESS AND KEEP YOU!

CONCLUSION – CONQUERING CUPIDITY

General Smedley Butler had a suggestion for the industrialists and arms merchants, who profit when the lads in the trenches have been sent into the fray. Let them also be drafted. (Butler: 33). He wrote, "They aren't running any risk of being killed or of having their bodies mangled or their minds shattered. They aren't sleeping in muddy trenches. They aren't hungry. The soldiers are!" (Butler: 34).

In history, the methodology of operation of arms merchants is defined "… by cultivating governmental connections, by playing the complicated game of international banking, by stimulating war scares and by manipulating the press." (Engelbrecht:139).

What can be done? "They can support every move made for the peaceful settlement of international disputes; they can help to reduce the exorbitant budgets of war and navy departments; they can work for regional limitation of armaments and back all treaties which tend to avoid competition in arms; … they can strive to bring order into the chaotic and political conditions of the world." (Engelbrecht: 272).

It requires that all citizens must be informed and active in politics and government. Citizens must pay attention to national and international issues and question seriously and severely all situations possibly leading to warfare and the shedding of blood of our young men and women much less all those who will suffer in collateral damage.

As an American citizen, who has answered the clarion call of volunteering to go off to war and suffered severe wounds, I ask earnestly that we be involved with our elected officials when the drums of war begin to be played!

Well-documented has been the history of religious wars. In modern day society there is a decided amount of religious competition/non-violent conflict (for membership counts, conversions, enrichment of religious leaders, massive edifices). One of the cited authors proclaims his opinion of sectarian clashes:

> Religious competition approaches the day of its doom. Under rational analysis it is found that the warring denominations provide sectarian distinctions without fundamental difference, just as opposing political parties create campaign issues of negligible consequence. Struggle for institutional influence and financial gain by the churches is obstructive in the spiritual development of men. Impatient of ceaseless controversy among their ordained leaders, the laity have taken matters into their own hands, and already creedal dissension is declining." (Hurt: 228,239).

Candidly, that may be his opinion, but mine is not so much optimistic about lay people taking responsibility. As it should be in citizenship, it should likewise be in our places of worship. We should stand by our tenets of faith, but, reflect in our character and actions true civility, integrity, morality, and ethics, but not degrade nor dismiss the faith of others.

The following passage, written by two good friends of mine, encapsulates where we are in our society. The first is a recent quote from Kenny Wayne, Army veteran and retired Special Agent in Charge for an office in law enforcement, after decades of service to our nation:

> From Obama on down; career politicians, global leaders, Attorney Generals, past presidents, probably Trump himself, foreign governments. ... These types all operate on a theory of 'Mutually assured political/power-base destruction.' ... It's so broken and crooked in the District of Columbia Federal Government (bureaucracy and Congress) that I doubt it can ever be fixed. Only a genuine political revolution would have any impact. The conspirators always

cover for each other, it's 'you owe me. I owe you' etc. and on and on it goes.[1]

Writer Kelleigh Nelson quoted my friend and added her own summary in an article, "The Rule of Law" obviously does not affect global elites, not even when there are thousands of deaths of innocents."[2]

The book *War! War! War!*, published in 1940 during the prelude to our entry into World War II, states extraordinarily clearly the essence of the thesis behind this book:

> May I give the thoughts, if not the words, of our fine, patriotic young America. (When) ...its radios and suggestive movies, its big business and Anglophiles, its indecent shows and sly orations, its blatant demagogues, its warmongers, its corrupt politicians and its grafting office-holders, has flattered and threatened a timid, spineless, and unresisting Congress into a declaration of war, we will enlist at once for the supreme sacrifice under the Stars and Stripes even on foreign soil; but when the war is over our families and friends, the common people of the true America, will remember and hold sternly responsible for the 'deep damnation of our taking off,' our real foes, operating behind the closed doors in the White House, the Halls of State, and the curtained, paneled palaces and citadels of New York and Washington. We say to you despite your treachery and cupidity, your love of aliens and alien ideas, we will not allow our country to be disgraced. When the flags fly and the bands play, we shall enlist at once and fight as bravely as did our ancestors. You know and we know there is no such thing as a half-way war. If we fight, we must and should win at any cost. When you palaver and deceive, and cheat, and trick, and shout this country into war for your alien friends, war-mongers, foreign allies and cushioned pashas, you who are too old to fight, you will secure for your sons easy berths far from the front, we shall enlist and fight and suffer and die for America. We

shall say 'morituri te salutamus,' but when our maimed, tortured, or dead bodies return, our relatives, friends, associates and real America will call to mind your honeyed words, your greed, your concealed cruelty, and will hold you to strict accountability, as meriting the severest punishment that our country can inflict, because you made us fight not for our America, but for your sordid foreign interests, your love of power. (Cincinnatus: 7-8).

With these words, I rest my case for the "Usual Suspects" and their CUPIDITY!

Perhaps the words in these hymns should become our prayers:

Almighty Father, who dost give the gift of life to all who live, look down on all earth's sin and strife, and lift us to a nobler life.
The world is weary of its pain; of selfish greed and fruitless gain; of tarnished honor falsely strong, and all its ancient deeds of wrong." (Hymnal: 530).[3]
God of grace and God of glory, on thy people pour thy power;
From the fears that long have bound us Free our hearts to faith and praise;
Cure thy children's warring madness,
Bend our pride to thy control;
Shame our wanton, selfish gladness,
Rich in things and poor in soul." (Hymnal: 524).[4]
Bring to our world of strife
Thy sov'reign word of peace,
That war may haunt the earth no more
And desolation cease." (Hymnal: 525).[5]
Give peace, O God, the Nation's cry, From evil man and deed;
But peace they ask from war's alarms, Surcease from earthly care,
And peace that rests on fighting arms of land and sea and air.

We need the peace of heart and mind
In men from hate set free,
Who by their love for human kind
Show deeper love for thee.
O cleanse all hearts of pride and greed,
Remove all lust and sin,
That man from chains of wrath be freed,
Eternal peace to win. (Hymnal: 526).[6]

AMEN

AFTERWORD

This book documents individuals whose actions reflected greed, selfishness, and the pursuit of power, far from altruistic motivations. We recognize that the underlying character and actions of many of those of whom we wrote were in many instances actions and expressions that were divorced from some overall nefarious, organized, and concerted evil efforts. However, others took part in the concerted effort in secular world history through their actions to be participants in the larger political goal of constantly consolidating and amassing central power and accumulation of wealth. Recorded history is replete with attempts to control and acquire power at the expense of others, especially the powerless or uninformed. We have attempted to unveil and reveal true history, revised from that written by those allied with the elite. It is always an attempt to Follow the Money!

Writers such as I may pen books and write opinions to our hearts' and consciences' delight, but, that, about which we have written, has had Millenia to build and be fine-tuned under the command of God's arch-conspirator adversary, Satan himself. Admittedly he has done a most credible job, witnessed by the blood of his victims soaked into the soil of so many places. In my once youthful naivete I had thought enough good people, inspired by the positive precepts and principles of God, could band together to change the course of the End Times prophecies.

In my senior years, I have disabused myself of this starry-eyed quest. Only upon the Second Coming of our Lord, Jesus, the Christ, at the end of the Seven Year Tribulation period, will finally cease the horrors and bloodshed perpetrated by the characters above. All that authors, preachers, and philosophers can accomplish is to identify what are the truths of the manifold transgressions of the history's "Usual Suspects." Only God can put His adversary into "Checkmate."

One of my strongest loyalties is to our military members, our veterans, and the families, who have lost our patriots in warfare or suffer with our veterans, who have returned with bloodless wounds of the heart. We do not endure combat for the president, politicians, or "mom and apple pie." We take care of each other on the battlefield. It is a noble cause. We brothers and sisters under arms believe in a creed of Duty, Honor, and Country.

"That which a man saith well is not to be rejected because it hath some errors. No man, no book is void of imperfections. And, therefore, apprehend who will in God's name; that is, with sweetness and without reproach." - John Cowell

ACKNOWLEDGMENTS

Linda, my wife, has endured many hours of separation as I have read many books and remained voluntarily imprisoned in my office writing the book. I am grateful to her for her forbearance. She has been my patient muse for this third book and many other endeavors of my undertaking.

My daughter Elizabeth has been my extraordinary wordsmith and editor, volunteering to help bring it to publication and oversee my marketing efforts.

My long-time friend Elliott Snyder, M.D. (deceased in the spring of 2018) has been by my side throughout the past few years as my thesis evolved and he contributed much valuable input.

Larry Kryske, an author in his own right and a Winston Churchill scholar, has been of inestimable value in guiding me through the publishing process.

I'm thankful to LTC Allen B. West and all eleven of my friends who contributed endorsements with the knowledge that the book covers some very sensational and controversial subjects of history. They were courageous enough to join me in my quest to research through history the origins and casualties of the world's wars.

CHAPTER NOTES

Prefaces
1. https://www.nytimes.com/2016/11/27/us/politics/steve-bannon-white-house.html.

Introduction
1. W.T. Stead was a close friend of Cecil Rhodes and wrote a book titled *The Last Will and Testament of Cecil John Rhodes.* London. 1902. Pp. 73-77. The quote is from a letter sent to Stead in 1891.

SECTION I: CONFLICTS – SECULAR AND SPIRITUAL

Chapter 1: The Personal Appearance of Jesus on the Stage of History

1. Copyright 2001: Integrity's Hosanna! Music Words & Music by Lynn Deshazo. CCLI #54921
2. Ibid.

Chapter 2: Between Two Worlds – Spiritual Warfare

1. Original source: Billy Graham, *Angels*, p. 124.

Chapter 3: Connecting the Dots – Conspiracies and Prophecies

1. Original source: Ed Young, Dare to be a Daniel. Taped message #A1075.
2. Original source: Grant Jeffrey, *Final Warning*, p. 158.
3. Original source: John Robison, *Proofs of a Conspiracy*, pp. 106, 107).

SECTION II: CUPIDITY – PLAYERS AND CONSEQUENCES

Chapter 4: Cupidity and the "Usual Suspects"

Chapter 5: Warfare and Casualties

1. Hemingway, Ernest. *A Farewell to Arms*. Scribner (Now Simon & Schuster): NY. 2012. p. *ix*. Hemingway Library Edition.
2. Vickers, *op.cit.*, 7.
3. https://en.wikipedia.org/wiki/United_States_military_casualties_of_war.

Chapter 6: Arms Merchants

1. Original source: Bethlehem Steel Company, *Ordnance Material* (1914), p. 85; American Iron and Steel Association, History of the Manufacture of Armor Plate for the U.S. Navy, p. 5.
2. Original sources: John K. Winkler. *Incredible Courage*. pp. 226-235; Allan Nevins. *Grover Cleveland: A Study in Courage*, pp.673-674.
3. Original source: H. Murray Robertson. *Krupp's and the International Armaments Ring. The Scandal of Modern Civilization*. Holden and Hardingham: London. 1915. P. 173.
4. Original source: H. Murray Robertson, *op. cit.*, pp. 150ss.
5. Original source: Francis McCullagh. *Syndicates for War. World Peace Foundation Pamphlets*, Series No. 2, Part III, Jul. 1911. P. 5.
6. Original source: Viktor Niemeyer. *Alfred Krupp: A Sketch of His Life and Work*. (Translation from the German). Prosser and Son: New York. 1888. P.26.
7. Original source: H. Murray Robertson, *op. cit.*, p.31.
8. https://www.britannica.com/biography/basil-zaharoff. (Accessed Feb. 3, 2018.)
9. "Report of the Special Committee on Investigation of the Munitions Industry (The Nye Report), U.S. Congress,

Senate, 74th Congress, 2nd Session, Feb. 24, 1936, pp. 3-13. https://astro.temple.edu/~rimmerma/nye_commission_report.htm. (Accessed Oct. 16, 2017.)

10. http://www.ourdocuments.gov/doc.php?doc=90. (Accessed August 23, 2019).

Chapter 7: Bankers – Morgans and Rothschilds

1. http://www.goodreads.com/quotes/296162-when-a-government-is-dependent-upon-bankers-for-money-they-and-not-the-leaders.htm. (Accessed March 8, 2017).
2. http://www.newswithviews.com/spingola/deanna119.htm. (Accessed August 19, 2016).
3. https://www.amazon.com/Jacob-H-Schiff-American-Leadership/dp/0874519489/. (Accessed Jul. 7, 2017).
4. http://nytimes.com/1863/10/11/news/the-house-of-rothschild.html. (Accessed Jan. 23, 2018).
5. https://www.rothschildarchives.org/exhibitions/timeline. (Accessed January 23, 2018).
6. Original source: Niall Ferguson. *The House of Rothschild The World's Banker, 1848-1999*. Penguin Books: London. 1998. Pp. 38, 251.
7. Original source: Stanley Chapman. *The Rise of Merchant Banking*. George Allen and Unwin: London. 1984. P. 25).
8. https://www.cheatsheet.com/money-career/real-richest-man-world-other-secret-billionaires.html/16/. (Accessed January 19, 2018).

Chapter 8: Industrialists

1. Original source: John D. Rockefeller, *Random Reminiscences of Men and Events* (New York: Doubleday, Page & Co., 1909), p. 81. ("I'll go no higher"); Allan Nevins, *Study in Power: John D. Rockefeller, Industrialist and Philanthropist* (New York: Scribners, 1953), vol. 1, pp. 35-36 ("I ever point"). Nevins remains the standard biographical source.

2.   Original source: Warren Zimmerman, *First Great Triumph, How Five Americans Made Their Country a World Power*. Farrar, Strauss and Giroux, New York, 2002, pp. 25-28.

3.   https://libertyconservativenews.com/president-trump-calls-out-military-industrial-complex-while-shooting-down-endless-war/. Shane Trejo. May 20, 2019. (Accessed May 22, 2019).

Chapter 9: Elitists – Rockefellers, Politicians, Lawyers and Masons

1.   www.azquotes.com/author/49031-walter-rathenau (Accessed Nov. 4, 2017).

2.   http://www.nytimes.com/1995/03/03/obituaries/f-lundberg-92-author-who-wrote-of-the-rich.html (Accessed Sep. 7, 2015).

3.   Original sources: Henry Demarest Lloyd. *Wealth Against Commonwealth*. Home Library Foundation, 1936; Gustavus Myers. *History of the Great American Fortunes.* 3 vols. Charles H. Kerr and Company. 1909-1911; Charles Edward Russell. *Stories of the Great Railroads*; Claude G. Bowers. *The Tragic Era*; Don C. Seitz, *The Dreadful Decade, 1869-1879*. The Bobbs-Merrill Company. 1926; Ida Tarbell. *The History of the Standard Oil Company*. 2 vols. The Macmillan Company. 1925; Henry Adams. *Chapters of Erie*; Matthew Josephson. *The Robber Barons*. Harcourt, Brace and Company, 1934.

4.   Original source: David Saville Muzzey. *The American Adventure*. II, Harper and Brothers. 1927. p. 443.

5.   http://www.mcclatcheyde.com/news-nation-world/national/article69943337.html. (Accessed November 24, 2017).

6.   https://www.nytimes.com/2016/04/05/world/panama-papers-explainer-html. (Accessed November 2, 2017).

7.   https://www.nytimes.com/2017/10/16/world/europe/daphne-caruana-galizia-journalist-malta.html?action=clic. (Accessed March 12, 2018.

8.   Original source: John T. Flynn. *God's Gold*. Harcourt, Brace and Company. 1932. p. 254.

9. Ibid. p. 254.
10. Original source: Herbert Croly. *Marcus Alonzo Hanna.* The Macmillan Company. 1912. p. 383.
11. John T. Flynn, *op. cit.*, p. 383.
12. Deanna Spingola. http://www.newswithviews.com. Article, June 22, 2007. "The Rockefellers, Funding Fathers of the New World Order." (Accessed Aug. 19, 2016).
13. http://www.newswithviews.com/spingola/deanna87.htm. (Access date unrecalled).
14. Andrew Carnegie. *Triumphant Democracy, or Fifty Years' March of the Republic.* First published, Charles Scribner's Sons: New York. 1886. pp. 447-448. Cosimo Classics. Nov. 1, 2005. pp. 447-448. https://archive.org/details/triumphantdemocr00carn. (Accessed February 22, 2018).
15. Kelleigh Nelson. www.newswithviews.com. Nov. 27, 2017. (Accessed Nov. 27, 2017).

Chapter 10: Media and Propaganda

1. David Uberti. December 15, 2016. http://www.cjr/special_report/fake_news_history.php. (Accessed March 8, 2018).
2. Michael Snyder. October 17, 2017. http://investmentwatchblog.com/how-the-elite-dominate-the-world-part-3-of-what-you-watch. (Accessed Oct. 29, 2017).

SECTION III: RELIGION – GOD AND WAR

Chapter 11: Protestant Reformation and Religious Wars
1. http://libertymagazine.org/article/-the-reformation-and-wars-of-religion. Article draws substantially from D.J.B. Trim, "Conflict, Religion, and Ideology," in Trim and F. Tallett, eds. *European Warfare*, 1350-1750. Cambridge University Press: New York and Cambridge. 2010. Chapter 13.

2. Trim (3). Original source: A summary overview has appeared in an earlier article: D.J. B. Trim, "Tumults, Riots, and Seditions: Persecution and Violence in France During the Wars of Religion," *Liberty*, May/June 2007, pp.16-21.
3. Trim (4). Original source: Peter H. Wilson. *Europe's Tragedy: A History of the Thirty Years' War.* Penguin: New York. 2009.

Chapter 12: Protestantism, Anglicanism, Pilgrims, Puritans, Congregationalists, and Unitarians

1. http://anglican.org/church/churchhistory.html. (Accessed Dec. 8, 2017).
2. http://www.patheos.com/library/Anglican/origins/founders.aspx?. (Accessed Dec. 8, 2017).
3. http://www.themainlesson.com/php?. The Baldwin Project: The Tudors and the Stuarts by M.B. Synge. "Thomas Cromwell and the Destruction of the Monasteries." p. 11. (Accessed December 8, 2017).
4. Ibid., 16.
5. https://www.biography.com/people/mary-tudor-9401296. (Accessed December 8, 2017).
6. Trim (4). Original source: D.J. B. Trim, "Oliver Cromwell: The Intolerant Inheritance of America's Religious Extreme," part 1, *Liberty*, Nov./Dec. 2006.
7. http://www.eyewitnesstohistory.com/spanishmassacre.htm. (Accessed Feb. 27, 2018).
8. https://www.history.org/Almanack/life/religion/religionfn.cfm. "The Anglican Church in Virginia." (Accessed February 27, 2018).
9. http://8townsquare.org/newhistory.html. (Accessed February 27, 2018).
10. Ibid.
11. Ibid.
12. Ibid.

13. http://uudb.org/articles/unitariancontroversy.html. "The Unitarian Controversy and Its Puritan Roots." (Accessed February 27, 2018).
14. Ibid.
15. Ibid.
16. Ibid.
17. Ibid.
18. https://wwwnewenglandtravelplanner.com/religion/unitarianism.html. (Accessed February 27, 2018).

Chapter 13: Catholicism

1. https://www.scribd.com/document/126943758/Fourteen-Years-a-Jesuit-volume-2-by-count-Paul-Von-Hoensbroech.
2. Paris (26) as quoted from Huber, J., Professor of Catholic Theology in Munich, "Les Jesuites." (Sandoz et Fischbacher, Paris. 1875. p. 127).
3. Paris (29) as quoted from H. Boehmer, Professor at the University of Bonn, *Les Jesuites.* (Armand Colin, Paris. 1910. pp. 20-21, 25).
4. Ibid., pp. 25, 34-35
5. Paris (44) as quoted from Pierre Dominique, Le Politique de Jesuites (Gresset, Paris. 1955. p. 37).
6. Paris (44) as quoted from J. Huber, *op. cit.*, p.165.
7. Paris (45) H. Boehmer, *op. cit.*, pp. 85-88.
8. Paris (46) H. Boehmer, *op. cit.*, pp. 85-88.
9. Paris (47) H. Boehmer, *op. cit.*, pp.89, 104, 112, 114.
10. Paris (48) as quoted from Rene Fulop-Miller. -*Les Jesuites et le secret de leur puissance* (Plon, Paris. 1933, II, pp. 98, 102).
11. Ibid.
12. Paris (49) H. Boehmer, *op. cit.* pp. 89, 104, 112, 114.
13. Paris (51) Rene Fulop-Miller*, op. cit.*, II, pp. 104-105.
14. Paris (54) J. Huber*, op. cit.*, p.184ff.
15. https://www.manresa-sj.org/stamps/-Switzerland.htm. "Jesuit Institutions in Switzerland." (Accessed January 7, 2018).
16. Paris (56) H. Boehmer, *op. cit.*, p. 135.

17. Paris (58) H. Boehmer, *op. cit.*, p.135ff.
18. Paris (62) Pierre Dominique, *op. cit.*, pp. 101-102.
19. Paris (63) Gaston Bally. *Les Jesuites* (Imprimerie Nouvelle, Chamberg, 1902, p.69).
20. Paris (65) Pierre Dominique, *op. cit.*, pp. 85, 86, 89.
21. Paris (82) F. Charmot, SJ.: "La Pedagogie des Jesuites" (Edit. Ses, Paris. 1943. P. 39).
22. Paris (92) H. Boehmer, *op. cit.*, pp. 244-246.
23. Ibid.
24. Paris (94) H. Boehmer, *op. cit.*, pp. 238, 241.
25. Paris (97) Pierre Dominique, *op. cit.*, p. 191.
26. Paris (100) Baron de Ponnat, "*Histoire des Variations et Contradictions de l'Eglise romaine,*" G. Charpentier. Paris. 1882. p. 215. T. 11.
27. Paris (101) Louis de Potter-*Vie de Scipion de Ricci* (Bruxelles 1825. I, p. 18).
28. Paris (102) Ponnat*, op. cit.*, p. 224.
29. Paris (107) Dominique, *op. cit.*, p. 220.
30. Paris (107) H. Boehmer, *op. cit.*, p.285.
31. Paris (107) Fulop-Miller, *op. cit.*, pp. 149-150.
32. Paris (112) Adolphe Michel. *Les Jesuites* (Sandoz et Fischbacher, Paris. 1879. pp. 71-72).
33. Paris (113) Paul Leon, of the Institute, "La guerre pour la paix," (Ed. Fayard. Paris. 1950. pp. 321-323).
34. Paris (113) As quoted by Monsignor Journet: "Exigenses chretiennes en politique." (Ed. L.V.F. Paris. 1945. P. 274).
35. Paris (114) Albert Bayet. *Histoire de France* (Ed. Du Sagittaire Paris. 1938. p. 282).
36. Paris (115) Gaston Bally, *op. cit.*, pp. 100, 101).
37. Paris (121) Louis Roguelin: "L'Eglise cretienne primitive et le catholicisme" (Albin Michel, Paris. 1927. pp. 79-81).
38. https://catholiceducation.org/en/culture/history/-the-Catholic-Church-in-the-United-States-of-America.html. (Accessed February 27, 2018.)

Chapter 14: Judaism

1. *Life Application Study Bible.* (KJV). Notes on Book of Hebrews. p. 2154.
2. https://britannica.com/topic/semite. (Accessed January 13, 2018).
3. As related by Jim Wald, March 18, 2014. http://blogs.timesofisrael.com. p. 1. (Accessed May 11, 2016).
4. Reference: Behar, Doron M.; Metspalu, Mait; Baran, Yael; *et. al.*, "No Evidence from Genome-Wide Data of Khazar Origin for the Ashkenazi Jews," *Human Biology.* Vol. 85: Iss. 6, Article 9. http://digitalcommons.wayne.edu/humbiol/vol85/iss6/9. (Forwarded by friend. Not accessed by author).
5. http://louisville.edu/law/library/special-collections/-the-jewish-problem-how-to-solve-it-by-Louis-D-Brandeis. p. 2. (Accessed January 19, 2018).
6. Ibid, p. 6.
7. http://www.zionism-israel.com/bio/biography_herzl.htm. (Accessed January 19, 2018).
8. Ibid, p. 2.
9. Sombart, Werner (172-173) as quoted from *Revue Historique*, vol. 44. 1890.
10. http://www.bibleprophecyblog.com/2015/12/Zionism-what-it-is-and-what-it-is-not.htm. "Zionism: What It Is and What It Is Not." Dr. Arnold Fructenbaum. *Ariel Ministries.* Dec. 26, 2015.
11. http://tourosynagogue.org/history-learning/jew-in-colonies. (Accessed February 27, 2018).
12. http://freebeacon.com/national-security/un-watch-blasts-un-human-rights-council-defining-practice-judaism-war-crime/. "U.N. Watch Blasts Human Rights Council for Defining Practice of Judaism as 'War Crime.'" Jack Heretik, March 28, 2018.
13. "The False Prophet" by Edward Hindson. At time of publication he was Professor of Religion, Dean of the

Institute of Biblical Studies, and Assistant to the Chancellor, Liberty University, Lynchburg, VA.

14. "Israel in Tribulation" by David Allen Lewis. At time of publication he was president of Christians United for Israel, Springfield, MO.

15. "The Battle of Armageddon" by John F. Walvoord. At time of publication he was Chancellor of Dallas Theological Seminary, Dallas, TX.

SECTION IV: AMERICA'S WARS – MONEY AND BLOODSHED

Chapter 15: American Revolutionary War (1775-1783)

1. Wandrei, Kevin. "Which European Nations Fought With the Americans Against the British in the Revolutionary War?" http://classroom.synonym.com/european-nations-fought--americans-against-british-revolutionary-war-22011. (Accessed June 28, 2017).

2. Moran, Donald N. "Haym Salomon-The Revolution's Indispensable Financial Genius." Reprint from October 1999 edition of the Liberty Tree and Valley Compatriot Newsletter. Sons of Liberty Chapter. Sons of the American Revolution. http://www.revolutionarywararchives.org/salomon. (Accessed June 27, 2017).

3. Mueller, Jennifer. "What is an Example of Propaganda in the American Revolution?" http://classroom.synonym.com/example-propaganda-american revolution-17805. (Accessed June 28, 2017).

4. Levy, Janet. "The Forgotten War that Changed American History." June 23, 2017. From original source book *Thomas Jefferson and the Tripoli Pirates*. (Sentinal, 2015). http://www.familysecuritymatters.org/publications/detail/print/the-forgotten-war-that-changed-american-history. (Accessed June 23, 2017).

5.   Watkins, Thayer. "The First Bank of the United States." Department of Economics San Jose State University. http://www.sjsu.edu/faculty/watkins/BofUS. (Accessed June 29, 2017).

Chapter 16: The Civil War (1861-1865)

1.   http://www.Blackpast.org/primary/declaration-independence-and-debate-over-slavery. (Accessed December 22, 2016). Original source: (Taylor & Manny, 1853-1854 Washington, D.C.. Thomas Jefferson, The Writings of Thomas Jefferson).
2.   http://www.usconstitution.net/consttop_slav.html. (p. 7). (Accessed March 5, 2017).
3.   Ibid, 8.
4.   Ibid, 9.
5.   http://www.wnd.com/2010/213757. (Accessed March 8, 2017).
6.   https://millercenter.org/the-presidency/presidential-speeches/July-10-1832-bank-veto. (Accessed March 8, 2017).
7.   Author's note: David Keehn's book regarding the Knights of the Golden Circle has extensive notes the inclusion of which would be laborious, so license is taken to simply note the page on which Keehn relates his information, not the original sources.
8.   Graham as noted in Scheele v. Union Finance & Loan Co., 200 Minn. 554 at 560, 274 N.W. 673 AT 678 (1937).
9.   As quoted from John R. Elsom. *Lightning Over the Treasury Building.* (Meador Publishing Co.: Boston). 1941. pp. 51-52.
10.   As quoted from I. Katz. *August Belmont: A Political Biography.* New York: 1968. pp.144-145.
11.   Original source: Reinhard H. Luthin. "Abraham Lincoln and the Tariff," The American Historical Review, Vol. XLIX, No. 4, July 1944, pp. 610-627.

12. Original source: Terry L. Jones, "The Jewish Rebel," in http://opinionator.blogs.nytimes. April 18, 2012. (Accessed April 17, 2017).
13. https://www.dmdc.osd.mil/dcas/pages/report_principal_wars.xhtml. (Accessed April 20, 2017).
14. As quoted in *The Collected Works of Abraham Lincoln* edited by Roy P. Basler, Volume VIII, "Letter to Mrs. Lydia Bixby." (November 21, 1864), pp. 116-117.
15. Byars, Steve. "Uncivil War." *The New American*. January 25, 2016. Pp. 34-38.
16. *Vancouver Daily Province*, May 2, 1934.
17. Ibid.
18. Phil Leigh, "The Confederate Diaspora." May 14, 2015. Opinion Pages. *New York Times.*

Chapter 17: Spanish-American War (1898) – The Beginnings of American Imperialism

1. As quoted in William A. Williams. *The Tragedy of American Diplomacy*, (New York: Dell Publishing Co., Inc., 1962), p. 26.
2. Ibid, 16.
3. As quoted in William A. Williams. *The Contours of American History*, (Cleveland: The World Publishing Company, 1961), p. 346.
4. Original source: R.S. Waddell, "Brief on Smokeless Powder," February 1907 (sent to all members of Congress), *Selections from the National Archives*, File Folder No. 4480, "Complaints Against the Powder Trust by Buckeye Powder Company," Eleutherian-Mills Library.
5. *American Heritage* 53(6). November-December 2002.
6. Home of Heroes, "Fighting a New Enemy," p. 5. http://homeofheroes.com/wallofhonor/spanish_am/15_closing.html. (Accessed February 10, 2016.)
7. Ibid, 3.
8. Ibid.
9. Ibid.

10. Stratfor Worldview. "Visualizing the Fierce Battle for Marawi City." July 5, 2017.
11. Original source: Leland Hamilton Jenks. *Our Cuban Colony: A Study in Sugar.* (New York: Vanguard Press, 1928), p. 165.
12. Original source: Julie A. Tuason, "The Ideology of Empire in National Geographic Magazine's Coverage of the Philippines, 1898-1908," (*The Geographical Review*, Volume 89, Issue 1, 1999).
13. *Purple Heart Magazine,* May/June 2016. pp. 20-21.

Chapter 18: Banker, Oil, and Banana Wars – Mexico and Central America

1. Monroe Doctrine-Facts & Summary. http://www.history.com/topics/monroe-doctrine. (Accessed Oct. 9, 2017).
2. [American Diplomatic Code, 1778-1884, vol. 2; Elliott, p. 179]. Entered in Congressional Record-Senate, 64th Congress, 1st Session, vol. 53, part 7, page 6781.
3. Ibid.
4. Ibid.
5. "Mercury's Agent. Lionel Davidson and the Rothschilds in Mexico" by Alma Parra, pp. 27-32. As related in https://www.rothschildarchive.org/materials/ar2008mexic o.pdf. (Accessed Oct. 9, 2017).
6. https://tshaonline.org/handbook/online/articles/bmc72. (Accessed October 5, 2017).
7. http://www.sanantonio.gov/mission-trails/Prehistory-History/History-of-San-Antonio/Mexican-and-Texas-Republic-Periods. (Accessed Oct. 5, 2017).
8. http://www.history.com/topics/mexican-american-war. (Accessed Oct. 9, 2017).
9. "The 'Reconquista' Mexico's Dream of 'Retaking' the Southwest" by John Tiffany. THE BARNES REVIEW. http://barnesreview.org/pdf/TBR2001-no2-4-9.pdf.
10. https://www.dmdc.osd.mil/dcas/pages/report_principal_ wars.xhtml. (Accessed April 20, 2017).

11. As related in *Arkansas True Democrat.* Sep. 7, 1859. "The K.G.C. in Action."
12. As related in "Laws of the American Legion, K.G.C. Military Department," in *Rules, Regulations, and Principles of the K.G.C.,* 9-19.
13. As related in *Degree Book,* George Bickley Papers. National Archives.
14. As related in "Third Annual Message." December 19, 1859, in *Works of James Buchanan,* ed. J. Moore, 10:339, 353-59.
15. https://www.britannica.com/print/article/307025. (Accessed August 30, 2017).
16. https://history.state.gov/milestones/1861-1865/french-intervention-in-Mexico. Office of the Historian U.S. Department of State. (Accessed January 7, 2016).
17. Ibid.
18. http://www.geni.com/projects/French-intervention-in-Mexico-1862-1867/13007. (Accessed January 26, 2016).
19. https://www.cia.gov/library/center-for-the-study-of-intelligence/kent-csi/vol2no3/html/v02i3a12p_0001.htm, p.2. by Edwin C. Fishel. Approved for Release CIA Historical Review Program 22 Sept. 1993. Posted May 8, 2007. Updated Aug. 3, 2011 (Accessed Aug. 28, 2017).
20. Ibid. Source: J. Fred Rippy, *The United States and Mexico* (New York: 1926), p. 261, citing Genaro y Carlos Pereya Garcia, Documentos ineditos o muy raros para la historia de Mejico (20 vols., Mexico City, 1903, XIV, pp.8-20.
21. *Op. cit.* CIA Report.
22. *Op. cit.* history.state.gov.
23. https;//www.britannica.com/biography/Porfirio Diaz. (Accessed Aug. 31, 2017).
24. As related in Stone, Oliver, p. 2. George C. Herring. *From Colony to Superpower: U.S. Foreign Relations Since 1776.* (New York; Oxford University Press, 2008), 390.
25. As related in Stone, Oliver, p.2. Walter LaFeber, *The American Age: United Stated Foreign Policy at Home and Abroad Since 1750.* (New York: W.W. Norton, 1989), 262; Lloyd C. Gardner, Walter F. LaFeber, and Thomas J.

McCormick, *Creation of the American Empire,* vol. 2: *U.S. Diplomatic History Since 1893.* (Chicago: Rand McNally, 1976), 305.

26. As related in Josephson *Rockefeller,* p. 189. Senate Foreign Relations Committee Hearing 1913, "Revolution in Mexico," pp. 104, 146.
27. https://www.britannica.com/print/article/96883. (Accessed Aug. 30, 2017).
28. As related in Josephson *Rockefeller,* p. 50. State Department, Foreign Relations of the United States, 1914, p. 444.
29. As related in Denny, *We Fight for Oil,* p. 51. Scott Nearing and Joseph Freeman, *Dollar Diplomacy.* 1925. pp.100-111.
30. As related in Denny, *We Fight for Oil, p. 52.* 66th Congress, 2nd Session, Senate Documents, vol. 9, p. 284.
31. As related in Sutton, *Wall Street and the Bolshevik Revolution,* p. 52. United States Senate, Committee on Foreign Relations, *Investigation of Mexican Affairs,* 1920.
32. Ibid. Pts. 2, 18, p. 681.
33. As related in Sutton *Bolshevik,* p. 53. *New York Times,* January 23, 1919.
34. As related in Sutton *Bolshevik,* p. 53. U.S. Senate, Committee on Foreign Relations, 1920. pp.795-96.
35. As related in Sutton *Bolshevik,* p. 51. United States, House Committee on Foreign Affairs. *The Story of Panama,* Hearings on the Rainey Resolution, 1913, pp. 53, 60.
36. As related in Langley p. XVIII. Herbert Croly, *The Promise of American Life,* (New Brunswick, 1996; orig. pub. 1909), 302.
37. As quoted in Stone p. 40. "The Republic of Brown Bros.", *Nation,* June 7, 1922. 622.
38. Ibid.
39. https://www.theguardian.com/news/1999/aug/10/ guardianobituaries3. (Accessed February 3, 2018).

SECTION V: CASUALTIES – HEALING AND TRIUMPH

Chapter 19: A Spiritual Approach to Healing

No references.

Chapter 20: My Personal Healing Story

No references.

CONCLUSION: CONQUERING CUPIDITY

1. https://newswithviews.com/bill-clinton-and-the-deadly-Arkansas-tainted-blood-scandal. (Accessed Jan. 29, 2018).
2. Ibid.
3. Hymnal #530 (Composer: Mark Dickey, 1941; and Author: J.H.B. Masterman, 1922).
4. Hymnal #524 (Composer: *Congregational Church Music,* 1853, adapted from Friedrich Filitz, 1847; and Author: Harry Emerson Fosdick, 1930).
5. Hymnal #525 (Composer: James Hopkirk, 1938; and Author: R.B.Y. Scott, 1937).
6. Hymnal #526 First Tune (Composer: Anne L. Miller, 1941; and Author: John W. Norris, 1939).

BIBLIOGRAPHY

[Author's note: In various instances backgrounds of some of the principal authors upon whom much of the research is based will be specified as well as some selected book endorsements.]

Abbott, John S.C. *The History of the Civil War in America*. Published by Gurdon Bill: Springfield, Mass. Vol. 1. 1864.

Acemoglu, Daron and James A. Robinson. *Why Nations Fail*. Crown Business: New York. 2012.

Bernays, Edward. *Propaganda*. Ig Publishing: Brooklyn, New York. 1928. Renewed 1955.

> "Edward Bernays (1891-1995), nephew of Sigmund Freud, pioneered the scientific technique of shaping and manipulating public opinion, which he called 'engineering of consent.' During World War I, he was an integral part...(of) a powerful propaganda machine that advertised and sold the war to the American people..."

Bible (ASB). *Archaeological Study Bible*. Zondervan: Grand Rapids, MI. 2005.

Bible (KJV). *Life Application Study Bible*. Tyndale House Publishers: Wheaton, IL. 1984.

Bible (NIV). *Life Application Study Bible.* Tyndale House Publishers: Wheaton, IL. 1984 and Zondervan: Grand Rapids, MI.

Bible (PSB) Tim LaHaye. *Prophecy Study Bible*. (KJV). Power Publishing: 2000.

Brands, H.W. (Ed.). *The Selected Letters of Theodore Roosevelt*. Cooper Square Press: New York. 2001.

Butler, Brigadier General Smedley Darlington. *War is a Racket*. Skyhorse Publishing: New York. 2013.

> "...at the time of his death (he) was the most decorated Marine in U.S. history....He is one of nineteen people to be

twice awarded the Medal of Honor..."

Butler: "I spent thirty-three years and four months in active military service, and during that period I spent most of my time being a high-class muscle man for Big Business, for Wall Street and the bankers. In short, I was a racketeer, a gangster for capitalism...How many of these war millionaires shouldered a rifle? How many of them were wounded or killed in battle?"

Cahn, Jonathan, Rabbi. *The Harbinger*. Charisma Media: Lake Mary, FL. 2012.

Cherep-Spiridovich, Major General Count. *The Secret World Government or the "Hidden Hand."* The Book Tree: Escondido, CA. 2000. Originally published 1926.

"Nordic tradition, coupled with exceptional education and training have given Count Cherep-Spiridovich a unique perspective on Russian history. The author has significant biases 'but, there really is some good information here, primarily about government, religion, world power, the Rothschilds, and money.'" (Publisher).

Chernow, Ron. *The House of Morgan an American Banking Dynasty and the Rise of Modern Finance*. Touchstone: New York. 1990.

Cincinnatus. *War! War! War!* Sons of Liberty: Metairie, LA. Third Edition Revised. 1984.

Clark, Allen. *Wounded Soldier Healing* Warrior. Zenith Press: Minneapolis, MN. 2007.

Clark, Allen. *Valor in Vietnam*. Casemate: Philadelphia & Oxford. 2012.

Colby, Gerard. *Dupont Dynasty*. Lyle Stuart, Inc.: Secaucus, NJ. 1984.

Coleman, Dr. John. *The Conspirator's Hierarchy: The Committee of 300*. 4th Ed. World Intelligence Review, Inc.: Carson City, NV. 2006.

[Author's note: Dr. Coleman was formerly employed by British intelligence (MI6), stationed in fourteen countries around the world. He spent five years in study at the British Museum in London in the inner sanctum, not open to the general public.]

Coleman, Dr. John. *Diplomacy by Deception*. World Intelligence Review, Inc.: Las Vegas, NV. Second Edition Updated and Revised. 1993.

Coleman, Dr. John. *The Illuminati in America 1776-2008*. World in Review: Carson City, NV. 2008.

Coleman, Dr. John. *Tavistock Institute of Human Relations*. World Intelligence Review, Inc. First Edition: Las Vegas, NV. 2006.

Coleman, Dr. John. "How the Earth was Created." Monograph. World in Review: Carson City, NV: 2004.

Cooper, Kent. *Barriers Down: The Story of the News Agency Epoch*. Farrar & Rinehart, Inc.: New York. 1942. (Cooper was General Manager of the Associated Press).

Cox, Caroline. *A Proper Sense of Honor: Service and Sacrifice in George Washington's Army*. The University of North Carolina Press: Chapel Hill. 2004.

Dall, Curtis B. *F.D.R. My Exploited Father-in-Law*. Institute for Historical Review: Torrance, Calif. 1982.

[Author's note: This author was the son-in-law of President Franklin Delano Roosevelt and had exposure in meeting many of the individuals who were associates of the President.]

Davenport, Guiles. *Zaharoff High Priest of War*. Lothrop, Lee and Shepard Company: Boston. 1934.

DeVoto, Bernard. *The Year of Decision 1846*. Truman Talley Books St. Martin's Griffin: New York. 2000.

Docherty, Gerry and Jim Macgregor. *Hidden History the Secret Origins of the First World War*. Mainstream Publishing: Edinburgh and London. 2013.

Dolin, Eric Jay. *When America First Met China.* Liveright Publishing Corporation: New York. 2012.

Duck, Daymond R. *Daniel: God's Word for the Biblically-Inept.* Starburst Publishing: Lancaster, PA. 1998.

Duck, Daymond R. *Revelation: God's Word for the Biblically-Inept.* Starburst Publishing: Lancaster, PA. 1998.

Duck, Daymond. *God Has Spoken (And We Know It).* Icon Publishing Group: Noble, OK. 2013.

Dye, John Smith. *The Adder's Den or Secrets of the Great Conspiracy.* The Cornell University Library Digital Collections. 2011. Originally published by author in 1864.

Emerson, Edwin, Jr. and Marion Mills Miller. *The Nineteenth Century and After.* P.F. Collier & Son: New York. In three volumes. 1906.

Engdahl, F. William. *A Century of War.* Progressive Press: Palm Desert, CA. 2012.

Engdahl, F. William. *Gods of Money.* edition.engdahl: Wiesbaden, Germany. 2009.

> "F. William Engdahl ...discusses little-known details of wars and manipulations designed over the past world's known oilfields. The myth of scarcity has been a pillar of their power and in fact of the power-projection of the United States as sole superpower." (Jacket).

Engelbrecht, H.C. and F.C. Hanighen. *Merchants of Death.* Dodd, Mead & Company: New York. 1934.

> "They (the authors) expose all the evils of the armament industry, but they remain at all times conscious that broader forces, such as patriotism, imperialism, nationalistic education, and capitalistic competition, play a larger part than the armament industry in keeping alive the war system." (Foreword by Harry Elmer Barnes).

Erdmann, Martin. *Building the Kingdom of God on Earth.* Wipf and Stock Publishers: Eugene, OR. 2005.

"The book shows the detailed influence of the Round Table Group and its affiliated organisations---such as the Royal Institute of International Affairs (London) and the Council on Foreign Relations (New York City)-on the ecumenical movement, using it successfully for their purpose of creating an international community of nations." (Back jacket).

"Martin Erdmann's study of John Foster Dulles' vision of a new world order breaks new ground by uncovering the close connections between the internationalist and ecumenical movements in the first half of the twentieth century. It will be of equal value to historians of international relations, American politics, and the Christian churches." Dr. Brian Stanley, University of Cambridge.

Evans, Tony. *The Best is Yet to Come.* Moody Press: Chicago, IL. 2000.

Ferguson, Niall. *The House of Rothschild the World's Banker 1849-1999.* Penguin Books: New York. 1998.

Forrester, Izola. *This One Mad Act.* Hale, Cushman & Flint: Boston. 1937.

Fuller, R. Buckminster. *Critical Path.* St. Martin's Press: New York. 1981.

"Critical Path traces the origins and evolution of humanity's social, political, and economic systems from the obscure myths of prehistory, through the development of the great political empires, to the vast international corporate and political systems that control our destiny today..." (Back cover).

Gates, Frederick T. *Occasional Paper, No. 1.* "The Country School of To-morrow." General Education Board: New York City. 1916.

Getz, Gene. *Moses.* Broadman Holman Publishers: Nashville, TN. 1997.

Getz, Gene. *Joshua.* Broadman Holman Publishers: Nashville, TN. 2005.

Goodson, Stephen Mitford. *A History of Central Banking*. Black House Publishing Ltd.: London. 2015.

Graham, John Remington. *Blood Money the Civil War and the Federal Reserve*. Pelican Publishing Company: Gretna, LA. 2006.

Griffin, G. Edward. *The Creature from Jekyll Island*. American Media: Westlake Village, CA. Fifth Edition. 40TH printing. May 2016.

Hamill, John. *The Strange Career of Mr. Hoover Under Two Flags*. William Faro, Inc.: New York. 1931.

Higham, Charles. *Trading With the Enemy*. Delacorte Press: New York. 1983.

"Charles Higham, biographer and former New York Times writer, presents a meticulously documented, dispassionately told behind-the-scenes picture of American involvement with the Nazis before, during, and after World War II." (Book jacket).

Hobart, Mary E. *The Secret of the Rothschilds*. Reprint of self-published book by the author. 1900.

Hoensbroech, Count Paul Von. *Fourteen Years a Jesuit*. Trans. from the German by Alice Zimmern (Girton College, Cambridge). Cassell and Company, LTD.: London, New York. 1911.

In the introduction, Count Hoensbroech wrote of his book: "Within it are comprised religious enthusiasm, lofty idealism, and complete disenchantment; religious despair and the very depths of pessimism; ardent faith and stubborn unbelief; spiritual struggles, self-denial, verging on self-annihilation, suffering that penetrated the very marrow of my being, stabbing me to the quick and crushing me as with the weight of a millstone ..."

Holt, Dean. *American Military Cemeteries*. McFarland & Company, Inc.: Jefferson, North Carolina, and London. 1992.

Hurt, Walter. *Truth about the Jews*. Horton and Company: Chicago. 1922.

Hymnal. The Church Pension Fund. Protestant Episcopal Church of the U.S.A. 1961.

Jacobson, Arni. *The Favor Factor*. Charisma House: Lake Mary, FL. 2007.

Josephson, Emanuel M. *The Strange Death of Franklin D. Roosevelt*. Chedney Press: NY, NY. 1948.

Josephson, Emanuel M. *Rockefeller Internationalist the Man Who Misrules the World*. Chedney Press: New York. 1952.

Keehn, David C. *Knights of the Golden Circle: Secret Empire, Southern Secession, Civil War*. Louisiana State University: Baton Rouge. 2013.

Kinzer, Stephen. *Overthrow America's Century of Regime Change from Hawaii to Iraq*. Times Books: Henry Holt and Company, New York. 2006.

> [Author's note: Stephen Kinzer is a longtime foreign correspondent who has reported from more than fifty countries on four continents. He has served as the New York Times bureau chief in Turkey, Germany, and Nicaragua.]

Knuth, E.C. *The Empire of the City.* Published by author 1983. Originally published 1944.

> "At the end of World War 1, the writer then 27 years old, was released from the U.S. Army as a second lieutenant of the Coast Artillery Corps. Like many more servicemen, he was filled with resentment as the deluge of utterly obvious and brazen falsehood, by which participation in that war had been forced upon the American people, was exposed, and became more evident day after day after the war was won." (Introduction).

Koestler, Arthur. *The Thirteenth Tribe*. Random House: New York. 1976.

Langley, Lester D. *The Banana Wars United States Intervention in the Caribbean, 1898-1934*. Scholarly Resources, Inc.: Lanham, MD. 2002. First published in 1983 (revised 1985) by The

University Press of Kentucky.

Lewis, C.S. *The Screwtape Letters*. Simon & Schuster: New York and London. 1996.

Lindsey. *The Late Great Planet Earth*. Bantam Books: Toronto New York. 1981.

Lisagor, Nancy and Frank Lipsius. *A Law Unto Itself The Untold Story of the Law Firm Sullivan & Cromwell*. William Morrow and Company, Inc.: New York. 1988.

Lundberg, Ferdinand. *America's 60 Families*. Unknown publisher (Reprint). Originally published 1937.

> Mr. Lundberg's *New York Times* obituary on March 3, 1995, reported, "'America's Sixty Families (1937) proposed that a small group of wealthy families held sway over the economy and the body politic, while their financial interests controlled the press. 'The United States,' Mr. Lundberg wrote, 'is owned and dominated today by a hierarchy of the richest families, buttressed by no more than 90 families of lesser wealth.'"

Marsh, Daniel L. *Unto the Generations*. The Long House, INC.: New Canaan, Connecticut. 1968.

Martin, Malachi. *The Jesuits*. Simon & Schuster Paperbacks: New York. 1987.

> Writeup in Martin's *Keys of the Kingdom*: "Martin ...is widely known for his intimate knowledge of the Vatican and its politics...A Vatican insider for many years, Martin...opens up one of the strangest and most lethal deceptions since the Trojan horse...The most chilling and controversial portrait of the Society of Jesus in over 300 years."

McCann, Thomas P. and Henry Scammell. *An American Company the Tragedy of United Fruit*. Crown Publishers, Inc.: New York. 1976.

> [Author's note: This author was an ultimate insider to the story of United Fruit Company and its operations in Central America having departed the company in 1971, but

remaining affiliated in the capacity of a public relations executive for a longer period of time.]

McCarty, Burke. *The Suppressed Truth about the Assassination of Abraham Lincoln*. Reprint by Library of Congress. Burke McCarty, Publisher: Washington, D.C. 1922.

Messervy, George P. *The Quick-Step of an Emperor: Maximilian of Mexico*. Grant Richards Ltd: London. 1921.

> "The scope of the present work is that neither of history nor yet of a historical novel. While observing a strict regard for well-authenticated fact, the writer has principally endeavored to present a fresh and living portrait of the Emperor as a man." (Preface)

Miller, John Chester. *Sam Adams Pioneer in Propaganda*. Stanford University Press: Palo Alto, CA. 1936.

Millis, Walter. *The Martial Spirit*. Ivan R. Dee, Inc.: Chicago, IL. 1987. Originally published by Houghton Mifflin Company. 1931.

> "Walter Millis (1899-1968) wrote for many years for the New York Herald-Tribune and later joined the Center for the Study of Democratic Institutions."

Musicant, Ivan. *The Banana Wars*. Macmillan Publishing Company: NY. 1990.

Musmanno, Michael A. *The Glory & The Dream Abraham Lincoln, before and after Gettysburg*. The Long House Inc.: New Canaan, Conn. 1967.

O'Connor, Harvey. *The Empire of Oil*. Monthly Review Press: New York. 1955.

100 Prophecies Fulfilled by Jesus. (Pamphlet). Rose Publishing: Torrance, CA. 2005.

Owen, Robert L. *National Economy and the Banking System of the United States*. 76th Congress. No Patriots. 28-January 24, 1939.

Palmer, Dave R. *George Washington and Benedict Arnold A Tale of Two Patriots.* Regnery Publishing, Inc.: Washington, DC. 2006.

Palmer, Dave R. *George Washington's Military Genius*. Regnery History: Washington, DC. 2012.

Paris, Edmond. *The Secret History of the Jesuits*. Chick Publications: Ontario, CA. Unknown date.

"About the Author. This study is based on irrefutable archive documents, publications from well-known political personalities, diplomats, ambassadors and eminent writers, most of whom are Catholics, even attested by the imprimatur." (Amazon listing)

From an April 8, 2012, review on Amazon (Truth in History) of this work: "First of all, THIS BOOK IS NOT WRITTEN BY JACK CHICK. It is only published by him. The catholics and coadjutors posting reviews here did not even read the book. This book was written (as Jack Chick notes on the back cover) by a SECULAR French man who has done an incredible amount of research on this subject. "...the book is HEAVILY cited and referenced with MAINSTREAM (mainly French) and CATHOLIC ...sources!"

Perkins, John. *Confessions of an Economic Hit Man*. Berrett-Koehler Publishers, Inc.: San Francisco. 2004.

Perloff, James. *The Shadows of Power the Council on Foreign Relations and the American Decline*. Western Islands: Appleton, WI. 1988.

Preston, John Hyde. *A Short History of the American Revolution*. Pocket Books, Inc.: New York. 1952.

Prince, Derek. *Rules of Engagement*. Chosen: Minneapolis, MN. 2012.

Quigley, Carroll. *Tragedy and Hope*. Wm. Morrison. 2nd Ed.: Los Angeles, Ca. 1974.

Reeves, John. *The Rothschilds: The Financial Rulers of Nations*. Forgotten Books. 2012. Originally Published by A.C. McClurg & Co., Chicago. 1887.

Richardson, Don. *Eternity in Their Hearts*. (Rev.) Regal Books: Ventura, CA. 1981.

Sampson, Anthony. *The Money Lenders*. Coronet Books: Great Britain. 1988.

Schaeffer, Francis A. *How Should We Then Live?* The Rise and Decline of Western Thought and Culture. Fleming H. Revell Company: Old Tappan, NJ. 1976.

Scherman, Nosson and Meir Zlotowitz (Rabbis and General Editors). *The Chumash Torah*. Stone Edition. Mesorah Publications, Ltd.: Brooklyn, NY. 2000.

Search, R.E., Dr. *Lincoln Money Martyred*. GSG & Associates: San Pedro, CA. Reprinted 1989. Originally published in 1935.

Sexton, Jay. *Debtor Diplomacy: Finance and American Foreign Relations in the Civil War Era 1837-1873*. Clarendon Press: Oxford. Reprint 2007.

Shuckford, Samuel. *The Sacred and Profane History of the World Connected*. Vol. 1. Tolle Lege Press: White Hell, WV. 2009.

Sombart, Werner. *The Jews and Modern Capitalism*. Martino Publishing: Mansfield Centre, CT. 2015. Reprint. T. F. Unwin: London. 1913. Translated, with Notes, by M. Epstein.

> [Author's note: This author in 1913 held the Chair of Economics in Berlin at the Handelshochschule.]

Spingola, Deanna. *The Ruling Elite: The Zionist Seizure of World Power*. Trafford Publishing. 2012.

> "The winners sanction the plunder of land and resources on behalf of multinational corporations and international banks. Nations wage total warfare to impose policy, eliminate local leaders who are unwilling to forfeit the country's resources, and exterminate the population." (xiv).

Spingola, Deanna. *The Ruling Elite: Death, Destruction, and Domination.* Trafford Publishing. 2014.

Spingola, Deanna. *The Ruling Elite: A Study in Imperialism, Genocide and Emancipation*. Trafford Publishing. 2011.

Steed, Henry Wickham. *Through Thirty Years 1892-1922*. Vol. 1. First published in 1924 by William Heinemann LTD.: London.

Reprint Facsimile Publisher: Delhi, India. 2015.

[Author's note: Reflects observations over thirty years of travel by a journalist from Great Britain.]

Sutton, Antony C. *The Federal Reserve Conspiracy*. Dauphin Publications: (Reprint). 2014. Originally published 1995.

Sutton, Antony C. *Wall Street and the Rise of Hitler*. GSG & Associates: San Pedro, CA. 2002.

Sutton, Antony C. *Wall Street and the Bolshevik Revolution*. Buccaneer Books: Cutchogue, New York. 1974.

[Author's note: Antony Sutton was originally a British citizen but became an American in 1962. He taught economics at California State University. He was a research fellow at Stanford's Hoover Institution on War, Revolution and Peace. His book on aid to the Soviet Union proved to be too controversial for the Hoover and he was forced out.]

Taylor, Lieutenant Colonel Waters. *Eighth Crusade*. Reprint of 1939 Edition. Sons of Liberty: Hollywood, CA. n.d.

[Author's note: Taylor is the mouthpiece for the true author, a British Staff officer, who preferred to be anonymous and whose writings are termed "Uncensored Disclosures."]

Tenney, Merrill C. (General Editor). *Pictorial Bible Dictionary*. Zondervan Publishing House: Grand Rapids, Michigan: 1963.

Thompson, Arthur R. *To the Victor Go the Myths & Monuments*. AOF Publishing: Appleton, WI. 2016.

Trim, David J.B. (See Chapter Notes in Chapter 11: Protestant Reformation and Religious Wars.)

Van Doren, Carl. *Secret History of the American Revolution*. The Viking Press: New York. 1941.

Vickers, Vincent C. *Economic Tribulation*. Bodley Head Limited: London. 1941. Stephen Austin and Sons, Ltd.: John Lane.

Webster, Nesta H. *World Revolution or the Plot Against*

Civilization. Kessinger Publishing. Date Unknown.

Webster, Noah. *American Dictionary of the English Language*. First Ed. 1828. Republished in Facsimile Edition by Foundation for American Christian Education. Seventh Ed. 1993. www.face.net.

Whitt III, Robert Ampudia. *Expat Survival of an Expatriate in Latin America.* Tate Publishing & Enterprises, LLC: 2007.

Wilson, Derek. *Rothschild: The Wealth and Power of a Dynasty*. Charles Scribner's Sons: New York. 1988.

Yergin, Daniel. *The Prize: The Epic Quest for Oil, Money, & Power*. Free Press: New York. 2009.

> "The canvas of his narrative history is enormous-from the drilling of the first well in Pennsylvania through two great world wars to the Iraqi invasion of Kuwait, Operation Desert Storm, and now both the Iraqi War and climate change." (Book Jacket)

Zagami, Leo Lyon. *Confessions of an Illuminati*. Vol. 1. CCC Publishing: San Francisco, CA. 2016.

Zinn, Howard. *A People's History of the United States*. Harper Perennial Modern Classics; Reissue edition: New York. 2015.

INDEX

Britain, 98, 124, 139, 145, 172, 193, 213, 262–63, 268, 282–84, 287–89, 320–22, 325, 347, 393
British East India Company, 169, 265
Brown Brothers, 143, 402, 407
Buddhism, 63
Buffalo Soldiers, 366, 370
Butler, MG Smedley, CMOH, 111, 114, 162, 381, 394, 400–02, 407,
  427, 453

C

Calvinism, 208–9, 219–21, 230, 238
Cambodia, 27, 96, 185
Canada, 273–74, 288, 334, 337, 347
capitalism, 43, 155, 406–7, 454
Carnegie, Andrew, 122, 181–82, 327, 350, 441
casualties, 7, 18, 23, 25–26, 30, 32–33, 48, 69, 113, 118, 174, 205, 214, 228, 272, 294, 328–29, 332, 363, 367, 370–71, 402, 404, 408, 411, 435, 438, 452
Casualties, Missing in Action (MIA), 118, 338
Catholic Church, 100, 119, 205–9, 211–12, 221, 224, 227–28, 231, 234, 238, 248, 313, 361, 386, 388, 462
Central America, 34, 159, 304, 348, 387, 398, 401–2, 449, 461
Central Intelligence Agency (CIA), 167, 185, 376, 394, 398, 400–402, 450–51, 460
Christianity, 5, 7–8, 16–17, 23, 30, 50–51, 58, 62–63, 69, 71, 73–75, 78–79, 81, 85–86, 88, 90, 94, 96, 98, 100, 104, 111, 137, 145, 166, 215, 217, 220, 222–23, 227, 239, 241, 243–44, 246–47, 295, 297, 311, 405–6, 418, 420, 424–25, 433, 446
Church of England, 216, 238
Civil War, 26, 31, 38, 47, 120–21, 144, 147, 170, 177, 208, 212–13, 232, 274, 288, 299, 301, 304, 309–10, 312–15, 317, 319–21, 326–27, 334, 338–39, 341, 343–44, 367, 381, 389–90, 392, 398, 401–2, 447, 453, 458–59
Communism, 27, 34, 35, 39, 43, 102, 159, 242, 249, 405
Confederacy, 306, 313, 315, 323–25
Congregationalism, 215–17
conspiracies, 47, 49, 83, 88–89, 99–101, 135, 167, 170, 189, 201,

291, 304, 306–7, 315, 334, 437

Genesis, 58, 62, 64, 69, 260
Germany, 34, 122–24, 126–27, 141–42, 157, 187–88, 193–94, 200, 206–8, 222, 224, 230, 236–37, 247, 311, 317–18, 324–25, 345, 347, 358, 361, 366–67, 372, 377, 379, 397, 400, 438, 456, 458–59
Gettysburg, 19, 299, 325, 327–28, 332–33, 461
Getz, Reverend Gene, 16, 66
Golden Circle, 304, 306–7, 313, 336, 386, 447, 459
Great Britain, 49, 123, 127, 147, 151, 200, 215, 257–58, 270, 282, 287–88, 322–24, 347, 381, 389, 392, 463–64

H
Haiti, 399–400, 402, 407
Heaven, 23, 51, 58, 61, 63, 65, 71, 73, 76, 78, 96, 103, 295, 408
Henry, Patrick, 257, 266, 301
Henry VIII, 211–12, 221

I
Illuminati, 47, 93–95, 99–100, 189–90, 291, 455, 465
illumination, 95–97, 100, 381
independence, 136, 261, 263–64, 270–72, 279, 288, 349, 371–72, 376–77, 383
Indian Wars, 258, 262, 275, 341–42
International Telephone and Telegraph (ITT), 157, 159
Iran, 116, 184 Iraq, 8, 19, 40, 63, 459, 465
Islamists, 251, 258, 292, 372
Israel, 64–65, 67, 80, 103, 239–42, 245, 250–53, 293, 446
Italy, 32, 39, 113, 122–24, 127, 157, 178, 206, 230, 313, 382

J
Jesuits, 93–94, 189–90, 209, 221–26, 228–38, 313, 404–6, 458, 460, 462
Jesus, 23, 50, 55, 58, 63, 68, 73–74, 76–78, 86, 97, 103, 217, 221–25, 228, 236–38, 251, 405–6, 419, 423–25, 433–37, 460–62
Juarez, Benito, 237, 305, 388, 390
Judaism, 26, 47, 56–57, 63, 65–66, 74, 78, 86, 145, 169, 189, 201, 205, 208, 239–51, 283–84, 321, 408, 445–46, 459

K

Korean War, 29, 39, 47, 172, 197, 377
Krupp, Alfred, 125–27, 438

L

Latin America, 197–98, 289, 314, 319, 381, 398, 402, 404, 465
Lincoln, 305, 307, 309, 312, 322, 325, 332–34, 337
London, 100, 144–47, 151, 157, 167, 181, 190, 194, 266, 268–69, 287, 292, 313, 315, 317, 320, 322, 324, 383, 391, 437–39, 455–58, 460–61, 463–65
Luther, Martin, 81, 205–7, 213

M

MacArthur, General Douglas, 6, 132, 368, 377
Macmillan Company, 440–41
Magna Carta, 211
Marxism, 88, 245, 404, 406
Mexican-American War, 343, 383–86
Mexico, 47, 121, 151, 222, 235–37, 303–5, 313–14, 325, 339, 378, 381, 383–96, 398, 402, 407–9, 449–50, 461
Mexico's Oil Wars, 392, 395
Middle East, 47, 93, 166, 184
Monroe Doctrine, 313–14, 350, 381–82, 392, 398
Morgan, John Pierpoint, 182, 326
Morgan, Reverend Hugh, 76
Moros, 372

N

Napoleon, 120, 125, 144, 148–49, 222, 250, 324–25, 389–92
National Guard, 363, 365
Nazism, 98, 152, 155, 158, 173–74, 187, 458
Nelson, Kelleigh, 182, 429
New England, 215, 217–18, 220, 238, 266
New Testament, 68, 85, 92, 251
New World Order, 47, 86–87, 89, 92, 98, 105, 190, 441
Nicaragua, 342, 396–99, 401–4, 406, 459

O

Old Testament, 55–58, 60, 63, 66–69, 73, 85–86, 240–41
Ottoman Empire, 104, 245, 292

P

Palestine, 56–57, 73, 104, 152, 240, 244–45
Palmer, LTG Dave, 2, 11, 16, 268, 269, 272, 274, 279, 281
Panama, 121, 172–73, 187, 374, 396–97, 401–2, 451
Paraguay, 234–35, 404
patriotism, 14, 94, 110, 119, 126, 128, 136, 157, 183, 274–75, 293, 364, 456
patriots, 5, 14, 16–17, 133, 220, 261–63, 269, 272–78, 284, 286, 288–89, 355, 372, 434, 462
Perot, Ross, 2, 11, 13, 423
Pershing, General John, 38, 366, 368, 395
Peru, 61, 402
Philadelphia, 2, 144, 257, 268–69, 272–73, 277–78, 284
Philippines, 341, 350–54, 358, 361–64, 366–68, 371–73, 377–78, 449
Pilgrims, 14, 26, 211, 215–16, 260, 442
Poland, 230, 233, 284
Popes, 198, 205, 211, 222, 225–26, 235–37, 391, 404–5
Prisoners of War (POW), 174, 288, 331, 415
Protestantism, 26, 92, 198, 205–9, 211–14, 227, 230–31, 234, 297, 419, 441–42, 459, 465
Prussia, 126, 144, 227, 280, 391
PTSD (Post-Traumatic Stress Disorder), 16, 50, 177, 293, 413–14, 416–18, 423
Puerto Rico, 121, 162, 341, 364, 366–67, 369, 371–72, 374, 376–77, 404
Puritanism, 26, 208, 211, 213, 215–16, 218–19, 258–60, 442–43
Purple Heart, 6, 13, 16, 27, 36, 69, 449

Q

Queen Elizabeth I, 168, 212

R

religion, 26, 58, 63, 77, 88, 90, 93–94, 96–97, 190, 203, 205,

Sullivan & Cromwell Law Firm, 47, 184, 186–88, 374, 396–97, 460
Switzerland, 123, 141, 207–8, 222, 231–32, 236, 313, 444

T

Taliban, 93, 161
Texas, 16, 28, 40, 57, 180, 183, 303, 305–6, 313, 339, 362, 371, 378–79, 383–84, 387–88, 390, 395, 405, 409, 423
Thompson, Arthur, 195, 196, 281, 282, 306
Trump, President Donald, 29, 163, 164, 428

U

United Fruit Company, 159, 373, 401, 461
United Nations, 96, 98
United States Army, 14, 21, 27, 33, 38–39, 118, 121, 183, 227, 283, 285, 288, 306, 341–42, 358, 362–64, 371, 373–74, 377, 394, 407, 413, 420, 459
United States Congress, 37, 42, 136, 182, 232, 266–67, 271, 278, 288, 301–2, 309, 316, 319, 353, 359–61, 381, 387, 402, 428, 439, 448–49, 451, 461–62
United States Constitution, 232, 272, 284, 289–91, 294, 300–301, 311–12
United States Declaration of Independence, 136
United States Marine Corps, 39, 407
United States Military Academy (West Point), 1, 2, 6-7, 11, 13-14, 16, 18-20, 29-30, 56, 65, 69, 120-121, 144, 229, 268, 274, 306, 330, 363, 365-366, 368, 403
United States Navy, 38, 121, 307, 322, 353–54, 357, 374, 394, 397, 400
United States Senate, 14–15, 121–22, 130, 156–57, 162, 182, 308– 9, 311, 324, 344, 346, 348–49, 355, 358, 361, 368, 382, 394, 397, 439, 451
U.S. Presidents, 29–30, 87, 91–92, 163–64, 184–86, 188, 215, 222, 236, 257, 259, 264, 266–67, 269, 271–74, 277–78, 281– 82, 285, 287–92, 294–96, 300–307, 310–11, 313, 316–17, 319– 22, 332–37, 339, 341, 344–45, 347, 349–55, 357–58, 360–62, 364–65, 368, 375, 381–84, 387–88, 390, 396, 398– 99, 404–5, 428–29, 447–48, 450, 453, 455, 458–59, 461–62, 464–65
U.S. State Department, 187, 353–54, 367, 374, 451

V

W